Cultural Agency in the Americas

Cultural Agency in the Americas

DORIS SOMMER, EDITOR

Duke University Press
Durham and London
2006

Designed by Erin Kirk New

Typeset in Ehrhardt and Frutiger

by Keystone Typesetting, Inc.

Library of Congress Cataloging-in-Publication Data appear on the
last printed page of this book.

THIS BOOK WAS ORGANIZED BY THE SOCIAL SCIENCE RESEARCH COUNCIL WITH
FUNDS PROVIDED BY THE FORD FOUNDATION.

DIANA TAYLOR'S CHAPTER WAS PUBLISHED PREVIOUSLY IN *THE ARCHIVE AND
THE REPERTOIRE* (DUKE, 2003).

Contents

Introduction: Wiggle Room

DORIS SOMMER

> Culture is the area in which humanist values are created and established. . . . That
> is why we interpret it in the broadest possible way to include everything from cus-
> toms and traditions of distinct sectors that make up Chilean society to the most
> developed forms of creative and artistic expression: from mass entertainment
> and recreation to the most specialized manifestations of art. . . . In culture thus
> conceived tradition lives alongside novelty, historical memory alongside utopia,
> what we have been and what we can be. . . . Culture is, therefore, a dimension of
> life that involves all the inhabitants of the country, that which confers a sense of
> belonging, or a project, of community and nation, and that which spiritually binds
> them all with the rest of humanity.—Concertación de partidos por la democracia,
> "Programa de gobierno" *Documentos diario La Época* (Santiago, 1989)

Some years ago, Bogotá, Colombia, was the most dangerous city in Latin
America, if you believed the U.S. State Department advisory not to go there.
At airports, official warnings singled out Lagos, Nigeria, and Bogotá as
places too troubled to traffic in tourism. On this count, Bogotanos themselves didn't doubt the North American advice to keep a safe distance from
their own city. Many had lost confidence altogether, and those who were not
emigrating tended to live very sheltered, private lives. The situation seemed
hopeless, given the general level of corruption that could turn any investment against itself. More money for economic recovery might deepen the
pockets of drug dealers; more armed police would increase the number of
guns and the level of violence. What intervention could possibly make sense
in this stagnant and volatile situation?

In 1995, the newly elected mayor of Bogotá, Antanas Mockus, proposed a
bold program of cultural agency, a term this book proposes to name and
recognize as a range of social contributions through creative practices. Simply stated, Mockus put culture to work. If civic spirit had worn so thin it
would not sustain a body politic that could take fiscal cures or demand

security, the first prescription was to revive the spirit through art, antics, and accountability. First a mathematician and philosopher, and then a public servant, the mayor made theory yield practices that would themselves yield to more reflection. He sidestepped conventional sites of struggle that stayed stuck between fear and opportunism. Like Antonio Gramsci, Mockus refused to wait for better conditions and instead promoted a "passive revolution" through the power of culture. Gramsci's response to unbeatable odds makes him something of a patron saint of cultural agency. Using culture as a wedge to open up the civil conditions necessary for decent politics and economic growth, workers would get beyond economistic deadlocks and move toward the goal of emancipation.

For Mayor Mockus civility was goal enough, and getting there became an experiment that mixed fun with function (imagine combining Friedrich Schiller's playful education for self-made subjects with Immanuel Kant's appeal to intersubjective judgment inspired by aesthetics). For example, the municipality's inspired staff hired pantomime artists to make spectacles of good and bad performances at traffic lights. Skeptical subjects suddenly became an interactive public of spectators. The mayor's team printed thousands of laminated cards with a green thumbs-up on one side and red thumbs-down on the other, for drivers to flash in judgment of the safe (or reckless) actions of their fellow drivers. Vaccination against violence was one citywide performance therapy against the "epidemic" that had become a cliché for aggression. Arts programs in schools, rock concerts in parks, a monthly *ciclovía* that closed streets to traffic and opened them to bikers and walkers have, among other civic games and alongside rigorous educational programs, helped to revive the metropolis.

Citizens now pay their taxes, often over and above what they owe in order to support a library, park, or senior program. Between 1993 and 2003, the end of Mockus's second term, one stunning indicator of change was the rate of homicide, which fell by 65 percent. Today, Bogotá feels the strain of migrants who flee zones of conflict for this newfound haven. As they overload the city's systems, planners suggest that migration might slow down if cultural agency were stepped up in still-troubled areas of the country.

Throughout the Americas, culture is a vehicle for agency. Photographers are teaching visual literacy and whetting young appetites for other arts and sciences. Nancy McGirr began with a few children from the city dump in

Guatemala City and now counts one of them as a colleague with a college degree. João Kulcsar trains art students as facilitators of photography in the *favelas* of São Paolo. In theater, improvisations foster collaboration and find dramatic outlets for frustration while rehearsing roles that rise to daunting challenges. Without the Teatro campesino, reports a labor organizer who worked with César Chávez, there would be no United Farm Workers' Union.[1] Perhaps the most far-reaching case is Augusto Boal's Theater of the Oppressed. The multiplier effect of his lessons in listening to disadvantaged social actors and encouraging them to take the stage resulted, for example, in his two-term election to the city council of Rio de Janeiro. There, he promoted legislation suggested by audiences and actors in marginal neighborhoods; thirteen laws passed, and several were adopted at the national level. Alongside these artist-activists are many others. Musicians, dancers, poets, and painters past and present do not yet figure as subjects of academic studies perhaps, but they may well inspire the kind of creative reflection that amounts to a civic contribution.

In Bogotá, no one asks what *cultural agency* means. The concept resonates with a variety of public practices that link creativity with social contributions. But elsewhere the term can beg definition. Maybe this shows a lack of activity, but I suspect that activity is almost everywhere. What we lack instead is perspective on the family resemblances among a variety of repertoires and remixes. Recognizing these resemblances and giving them the name *cultural agency* will, perhaps, make these arts and their effects more visible to scholarship and to activists who stay alive to inspiration.

Culture enables agency. Where structures or conditions can seem intractable, creative practices add dangerous supplements that add angles for intervention and locate room for maneuver. Social movements have learned this and occasionally taught it to social scientists. Humanists might take a lesson from Sonia Alvarez, Evelina Dagnino, and Arturo Escobar, the editors of the important collection *Cultures of Politics, Politics of Cultures.*[2] The editors welcome experiments in cultural studies because scholars who venture beyond disciplinary limits can tell how a change of heart can lead to a change of mind. Strangely, students of creativity seem slower to study the material effects of art and interpretation.

Changing cultures often cause conflict, but they can also offer remedies. Yet culture can fall out of focus both for social scientists, who do not deal in art, and for students of art, who imagine they have little effect on the world. Humanists tend to be timid about what their scholarship can do regarding rights and resources. The oversight limits both theory and practice. Until now, concern about material conditions has produced "cultural studies" to describe, or to denounce, political and economic asymmetries. But critique can dead-end if it doesn't nudge toward change. As an end product, Rigoberta Menchú quipped informally at the Latin American Studies meeting in 2002, critique is a sign of privilege. Poor people need a next step.

While wealth concentrates, state services dwindle, and a war on terror constrains everyone's civil liberties, people can feel squeezed toward despair. Forces beyond anyone's control seem to cancel any capacity to defend rights and resources, least of all through culture. But some of us prefer to notice the gaps in destabilized systems as they scramble to make adjustments. This is wiggle room. Recognizing it amounts to anticipating and (as a corollary) promoting moments and manners of acting up through cultural practices. We may win material gains, but the purpose is also to reinforce what a growing number of political theorists acknowledge as "the cultural background" for winning hearts and minds in democratic life.[3] This does not yet bring background to the fore, but it is an advance over standard politics, which hardly notices culture at all.[4] Is humanism too shy to step forward?

Students of art and culture who denounce injustice usually stop short of asking about the effects of their scholarship. No wonder cultural studies has been a topic of familiar and now tired debate among Latin Americanists. Defenders have called cultural studies a new label for standard interdisciplinary practices that North America recently discovered; and detractors resent the uses of Latin American culture as mere raw material for foreign theorists. Cultural agency takes a detour around this debate and adds the question of scholarly contribution to its subjects. Does paying attention to particular arts promote or deform them? In what ways do cultural activists use academics to gain attention and legitimacy? And how do academics use artist-activists to teach one or another culturally conditioned aesthetic value that conditions political predispositions? Culture can do damage, for example, by closing ethnic ranks to breed intolerance. And it can do good, for example, by developing strategies to reach specific goals and more generally by promoting the respect for self and others that enables democratic engagement. In either case, human values and desires develop through cultural practices that constitute vehicles for change.

The politics of culture is often indirect and delayed, which can make it vulnerable or invisible to scientific research. Consider for example how long it took the U.S. Supreme Court to "consolidate cultural developments" in favor of minority and gay rights. Yet the Court finally did respond to developing definitions of the good by establishing them as binding law.[5] Attention to the agency of culture shows that resistance is only one response to oppression. Michel Foucault taught us to be skeptical about any possible escape from the repressive power of politics, medicine, and the law because fighting discursive power with more discourse was a sure way to increase the volume of arguments in a spiral of repression and refusal. But Foucault hardly noted what Michel de Certeau called "the practice of everyday life," or "domination and the arts of resistance," in James Scott's term.[6] Despite material constraints and customs that can cramp creativity, a kind of cautious confidence in cultural agency comes from the very openness of culture to variation and to multiple interpretations.[7] Like civil society itself, agency operates at many levels of association and belonging, often providing more than one anchor of identity for each subject. In the contradictions among those anchors is wiggle room to act up.

Now more than ever, says Néstor García Canclini, crosscurrents and crosspurposes reveal the totalizing design of modernity to be only virtual. It is an *Imagined Globalization*, to use the title of his book.[8] That is why García Canclini exhorts readers to take creative advantage of the incoherence, while wiggle room exists. Jesús Martín Barbero endorses the exhortation with his own description of a multilayered field of media options in Latin America that allow for surprisingly autonomous messages. The advice is to develop spaces for what Brazilians call *jogo de cintura*, a move from the waist (or hip) not forward or backward, but sideways. A Puerto Rican equivalent, the crablike *jaibería*, and the English *wiggle room* suggest this same preference for caginess over confrontation. The preference admits that opponents have greater weight and force, so that heroism is foolhardy and good sense demands creative options.

"Passive revolution" was Gramsci's *jogo de cintura*. He veered away from the "scientific" marxism that awaited capital's demise and suggested a way to get past historical determinants.[9] Using peripheral vision from Italy (and by extension from other subaltern spaces) and hindsight following the Russian Revolution (which succeeded where marxists least expected it to), Gramsci saw that workers could force change when the forces of history didn't line up right.[10] He detoured around economic determinism on one side and Lenin's political authoritarianism on the other, and made a sidestep toward cultural incitations.[11] Since Marx had appreciated the mutual effects of the economy and ideology, Gramsci underlined the relative autonomy of each sphere to get more play between them and to make culture count.[12] His *jaibería* avoided both the fatalism of academic marxism and the deadlock of proletarian dictatorship.[13] To Lenin's anti-economism and political vanguard, Gramsci added the wiggle room of consensual hegemony. Unlike dictatorship, hegemony requires compromise and a new culture that counts everyone in. Uneven and codependent class interests disturb the supposed laws of marxism and turn it into an artful practice something like juggling sticks of fire. This is the challenge for organic cultural-intellectual leaders.[14]

Gramsci made mischief with historical fatality. He saw that the unity of an emergent class would depend on ideology, so he practically inverted its relationship to the base.[15] The push of economic constraints and the pull of a usable culture describe Gramsci's dynamic interdependent two-step. For literary critics, it might evoke the "dialectical allegory" of desire and disaster that Walter Benjamin described as history; and also the alternating rhythm of "slaps and embraces" between particularity and universality that Toni Morrison describes in peripheral or minority artists. (Should I mention that Gramsci used *estrangement*, a familiar term from formalist aesthetics, to describe the workers' refreshing perspective on history?)[16] Gramsci's inside-outside movement toggles between science and creativity to improvise emancipatory politics.

For Gramsci, the salve or glue of antagonistic classes that were stuck with one another is a shared ideology or a "popular religion."[17] This expressive form of the "people-nation" is a new culture, a first step toward political and economic hegemony. But for today's multicultural Italy, and for other European, Asian, and American states, Gramsci's insistence on *one* cultural language and his impatience with interference from regional dialects are disastrous. The singular ending of the word "emancipation"[18] shows the single posture in his war of positions or passive revolution toward a single, coherent, and outdated outcome.[19]

Outcomes are more than one, Ernesto Laclau glosses. Liberally, he reinterprets Gramsci's "emancipation" when he pluralizes the term and multiplies the possible results of unhinging science from marxism: "By playing within the system of logical incompatibilities; . . . [b]y looking at the effects which follow from the subversion of each of its two incompatible sides by the other," struggle can "drift away" from any single operation.[20] Here is room to wiggle. Gramsci had already abandoned fantasies of absolute freedom (Emmanuel Levinas dreaded freedom as egolotry) when he embraced compromise between the ruling class and the ruled. But this very defense of democracy as antagonism leads Laclau another step back from a single utopian endgame into plural "emancipation(s)." Between the singular and the plural political grammar is a difference that Gilles Deleuze and Félix Guattari also heard, as the contrast between the right line from origin to end and maps that multiply routes.[21]

For some activists and intellectuals, including the contributors to *Cultural Agency in the Americas*, the goal is no longer the dusk of capitalism before the dawn of an egalitarian utopia, but rather many smaller foci of reform. For others, losing sight of that goal means losing one's way. Yet the post–cold war world makes radicalism sound more like religious extremism than a leftist movement, maybe because monotheism migrates so easily from single-minded religious devotion to single-minded sacrificial ideology.[22] Utopian dreams may be too perfect and encompassing for the dangerous supplements of dissent and politics. Struggles for particular freedoms don't presume to destroy the state; they need it as an antagonist to struggle against in a contest for concessions. In the absence of a power to oppose, there are no struggles and no victories. The object is to win ground in hegemonic arrangements that depend on popular consent. And the mechanism is to irritate the state in ways that stimulate concessions of more freedoms and resources. Reformism is of course disappointing to those who prefer systemic responses to an unfair system. But the virtue of this pluralized approach is to recognize multiple if modest agendas.

To take Argentina as a dramatic example, a pragmatic spirit has been pointing activists beyond the standard polar opposition between reform and revolution, Claudia Briones explains.[23] Recent theoretical reflections of the *Colectivo Situaciones* ("Situations Collective") and of the *Movimiento de Trabajadores Desocupados de Solano* ("Movement of Unemployed Workers of

Solano") show how widespread the development has become. Although reform and revolution appear to be opposing options, the collectives of intellectuals and (other) unemployed workers point out that the conventional difference is muted by a fundamental element the competitors share as they produce political meanings. The two approaches to politics are informed by the same general situation and by the particular requirements of this political conjuncture. From the perspective of subalterns forced to derive legitimacy from the available meanings in the general context, both reformers and revolutionaries adopt a "rationality conditioned by socially institutionalized forms of legitimacy." The goal can be either the reformist inclusion of all sectors of society, based on the potential of the democratic state to represent differences and to form consensus, or the revolutionary creation of social alliances in order to take state power. But when the primary purpose is to "activate the production of values towards a new non-capitalist sociability," a third possibility emerges, one based on situational thought and unconventional premises for politics. Therefore, "affirm[ing] situational meanings in order to make room for social change" leads to thinking oppositionally in terms that "depart from general principles in order to affirm a clear and irreducible point of view: the situation is not part of a whole, but a concrete totality that cannot be subordinated to any abstract totalization. This departure opens the way towards a process of ethical subjectification, that is, to a recovery of agency that renders the difference between reform and revolution secondary to the general practices of empowerment." This suggestive formulation, which straddles the discursive operations of description of existing practices and of programmatic manifestos for legitimating them, promotes a multiplicity of insertions to take advantage of the fissures in existing structures. It is precisely this kind of collaboration between research and activism that the following essays mean to capture through the idea of cultural agency.[24]

A focus on cultural agency is not only possible; it is urgent, whether agency is direct, indirect, or even seems plausible for scholars who have many motives for pessimism. Pessimism about what scholarship can or should do brings a kind of despair that is close to complacence. As an alternative to agency, despair feels like a failure of vigilance and of obligation. It is easier, after all, to be right about a bad situation than to make a difference in it.

Against our own skepticism, sometimes, observing activity where passivity is sure to lose, expands skepticism to include the skeptics themselves.

The collective effort to notice and to promote some promising cultural practices is meant to work in a reciprocal and mutually reinforcing dynamic. Self-critical practitioners will worry that, when Westernized intellectuals use indigenous informants, the dynamic ends in the familiar traps of vampirism and co-optation. During our first Cultural Agency meeting, concerns over vampirism haunted several discussions. A paradoxical effect of intellectual self-reflection was the near blocking from view of the demonstrated agency of underprivileged people. Asymmetry is not news to the poor; their challenge is to make advantageous alliances even when equality doesn't enter into the bargain. Perhaps we worry too much, as Barbara Johnson pointed out, because "using people" is an effect of normal, healthy relationships as well as of mutually interested deals. Using others attests to their sturdiness.[25] Perhaps other people are using us, too, as I have been pointing out in the case of Rigoberta Menchú's testimony.[26] If she were not hoping to use us to change public opinion, influence governments, and stop a genocidal war in Guatemala, she would not be addressing us through a book that may well be, in some measure, an appropriation of her voice. Vampirism turns out to have the double dealing and uneven logic of hegemony (including traditional marriage): it binds together agonistic sectors for mutual but unequal advantage. Diane Nelson shrewdly commented that vampires do drink other people's blood. There's no denying it. But the victims can get eternal life in exchange.

When the reciprocal dynamic between cultural activists and scholars works productively, a creative practice can inspire an original scholarly essay. Cultural agents confirm their power to be heard, and listeners display their own training and talent to read performances as social speech acts. This means, as Martín-Barbero spells out, that essays represent a kind of reflective agency to stimulate civic debate.

Raymond Williams was a model of reflexive scholarship when he named a certain "structure of feeling" as emergent in works of literature that would become classics.[27] Important works, he said, anticipate and give voice to a still-inchoate set of rising assumptions about the world, and by so doing they promote progress. Williams's antennae located a kind of will that reframed social relationships. But the limitation of his talent and training as a literary historian was that he worked backward from results. History doesn't normally take risks when it comes to naming which structures of feeling might merit support before they take hold. Williams wrote after the fact. He identified works that became classics and asked why they did. The answers may be circular, since a new dominant feeling will warm its cultivators with the glow of having been right all along, like winning armies that turn wartime narrative into national epic. For Williams, history was a fundamentally coherent story that moved from one dominant set of assumptions to another. Gramsci wanted more intervention than etiology.

Is there a reigning structure of feeling today? It would miss the point of our fragmented multicultural be-longings to give them a single name. Fragmentation is one feeling; dangerously intense dedication to one ideal is another, alongside undirected irony. Like the plural ending that Laclau adds to the politics of emancipation, feelings today develop in a variety of structures. Do we celebrate them all? Or do we tune our antennae to pick up structures, or frames (in William Rowe's formulation), that appreciate or anticipate democratizing, emancipatory practices?[28] Tuning and trying show through this collection of essays on cultural agency.

One effort is to shift the center of cultural gravity from North to South. The organizers of the first conference on cultural agency decided to convene in Cuzco in January 2001. The indestructibly indigenous city overlaid with Spanish constructions provided the site for confronting some paradoxes of cultural politics. Built in one grand design to resist earthquakes and aggressions, Cuzco is the sum of architectural lessons learned from several conquered peoples in the vast territories of Tawantinsuyu.[29] "Here are eternal *Inca* walls," a self-appointed teenage guide told us, "facing the crumbling constructions of *inca-pable* (Spaniards)." The pride of an autochtonous world that owed nothing to Europe was visible and audible everywhere, as were the Hispanic interruptions. In Cuzco, we were all foreigners (except for Juan Carlos Godenzzi), including those Peruvians who live in the capital. To different degrees we shared the *unheimlich* sense of a city that was both familiarly Hispanic and also unavailably Andean in its local lineage, however besieged it may be politically and economically.

Then, suddenly, a casual comment added a dangerous supplement to

Incan pride. The place itself shifted its point of gravity when Rosamel Milla-mán Reinao, a Mapuche activist anthropologist trained in the United States, referred to the Chilean authorities as *wincas*. The word is a peripheral, Ma-puche variation on *Incas*, naming enemies of the Mapuches of any stripe,[30] the way *gentiles* names non-Jews or Blacks or the way indigenous Andeans use *mistis* to keep Creoles at the distance between "us" and "them." Mil-lamán's comment remembered Inca as an aggressively imperial sign.

To acknowledge one's complicity in certain games of naming may give pause in a conversation. But to pause is not to stop; it is a stage of respectful engagement. Insider and outsider are not easily reversible positions, given the barriers of language and the asymmetries of power. The reference to old and new empires was a sign to keep differences in focus and to take lessons from cultural agents who manage to enter and exit disparate codes with an agile *jogo de cintura*.

A troupe of agents had begun to train us the night before our Cuzco meeting. Yuyachkani, a longstanding theater collective in Lima, staged *Santiago* for us. The play is about an indigenous sacristan who lives somewhere in a rural Peru devastated by the *Sendero Luminoso* (Shining Path) and counterattacks by government forces. For the first time, the sacristan refuses to play the Moor crouching at the hoofs of Santiago's (Saint James's) horse during the holy procession planned for the next day. He must submit, insists the Creole who will impersonate Santiago. The debate between the charac-ters developed historical, cultural, racial, and religious arguments for and against the tradition of Indians who play vanquished Moors.

At the level of artistic success, the play may have been uneven. Some found it slow, or long perhaps, too dimly lit, and a bit unconvincing in the character development of the two antagonists and the one-woman chorus. Others speculated that the play was designed for performances in open, public places, where religious processions could be re-presented and resig-nified. But at the level of impact, all of us felt moved by the confrontation.

We *felt* more than we understood. This is the stunning point: The lan-guage that played out the tension between indigenous refusal and Creole au-thority was a language we didn't understand. Most of the debate took place in Quechua, without translations.[31] Although the conversations slipped into Spanish often enough for outsiders to understand the argument, we also understood how ignorant and excluded we were from the scene. The act of excluding us performed the kind of cultural *estrangement* that was at play on- and offstage. Paradoxically, it made us participants in the standoff.

Afterward, when the director, Miguel Rubio, and the actors engaged us in a discussion of *Santiago*, we learned the dimensions of our exclusion through two revealing details: first, that each antagonist spoke a very different dialect of Quechua. The Catholic traditionalist spoke elite Cusqueño, while the indigenous rival used a popular version from Puno, mixed with Aymara. The distances (of taste, class, race) signaled by these registers of Quechua ex- panded the religious rancor to include practically every other cultural con- test, for those who could hear the differences.

The second point of information was the astounding response of Lima's teenagers. Yuyachkani had contracted with an anthropologist to survey au- diences, and the result was dramatic. In contrast to our despair at the double defeat of religion (as Catholic and as local cult), the youth felt inspired. Born mostly of migrant parents who worry that their children may retain the highland accent that holds them back in the capital, the teenagers were used to feeling defeated. The play acknowledged that feeling but refused, in Quechua, to submit. The language became a protagonist of collective pride, and the teens desired to learn it.

The resilience of Quechua, in the capital and elsewhere, continued to intrigue us. We learned, for example, of several radio stations that broadcast in Quechua during early morning hours to coincide with lively migrant markets, a phenomenon that repeats in Bolivia and surely elsewhere. These are networks that Martín Barbero helps us appreciate, in "Communication and Modernity," as structural resilience in Latin American communications.

What can culture do in a world that has become a field for games of ag- gressive brinkmanship? Very little is an easy—and irresponsible—answer. It is true that people everywhere may feel unhinged as globalization dis- mantles familiar relationships, and true that we are shaken after the attacks of September 11, 2001, and the sequel of spiraling aggression and terror. September 11 is a date that retraumatizes Latin Americans who remember 1973, when the democratic Left of President Salvador Allende in Chile succumbed to right-wing terror incited by the United States. This time, the blasts brought down New York's Twin Towers and left a gash in U.S. military headquarters, reducing it to what callous punsters were calling the Penta-gone. Picking up the pieces and patching up the holes won't be easy, as the menace circles the world.

Now, cultural responses don't seem urgent, to say the least. And those of us in the business of offering them may elicit interest only for the potential savings we represent in budgets that can be cut in the name of a greater cause. But culture is at the core of this crisis, and nothing excuses us from taking the core to heart. While Islamic extremists engage in a holy war against the evil West, calls go out for a Christian crusade against the evil East.[32]

All this makes finding an alternative to single-minded passion increasingly vital but delicate. A capacity to think and to feel more than one idea and preference, a taste for secular heterogeneous states that can embrace religion without getting carried away with it, will be vital because democratic so-cieties need stamina when terror makes everything precarious. If we manage to banish dissension altogether and be rid of the "negative"[33] irritating mo-ments that risk violence, there will be little democracy left to defend.[34]

Humanists almost always take culture to mean creativity, which supposes a degree of liberating iconoclasm, and therefore we may miss the sometimes repressive agency of culture. On the other hand, anthropologists can define culture as collective practices and beliefs, a repository of repetitive traditions and ready-to-hand responses. Culture can therefore mean a strategy of con-tainment for irritating change, material for fetish-making observer-voyeurs. Indian reservations, or *reducciones*, did more harm than merely to contain indigenous populations in controlled territories; they also reduced the defi-nition of authentic culture into something uncontaminated and lifeless.[35] But living traditions appropriate foreign elements into multiple modernities. Culture becomes a vehicle for agency.[36] The two meanings of culture, as collective practice and as artistic rupture, differ enough for Raymond Wil-liams to have listed them both among his keywords.[37] In fact, they are often blind to one another since a monocle on continuity can miss creativity,[38] and an eye for originality often squints at context.[39]

A focus on art reveals the charm of unpredictable moves as evidence of autonomous subjects, since a creative gesture literally becomes a per-sona; that is, a device to project to the human voice. Culture in the broad and continuous sense may also add dangerous supplements to systems that prefer to be left alone. Agency runs interference, demands flexibility, tolerance, and humor, all of which are inimical to coercive regimes. Quechua on stage, a man in woman's dress, bolero divas who turn misogyny into female power,[40] oral traditions that survive beyond a lettered city,[41] these are some of the small irritants that pry open room for maneuvering. They make just enough trouble to get a rise out of people for whom difference had looked like an obstacle to level and to leave behind.

Another way to approach cultural agency is to take a step back from politics and notice that "reason is not enough" to settle debates, as political philosophy has noticed from Kant on.[42] The "scandal of reason" demands something more, the common, collective sense of intersubjective agreement, difficult to achieve today because of asymmetries of power and culture.[43] Political theory seldom considers the iconoclastic uses of culture or of *feeling* as residues of reason.[44] Do we feel good about compact and cozy communities based on "likeness" of belief and taste? or do we prefer the heterogeneous, always irritating, and risky public life that demands creativity? Democracies depend on these risks, as I said, especially today when mass migrations leave little likeness among residents of the same country. Taking this step back from political theory that senses the damage culture can do and even acknowledges the need for a cultural background to support democratic engagements, we should ask what good it can do. How can initiatives and reflections on cultural agency actually promote the kind of agonistic, nonviolent politics that describe democratic arrangements?

The first section of this book, "Media," suggests a range of vehicles for cultural agency. The next, "Maneuvers," tracks some exemplary moves; and the final note, "Cautions," asks what can be gained or lost through cultural agency. Two afterwords contribute reflections on the collection in the best spirit of participant observers.

"Media" begins with a double contribution from Jesús Martín Barbero, perhaps Latin America's most innovative and influential author on the mixed messages of mass media.[45] His first step is itself a double-take, a reflection on the necessary relationship between scholarship and agency. To observe is to participate. Then he observes local creativity as it veers away from the homogenizing pressures of mass media. The asymmetrical, heterogeneous, multiform modernity that lacks a clear trajectory is richness, according to

Martín Barbero, and, as he shows in his essay "Between Technology and Culture," is worthy of celebration. Given the importance of cultural politics today, the heterogeneity augurs flexibility, technological experiments, and tolerance, to make local cultures flourish in ways that scholars have hardly known how to track. Were coherence a goal, it would entrench ethnic and racial particularism and refuse the opportunities that global movements offer.

In any case, globalization, as a single concept, is "imaginary," to recall Néstor García Canclini. Here he adds a case study of a city that takes advantage of wiggle room to renovate deteriorated public life through the lively trade in culture that comes with globalization. The example should conjure others. Mexico City may not be New York, London, or Tokyo, but it measures up to any second city (like Barcelona, Berlin, Brussels, Paris, Hong Kong) and, like them, feels the refreshing currents of finance, consulting, advertising, design, and communication. How to formulate cultural policies that account for and take advantage of this new life is the challenge posed by his essay.

Another challenge is how to reckon academically with embodied memory. Diana Taylor calls it the "DNA of Performance." Her essay makes a lateral move from trauma theory to performance theory in order to resignify personal pathology as a collective burden, when social disaster lingers and passes on to new generations. The intervention, then, is to offer a therapy of recognition for historically conditioned sadness as an antidote to narrow personal prescriptions for emotional hygiene that would pathologize normal pain and transfer the burden of therapy to the patient. By emphasizing the public, pain can turn into an engine of cultural agency. The risk that lies within memory and possible retraumatization was a concern at the conference, as was the creativity that compensates for lack, like prosthetic limbs for damaged bodies.[46]

"Maneuvers" starts with this compensatory art of putting a political body together from disarticulated members. Diane M. Nelson teases out the theme in her essay "The Cultural Agency of Wounded Bodies Politic: Ethnicity and Gender as Prosthetic Support in Postwar Guatemala." To hobble along until strength can be regained, Guatemalans employ prosthetic devices, in Nelson's formulation. And Mayan women become useful cover-up devices both for the government that claims to represent them and for the cultural rights movement. But in the process, the women can sometimes take advantage of being "stumped," because the verb also means "to make political speeches or support a cause."

Applying a different twist to the conventions of sex and gender, J. Lorand Matory makes a move that will unhinge both women-centered and African-centered scholarship. He dares to recover the transvestism of Afro-Brazilian religious traditions. To the standard defense of women's preeminence in those traditions, and also to the patriarchal denial of homosexual priests who stand in for women at a higher level of authority, Matory responds with a refreshing focus on gender crossing as an important function of African spirituality. (See also Richard Trexler's *Sex and Conquest*.)[47] The crossings that open up bodies to receive the spirits depend on a cultural memory that passes through ritual, not through written texts.[48]

Thanks to Juan Carlos Godenzzi, Peru's multilingual repertoire gets a hearing. The complexity may be a promising response to the deadlock between minority and majority languages in official bilingualism. (Canada, for example, might focus more on its multilingual immigrant populations.) Diversity is the new banner for progressive Peru (as it is in Carlos Iván Degregori's collection, *No hay país más diverso*).[49] In light of Peru's forty plus indigenous language groups, the officializing of Quechua is no response to demands for language rights, especially given the debates about what counts for correct Quechua that we glimpsed on stage in *Santiago*. Godenzzi's brilliant *jogo de cintura* beyond binarism was to promote successful legislation that made bicultural education mandatory for all children. In practice this means that indigenous children would perfect their native language and Spanish, while Creole children would perfect their Spanish and learn at least one indigenous language.[50]

The Gramscian two-step, this time between home and host languages, also describes the Maya movement during the Guatemalan wars of the 1980s. Arturo Arias makes that double play available to other activists by offering the strategy and the slogan of the Maya participants: theirs was "the conspiracy inside the conspiracy." While the Left tried to force political and military concessions from the Guatemalan state, Maya militants were gaining cultural ground to renew their nation during the murderous campaigns against it. The doubled formulation of *conspiracy* recalls Regis Debray's description of Cuba's political radicalization as the *Revolution in the Revolution* (1967), though the Maya version put armed struggle in the service of cultural reaffirmation. Their success is a counterpoint that cannot be gauged, as Kay Warren observed, by standard political measures such as demonstrations or voting patterns.[51]

Counterpoint may be the most American form of art and life, to follow Fernando Ortiz's description of Cuba's dynamic tussle between tobacco and sugar, black slaves and white masters, macho men and seductive women. Counterpoint performs a codependency between one rhythm and its apparent antagonist, so that music lovers hardly hope for resolution. From the imported taste for rock bands that Martín Barbero finds in Mexico to the *chicha* that spikes the airwaves in Lima with hybrid sounds from the highlands, music has the ungovernable charm of improvisation. Official airways are therefore wary, and often cleverly controlling, when they broadcast *descargas* (meaning jam sessions, but also volleys of shots).

Ariana Hernández-Reguant shows that Radio Taíno improvised *jogo de cintura* between its double consciousness as "official culture" and its heterogeneous appeal. Originally established to stretch a cultural bridge between Cuba and ex-patriots abroad, the state-controlled station has also become a vehicle of cultural reaffirmation for the island itself. This politics of inclusion avoided slogans and instead tried to perform a continuous national imaginary through commercial advertisements and Latin music from around the hemisphere, including dissonant voices of youth, Blacks, and business.

Dissonance is a musical name for irritation, for example, in the inharmonious performances that upset official scores of national or folkloric music. The essay by Denise Corte about Olodum's Afro-Brazilian theatrical interferences suggests a whole range of counterpuntal moves that make the stage a space for contestation. Banished from Bahia's newly refurbished colonial tourist center, the displaced actors of Olodum literally embody the conflicts over housing and related complaints that they represent on stage. But their theatrical success, Corte worries, may produce the unpleasant irony of underwriting marginalization as a ground for creativity.

Alcida Rita Ramos knows how fragile the difference can be between worry about cultural agency and hopes for effectiveness. Scholars come down on one side or on the other soon enough. Her masterful contribution was to do both, successively, and thereby to demonstrate that much of the work of cultural agency is interpretative. The conference version of her essay, "Cultural Instrumentalities of Indigenism in Brazil," decried the manipulations of government and mass media as they neutralized the Indigenist protests meant to disrupt the quincentennial celebrations in 1993. Her second take—included here—pulls on the loose ends that protesters exposed and that the government tried to sew up.

Claudia Briones also moves deftly between considerations of intended agency and real effect. Her work with Mapuches in Argentina begins by noting a paradox of neoliberal reform: Decentralizing power gives some degree of autonomy to the provinces, a corollary to market interests that promote traditional rights. Mapuches had achieved international visibility along with some efficacy through the 1990s, and the global dimension encouraged cross-border alliances of Mapuche peoples. But toward the end of the decade, alliances fragmented as leaders explored the traps of ethnic essentialism and developed other political skills to intervene "sideways" in local government.

"Cautions" alerts readers that agency can backfire. If Briones is impressed with the flexibility of Mapuche strategists, Charles R. Hale and Rosamel Millamán worry that trial and error can lead astray. Like Nelly Richard, who reminded us that losing an interpretive vector may mean following a line of flight into another circle of control, Hale and Millamán report that resistance can grind down into reinforcement of discrimination.[52]

They fear capital that concentrates in capital cities and ignores the countryside. Sometimes desperate need, having little recourse to resources at the national level, encourages rural residents to organize at the local level. Then the fissures between citizen and state can broaden into trenches of local bases from which to broadcast demands at national and international levels. Briones sees this too. But Hale and Millamán conclude that trenches are too cramped and precarious to be strongholds. Successfully argued demands can become mechanisms of state integration, and the trenches turn into branch offices of power.

Brave intentions at the national level can lead astray because the state is a very risky partner. Santiago Villaveces-Izquierdo documents the convoluted history of Colombia's "violentologists," the social scientists whose object of study gave them a haunting name. They began as radical critics of the state in the late 1970s, became counselors of the Colombian government in the eighties and early nineties, and ended up as victims of war and political exile in the late nineties. The success intellectuals achieved in formulating government policies ("feeding the hand that bites it," as one of my colleagues quipped when solicited for a donation to our college) hid, for a while, the political fragmentation that finally neutralized academic activists.[53]

Hale, Millamán, Villaveces-Izquierdo, and others are mindful of the many dangers related to cultural agency, ranging from co-optation to aggression. Still, they conclude that the political promise of cultural activism may justify the risks. The challenge is to voice demands without spiraling into self-defeating frameworks of repression and resistance. The essays collected here describe some deft moves alongside those spirals, to catch opponents off guard and win a right or a resource before the structure manages to neutralize the demand.

Mary Louise Pratt's afterword reads more like a fresh beginning than like the end of a project. Adding her own brilliant case of cultural agency, she also reflects on how the term recasts cultural studies by training light on everyday practices that work. For example, she describes the "artful, risk-ridden, intensely human circuit board" that connects indigenous traditions with scholarly interpreters and the state apparatus in ways that can save us from procedural disasters. Pratt suggests that losing those connections, as if they were impossible instead of conflictual, misses the everyday agency that academics might otherwise engage. Like her, Claudio Lomnitz puts his finger on the pulse of the invitation to think of agency when he commends its minor key, the small interventions that many of us can achieve and that therefore oblige us to act. Lomnitz lauds the *modesty* of the project, in contrast both to Latin American pride in intellectuals as public figures and to North American despair about the irrelevance of the national intelligentsia. He explains that cultural agency avoids inflated expectations and also paralysis; it incites and reflects on quotidian engagements as "necessary efforts to give teeth and claws to democratic process."

Creativity is a condition of that process, if you consider that democracy describes procedures (through techniques associated with art: selection, re-combination, judgment) rather than orders and outcomes. Agency through culture is almost second nature to democratic life, whether we take culture to mean collective and flexible everyday practices or the individual departures from convention that we call art. Cultural agency is a name for the kind of political voice that speaks through aesthetic effects and that can renew love for the world while it enhances the worth of artist-agents. Instead of tracing the familiar routes from inequalities back to power, where movement gets stuck and protestors can feel paralyzed, cultural agency pursues the tangents of daily practices to multiply creative engagements with power and to get some wiggle room.

Notes

The epigraph is from statements made by *Concertación de partidos por la democracia*, the coalition against General Augusto Pinochet, which managed to gain a surprising majority vote of no confidence in the government while the dictator was in full power. The original Spanish reads:

> La cultura es el ámbito donde se crean y se instauran los valores humanistas. . . . Por eso la entendemos en un sentido amplio, que abarca desde las costumbres y tradiciones de los distintos sectores que componen la sociedad chilena, hasta las expresiones creativas y artísticas en sus más diversos grados de elaboración; desde la diversión y recreación masiva hasta las manifestaciones especializadas del arte. . . . En la cultura así concebida conviven la tradición y la novedad, la memoria histórica y la utopía, lo que hemos sido y podemos ser. . . . La cultura es, por lo tanto, una dimensión de vida que involucra a todos los habitantes del país, que les confiere sentido de pertenencia, de proyecto, de comunidad, de nación, y que los vincula con la espiritualidad de todos los demás seres humanos.

My thanks to Saritha Komatireddy for sharing this with me from her manuscript "Culture in Action: Chile's Ousting of General Augusto Pinochet." (April 2005), 20.

1. Prof. Marshall Ganz, during GSAS workshop in Cultural Agency. Harvard University, November 17, 2003.

2. *Cultures of Politics, Politics of Cultures: Re-visioning Latin American Social Movements*, ed. Sonia E. Alvarez, Evelina Dagnino, Arturo Escobar (Boulder: Westview Press, 1997).

3. One particularly noteworthy contribution is Gary Gereffi, ed., *Who Gets Ahead in the Global Economy: Industrial Upgrading in Theory and Practice* (forthcoming). Several studies of Central American economy and society reach similar conclusions (e.g., Juan Pablo Pérez Sáinz, ed., *Encadenamientos globales y pequeña empresa en Centroamerica* [FLACSO-Costa Rica, 2002]). A growing number of critical economists, though mindful of the adverse distributive ramifications of globalization, also note that it presents opportunities for greater autonomy as well as risks of subordination for traditionally vulnerable segments of the world's population.

4. For a critique of the discipline's approach to the study of contemporary Latin American politics, see Eric Hershberg, "Latin American Studies Sans Political Science?" Paper presented at the conference "The New Latin Americanism: Cultural Studies Beyond Borders," University of Manchester, U.K., June 2002.

5. "To some extent the court was leading the country, and to some extent it was playing catch-up, but the most significant aspect of the term, Professor Gewirtz said in an interview, was the court's role in 'consolidating cultural developments,' legitimizing them and translating them into 'binding legal principle.' Justice Antonin Scalia, in a bitter dissenting opinion in the gay rights case, accused the court of having 'taken sides in the culture war.'" Quoted in Linda Greenhouse, "In a Momentous Term, Justices Remake the Law, and the Court," *New York Times*, July 1, 2003, 1.

6. Michel de Certeau, *The Practice of Everyday Life*, trans. Steven F. Rendall (Berkeley: University of California Press, 1988); James Scott, *Domination and the Arts of Resistance: Hidden Transcripts* (New Haven: Yale University Press, 1990). While Scott's project is analogous to the theme of wiggle room, he seldom considers the cumulative effect of what he calls "the weapons of the weak; they seem to let off steam rather than lead to a veering off from domination's course" (*Weapons of the Weak* [New Haven: Yale University Press, 1985]).

7. This is also the conclusion of Alvarez et al., *Cultures of Politics*, 20: "Nonetheless, we maintain that, however contradictory, the sustained public presence and proliferation of social movement webs and alternative publics has been a positive development for existing democracy in Latin America."

8. Néstor García Canclini, *La globalización imaginada* (Buenos Aires: Paidós, 1999).

9. See Leonardo Paggi, "Gramsci's General Theory of Marxism," in *Gramsci and Marxist Theory*, ed. Chantal Mouffe, 113–67, at 131 (London: RKP, 1979). Also, Antonio Labriola, "Gramsci's Teacher," in *Socialism and Philosophy*, trans. Ernest Untermann (Chicago: Charles Kerr, 1907).

10. Gramsci's critique of economism was not abstract; it responded to the Second International, where the working class in Germany and Italy suffered defeats. Spokespersons such as Karl Kautsky considered the proletarian revolution inevitable and so adopted a "wait and see" attitude. See Chantal Mouffe, "Hegemony and Ideology in Gramsci," in *Gramsci and Marxist Theory*, 168–204, at 172, 176.

11. See Norberto Bobbio, "Gramsci and the Conception of Civil Society," in *Gramsci and Marxist Theory*, 21–47, at 39. To Lenin's "political leadership" Gramsci adds "cultural leadership."

12. In 1918, Gramsci wrote, "[It is] not only by economic facts that the history of a

people can be documented. It is a complex and confusing task to unravel its causes and in order to do so, a deep and widely diffused study of all spiritual and practical activities is needed." *Studi Gramsciani*, ed. F. Andreucci and T. Detti (Rome: Editori Riuniti, 1958), 280–81. Quoted in Bobbio, "Gramsci and the Conception of Civil Society," 33. Bobbio (35) concludes that Gramsci inverted Marxism, favoring the determinance of superstructure (including civil society for Gramsci) over structure, and within the superstructure, claiming that ideologies are the primary moment of history and institutions secondary. This is a scandal for Jacques Texier, in "Gramsci, Theoretician of the Superstructures: On the Concept of Civil Society," in *Gramsci and Marxist Theory*, 48–79. The only difference between Marx and Gramsci is emphasis. Otherwise, you could misread him as saying that the working class will "turn the revolutionary party into a House of Culture!" (52). Mouffe and Paggi underline the young Marx's emphasis on expressive culture. See their essays in *Gramsci and Marxist Theory*.

13. Antonio Gramsci, *Prison Notebooks*, trans. Quintin Hoare and Geoffrey Nowell-Smith (London: Lawrence and Wishart, 1973), 437: "The historical dialectic is replaced by the law of causality and the search for regularity, normality, and uniformity. But how can one derive from this way of seeing things the overcoming, the 'overthrow' of praxis?" See *Prison Notebooks*, no. 4, and Mouffe, "Hegemony and Ideology," 181.

14. Gramsci, *Prison Notebooks*, 3–43. See also Nicola Badaloni, "Gramsci and the Problem of the Revolution," in *Gramsci and Marxist Theory*, 80–109.

15. "What was previously secondary and subordinate, or even incidental, is now taken to be primary—becomes the nucleus of a new ideological and theoretical complex" (Gramsci, *Prison Notebooks*, 195).

16. See Badaloni, "Gramsci and the Problem of the Revolution," 85: "The extraneity [*estraneita*] of consciousness of the producers was affirmed historically with a suddenness which imposed on the new political groups tasks of political leadership." Later, Gramsci abandoned extraneity, which seemed too pure and simple an opposition, adopting an articulation based on antithesis (88). She cites Gramsci, *Selections from Political Writings (1921–1926)*, trans. and ed. Quintin Hoare (London: Lawrence and Wishart, 1978), 36, 48. Can we speculate that this movement from strangeness to articulation is parallel to the shocking surprise of the sublime, followed by the satisfaction of recovering balance through reason?

17. Mouffe, "Hegemony and Ideology," 194, cites *Quaderni del carcere*, ed. V. Gerratana (Turin: Einaudi, 1975), 2:1084, 3:1724; *Prison Notebooks*, 241; 2:1084.

18. Gramsci, *Prison Notebooks*, 114.

19. E. Laclau and C. Mouffe, *Hegemony and Socialist Strategy: Towards a Radical Democratic Politics* (London: Verso, 1985), 69–70.

20. Laclau, *Emancipation(s)* (London: Verso, 1996), 2, 8.

21. Charles R. Hale articulated these differences in a reflection written after the Cuzco conference on cultural agency in January 2001.

22. Jesús Martín Barbero, "Desencantos de la socialidad y reencantamientos de la identidad," 9, paper presented at the conference "Cultural Agents and National Belonging" at New York University, October 3, 2001.

23. Claudia Briones in a letter of January 5, 2003.

24. See Colectivo situaciones 2002, "Multiplicidad y contrapoder en la experiencia piquetera," in MTD de Solano and Colectivo situaciones, *La Hipótesis 891. Más allá de los piquetes* (Buenos Aires: Ediciones de Mano en Mano), 121–22.

25. Barbara Johnson, "Using People: Kant with Winnicott," in *The Turn to Ethics*, ed. Marjorie Garber, Beatrice Hanssen, and Rebecca Walkowitz, 47–63 (New York: Routledge, 2000).

26. "No Secrets for Rigoberta," the latest version of an essay begun in 1986. In *Proceed with Caution, When Engaged by Minority Writing in the Americas* (Cambridge, Mass.: Harvard University Press, 1999), 115–59.

27. Raymond Williams, *Marxism and Literature* (New York: Oxford University Press, 1977), 132. I thank Tomás Ybarra Frausto for reminding me of Williams's relevance for us.

28. William Rowe, *Hacia una poética radical; ensayos de hermenéutica cultural* (Rosario Argentina: Beatriz Viterbo Editora, 1996), 26.

29. "Lo más probable es que las innovaciones arquitectónicas se deban a las reformas del Transformador del Mundo (Pachakutiq Inka Yupanqi), que gobernó entre 1438 y 1471, según Brian Bauer" (*El desarrollo del estado inca* [Lima: CBC, 1996], 61). "Esto no quita, ciertamente, que la fecha del terremoto pueda haber sido anterior. También puedes encontrar datos confiables en *Arquitectura inca* de Graziano Gasparini y Louise Margolies, que es el libro clásico para el tema."

30. Elicura Chihuailaf, *Recado confidencial a los chilenos* (Santiago, Chile: LOM Ediciones, 1999), 52: "De ahí que decimos que han existido, existen y existirán los winka, es decir, los no mapuche invasores, usurpadores, que no serán desde luego nuestros amigos; y los kamollfvñche, la gente de otra sangre, es decir, gente no mapuche–como usted–que puede ser o no amiga nuestra."

31. Miguel Rubio claimed, during the discussion session with the Cultural Agents conference participants after the play *Santiago*, that the decision to stage the linguistic opacity was inspired by Doris Sommer's *Proceed with Caution, When Engaged by*

Minority Writing in the Americas (Cambridge, Mass.: Harvard University Press), 1999.

32. Front page article in the *New York Times*, November 25, 2002, on enmity between Christian evangelists and Muslims, after the killing of a young woman in Lebanon. Bernard Lewis admits that President Bush's use of the word "was unfortunate, but excusable." In the West, *crusade* has "long since lost its original meaning of 'a war for the cross' "; it "almost always means simply a vigorous campaign for a good cause, . . . rarely, if ever, religious." But in the Middle East, the word refers to medieval precursors of European imperialism, a misleading association, for Lewis, since the Crusades were a belated and rather ineffectual response to the *jihad*. See his "Jihad vs. Crusade," *Wall Street Journal*, September 27, 2001, A18. Nevertheless, some Western leaders are neither reluctant nor sorry to revive the original intent of crusade. For example, on September 26, 2001, during a briefing in Berlin, where he met with Russian president Vladimir V. Putin and German chancellor Gerhard Schroeder to discuss international cooperation against terrorism, the Italian prime minister, Silvio Berlusconi, urged Europe to "reconstitute itself on the basis of its Christian roots." "We should be confident of the superiority of our civilization" against that of the Islamic world. Quoted by Steven Erlanger, "Italy's Premier Calls Western Civilization Superior to Islamic World," *New York Times*, September 27, 2001, A8. A week earlier, in a chat with CNN website readers on September 22, 2001, General Wesley Clark said, a bit less categorically, "I hope that people will understand that this is a threat to Western civilization, not to the U.S. And it is a threat that cannot be appeased by apologies or changing policies toward Israel. It is derived from fundamental conflicts within Islam itself." This ignores the secular tradition in Arab countries. Stephen Zunes begins his article, "U.S. Policy Toward Political Islam," with a reminder that "ugly stereotypes of Muslims" don't take into account "the existence of moderate Islamic segments and secular movements that are at least as influential as radicals in the political life of Islamic countries" (in *Foreign Policy in Focus*, September 12, 2001).

33. T.W. Adorno, *Negative Dialektic* (Frankfurt: Surkamp, 1966), 172. The paradox of striving for complete understanding is that it misunderstands the particularity of its object. To understand is to establish identity; and this requires conceptualization that generalizes away otherness. Identifying, therefore, turns out to be a trap at two levels: empathic identification violates the other person; and ontological identification eliminates particularity for the sake of unity. The greedy subject is Freud's formulation. See Diana Fuss, *Identity Papers* (New York: Routledge, 1996).

34. The Israeli author David Grossman reckons the loss in "Terror's Long Shadow," *The Guardian*, September 20, 2001: "Terror also sharpens one's awareness

that a democratic, tranquil way of life requires a great deal of goodwill, the truly good will of a country's citizens. That is the amazing secret of democratic rule, and it is also its Achilles heel. All of us are, when it comes down to it, each other's hostages. Terrorists act on this potential, and so unstring the entire fabric of life."

35. Chihuailaf, *Recado confidencial a los chilenos*, 46.

36. Ibid., 48: "La cultura no es solo los elementos que poseemos y las manifestaciones visibles. Hay que entender la cultura como la forma de pensar, avanzar y progresar en el desarrollo y en la interrelación del grupo social. La cultura es la que nos permite transformar nuestras comunidades en lo económico, social y político sin dejar de ser indígenas, la que nos permite mantener nuestra identidad como grupos diferentes a la vez que intercambiamos elementos de otras culturas, por ejemplo, el uso de la tecnología, que facilita nuestra labor organizativa."

37. Raymond Williams, *Keywords* (rev. ed.; New York: Oxford University Press, 1983), 90–91:

It is especially interesting that in archaeology and in *cultural anthropology* the reference to culture or a culture is primarily to *material* production, while in history and *cultural studies* the reference is primarily to *signifying* or *symbolic* systems. This often confuses but even more often conceals the central question of the relations between "material" and "symbolic" production, which in some recent argument—cf. my own *Culture*—have always to be related rather than contrasted. Within this complex argument there are fundamentally opposed as well as effectively overlapping positions; there are also, understandably, many unresolved questions and confused answers. But these arguments and questions cannot be resolved by reducing the complexity of actual usage. This point is relevant also to uses of forms of the word in languages other than English, where there is considerable variation. The anthropological use is common in the German, Scandinavian and Slavonic language groups, but it is distinctly subordinate to the senses of art and learning, or of a general process of human development, in Italian and French. Between languages as within a language, the range and complexity of sense and reference indicate both difference of intellectual position and some blurring or overlapping. These variations, of whatever kind, necessarily involve alternative views of the activities, relationships and processes which this complex word indicates. The complexity, that is to say, is not finally in the word but in the problems which its variations of use significantly indicate.

38. Thanks to Craig Calhoun for this observation.

39. Conversation with Craig Calhoun, October 29, 2001.

40. In "La Tirana y La Divina: Gender, Agency, and the Mexican Bolero," Mark Pedelty presented this theme at the Cuzco conference in 2001.

41. Deborah Cohn's conference contribution, "Nationalism, Cosmopolitanism, and the Intelligentsia: Mexico, 1950–1968," about the Mexican intelligentsia, showed how official literary creativity can also serve as a mechanism of control. In debates about style and matter between elite Creole internationalists and popular defenders of "lo mejicano" during the 1950s and 1960s, internationalism became official through agencies that gave the elite a practical monopoly on culture. Lidia Santos held out for a different dynamic that doesn't fold into one airtight style. "Stories of the *post-everything* and the *with-nothing*" describe a multicentric and unruly Brazil with parallel movements that reinforce one another. They are the landless movement (material condition turned into speech act) and concrete poetry (language that counts for material interventions beyond colonial traditions).

42. "There is always 'more than reason,'" Seyla Benhabib summarizes from essays by Richard Rorty, Jane Mansbridge, Chantal Mouffe, Benjamin Barber, and Bonnie Honig, "whether this be power, nonnegotiable and axiomatic value differences, or the never-ending assertions of conflict and alterity." See "Introduction," *Democracy and Difference: Contesting the Boundaries of the Political*, ed. Seyla Benhabib, 3–18, at 14 (Princeton: Princeton University Press, 1996). Sentiment is more directly addressed by Sheldon Wolin's contribution, "Fugitive Democracy," ibid., 31–45: "To contain that contradiction, the state cultivates the political education of its citizens to instill the virtues of loyalty, obedience, law-abidingness, patriotism, and sacrifice in wartime" (33). Here, of course, education is instrumental rather than formative of democratic predisposition. And John Rawls nods in the direction of a "vital . . . background culture" for liberal democracy without exploring its sensibility (*Political Liberalism* [New York: Columbia University Press, 1993], 215).

43. Hannah Arendt, *Lectures on Kant's Political Philosophy*, ed. Ronald S. Beiner (Chicago: University of Chicago Press, 1982).

44. See Seyla Benhabib, *Claims of Culture: Equality and Diversity in the Global Era* (Princeton: Princeton University Press, 2002).

45. Jesús Martín Barbero, *De los medios a las mediaciones: Comunicación, cultura y hegemonía* (Mexico City: Gustavo Gili, 1987); "Innovación tecnológica y transformación cultural," *TELOS*, no.10 (Madrid, 1989); and "Identidad, comunicación y modernidad," in H. Herlinghaus and M. Walter, eds., *Posmodernidad en la periferia. Enfoques latinoamericanos de la nueva teoría cultural* (Berlin: Langer Verlag,1994).

46. Irina Carlota Silber, "Recordando lo Pasado y Haciendo lo Presente: Between Remembering and Forgetting in Post-War El Salvador."

47. Richard C. Trexler, *Sex and Conquest: Gendered Violence, Political Order, and the European Conquest of the Americas* (Ithaca: Cornell University Press, 1995).

48. Crossover arts include queer uses of language that maneuver between the relatively stable identity markers of one language and another. But queerness presents a paradox for protests against official monocultures. If the protest succeeds, doubleness may become legitimate or even required and a vehicle for control rather than for irritating creativity. Consider the case of Paraguay, where native speakers of Guaraní strive for inclusion and where inclusion can mean containment. Bartomeu Meliá wrestled with this double bind at the Cuzco conference. His Jesuit order has a long history of paradoxical contributions to Paraguay. Indigenous Guaraní is, in effect, a general language forged through Jesuit efforts to facilitate collaborations between priests and Indians during the years of conquest and settlement. I should add that today, Paraguay is the hemisphere's only officially bilingual country south of Canada, and the only one to rescue a local language for national use. The two countries have corollary concerns in common: one is the still subaltern sound of the second "official" language to the powerful center; another problem is the capacity for cooptation of minority speakers by powerful sectors who know enough Guaraní (or French) to set agendas. But the traps, risks, and contradictions did not keep Meliá from promoting bilingual policies, through his scholarship and through the Ministry of Education. Despite the constraints, he concluded that bilingual games have a delightfully unpredictable and ungovernable quality that finds wiggle room in tight spaces. Imagine a field where people are playing baseball and basketball at the same time, he suggested; the moves are always surprising, demanding of vigilance, agility, and admiration (Meliá, *Elogio de la lengua guaraní* [Asunción, Guaraní raity, 1995]).

That metaphor of the double playing field summarizes my own work on bilingual be-longing. Living in two languages forces open a range of assumptions in politics, philosophy, and aesthetics for scholarship that tends to narrow the fields through a monolingual focus. Code switching to maneuver out of a tight situation (for example, "Hispanic students find a way around Affirmative Action Ban") or to turn the tables on a monolingual agonist who loses a step or doesn't laugh on cue, or to refresh perception with the foreign-making (*Verfremdung*) effect that amounts to aesthetic pleasure, are all moves that most people make. But the moves fall out of focus in academic disciplines that take monolingualism to be normal, and also in cultural paradigms of belonging either to one culture or to another.

49. Carlos Iván Degregori, ed., *No hay país más diverso. Compendio de antropología peruana* (Lima: PUCP, IE, 2000).

50. No one would be stuck in the dogmatism that follows from monolingualism, as Mikhail Bakhtin put it; nor would anyone presume to have mastery over all communication in Peru. In what Mary Louise Pratt called the American contact zones,

where European, Indigenous, and African cultures collide, any one language or style cannot capture the dynamism. Mary Louise Pratt, "Arts of the Contact Zone," *Profession*, 91 (1991): 37.

51. Kay Warren, quoted in *Cultures of Politics*, 4: "But there will be new generations of students, leaders, teachers, development workers, and community elders who have been touched in one way or another by the pan-Mayan movement and its cultural production."

52. That lesson of circularity repeated in Sergio Villalobos-Ruminott's conference paper about the possibility of adjudicating Mapuche rights in newly democratized Chile: When those rights are argued inside the legitimating mechanisms of the state, they lose their force and purpose by the very gesture of submitting to that juridical logic.

53. In "Antropólogos, crítica cultural, in/disciplina y agencia intelectual en el Perú (1946–2001)," Javier Avila Molero told a similarly twisted story at the Cuzco conference, about Peruvian anthropologists who identified themselves as cultural agents on behalf of the country's indigenous populations, meaning mostly Andean populations.

1 Media

Intervening *from* and *through* Research Practice: Meditations on the Cuzco Workshop

JESÚS MARTÍN BARBERO

The Ambiguous Burden of Our Own Skepticism

In spite of widespread use among its foes, globalization describes a social imaginary that functions in the process of globalization. The image derives from a monotheistic conception of society and history according to which all events gravitate around a single point and are motored by a single, uniform subject. But if anything characterizes globalization today, it is the multiplicity of processes and actors, rhythms and logics. The 2001 scare at the New York Stock Exchange and the sharp decline in the value of "new economy" stocks (e.g., Yahoo's stocks today are worth 10 percent of their value of a year ago!) speak to the presence of logics that are neither *radical alternatives* nor hegemonic. And if I use examples from the financial world, it is because finances seemed to be going at top speed and in a single direction. Yet not even this arena is uniform or mono-rhythmic. There are demobilizing skepticisms as well as mobilizing ones. Not believing in a single globalizing logic liberates us from the heavy burden of causality and, at the same time, burdens us with the responsibility to pry open spaces, recognize, anticipate, and promote the fissures that traverse and destabilize the global, in order to intervene toward the development of multiplicity.

Intervening through Research Practice

Here I refer to intervention that can be exercised from the practice of research itself and which begins, as Charlie Hale proposes, with the theoretical development of *cultural protagonism* or of "the cultural." My essay included here on the political and cultural dimensions that bring communications studies beyond instrumental rationality is a contribution in this direction. We are witnessing the emergence of *cultural citizenships* that signal the growing presence of strategies of exclusion and empowerment, exercised in and from the cultural arena. The strategies of empowerment not only inscribe "identity politics" within the politics of human emancipation, but also re-open the very meaning of politics, giving rise to new agents and new types of political subjects—agents and subjects that have been visible since feminism subverted the metaphysical *machismo* of the various Lefts with the assertion that "the personal is political." What those new citizenships prove is that the liberal-democratic institutions have been loath to incorporate the multiple forms of cultural diversity that may strain and rupture social life precisely because these do not fit into a particular institutional framework. In the face of the citizenship of "the moderns," which was conceived and exercised *above* the level of identities based on gender, ethnicity, race, or age, the kind of democracy that is necessary today is one in which multiple citizenships assume responsibility for identities and difference. The necessary starting point for creatively sustaining the tension between difference and equality is our ability to mediate that other tension, between our identities as individuals and as citizens.

Another line of intervention from or *through* is the one that locates the construction of maps with crossing lines, multiple entrances, where simultaneous narratives enter into conflict and look for alternative lines of escape at the center of our research efforts. On this subject I have written the following: Who said that cartography can only depict borders and not construct images of the relationships and the intertwining of the paths and labyrinths? A cartographic expert like M. Serres has written:

> Our history, singular and collective, our discoveries as our loves, look more like the risky weather forecasts or seismic activity charts than an organized travel itinerary with an insurance policy. . . . For this reason, rapidly changing meteorological maps, or the slow and patient sciences of the earth, with its deep and shifting plates, fracture lines, and hot points, are of more interest to the philosopher than the old highway maps.[1]

We encounter a cartographic logic that becomes *fractal*, allowing the maps of the world to recuperate the diverse singularity of the objects—mountain chains, islands, jungles, oceans—a logic that expresses itself *textually* in folds, reverses, intertexts, and intervals—a cartography in which the spaces of geography, of history, and of the psyche are not discrete but overlap, illuminating, without elitism or postmodern eclecticisms, new questions that "philosophically" liberate cultural studies from its concealed borders and make them able to accept the elements and the notion of diaspora as new perspectives from which to think.

The new forms of mapping the sociocultural also require a transformation of writing which places the reader before questions and narratives that account for the decentering of the researcher's voice with respect to the multiplicity of voices and experiences. What is needed here are both hard data and metaphors that can together construct more or less powerful articulations of the economic and the political which may reveal the strategic intersections between the economy and culture—focal points for the reorganization of institutions and socialities. The gains in this are enormous—the resulting *nocturnal map* can lead to a demand for cultural policies which, in order to be formulated, must rearticulate the meaning of the public and the political. The current reconstruction of the public sphere has, without a doubt, much to do with profound changes in mental maps, in languages and in policy design, brought about by the new forms of complexity that characterize the reconfigurations and hybridizations of the public and the private. For example, the Internet represents a new complexity: private contact between interlocutors which is at the same time mediated through the Net's public space in a process that simultaneously introduces an explosion of public discourse while mobilizing a large number of very heterogeneous communities, associations, and tribes. At the same time, these heterogeneous social groups can free political narratives from the multiple logics of specific life worlds, weakening the bureaucratic centralism of institutions by infusing creativity into citizenship and participation.

Intervening with Research Practice

What I am referring to here is not the political instrumentalization of research. We have already learned about the excessive and sometimes tragic effects of that particular perversion. What I am referring to is the utilization of research to promote both social creativity as well as the political productivity of culture by strengthening its own capacity for experimentation. I see this taking place in two strategic arenas and two different dimensions of culture:

The local sphere, which is currently undergoing, both in the rural areas and in small cities, a kind of social prostration, political co-optation, and cultural devastation that is extremely dangerous for the survival of communities. We need to encourage research projects that accompany concrete experiences of social revitalization through cultural agencies—be it through arts and craft production or mass media and tourism. An example: research projects that take on patrimony as "cultural capital." It is necessary to expropriate it from its old or antiquated owners so that municipal or neighborhood communities can reclaim their patrimony. Then the right to cultural memory is awakened, recognized, researched, protected, amplified, interpreted, put to use, and even made profitable in all senses of the word.

The regional Latin American sphere. There is no doubt that Latin American economic and cultural integration is affected by the dynamics and ambiguities of the culture industries. If this was the case in the past—in Latin American film, with its myths and stars, in bolero, tango, and the ranchera—it is as much or more so today with telenovelas and salsa, Latin rock and even the Latino version of MTV, boasting its own stars and myths. Focused on preserving patrimonies and promoting the elite art forms, the cultural policies of Latin American states have completely disregarded the decisive role that the audiovisual industries have played in everyday culture. Yet the major culture industries are successfully penetrating personal and family life, organizing free time through the offer of entertainment and the strategic management of information in the home. Anchored in a fundamentally preservationist conception of identity and in a lack of understanding of and engagement with the practices of companies and independent groups—that increasingly powerful "third sector"—public policies are responsible, to a large extent, for the unequal segmentation of consumption and for the impoverishment of national production. This occurs at a time when heterogeneity and multiculturalism can no longer be seen as problems but as the basis for the renovation of democracy. Meanwhile, as liberalism expands deregulation to the cultural sphere, it also demands the reconstruction of a public sphere from States and international agencies. Economic integration itself will be impossible without the creation of *cultural space*, through which public communications policy is able to promote and sustain the circulation of production and programs among all countries in the region, creating a real opening that can link media in each country to those in other countries in the region. These various linkages would intensify cooperation between different media, especially the strategic cooperation between television companies and film. They would also promote increased contact between such media professionals as programmers, scriptwriters, and directors across national boundaries and create networks of exchange and cooperation between independent producers throughout the region.

The sphere of narrative logic(s). A good part of the political frustration and demoralization of the young generation comes from the political and cultural exclusions still generated by the "lettered city," despite the multiplicity of narratives and writings through which new sensibilities are expressed. There is a strategic need to expand the range of discourses through which politics are named and performed and through which cultural creativity takes place. In a society that is suffering what is perhaps the greatest symbolic deficit in history, and which compensates for it by saturating itself with signs and noise, young sensibilities ally themselves with the new languages through which both our fears and our nightmares are expressed. It is this feeling that imbues the notion of youth with its symbolic meaning. And if youth *symbolizes*, it is not because of the market's crooked operations but because it condenses—in its unrest and miseries as much as in its dreams of liberty or its cognitive and expressive complicities with the language of technologies—some of the keys to the cultural mutation that is currently crisscrossing our world.

The sphere of aesthetic innovation and technical experimentation. The blurring of boundaries between technical experimentation and aesthetic innovation is producing profound dislocations in art while at the same time making the emergence of a new standard for evaluating both art and technology possible. In its new relationship with art, technology appears in a new light, that of its capacity to *signify* some of the deepest epochal transformations being experienced in our society. On the other hand, the dislocation of art by technology is making it possible for art to subvert the destructive fatality of a technological revolution that has for many years been directly or indirectly strengthening military power. This new relationship between art, technology, and communications points to more than the circulation of fashion and style. It signals the reaffirmation of cultural creativity as the appropriate space of that utopian minimum without which material progress loses its sense of imagination and turns into the worst kinds of alienation. In the face of the trivialized and trivializing aestheticization of everyday life—and also in the face of its other pole, that ecstasy of form that confuses art with provocative gestures and mere extravagance—there do not appear to be any clear signs of a "way out." We have, however, been learning that any such way would inevitably pass through an opening of the aesthetic to the cultural question: that which seizes the density of the heterogeneity to which different sensibilities and tastes expose us to, in alternative lifestyles and in social movements.

Note

1. Michel Serres, *Hominescence* (Paris: Le Pommier, 2001).

Between Technology and Culture:
Communication and Modernity in Latin America

JESÚS MARTÍN BARBERO

> To abstract modernization from its original context is to see that its processes have
> lost their center and multiplied throughout the world, in capital accumulations,
> the internationalization of markets, the spread of technology and schooling, the
> globalization of mass media, and the dizzying circulation of fashion that comes
> with universalizing certain patterns of consumption.—J. Joaquin Brunner

Clues to the Debate

From the beginning, but especially since the mid-1960s, Latin American
communication studies have been rent between two poles: technology—the
"fact of technology" with its modernizing or developmental logic—and culture, meaning memory and identities as they struggle to survive and regroup
through resistance and reappropriation. The theoretical and political vacilla-
tion of communication studies derives from this ambivalent, mestizo discourse that pulls in the opposite directions of (1) *knowledge* regulated by the
laws of accumulation and compatibility and (2) *acknowledgment* of cultural
differences and variable truths. At stake in the relationship between communication and modernity is the very story line of modernity and cultural
discontinuities, the anachronisms and the utopias that mass media both
deliver and resist.

The debate about modernity has a very particular interest for Latin America because it recasts the linear model of progress that had run past modernity's variations and temporal discontinuities, the long durée of deep collective memory "brought to the surface by sudden changes in the social
fabric torn by modernity itself."[1] The debate is about our crises, and this
debate engulfs Latin America in "resistance" through traditions, the con-
temporaneousness of its "backwardness," and the contradictions of development. Modernism came early and modernity came late, in heterogeneous

pieces. These concerns have joined social sciences with philosophic reflection. Everyday experience demands more than shifting paradigms for analysis; it needs new questions.

One key question, unavoidable for understanding the folds in the fabric of Latin American development, is the cultural question. It is crucial, since constructions of identity take on decisive dimensions when cultural communities retrench themselves against modernity and refresh ethnic and racial labels. If development means the capacity for societies to act for themselves and to modify the course of events, the undifferentiated form of global modernization today clashes with cultural identities and exacerbates fundamentalist tendencies. We need a new notion of identity, "not static or dogmatic, but one that assumes continuous transformation and historicity as part of a substantive modernity."[2] The improvement would get beyond purely instrumental reason and would renew the pursuit of universality as the counterpoint to particularism and cultural ghettos. All this requires a new concept of development capacious enough for culturally different modes and rhythms of insertion.

Globalization delegitimizes the traditions and customs that, until very recently, served our societies as "contexts of confidence";[3] it dismantles our bases for ethics and cultural habitat. This is at the root of so much inner seething and also of surface violence. People can easily assimilate technological advances and images of modernization. But recovering a system of values and civic norms is a long and painful process. The uncertainty of epochal change compounds the ideological shifts with an erosion of cognitive maps, leaving one without interpretive categories to capture the dizzying transformations. This is most patent in the changes suffered by traditional cultures (agricultural, indigenous, and Black) during the intensification of communication with other cultures in each country and with other countries in the world. From within traditional communities, communication is perceived simultaneously as yet another threat to cultural survival and as a chance to break through isolation. If interaction is risky, it also creates opportunities. The fact is that traditional communities show a dynamism today that outstrips the interpretive frameworks of anthropologists and folklorists: there is less nostalgia and more consciousness that symbolic life needs to be adjusted for the future.[4] Consider the diversification and development of artisanal production in open interaction with modern design and even with some dynamics of cultural industries, the growing number of radio and television stations run by communities themselves, or the Zapatista movement making proclamations over the Internet about the utopia of indigenous Mexicans in Chiapas. On the other hand, these traditional cultures offer modern society an unsuspected strategic relevance by helping to offset a purely mechanical replacement of values. In their diversity, traditions represent a challenge to the allegedly universal and ahistorical homogenizing pressure of modernization.

If economic and technological globalization discounts the importance of place and peoples, a complementary pressure from local cultures raises the ante with daily demands for more self-determination. They claim rights to count in decisions about economics and politics, to construct their own images, and to recount their own stories. Identity is therefore no longer conceivable as separate or exclusive in ways that would resist homogenization; it is a narrated construction. The polysemia of the verb *re-count* cannot be more meaningful. It means the plurality of cultures that can be counted and the activity of dynamic cultures that tell their own unfolding stories.[5] Those stories respond both to the hegemonic language of mass media with its double movement of hybridization (between appropriation and mestizaje) and to translations from orality to audiovisual and informatic media as well as to writing. In its thickest and most conceptually daunting sense, *multiculturalism* points to this reciprocity: societies dynamized by the economy and cultural differences to support a heterogeneity of groups and their adjustment to global pressures, but also aware of the diverse range of codes and stories within a cultural group. What globalization puts into play, then, is not just the greater circulation of products, but also a deep reorganization of relationships among peoples, cultures, and countries. Cultural identity can be narrated and constructed through new media and genres, but only if communications industries get direction from creative cultural policies that take everyday culture into account. This would include an explicit transformation of the relationship between educational systems and the fields of experience that make up the new languages of the information age.

The debate has special connections with the field of communication for obvious reasons: modernization is ever more identified with technological advances in information, which makes communication the strategic site for reformulating modernity's viability and its repercussions for postmodernity. In recent years communication has become crucial for imagining and identifying new social models. The term *information society* signifies not only that information is vital to social life and development but that it organizes society at large through communication. What does this mean? Basically that all functions and spaces would be connected in a self-regulated, transparent way. Self-regulation means "well tempered functionality, solidarity among all the elements of the system so that all components stay informed about all others and about the system as a whole."[6] It is balance, retroactivity, constant circulation. In other words, self-regulation would mean a knot of complex relationships that tied each one of us down in incessant communication. Transparency is a corollary and alludes to the transformation of discourses into forms that become absolutely available to each other.[7] The result is to disturb the very nature of knowledge, understood now to be only that which is translatable to digitalized information. Society would then be transparent. Being and knowing would correspond to each other, with nothing left over.

Communication has also become paradoxically crucial in a sense opposed to the positivism of the informational model. Jürgen Habermas has expressly linked "communicative praxis" to the pursuit and defense of noninstrumental rationality, one that still sustains the liberating dimensions of modernity and questions the reduction of the project to its purely technical and economic aspects. Communicative reason is at the center of his reflection on society, filling the gap left by an "epistemological orphanhood" after the paradigms of production and representation came to crises.[8] This reorientation provides an ability to resist coercion and to promote new social movements, including ethnic, ecological, and feminist movements. From this perspective Habermas is a pioneer, despite critiques of his idealization of reason and communicative action. He established the relevance of communication as undeniable for reframing analyses of social action, a research agenda, and the epistemology and politics of critical theory.

From the other side of the crisis of modernity, where postmodernity enters, communication matters too. Communication is hardly a mere instrument or modality of action, but a constitutive element of the new conditions of knowledge, according to J. F. Lyotard.[9] This is where the fundamental change of epoch is being produced: in knowledge that no longer bows down to that modern reason that strives for unity, but on the contrary, reason that moves between gaps in a limitless horizon and in the limited forms of all knowledge, the impossibility of metanarratives and the irreducibly "local character" of all discourse. Similarly, but less austerely optimistic than Lyotard, G. Vattimo listens to a society of communication that emerges from a "weakening of reality"[10] as urban subjects are subjected to the constant crisscross of information, interpretation, and images. Mass society becomes an experience of declining values and diminishing power of modernity's central oppositions: tradition/innovation, progress/reaction, vanguard/kitsch. Instead of polarities we confront multiplicity through questions of the other: the political and cultural thickness of differences in ethnicity, sexuality, and locality.

Another link between analyses of the crisis and issues of communication is the challenge to the modernist rejection of mass culture: "The firm line that had separated 'classical' modernism from mass culture does not hold for the critical and artistic sensibility of postmodernity."[11] F. Jameson adds that the erosion is perhaps the most disturbing aspect of postmodernity from an academic viewpoint.[12] With that line of difference undone, we face a "field of tensions" between tradition and innovation, between high art and popular or mass culture. The field doesn't fit into the categories of modernity because the question of the other exposes a basic imperialism inside and out. Today, opposition is not limited to negation or rejection but includes "affirmative forms of resistance and resistant forms of affirmation."[13]

The Modernity of Communication

Latin America experiences, in particular ways, the generally ambiguous but strategic centrality of communication in modernity. During the "lost decade" of the 1980s the only industry that enjoyed major investments and notable development was communications. Suffice it to mention a few facts: the number of television channels grew from four hundred to fifteen hundred from the mid-1970s to the 1980s; Brazil and Mexico acquired their own satellites; radio and television linked onto global networks by satellite in most countries; data networks, parabolic antennae, TV cable networks were established; and several countries launched regional TV channels.[14] By the same token, since the eighties, telecommunications and information technologies have become beachheads for neoliberalism, as is evident from the priority given to the privatization of telecommunications (from Argentina and Colombia to Peru) and from the privatization of television in the few countries like Mexico and Colombia that still had some public channels. What accounts for this priority, except the fact that communication has become strategic not only at the level of technological advance but also in macro-economic decisions? In other words, the technological and political enclave of communication has become decisive in social design and reorganization as well as in economics. This implies that public institutions are incapable of managing the technological change in communications. Initiatives are left to market forces, and state intervention is seen as interference that borders on censorship! The purposeful confusion has unraveled what for years was called public service.[15] We will have to revive it if we hope to save some notion of democracy.

To think through the relationship between modernity and communication in Latin America is to let go of the theoretical and ideological baggage that refuses to accommodate the messy matrixes of disorganization and reorganization in urban life, including migrations, fragmentation, and dislocation. The dynamism scrambles the opposition between expansive democratizing massification and an elite fascination with modern technology. This experience of communicative thickness obliges us to rethink the relationship between culture and politics.[16]

What role has communication played in the process of interpellating social subjects? It has been a leading role, one which represents a fundamental change at the heart of modernization as we live it. The idea of modernity that promoted the construction of modern nations in the 1930s had an economic component—integration into international markets—and a political component to constitute a national culture, identity, and feeling for the nation. That project was conceivable only through communication between urban masses and the state. Media, especially the radio, became the state's spokesmen, interpellating masses into the people and the people into a nation. Populist *caudillos* used the radio to develop a new political discourse that abandoned the sermon and also parliamentary processes. Oscar Landi describes the modernity of Juan Perón's speeches, which, along with those of the Mexican Revolution, were the first to turn workers and farmers into citizens.[17]

Today, communication goes in the opposite direction to devalue the nation.[18] What the media broadcast, explicitly if you ask young people, is the emergence of cultures without territorial memory, or where place takes second place. New musical and visual cultures are unlike language-based cultures that are linked to a land. But just because transnational culture responds to transnational market strategies of television, records, and video, it should not be underestimated as an agent of particular identity formation. Today, identities live in short temporalities; they are precarious but also flexible enough to amalgamate elements from very different and discontinuous cultural worlds, including modernist residues and radical ruptures. It's easy to dismiss these new deterritorialized sensibilities as social agents, but that would make it harder to communicate the value that "the nation" may still have for them.

The media augur a world that doesn't fit into polar oppositions between national and antinational. They promote contradictory movements of globalization and cultural fragmentation through the revitalization of local cultures. The press as well as radio and, increasingly, television are invested in differentiating culture by region and age group, all the while creating links among them through global rhythms and images. The idea of nation is not only devalued as a result of deterritorialized economics and world culture; it also erodes from an internal liberation of differences. From one point of view, the nation seems provincial and tied down by the state; from another it is a homogenizing force of centralization. From both perspectives, culture resignifies the meaning of borders. What can borders possibly mean now that satellites can "photograph" underground resources and information needed for economic decisions circulates through informal networks? Of course frontiers still exist, but they are likely to describe old differences of class and race and the new frontiers of technology and generation rather than national borders. Nation can still have some purchase, if it doesn't get derailed into intolerant particularism as a reaction to dissolving frontiers; it can work as historical mediator to make intergenerational and interethnic communication possible.

> We know that struggle through cultural mediation doesn't make for immediately
> spectacular results. But it is the only guarantee that we won't go from a simula-
> crum of hegemony to a simulacrum of democracy where defeated oppressors come
> back through the complicit habits of thought and feeling.—N. García Canclini

Thinking about communication from the perspective of culture unsettles the instrumental thinking that has dominated the field of communication and that still legitimates itself today through a technological optimism based on an expansive concept of information.[19] At stake, beyond the academic legitimacy of communication studies, is *intellectual legitimacy*, the potential for communication to be a strategic site for social thought.[20] The paradigm of mediation and cultural analysis opens toward this social weight of research on the relationship between communication and society. Otherwise the expansion of our field and its deepening theoretical sophistication could turn into an embarrassing alibi for moral and practical bankruptcy.

Communication becomes more strategic every day in the development, or in the blockage, of our societies. Consider the links between information and violence, between the media and new authoritarian regimes, and new technologies for reorganizing productivity, public administration, and education. As a result, intellectuals face the task of struggling against a cult of immediacy. We need to recover historical context and critical distance in order to make sense of the transformations that affect the future of civil society and of democracy.

No wonder communication studies have become so important. In Latin America the field developed from the overlap between (1) a North American paradigm of information and instrumentalism, and (2) a Latin American social scientific critique, meaning ideological denunciation. Between these was a wedge of French semiotic structuralism. By the end of the 1970s developmentalists promoted a model of society that turned mass media communications into a beachhead for "spreading innovation" and for transforming society.[21] From Latin America, dependency theory along with a critique of cultural imperialism would lead to another kind of reductionism, one that identified communications with ideological reproduction and denied its specificity of domain and practices.[22] The mutual rejection of technological know-how and social critique during the seventies made for a dangerous excision. Communication studies started by theorizing the complicity between the media and domination, treating technical issues as so many instruments of power and leaving no room for contributions by the Frankfurt School or by semiotics. Theodor Adorno was reduced to denouncing the complicity between technological development and economic rationality and to identifying mass media with the death of art.[23]

Semiotics fared no better. It simply reinforced ideological refusals of the media on the grounds that they managed social control.[24] The combined result was to mire communication studies in what Mabel Piccini calls "a chain of totalities" that blocked any consideration of the culturally and socially constitutive dimensions.[25]

By the mid-eighties the field showed profound changes brought about mostly by a general movement in the social sciences. The question of instrumental reason was raised, including its hegemony as the political horizon of ideological marxism. At the same time, globalization and transnationalism overwhelmed theorists of imperialism and obliged analysts to rethink the roles of territory, actors, and contradictions. The stimuli for reconceptualizing communication came as much from the experience of social movements as from a reflection on cultural studies. Together they lifted the barriers that had demarcated the field of communication. Information, associated with technological innovation, gained scientific and operational legitimacy while communication migrated to the neighboring fields of philosophy and hermeneutics. But the breach between technological optimism and political skepticism remained.

In Latin America, the lifted barriers allowed for new relationships with a range of social sciences, often shaped by contributions from the very disciplines that reached out to study communication. Despite some misgivings, communication studies developed through methodological borrowings (from history, anthropology, aesthetics), while sociology, anthropology, and political science took on the media and cultural industries as central issues. From neighborhood histories of Buenos Aires to the transformation of Black Brazilian music into an urban and national sound, from accounts of symbolic artisanal crafts in market economies to the rhythms of continuity and rupture in urban carnival and religious practices, anthropology had to rethink the disorienting and hybridizing effects of globalization, and sociology had to consider the place of media in cultural transformation and cultural politics.[26]

Along with the theme of media in the social sciences came the growing consciousness that communication needed a transdisciplinary approach.[27] Otherwise the endlessly heterogeneous experience of big cities would stay out of focus. Through new practices of getting together and staying apart, the media acquire a density that doesn't fit into one discipline; they constitute the public by mediating the production of imaginaries and somehow integrating the fractured experience of urban life.

Integration and Construction of Cultural Space in Latin America

The cultural scene of the 1990s was characterized by two general contradictions: (1) the acceleration of technological change along with deregulation of markets, and (2) the discounting of culture's political value or social function while mass media offered new vehicles for social movements and civic expression.

The integration of Latin American culture takes place through cultural industries. This was true of the past, in the collective imaginaries of film, its mythologies and stars, the bolero, tango, and ranchera, and it is even more true today, as the industries offer telenovelas and salsa, along with Latin rock, including a Latin MTV channel with its own myths and stars. Nevertheless, up till now audiovisual industries have been only marginal to regional integration through the Andean Pact, the North American Free Trade Agreement (NAFTA), and Mercosur. Marginality derives not from the media's lack of economic importance but because of the complex relationship between media and culture, regional heterogeneity and the jealous interests that promote a single allegedly national identity. The debate between the European Union and the United States during a recent meeting of the General Agreement on Tariffs and Trade (GATT) over "cultural exceptions" shows that media accords fail in the absence of some political common ground. In Latin America this minimal ground has so far proved elusive. For one thing, the pressures of neoliberalism accelerate the privatization of telecommunications and the unraveling of regulations. At present multimedia conglomerates are consolidating their power and doing what they will, at times in self-serving defense of national culture and at others in favor of transnational flows.

The main obstacle to a minimal political accord about the culture industries is the survival of an outdated notion of national identity linked to the state and to elite practices.[28] On the other hand, cultural industries use mass media to reorganize personal and family life through free-time entertainment at home and strategic management of information. Against the effects both of media industries and of independent groups, a growing third sector, public policy, stays anchored in an old idea of nation that deepens the inequities of consumption and impoverishes local production. This happens at the same time that heterogeneity and multiculturalism are becoming the bases for renovating democracy and that liberalism (through deregulation even in the cultural industries) is requiring national and international administrations to rebuild the public sphere.

Economic integration itself won't be possible without the creation of a shared cultural space that depends on public policy to enable circulation and cooperation among media industries. In contrast to the surprising passivity of states, other forces are mobilizing the audiovisual integration of Latin America, most notably new agents and forms of communication: regional and even municipal and community-based radio and television stations and start-up video production groups that seem destined to attract global attention.[29] These participate in informal networks that connect local demand with global supply and should not be overlooked in deliberations about regional integration.

Meanwhile, some gaps in the multimedia conglomerates suggest political opportunities. I am referring to the appearance of subsidiaries of CNN and CBS—plagued though they are by schematic designs but also letting polyphony develop—in countries that have had very poor international communication, especially with the rest of Latin America. Out of place and frivolous as much of the programming may be, the opportunities for contact and exposure to alternative information are patent. Similarly, the rock and roll industry is experiencing a movement of cultural integration. Latino rock is more than a listening activity for youth; it generates unsuspected hybrid creativity that affects cultural, political, and aesthetic developments. From groups like Botellita de Jerez to Maldita Vecindad, Caifanes, and Café Tacuba in Mexico, Charly García, Fito Páez, or the Enanitos verdes and Fabulosos Cádillac in Argentina, to Estados Alterados and Aterciopelados in Colombia, rock has become a site for constructing symbolic unity for Latin America just as salsa was through Rubén Blades and the Nueva Trova in Cuba. This is no merely local phenomenon, as one can see from Latino MTV, where music and visual creativity develop through youth culture's favorite medium, the video clip.[30]

But in the absence of some minimal public policy on communication, a Latin American cultural space is unthinkable. And without that space, intergenerational and interethnic communication is also unthinkable. Policy would not be merely about media but about cultural communicative systems, since each medium has its particularities. Nor would appropriate policy be merely national, since internal and international diversity promote democratizing creativity. At stake are cultural politics, not simply technological policies. How can the relationship between state and culture change without an integral cultural policy? Can the state deregulate without reformulating the social, communicative contract? We need policies that address public and private interests. If deregulation is necessary, at least the state should provide a context for the democratic multiplication of voices through alternative radio and television channels that big business won't support.

Notes

1. G. Marramao, "Metapolítica: Más allá de los esquemas binarios," in *Razón, ética y política* (Barcelona: Anthropos, 1988), 60.

2. F. Calderon et al., *Esa esquiva modernidad: Desarrollo, ciudadanía y cultura en América Latina y el Caribe* (Caracas: Nueva Sociedad, 1996), 34. Key contributions along this line come from A. Touraine, *Critique de la modernité* (Paris: Fayard, 1992).

3. J. J. Brunner, *Bienvenidos a la modernidad* (Santiago: Planeta, 1994), 37.

4. N. Garcia Canclini, *Culturas híbridas* (Mexico City: Grijalbo, 1990), 280 ff.; G. Gimenez and R. Pozas, eds., *Modernización e identidades sociales* (Mexico City: UNAM, 1994); W. Rowe and V. Scheling, *Memory and Modernity: Popular Culture in Latin America* (London: Verso, 1991).

5. See Homi K. Bhabha, ed., *Nation and Narration* (London: Routledge, 1977); José M. Marinas "La identidad contada," in *Destinos del relato al fin del milenio* (Valencia: Archivos de la Filmoteca, 1996), 75–88.

6. J. Baudrillard, "El éxtasis de la comunicación," in H. Foster, J. Habermas, J. Baudrillard, et al., eds., *La postmodernidad* (Barcelona: Kairos, 1985); Ph. Breton, *L'utopie de la communication* (Paris: La Découverte, 1992).

7. G. Vattimo, *La sociedad transparente* (Barcelona: Paidos, 1989), 16–18.

8. J. Habermas, *Teoria de la acción comunicativa* (Madrid: Taurus,1986), and *El discurso filosófico de la modernidad* (Madrid: Taurus, 1989).

9. J. F. Lyotard, *La condición postmoderna: Informe sobre el saber* (Madrid: Cátedra, 1984), and *La diferencia* (Barcelona: Gedisa, 1988).

10. G. Vattimo, *El fin de la modernidad* (Barcelona: Gedisa, 1986), and *La sociedad transparente*.

11. A. Huyssen, *Guía del postmodernismo*, offprint from *Punto de vista*, no. 29 (Buenos Aires, 1987), 37.

12. F. Jameson, "Postmodernismo y sociedad de consumo," in *La postmodernidad*, 116.

13. Huyssen, *Guía del postmodernismo*, 40.

14. A. Alfonso, *Televisión de servicio público, televisión lucrativa en América Latina* (Caracas: Ministerio de Cultura, 1990).

15. T. Drago, ed., *Integración y comunicación* (Madrid: Turner, 1989).

16. O. Landi, *Reconstrucciones: Las nuevas formas de la cultura política* (Buenos Aires: Puntosur, 1988).

17. O. Landi, *Crisis y lenguajes políticos* (Buenos Aires: Cedes, 1982).

18. R. Schwarz, "Nacional por sustracción," *Punto de vista*, no. 28 (Buenos Aires, 1987), 22.

19. J. Martín Barbero, "Euforia tecnológica y malestar en la teoría," in *Dia-logos de la Comunicación*, no. 20 (Lima, 1988).

20. See Ph. Schlesinger et al., *Los intelectuales en la sociedad de la información* (Barcelona: Anthropos, 1987); S. Ramírez, *Culturas, profesiones y sensibilidades contemporáneas en Colombia* (Cali: Univalle, 1987).

21. E. Sanchez Ruiz, "La crisis del modelo comunicativo de la modernización," in *Requiem por la modernización* (Guadalajara: University of Guadalajara, 1986).

22. J. Nun, "El otro reduccionismo," in *América Latina: Ideología y cultura* (San José, Costa Rica: FLACSO, 1982). "En América Latina la literatura sobre los medios masivos de comunicación está dedicada a demostrar su calidad, innegable, de instrumentos oligárquico-imperialistas de penetración ideológica, pero casi no se ocupa de examinar cómo son recibidos sus mensajes y con cuáles efectos concretos. Es como si fuera condición de ingreso al tópico que el investigador olvidase *las consecuencias no queridas de la acción social* para instalarse en un hiperfuncionalismo de izquierdas."

23. T. Adorno, *Teoria estética* (Madrid: Taurus, 1980), 416.

24. J. Martin Barbero, *De los medios a las mediaciones: Comunicación, cultura y hegemonía* (Barcelona: G. Gili, 1987), 122; translated as *Communication, Culture and Hegemony* (London: Sage, 1990).

25. M. Piccini, *La imagen del tejedor: Lenguajes y políticas de comunicación* (Mexico City: G. Gili, 1987), 16; and "Industrias culturales, transversalidades y regímenes discursivos," in *Dia-logos de la Comunicación*, no. 17 (Lima, 1987).

26. L. Gutierez and L.A. Romero, *Sectores populares y cultura política* (Buenos Aires: Sudamericana, 1985); E. Squef and J. M.Wisnik, *O nacional e o popular na cultura brasileira: Música* (São Paulo: Brasiliense, 1983); R. Da Matta, *Carnavais, malandros, herois* (Rio de Janeiro: Zahar, 1981); Muñiz Sodré, *A verdade seducida: Por un conceito de cultura no Brasil* (Rio de Janeiro: Codecrí, 1983); J. J. Brunner, C. Catalán, and A. Barrios, *Chile: Transformaciones culturales y conflictos de la modernidad* (Santiago: FLACSO, 1989); R. Roncagliolo, "La integración audiovisual en América Latina: Estados, empresas y productores independientes," in N. Garcia Canclini, ed., *Culturas en globalización* (Caracas: Nueva Sociedad, 1996), 53; N. Garcia Canclini, *Culturas híbridas*, and *Las culturas populares en el capitalismo* (Mexico City: Nueva Imagen, 1982); N. Garcia Canclini, ed., *El consumo cultural en México* (Mexico City: Conaculta, 1994), and *Políticas culturales en América Latina* (Mexico City: Grijalbo, 1987); and N. Garcia Canclini and C. Moneta, eds., *Las industrias culturales en la integración latinoamericana* (Mexico City: Grijalbo / SELA / UNESCO, 1999).

27. For a review of two research approaches and theoretical developments up to the end of the 1980s, see J. Martín Barbero, "Retos a la investigación de comunicación en América Latina," *Comunicación y cultura*, no. 10 (Mexico City, 1980), and "Panorama bibliográfico de la investigación latinoamericana en Comunicación," *Telos*, no. 19 (Madrid, 1992).

28. Raúl Fuentes, "La investigación de la comunicación: Hacia la post-disciplinariedad en las ciencias sociales," in *Medios y mediaciones* (Mexico City: Iteso, 1994), 221–43.

29. Among works representative of the new tendencies are M. Wolf, "Tendencias actuales del estudio de medios," en *Comunicación social 1990, Tendencias* (Madrid: Informe Fundesco, 1990); Ph. Schlesinger, "Identidad europea y cambios en la comunicación: De la política a la cultura y los medios," *Telos*, no. 23 (Madrid, 1990); L. Grossberg, C. Nelson, and P. Treichler, eds., *Cultural Studies* (New York: Routledge, 1992); D. Morley, *Family Television, Cultural Power, and Domestic Leisure* (London: Comedia, 1986); G. Marcus and M. Fischer, *Anthropology as Cultural Critique* (Chicago: University of Chicago Press, 1986); Bhabha, *Nation and Narration*.

30. H. Schmucler and M. C. Mata, eds., *Política y comunicación: Hay un lugar*

para la política en la cultura mediática? (Córdoba: Catálogos, 1992); O. Landi, *Devórame otra vez: ¿Qué hizo la televisión con la gente, qué hace la gente con la televisión?* (Buenos Aires: Planeta, 1992); A. Rueda, "Representaciones de lo latinoamericano: Memoria, territorio y transnacionalidad en el videoclip del rock latino" (Thesis, Univalle, Cali, 1998).

DNA of Performance: Political Hauntology

DIANA TAYLOR

"Memory is a perpetually actual phenomenon, a bond tying us to the eternal present," Pierre Nora writes in "Between Memory and History: Les Lieux de Mémoire." Its affective power brings us fully into the here and now, for as Edouard Claparede observed in 1911, "It is impossible to feel emotion as past."[1] Trauma and posttraumatic stress particularly make themselves felt on and through the body long after the initial blow has passed. Trauma returns, with its emotional punch, through involuntary behaviors, flash-backs, and nightmares. The past revisits, full force, as present. The repeat characterizes trauma, which is always reexperienced viscerally, as a constant state of again-ness.

Performance proves vital to humans' understanding of trauma and social memory in part because it functions through a similar process of reiterative embodied behavior. Although not involuntary, performance does involve restored and, in Richard Schechner's words, "twice-behaved behavior." Like trauma, it is characterized by the nature of its repeats. "Performance means: never for the first time." It too makes itself felt affectively and viscerally in the present, capturing both the content (the dramatic / traumatic core) and the now-ness of reactivation. Thus, performance can transmit the meaning and the always-in-the-present experience of traumatic memory.[2]

Another connection: performance and memory rely on context for mean-ing. In one sense, they're always in situ. What Maurice Halbwachs wrote about memory aptly applies to performance: "No memory is possible outside frameworks used by people living in society to determine and retrieve their recollections."[3] Each intervenes in the individual / political / social body at a particular moment and reflects specific fears, anxieties, or values. When the context changes, they change, establishing a new specificity. The possibility for recontextualization and transmission, in performance and of traumatic memory, nonetheless points to an important difference. For performance, as Schechner points out, "behavior is separate from those who are behaving, the behavior can be stored, transmitted, manipulated, transformed" (36). The transmission of traumatic experience more closely resembles contagion—one assumes and embodies the burden, pain and responsibility of past behaviors and events. Traumatic experience may be transmittable, but it's inseparable from the subject who suffers it.

Perhaps the most important connection between performance and trauma/memory, however, remains the least explored: traumatic memory often relies on live, interactive performance for transmission. Even studies that emphasize the link between trauma and narrative, or witnessing and literature, make evident in the analysis itself that the transmission of traumatic memory from victim to witness involves the shared and participatory act of telling and listening associated with live performance.[4] The narrative, the story through which the victim attempts to process an event so horrible that it cannot be processed, comes into being only through the live interaction between testifier and listener. Giving testimony, Felman and Laub make clear, is not "a factual given that is reproduced and replicated by the testifier," but a "discovery of knowledge—its evolution and its very *happening* . . . an event in its own right." Bearing witness is a live process, a *doing*, an event that takes place in real time, in the presence of a listener who "comes to be a participant and a co-owner of the traumatic event."[5] The telling brings the "massive trauma" of the event into consciousness, into the shared repertoire of cultural experience, into existence. Through the process of telling and listening, those involved participate in the knowledge and experience of the traumatic injury.

This essay tries to bridge the gap between trauma theory and performance theory. While trauma scholars like Laub, Felman, and Caruth focus mainly on personal pathology and one-on-one interactions, performance studies allows us to explore the public, nonpathological cause and uses of trauma. By emphasizing the public, rather than just private, repercussions of traumatic violence and loss, social actors (such as the families of the disappeared in Argentina that I discuss here) turn pain into an engine of cultural agency.

The individual focus of trauma studies clearly overlaps with the more public and collective focus of performance studies. It might be helpful to think about the overlaps as three concentric circles, bound by performance and traumatic repeats.

At the very center of these circles, the individual experiences trauma as visceral and self-reflexive—springing from and aimed back at the self as nightmares, flashbacks, and other forms of emotional and physical disruption. Trauma makes evident that memory is stored in the body not just as visual memory or as written imprint, but also as a kinetic function. One victim of trauma I spoke with began to shake uncontrollably whenever there was an unexpected knock at the door. Trauma makes itself felt live—as embodied and as present. On this self-reflexive level, the individual cannot yet express or turn the trauma outward.

In the second circle, the victim of trauma reaches out to a therapist or witness. The live, structured performance plays an important role in the transmission of traumatic memory. Performance, unlike drama, does not connote mimetic representation but, on the contrary, relies on process, etymologically *parfournir*, meaning to *carry through thoroughly*. The telling and retelling offer victims a way of coping. That carrying through—the telling and bearing witness—is accomplished through the physical, live encounter of victim and listener. The telling and retelling constitute a performance, understood as reiterative, twice-behaved behavior. Thus, trauma can come into itself only through performance. Conversely, scholars have long argued that performance, here understood more narrowly as cathartic performance or ritual, comes into being as a healing practice. According to some, the ancient Greek theater at Epidaurus was originally a place of healing. And what is *catharsis* but the purging of noxious elements from the individual and social body? Trauma and cathartic performance, so mutually bound up in their origins, also share their end. If the disturbance or trauma were to end, cathartic performance would become unnecessary and, hypothetically, cease to exist.

On the third level, however, there is an enabling shift in performance modes that allows some victims of trauma to move out of the repetitive circle of (1) reliving the pain and (2) repeatedly testifying to enter (3) the contestatory, and no less reiterative, phase of performance protest. Cathartic, reiterative performances of sorrow and protest, such as the weekly marches of the Madres de la Plaza de Mayo, help the victims themselves deal with unspeakable loss. But by moving beyond the two circles of individual pain and pathology outlined above, they use the trauma to fuel their political activism. They have contributed to human rights efforts by successfully transmitting traumatic memory from one generation to another and from the Argentine political context to an international public that did not live the violence firsthand. Those acts of transfer prove vital to an understanding of cultural agency.

The physical presence of the body in the live experience of trauma and the interaction and exchange between people in the here and now, I believe, make a difference in the way knowledge is transmitted and incorporated. By this, I don't want to lessen the importance of the video and virtual testimonies that have gained currency in the past decade. The Video Archive for Holocaust Testimonies at Yale, for example (among many others), certainly expands our ability to archive and recapture the act of testifying. They store knowledge and make it available to a far greater number of people than any live scenario permits. But the *re-* in recapture is not the reiterative repeat of either trauma or performance, but rather a transfer into the archive—a different economy of storage and representation. In this case, as Peggy Phelan has compellingly argued, the live exchange cannot be stored. It becomes something else. The replay will always be the same, a record of an earlier moment, an anterior utterance that is frozen for posterior use.[6] I am not suggesting that the transmission of traumatic memory happens only in the live encounter, as this essay makes clear. However, I do want to distinguish between different, though intertwined, systems of knowledge—the archival and the embodied—that participate in distinct ways in the transmission of social memory.

Testimonial transfers and performance protest are two forms of expressive social behavior that belong to the discursive workings of what I have called the repertoire. The repertoire stores embodied memory—the traumatic shudder, gestures, orature, movement, dance, singing—in short, all those acts usually thought of as ephemeral, nonreproducible knowledge. Archival memory, on the other hand, maintains what is perceived as a lasting core—records, documents, photographs, literary texts, police files, digital materials, archaeological remains, bones—supposedly resistant to change and political manipulation. What changes over time, the archive claims, is the value, relevance, or meaning of the remains, how they get interpreted, even embodied. In-between and overlapping systems of knowledge and memory constitute a vast spectrum that might combine the workings of the permanent and the ephemeral in divergent ways. The recognition of the embodied nature of the traumatic experience—whether it's the body repossessed by the shudder or the live testimonial encounter—proves vital to our understanding of trauma. So, too, does the archival project that stores evidence and testimonies in less carnal, but more durable containers—video, books, forensic laboratories. Both change over time, and both are open to manipulation and erasure. Each system of containing and transmitting knowledge exceeds the limitations of the other. The live can never be contained in the archive; the archive endures beyond the limits of the live.

Performance works in the transmission of social memory, drawing from and transforming a shared archive and repertoire of cultural images. In some cases, performance functions as a symptom of history, part and parcel of the trauma. In others, it asserts a critical distance to make a claim, either affirming ties and connections or denouncing attacks on social contracts. Like trauma, performance protest intrudes, unexpected and unwelcome, on the social body. Its efficacy depends on its ability to provoke recognition in the here and now rather than rely on past recollection. It insists on physical presence—one can participate only by being there. The transmission entails more than content: performance *strategies* themselves have a history and also undergo change as the relationships of social actors shift in relation to the drama / trauma.

In this section, I explore the ways in which performance protest helps survivors cope with individual and collective trauma by using it to fuel political denunciation. Focusing on the highly performative protests that continue, uninterrupted, twenty years after the official end of Argentina's "Dirty War," I study the transmission of traumatic memory through performance and trace the strategies that get passed on, reformulated, or forgotten in transmission. The protest movements I examine developed along clear generational lines around the disappeared: grandparents (*las Abuelas*), parents (*las Madres*), and children of the disappeared, exiled, and political prisoners (H.I.J.O.S.). Just as the generations share genetic features, which these groups have actively traced through DNA testing, there are performance strategies (what I will provisionally call a DNA of performance) that link their forms of activism. One important feature is that these groups—Abuelas, Madres, and H.I.J.O.S.—see themselves as linked genetically, politically, and performatively. Here I look at various iterations of performance protest involving photography that have taken place over the past twenty years—the Abuelas of the Plaza de Mayo (fig. 1), the Madres (fig. 2), *los escraches* carried out by

H.I.J.O.S. (fig. 3), and an exhibit of photographs of Tucuman's children of the disappeared by Julio Pantoja (fig. 4).

From 1977, almost at the beginning of the Dirty War, the Abuelas and the Madres started calling public attention to the dictatorship's practice of "disappearing" those who opposed them in any way. Of the thirty thousand disappeared who were tortured and murdered, ten thousand were women, and three hundred of these women were pregnant. They were killed as soon as they gave birth. Their children, born in captivity, were adopted by military families. There are still about five hundred of these disappeared children— that is, children thought to be alive and living with their adopted families who may or may not know about the circumstances surrounding their birth. The military did not, however, usually abduct the young children of their victims. These, whom I will call children of the disappeared (as opposed to the disappeared children), were born before their parents disappeared and were raised by relatives. The Abuelas began tracing their disappeared grandchildren genetically, through their DNA. H.I.J.O.S., like Abuelas, actively look for their siblings, the disappeared children.

Much as the Abuelas relied on DNA testing to confirm the lineages broken by the military, they and the Madres used photo IDs as yet another way to establish truth and lineage. This representational practice is what I will refer to as the DNA of performance. This use of the term DNA, I will argue, is not simply metaphoric, but also functional. While related to what Joseph Roach, in *Cities of the Dead*, calls "genealogies of performance" ("the historical transmission and dissemination of cultural practices through collective representations"), it in fact refers to a different model of transmission. Roach outlines the "three-sided relationship of memory, performance, and substitution." He explores "how culture reproduces and re-creates itself by a process that can best be described by the word *surrogation*. In the life of a community, the process of surrogation does not begin or end but continues as actual or perceived vacancies occur in the network of relations that constitutes the social fabric. Into the cavities created by loss through death or other forms of departure . . . survivors attempt to fit satisfactory alternatives." His example: "The King is dead, long live the King." This process, as I see it, implies a narrowing down—instead of two royal individuals, we have one king. The act of substitution erases the antecedent. King is a continuous role that endures regardless of how many individuals come to occupy the

FIGURE 1. Photo by Guillermo Loiácono.

FIGURE 2.
Photo by Cristina Fraire.

FIGURE 3: The large placard photographs of the disappeared haunt the protest practice, 2000. Photo by Mariano Tealdi.

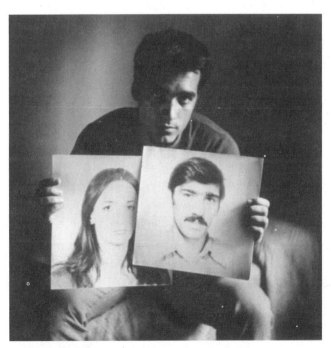

FIGURE 4. Photo exhibit by Julio Pantoja, "Los Hijos, Tucumán veinte años después," Tucumán, 1999.

throne. The model of surrogation stresses seemingly uninterrupted continuity over what might be read as rupture, the recognizable one over the particularities of the many.[7]

Roach makes clear he is not proposing a universalizing model for thinking about the relationship between performance, memory, and surrogation, and he carefully historicizes his argument for the centrality of surrogation in cultural self-fashioning. Roach's model, additionally, allows for scholars to think of performance as that which persists—through a process that assures a certain amount of stability and continuity—instead of that which disappears. Following his lead, I think it is equally urgent to note the cases in which surrogation as a model for cultural continuity and stability is rejected precisely because, as Roach notes, it allows for the collapse of vital historical links and political moves. Whether one sees cultural memory as continuous and coherent because it *relies on* or *rejects* surrogation might well depend on the beholder. There are many examples in the colonial history of the Americas of colonizers and evangelists clinging to the notion of surrogation when in fact there has been a performative shift that highlights, rather than erases, antecedents. One example will have to suffice: the Mesoamerican goddess Tonanztín, the early friars worried, had disappeared only to reappear in the cult of the Virgin of Guadalupe. Had the pre-Conquest goddess been successfully substituted by the Virgin? or did she in fact live on in the Christian deity? Did the noninterrupted pilgrimage to her shrine signal alliance to the old or to the new?[8] Further transformations of the Virgin into multiple, regionally specific figures—the Virgen del Camino, Virgen de la Soledad, and the Virgen de Zopopan (Guadalajara) that Mary Louise Pratt studies[9]—have, since 1734, multiplied into other manifestations of the same Virgin to reach her new worshipers. She most recently reappeared in Los Angeles in 1998 as La Viajera (the traveler), in order to be near the Mexican population that could not safely come to her. This strategy of doubling and staying the same, of moving and remaining, of multiplying outward in the face of constricting social and religious policies tells a very specific story of oppression, migrations, and reinvention that might be lost if the model of substitution, loss, and narrowing down were used to explain the continuities.

The strategy of using photographs of the disappeared that links these various movements, I will argue, is also a way of highlighting, rather than filling, those vacancies created by disappearance. Thinking about a DNA of performance helps one focus on certain kinds of transmission that refuse surrogation. The use of these images suggests, as does the analysis of DNA, that nothing disappears—every link is there, visible, resistant to surrogation. In this case, to think about the performances of disappearance through the model of surrogation would echo the attempts at disappearance through criminal violence. The phantasms, in the Aristotelian sense of the mental picture or the appearance inscribed physically on bodies as memory, can be seen, not only in the mind's eye, but by the eyes of the world. The phantoms of traumatic memory are externalized, performed, not to be forgotten or replaced (as in the case of surrogation) but in order to advocate for social recognition. Grandmothers, mothers, the disappeared, and the children establish a chain in and through representation.[10]

Moreover, these claims—the genetic and the performative—become vital in the absence of other social and legal structures that could redress the crimes against humanity committed by the armed forces. It is important, too, to recognize that these claims work together. Forensic specialists (and eugenicists, criminal detectives, and other scientists) have long relied on representation, performance, and live presentation to convey an understanding of their findings. A photograph taken during the so-called Trial of the Generals in 1985 shows how the scientific explanations and proofs depend for their validity on the way in which they are presented and viewed by jury and judge (fig. 5). The theatrical nature of this presentation is not metaphoric—rather it delivers the claim itself. So, too, thinking about a DNA of performance means that performance contributes to the proof of the claim itself. Thus it is functional, not simply metaphoric. While I share the widely expressed suspicion against reducing cultural complexity to biological determinism, I think there is another way of thinking about these cultural/biological relationships that does not reduce one to the other but tries to understand them as modes of thinking about and organizing knowledge—as interrelated, mutually informed, and sustaining discourses.

The photographs used by Abuelas, Madres, and H.I.J.O.S. present a kind of proof, evidence of the existence of the people in them. Like DNA, they strive to establish the uniqueness of each subject. DNA and photography offer radically disparate proofs of presence, of course, each making visible what is inaccessible to the other. One can't test a photograph for DNA any more than one can recognize physiognomies by looking at genes. But both DNA and the

FIGURE 5. This photograph, "Anatomy of Terrorism," shows the use of photography as evidence during the Trial of the Generals in 1985. Photo by Daniel Muzio.

photographs transmit highly coded cultural information. Like DNA, the images and strategies conveyed through these performances build on prior material, replicating and transforming the received codes. Not all the inherited materials get reused—some are incorporated selectively, others get discarded as "junk DNA." DNA, moreover, does not imply fixity or biological determinism. On the contrary, it is capable of changing codes, rather than simply transmitting them, in the process of cultural adaptation.[11] So, too, these performances change the sociopolitical environment even as they develop with it. The information conveyed through the performances, like the genetic information, appears in highly coded and concentrated, yet eminently readable, form. The images function as markers, identifying an entire movement.

Abuelas, Madres

On one level, the Abuelas' and Madres' spectacle looked relatively simple: a group of middle-aged mothers and housewives wearing white scarves and holding or wearing photographs of their missing children walked counterclockwise around the Plaza de Mayo.[12] By carrying or wearing the photos (usually official IDs) of their disappeared, they used their bodies to make visible the names and faces that had been stripped from the official archives. Photo IDs (like DNA testing in this respect) usually serve to situate and identify the individual vis-à-vis the state. Photographed in conditions of absolute sameness—white background, frontal pose, hair back, ears exposed, no jewelry—individual differences become more accessible to scrutiny and positive identification. The tight framing allows for no background information, no context, no network of relationships. The images appear to be artless and precise. Yet they are highly constructed and ideological, isolating and freezing an individual outside the realms of meaningful social experience. Normally categorized, decontextualized, and filed away in official or police archives, IDs grant the government power over the marked citizen. The images tend to be organized in nonaffiliative categories—that is, individuals may be classified as criminals or subversives but not as members of a certain family. Like DNA testing, photo IDs usually serve to identify strangers. Through photography, as Allan Sekula argues in his analysis of the nineteenth-century convergence of police work and eugenics, the body becomes constructed and contained in the archive.[13]

In Argentina, the photo ID has played a central role both in the tactics of the armed forces and in the protests by relatives of the disappeared. When a whole class of individuals (classified as criminals and subversives) was swept off the streets, the images in the archives disappeared with them. Although the government claimed not to know anything about the missing persons, witnesses have testified that they saw officials destroy the photo IDs and other photographic images of prisoners in their control. Families of the disappeared also testified that members of the military and paramilitary task forces raided their homes and stole photographs of their victims even after they had disappeared the victims themselves.[14] The idea, supposedly, was that by disappearing the documentary evidence of a human life one could erase all traces of the life itself. This strategy works as the negative image of what Roland Barthes has called the "special credibility of the photograph."[15] Destroy the photograph, destroy the credibility or the very existence of a life. Both the Madres and the military enact, each in their own ways, the faith in photography as one particular type of evidence.

When the Madres took to the streets to make the disappearance visible, they activated the photographs, performed them. The Madres needed to be mobile, and it was important that the photographs be visible from a distance, so the placards the women carried as they paraded around the plaza were oversized yet lightweight. The Madres' performance, like all performances, needed to engage the onlooker. Would the national and international spectators respond to their actions or look away? And by wearing the small photo IDs around their necks, the Madres turned their bodies into archives, preserving and displaying the images that had been targeted for erasure. Instead of the body in the archive associated with surveillance and police strategies, they staged the archive in/on the body, affirming that embodied performance could make visible that which had been purged from the archive.[16] Wearing the images like a second skin, the Madres highlighted the affiliative relationship that the military tried to annihilate. They created an epidermal, layered image, superimposing the faces of their loved ones on themselves. These bodies, the images made clear, were connected—genetically, affiliatively, and now, of course, politically. This representational tactic of indexability mirrored the more scientific one undertaken by the Abuelas: to establish the genetic link between the surviving family members and the missing children by tracing DNA.

The Abuelas, picking up the representational strategies used by the Madres, further developed the use of photography in searching for their disappeared grandchildren. While they have continued to use DNA testing to find these children, they have also begun to rely heavily on photography. In an exhibit "Memoria gráfica de Abuelas de Plaza de Mayo" at the Centro Cultural Recoleta in Buenos Aires (April 2001), they exhibited the same photographs the Madres have long paraded around the plaza. Here, the photos were set up in family units—the photos of the missing father and the missing mother. Next to it, however, they inserted a mirror (fig. 6). Spectators looking into that mirror are prompted to ask themselves: Am I the missing child? A photography exhibit might seem to belong more to the archive than to the embodied repertoire, yet this one stages a performance of shock and hopefully, on some level, recognition.

The spectator may not be the disappeared child, but five hundred children continue to be disappeared. Not just personal, or even national, issues of memory and identity are at stake. As the Abuelas put it, "encontrarlos es encontrarnos" (finding them is finding ourselves).[17] Multiple investigative

FIGURE 6. The placement of mirrors next to images of the disappeared in the photography exhibit "Memoria gráfica de Abuelas de Plaza de Mayo" at the Centro Cultural Recoleta in Buenos Aires (April 2001) forces spectators to ask themselves, Am I their disappeared child? Photos by Gabriella Kessler, courtesy of Paula Siganevich.

and reconciliation commissions have been set in place the world over, and international tribunals have been established to deal with the genocidal legacies that continue to tear communities and countries apart. Memory, as the Abuelas' exhibit "Memoria gráfica" makes clear, is an active political practice. "When they ask us what we do, we can respond, 'We remember.'" Memory intervenes, catches the spectators unaware, and places them directly within the framework of violent politics. The mirrors remind the onlookers that there are several ways of being there. Looking at an exhibition in a museum may constitute a different form of presence than the live participation demanded by performance, but this exhibit seizes the spectator, demanding live participation and identification. The DNA of performance reminds onlookers that they, too, are in the genealogical line, heirs to a continuing struggle for national identity and definition.

H.I.J.O.S.

Like the Abuelas and Madres, associations that politicize affiliative bonds, H.I.J.O.S. emphasizes its identity as an organization based on (but not reduced to) biological kinship. It identifies itself as "una organización de derechos humanos que agrupa a los hijos de desaparecidos y perseguidos políticos de la última dictadura militar Argentina" (a human rights organization that unites children of the disappeared and politically persecuted victims of the last military dictatorship in Argentina). Members of H.I.J.O.S. came to know each other by accident. Just as the Madres originally met in police stations and hospitals as they searched for their missing children, these children of the disappeared and political prisoners met at a conference on the disappeared held at the University of La Plata in 1995. Like the Madres, H.I.J.O.S. does not highlight individual or personal loss. Just as the Madres consider themselves sociopolitical mothers of all the disappeared, so too H.I.J.O.S. struggles to insure justice for all the disappeared by bringing criminals to trial: "Juicio y castigo" (Justice and punishment) is their motto (just as Madres used "Aparición con vida" [Live appearance or Live recovery] as theirs), and their sights are clearly set on the repressors. Memory, for most of these young people who grew up without their parents, is a political project.

Like the Madres, H.I.J.O.S. continues its fight against impunity and forgetting through the highly visible use of public spectacle, using their bodies to humiliate those in power. Like the Madres, H.I.J.O.S. meet at a predetermined time and place to carry out their protest en masse. They move in unison, yelling, singing, dancing, and holding hands to create a protective ring around the protestors even as they deliver their denunciation. Some of the visual features of their activism resemble those of the Madres: the use of a wide horizontal banner with their name on it (fig. 7) and the large placard photographs of the disappeared (fig. 8).

Nonetheless, their performance in fact looks and feels very different. Instead of the ritualistic protest and mourning of the Madres, confined to the Plaza de Mayo, H.I.J.O.S. organizes carnivalesque *escraches*, or acts of public shaming. *Escraches* (etymologically related to *scracè*=*expectorar*, meaning roughly to expose or to spit)[18] constitute a new type of guerrilla performance that forces Argentina's criminal politics into the open by targeting perpetrators. The perpetrators range from little-known physicians who assisted in torture sessions to the CIA, the School of the Americas, the infamous Campo Olimpo, where hundreds who opposed the military dictatorship were tortured and disappeared, and Plan Condor, a hemispheric plan of cooperation among right-wing military factions that ensured that activists targeted for disappearance would be abducted, tortured, and murdered even if they fled their country. The *escraches* aim to heighten public awareness that these unpunished crimes, criminals, and criminal organizations continue to exist in the context of a supposed return to democracy. Current neoliberal economic policies in Latin America, they argue, simply continue the economic policies of the dictatorship in more modern guise.

Usually, *escraches* are large, festive, humorous, and mobile demonstrations involving between three hundred and five hundred people. Giant puppets and military pigs-on-wheels parade through the streets (figs. 9 and 10). H.I.J.O.S. reproduces photographs of perpetrators on pamphlets (fig. 11), and with the help of the activist artists Grupo Arte Callejero they parade and post street signs marking the distance to a perpetrator's home (fig. 12). They paint the repressor's name and crimes in yellow paint on the sidewalk in front of his house. Vans with loudspeakers announce the aims of the protest as hundreds of people dance, jump, and parade down the main streets of Buenos Aires, Cordoba, and other major cities. The human rights violations have neither been punished, nor, in fact, have they ended. H.I.J.O.S. reminds its fellow citizens that they continue to live in proximity to criminal politics.

FIGURE 7. At protests, H.I.J.O.S., like las Madres, uses the long horizontal banner with their name on it, 2000. Photo courtesy of H.I.J.O.S.

FIGURE 8. H.I.J.O.S. uses the blown-up photo IDs of the disappeared in their rallies, 2000. Photo by Mariano Tealdi.

FIGURES 9 and 10. H.I.J.O.S. and Grupo Arte Callejero participate in an
escrache. *Escraches* are characterized by their rowdy and festive mood. A truckload
of protesters exhibit their signs and banners. The banner on the truck exclaims, "If
there is not justice, there will be an *escrache*." Photos courtesy of H.I.J.O.S.

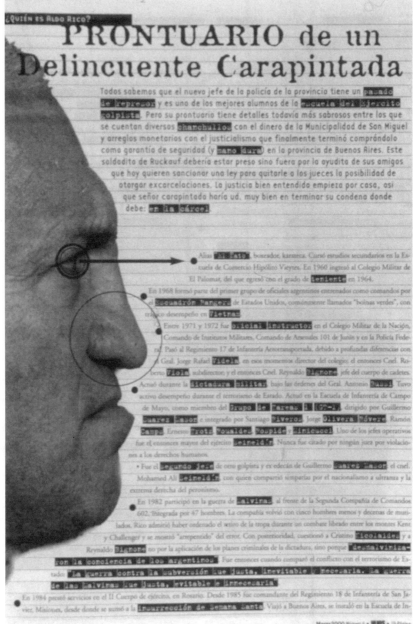

FIGURE 11. Courtesy of H.I.J.O.S.

FIGURE 12. Street signs with the photograph of the perpetrator to mark the distance to his home, 2000. Courtesy of Grupo Arte Callejero.

FIGURE 13. "You are here": 500 meters from a concentration camp, 2000. Courtesy of Grupo Arte Callejero.

Grupo Arte Callejero has developed a system of street signs that provide an alternative map of Argentina's sociohistorical space: a "You are here" sign placed five hundred meters from a concentration camp (fig. 13). Their performance, like the Abuelas' exhibits, reminds fellow citizens that there are different ways of being there—that is, of being caught up in criminal politics.

H.I.J.O.S. uses photographs in several ways. First, they hunt down recent photographs of their military targets to use in their *escraches*. Military repressors, not surprisingly, are the first to burn their own photographs as they struggle to change their appearance and reinvent identities. (To paraphrase Barthes again: eliminate the photograph, eliminate the criminal / crime.) If no recent photographs are available, H.I.J.O.S. follows its prey and furtively snaps pictures of them. A second use of photography, one which I will not discuss here, is far more personal. H.I.J.O.S. forms collages and installations in which they insert their own photograph next to that of their missing parent(s). The resulting "family photographs" give a sense of physical prox-

FIGURE 14. *Otro gobierno, la misma impunidad*: "Different government, the same impunity," 2000. Photo by Diana Taylor.

imity and intimacy that were denied in reality. Third, H.I.J.O.S. at times uses the blown-up photo IDs of the disappeared at their rallies.

I find H.I.J.O.S.'s use of the recognizably identical photographs of the disappeared displayed by the Madres is interesting, especially considering that they appear in the demonstrations after the Madres have stopped (for the most part) carrying theirs. The Madres continue to wear the small ID photo, encased in a plastic sleeve, around their necks. The large images on placards, however, belong to their performance past. The Madres' goal now is less to give evidence as to the existence of the missing than to denounce the politics of impunity (fig. 14). "We know who the disappeared were," the Madres said when they changed strategy in 1983. "Now let's see who the disappearers are." The members of H.I.J.O.S., on the other hand, never sought to give evidence in the same way. They entered the political arena long after the Madres had declared, "We know who the disappeared are." They never needed to prove, as the Madres did, that their loved ones were missing. When the protestors of H.I.J.O.S. carry photo IDs at their rallies, they index the continuity of a representational practice. They are quoting the Madres, even as they acknowledge the other influences, here the carnivalesque Goya and images from other cultural registers. They, like the Madres, take the archival photographs and doubly remobilize them: they signal both the archival use of the ID and the performative use associated with the Madres. The archival photos are performed again, but in a more complicated manner that signals various artistic and representational practices as well as the clearly defined political ones. The photographs of the disappeared, I contend, serve as placeholders in a sense, a way of assuring the place of the disappeared in the genealogical chain. The photographs assure that the victims are neither forgotten nor "surrogated." No one else will take their place. The members of H.I.J.O.S. continue the genetic line and to some degree the political trajectory of defiance, calling attention to the violence of the breaks.[19] Unlike surrogation in Roach's genealogy of performance, which covers up the vacancy by substituting one figure or person for another (the king is dead, long live the king), the DNA of performance demonstrates the continuity without surrogation. The specific link—though missing—can and needs to be identified for the genealogy, and the denunciation, to make sense.

Fotografía

Julio Pantoja's collection of portraits of the children of the disappeared, entitled "Tucumán, The Children: Twenty Years Later" represents another role of photography in performance activism, one that enables us to flesh out some of the nuances between the DNA of performance and Roach's genealogy. Pantoja's images occupy a different kind of space (the gallery wall) and form a different kind of archive (fig. 15). Here are portraits instead of photo IDs, and (of interest for my purposes) portraits that include photo IDs (figs. 16, 17). These portraits call for other forms of spectatorship and public response. They hang on walls, not people's bodies, and occupy interior viewing spaces rather than police files. They do not move in the same way as placards performed in public spaces. Unlike the photo exhibit organized by the Abuelas, these images do not participate in a direct intervention. They are portraits. Nonetheless, the images engage both the police and the contestatory uses of photography mentioned earlier.

Unlike the case of the Abuelas, Madres, and H.I.J.O.S., models of collective activism, Pantoja's "Tucumán" series constituted his own individual form of political intervention. When Antonio Domingo Bussi, a known torturer

FIGURE 15. Photo exhibit by Julio Pantoja, "Los Hijos, Tucumán veinte años después," Tucumán, 1999.

FIGURES 16 and 17. These children of the disappeared knew their parents only from photographs. Many of them are now the same age as their parents when they were disappeared. Photo exhibit by Julio Pantoja, "Los Hijos, Tucumán veinte años después," Tucumán, 1999.

during the dictatorship, was democratically elected as Tucumán's governor, Pantoja was moved to express his sentiments through his own instrument: photography.[20] The space and staging of Pantoja's resistance differ from those of the other movements: the Madres confront the whole governmental system by staging their denunciation in the Plaza de Mayo; the Abuelas shock spectators into reconsidering assumptions about personal and national identity; H.I.J.O.S. collectively denounces individual perpetrators and organizations. Pantoja's photographs, by contrast, call attention to the ongoing nature of the trauma lived day to day in the lives of the surviving children. While re-presenting some of the visual strategies associated with the Madres—particularly the insertion of the placards in the portraits—the photographs focus on individual pain (the thirty-three photographs of the children).[21] While photographs belong in what I have called the archive and need to be taken out of the archive to be performed, Pantoja reverses this scheme: he archives the embodied nature of traumatic loss. Some of these young people are activists, part of H.I.J.O.S. and other organizations. But these images capture the trauma outside of the solace of performance protest. Here, they, with their complicated and broken histories, are in focus. The trauma as well as the political activism lives on.[22]

Interestingly, Pantoja politicizes the traditional, usually elitist, genre of portrait photography as his form of intervention. Like the H.I.J.O.S. and its *escraches*, he turns the military's use of the ID against the military. His portraits work against the restrictions, the exclusions, and the isolation of the ID. In these images, the children have chosen to situate themselves in relation to their history, their environment, their interests. All but two of them choose to pose alone (there are two photos of young women with their children). In most cases, they introduce a complex personal life: music, religion, physics, pop culture, and politics all make their way into these photos. The cultural spaces under attack by the dictatorship—the home, the body, popular culture—participate in the denunciation. Pantoja's use of captions also merits attention. On one level, the simple labeling "Pablo Gargiulo, 20 años, 1996" (see fig. 4 above) echoes the use of photography to reduce and categorize subjects for the archive. On another, it reiterates the Madres' political use of the caption to defy erasure. The Madres marked the names of the disappeared and the dates of their abduction to resist the military's attempt to annihilate both the individual and the evidence. Now, it's the children's names and ages that appear, in Pantoja's captions. The photographs make the generational transmission visible, both as rupture and as continuity. This captioning practice, an allusion to social space and the practice of disappearance, would be clearly understood by Argentines who remember the representational trajectory.

The individual focus notwithstanding, Pantoja's images function as a form of denunciation (like those of the Madres), as a re-presentation of the evidence (police archives or DNA), and as works of art. As evidence, they prove that people and lives have been broken by military violence. The children who chose to be photographed holding photos or with photos in the background attest to the loss the military tried to deny. The trauma and the denunciation continue into the present. The perpetrators, still unpunished, enjoy their freedom outside the frame. These photographs constitute their own type of *escrache*. Julio Pantoja is, in one way, an *escrachador*, another term for a photographer who exposes the uglier side of life. In these images, the *escrache* works indirectly in that the target is not the person in the portrait but the criminal who, having escaped incarceration, flouts justice. The innocent faces looking out provoke a double-take and a visual layering or double exposure in the viewer—I see Bussi (and Rico and Videla and Massera and . . .) in each of those faces. The photographs, in their own way, interpellate the spectators and so urge them to act. The photos reach outside their frame, calling the viewer to take them outside the space of the gallery by making the connections.

Pantoja's weapon or tool of choice, photography, highlights the role of the arts in social crisis. Targeted by the armed forces, the arts played a central role in the articulation and transmission of collective memory both during and after the Dirty War. The galleries, Pantoja reminds us, are not a privileged elite space separated from the strife of civil conflict. The arts in Argentina, however censored, afforded one of the few spaces in which the population could rehearse a sense of identity and articulate a social memory. Photography, as these portraits illustrate, has long brought the seemingly separate worlds of arts and politics together in mutually defining ways. The black-and-white photographs brilliantly bring various visual worlds together—the black-and-white photo ID of the police archive, the black-and-white photos carried by the Madres as signs of resistance, the black-and-white photo of classic art photography. The tired binaries that posit art as being incompatible with politics collapse in the face of these photographs—so clearly art, so clearly politics.

In bringing this these children together as part of a series, a genetic pool of sorts, Pantoja asked himself what differentiated the children of the disappeared *visually* from others? The resulting group of photographs reveals some of the markers I suggest typify this DNA of performance. In twelve of the thirty-three photographs in the collection, the children locate themselves in relation to a photo of the disappeared parent. The centrality of the photographs, on one level, bespeaks a profound personal truth: these children, Pantoja tells us, knew their parents only from photographs. Many of them are now the same age as their parents were when they disappeared. But both genetically and visibly, the children resist the tugs of surrogation. While many of the children idealize their missing mothers and fathers, they haven't taken up their fight in any straightforward way—except as the fight for justice and human rights. Rather, they assume their place in a line that signals rupture and continuity. The place of the missing member of the family is reserved, made visible, through the photograph. In four of these cases, the children choose the same photos as those used by the Madres in their demonstrations. The isolated head-shots have a recognizable history. By including these particular images in their own portraits, the children acknowledge not just the existence of their parents but the violent history of political struggle surrounding the images of the disappeared. In these photos, the parents reappear as *desaparecidos*. Unlike the familial photographs chosen by the other eight children, these four are oversized, cropped, and mounted to be viewed in the public arena. Used formerly as weapons in a war of images, they (like the violent loss) prove impossible to domesticate. Like the Madres, the children struggle to repossess the images and recontextualize them, either by reintroducing them into the domestic space or by holding them against their bodies. They, like the Madres, have become the paradoxical living archive, the embodied home of the remains. We see the past reiterated, not as much in the photographs as in the positioning of the children themselves. The children, like the Madres, represent themselves as the conduit of memory.

This representational practice, to propose one possible reply to Pantoja's original question, is what visibly differentiates the children of the disappeared from other young people their age. More than their personal histories, perhaps, they share a cultural practice of embodying and performing that history. They, like the Madres and like other victims of trauma, carry what Cathy Caruth calls an "impossible history" within them. Yet what links them, the DNA of performance, is the way in which they make that history visible and politically efficacious.

Pantoja, who is not related to the disappeared, offers artists and activists an opportunity to think about how to intervene not only in the fight against ongoing criminal politics, but also in the representational practices that have stemmed from the Dirty War. Pantoja's portraits make clear that the images of the disappeared exist in dialogue with many other kinds of images. In his portraits, we recognize the children's links back to the Abuelas and Madres— that is one form of transmission. However, this form exists in relation to other forms of circulation. The wall plastered with advertisements featuring young, beautiful women-as-objects points to one commercial and gendered economy of representation. The young man wearing the Jim Morrison T-shirt signals another. He, too, illustrates the epidermal strategy associated with the Madres of wearing faces on the body. But here it is Morrison's face, in repeated poses, that serves as a second skin. Visually superimposed on this example of mass reproduction, the young man offers another model: a kind of genealogical family tree. His photograph highlights various family members at several points in their lives. The image signals the complexities of understanding and replicating the images of the disappeared in this wider system of representation. Pantoja's work thus offers both a model of intervention and a warning. Even images as specifically coded as those of the disappeared can become commercialized and performed in ways that cannot always be controlled.

Last, Pantoja's work sounds one further cautionary note. The warning here may be about limiting one's forms of intervention to some narrow or biologically deterministic understanding of the DNA of performance. With all the emphasis on collective action organized by survivors—Abuelas, Madres, Familiares, and H.I.J.O.S.—Pantoja suggests that we not forget the politics of the one: the one who has witnessed the violence and who accepts the responsibility of joining the ranks of resistance. Most of the people who look at these portraits are not victims, survivors, or perpetrators, but that is not to say they have no role to play in the global drama of human rights violations. The Dirty War, sponsored by the CIA and the School of the Americas and

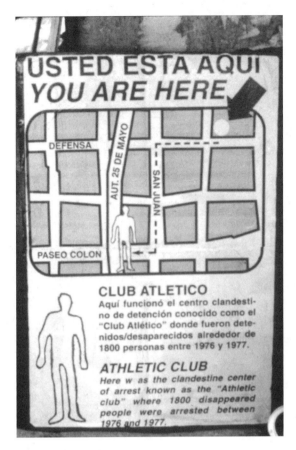

FIGURE 18. "Usted Está Aquí, You Are Here," 2000. Courtesy of Grupo Art Callejero.

organized through the workings of Plan Condor, was truly hemispheric. Thus, the DNA of performance, like current biological research, might expand, rather than limit, our sense of connectedness: we all share a great deal of genetic, cultural, political, and socioeconomic materials. As performance protest reminds us, we are (all) here (fig. 18).

Notes

1. Nora, "Between Memory and History: Les Lieux de Mémoire," in Genevieve Fabre and Robert O'Meally, eds., *History and Memory in African-American Culture* (New York: Oxford University Press, 1994), 284–300, quote on 285; E. Claparede, "La question de la 'mémoire' affective," *Archives de psychologie* 10 (1911): 361–77

(esp. 367–69), quoted in J. Bennett, "The Aesthetics of Sense-Memory: Theorising Trauma through the Visual Arts" (work in progress).

2. Schechner, *Between Theatre and Anthropology* (Philadelphia: University of Pennsylvania Press, 1985), 36.

3. Maurice Halbwachs, *On Collective Memory*, ed. and trans. Lewis A. Coser (Chicago: University of Chicago Press, 1992), 43.

4. See, for example, Cathy Caruth, *Unclaimed Experience: Trauma, Narrative, and History* (Baltimore: Johns Hopkins University Press, 1996), and Shoshana Felman and Dori Laub, *Testimony: Crisis of Witnessing in Literature, Psychoanalysis, and History* (New York: Routledge, 1992).

5. Felman and Laub, *Testimony*, 57, 62. Italics in the original.

6. "Performance's only life is in the present. Performance cannot be saved, recorded, documented, or otherwise participate in the circulation of representations of representations: once it does so, it becomes something other than performance" (Phelan, *Unmarked: The Politics of Performance* [New York: Routledge, 1993], 146).

7. Roach, *Cities of the Dead: Circum-Atlantic Performance* (New York: Columbia University Press, 1996), 2.

8. Bernardino de Sahagún was very suspicious and nervous about the new cult of the Virgin:

Where the [pre-Hispanic] basis of this Tonantzin was born is not known for certain, but what we truly know is what the word signifies from its first imposition, to that ancient Tonantzin, and it is something that should be remedied . . . this appears to be a satanic invention to lessen the idolatry under the equivocation of this name Tonantzin and they come now to visit the Tonantzin from far off, as far off as before, which devotion is also suspicious because everywhere there are many churches of Our Lady and they do not go to them and [but they do] come from distant lands to this Tonantzin as in the olden times.

From Sahagún's *Historia General*, 3:133–34, *Florentine Codex*, Intro. vol. I, 90. Trans. and ed. Arthur J. O. Anderson and Charles E. Dibble. Ed. Vol. Book 1–12 (Santa Fe: School of American Research and University of Utah, 1982). Also quoted in Florescano, *Memory, Myth and Time in Mexico*, 133–34.

9. Pratt, "Why the Virgin of Zapopan Went to Los Angeles: Reflections on Mobility and Globality." Lecture at King Juan Carlos II of Spain Center, New York University, April 16, 2001.

10. See Mary Carruthers, *The Book of Memory* (Cambridge: Cambridge University Press, 1990), 16.

11. For a succinct discussion of DNA, see Matt Ridley's *Genome* (New York: Harper Colllins, 1999).

12. See Diana Taylor, *Disappearing Acts: Spectacles of Gender and Nationality in Argentina's "Dirty War"* (Durham: Duke University Press, 1997), chap. 7.

13. Sekula, "The Body and the Archive," *October* 39 (1987): 3–64.

14. Taylor, *Disappearing Acts*, 277 n.13.

15. Barthes, *The Responsibility of Forms: Critical Essays on Music, Art, and Representation*, trans. Richard Howard (New York: Hill and Wang, 1985), 10.

16. The archive in the body is related to what I have elsewhere called the "repertoire"—the embodied images and behaviors that get transmitted through performance. Here, the embodied performance consciously displays the "archival" both as it promises to preserve materials, and it threatens to erase them.

17. "Teatro por la identidad," Postcard/flyer, Abuelas de Plaza de Mayo.

18. José Gobello, *Diccionario Lunfardo* (Buenos Aires: Peña Lillo, 1982).

19. While members of H.I.J.O.S. officially endorse the political activism of their parents, and vow to continue it, they have thus far avoided the schisms (between Montoneros, ERP, and other groups) that characterized their parents' movement.

20. "Durante los cuatro años que duró el formalmente democrático gobierno de Bussi, me dediqué sistemáticamente a retratar a los hijos de víctimas de la represión en Tucumán, que según los organismos de Derechos Humanos deben ser alrededor de mil. Al principio fue tal vez sólo un impulso casi ingenuo de resistencia empujado por la indignación, pero de a poco fue consolidándose y tomando forma de una toma de posición lúcida usando mi herramienta: la fotografía" (Pantoja, "Los Hijos, Tucumán veinte años después," Web site, http://juliopantoja.com.ar/).

21. In developing this series, Pantoja asked the children to choose their own setting, their own pose, their own objects. "Tomar cada una de estas fotografías llevó horas, y hasta días, de charlas y confidencias con desteñidos álbumes de fotos también descoloridos sobre nuestras manos . . . les proponía elegir un lugar que tuviese que ver con sus historias" (ibid.).

22. Caruth, ed., *Trauma: Explorations in Memory* (Baltimore: Johns Hopkins University Press, 1995).

A City that Improvises Its Globalization

NÉSTOR GARCÍA CANCLINI

For Martín and Silvia,
for their twenty-five years in Mexico.

If to write about globalization is, as Arjun Appadurai says, "a modest exercise in megalomania" (Appadurai 1996), then Mexico City, given its size, is an ideal place to start. Apart from its vast size, Mexico's megalopolis meets the four criteria that have typically defined a global city: a strong presence of transnational corporations, a multicultural mixture of populations drawn from diverse regions both within and outside of the country, a concentration of scientific and artistic elites from which the city derives prestige, and a high volume of international tourism.

Although the contradictory development of the capital denies Mexico City a ranking among the most recognized global cities (New York, London, and Tokyo), its economic influence in both the region and the world places it within a second tier, alongside Barcelona, Berlin, Brussels, Paris, and Hong Kong. Like these cities, Mexico's capital stands out for the prominence of its financial sector and of its consulting, publicity, and design industries and also for its headquartering of the audiovisual and communication industries (Borja-Castells 1997, Sassen 2001). It is only beginning to be recognized that these cultural and communicational resources could contribute to the socio-economic development of the capital and the renovation of its deteriorated public life. In this essay I suggest ways in which cultural policies would need to be reformulated to achieve these objectives.

Is Pollution All There Is to See?

The Museo de la Ciudad (City Museum) has no permanent collection of contemporary or historical Mexican art, and only in the past five years have attempts been made, albeit with a paltry budget, to revamp the museum with exhibitions highlighting themes related to urban life. Nor does the government of Mexico City have an acquisitions policy that would begin to develop a basic stock of materials and documents to conserve the memory of the city or that would establish collections of artistic works. The federal government has also paid only minimal attention to the preservation and celebration of urban culture, and what little effort it once made disappeared in the wake of the economic crisis of 1982.

As a consequence of this neglect, one of the capitals of Latin American art is losing the possibility that new generations will be able to view what has been created over the past forty years. Many valuable works of art have been sold abroad or disseminated among private collections. For the millions of tourists who visit Mexico City every year, there is no building where they can go to see a balanced overview of Mexican art after muralism and geometrism. This absence of contemporary cultural representations reinforces the stereotype of Mexican culture as nothing more than pyramids, murals, and Frida Kahlo. It is difficult to explain to friends from other places or to Mexican youth of today that the post-1968 period was replete with abstract expressionism, conceptual art, novel manifestations of public art, and experimentation in the visual arts. A city that attracted the attention of artistic and political journals, newspapers, and television because of its rebellious and innovative popular movements, its battles for democracy, and the feminism and youth movements of the sixties, eighties, and nineties is now noted only for its record levels of pollution and crime. As these cultural movements fade away and their protagonists die off, their works are becoming increasingly dispersed and unavailable to the public.

One of the challenges facing Mexico is what to do about the gaps in its recent cultural history. A nation cannot situate itself creatively and competitively in a globalized world if it cannot show the world what its culture has recently produced or how it prepared and improvised its entry into globalization. To fill these gaps, researchers will have to act as detectives of sorts, searching through private archives and traveling to libraries and art collections in the United States.

Mexico fascinates thousands of artists and intellectuals, businessmen and tourists, thanks to the potency of its pre-Columbian, colonial, and modern history. These attractions were seductive enough until a few decades ago, perhaps until the National Museum of Anthropology and the Museum of Modern Art were constructed in 1964. Yet in the twenty-first century, these museums do not suffice.

What other sources of cultural capital does Mexico boast today? One can identify at least three, including (1) a vigorous infrastructure for the production of radio, television, and, to a lesser degree, film and contemporary popular music; (2) multicultural communities created by internal migration and by the educational system itself as well as by exiled artists, intellectuals, and scientists from Spain and Central and South America and from Eastern Europe, the latter fleeing the World Wars and the collapse of the Soviet bloc; (3) a long history of existing *between* Europe, the United States, and Latin America and between legacies of indigenous culture and the heritage of modernity. Clearly, Mexico City is not only the capital of the nation. It is also the headquarters of these elements of cultural capital, though the country and the city have only recently begun to deploy these resources.

Mexico City has more museums (ninety-two) than New York (eighty-eight), Buenos Aires (fifty-five), Madrid (forty-seven), and São Paulo (thirty-two). It has more commercial outlets for artisanry and other crafts than all of these cities combined, and its repertoire of entertainment venues is on a par with those of the great cities. But for a city to globalize successfully, it must be safe, and it must feature commercial attractions, modern and postmodern cultures, and, above all, efficient services and adaptable electronic connections.

A survey of five hundred Latin American executives in 2001 highlighted the conditions they demanded of cities before they would consider doing business or residing there. At the top of the list were a combination of high educational and skill levels, security, efficiency, cultural life, ease of international communication, and business conditions (Berríos and Abarca 2001). Mexico City is well situated in terms of communication, cultural offerings, and workforce qualifications. With regard to the latter, one must recognize attempts by the Mexico City government to strengthen education through the newly opened University of Mexico City and its preparatory branches. The effort to broaden university access to the popular sectors is laudable, though it is troubling that admissions are governed by lottery. After all that it took to transition from utopian socialism to scientific socialism, and considering how problem-ridden that process was, Mexico should know better than to try to correct inequalities by trusting to chance.

The desired conditions of efficiency and security are not, as we all know, among Mexico City's strengths. Various government agencies have cited the slow pace of traffic (an average of three hours in transit per day per person to travel distances that should take an hour) as a cause of the city's low productivity. Of course, politicians and businessmen who are influenced by such details do not take into consideration the increase in cultural consumption that takes place during these delays. If residents of the capital lived in a faster-paced city, the shorter period of time they spent in cars and trains would deprive them of listening to an average of two hours of radio a day, they would have less time to hear CDs, and they would notice fewer billboards on the urban expressways. Unfortunately, this obligatory mode of cultural consumption is probably not what national and international investors are most concerned with.

In other words, the wealth Mexico offers to the globalized economy will continue to reside in its Zócalo and in the museums of Chapultepec Park. Yet the new commercial links, the growing patrimony of the cultural industries, and the scientific and technological economies that can articulate Mexico productively with the world are located in the region of Santa Fe, in the south and in the north of the capital. The city also needs cultural and communications policies for what is happening—or what should be promoted—in these areas.

With respect to the multicultural population that inhabits the capital, in 1999 the Mexico City Institute of Culture convened twelve round tables of artists, writers, philosophers, and social scientists to evaluate the presence of German, Argentine, Brazilian, Central American, Chilean, American, British, Jewish, and Asian communities in Mexico. How does having connections with so many countries become a source of wealth in scientific and cultural exchanges and a resource for regional leadership? Mexico has maintained a position of leadership in certain fields, as shown by the number of people who pursue graduate studies there. However, the city's capacity to be a cultural metropolis has been reduced by three main factors: the loss of most of the capital's publishing industry, the decay of the capital's international art exhibitions, and the low level of investment in studies of other regions of the world and of potential international relations strategies for Mexico. Only two institutions in the country are dedicated to researching American culture—the UNAM's Center for the Study of North America and the Colegio de la Frontera Norte—and few places produce work on Latin America and Europe. In other words, little scientific research is being done to learn about Mexico's principal partners in trade and in migration.

The third resource to which I referred—Mexico's intercultural position—has proven fruitful in efforts to mediate international conflicts and in reaching trade agreements (some perhaps too hastily) with other countries. There is very little study of how to take advantage of the city's cultural capital and communications skills through transactions that benefit the country as a whole, rather than two or three privileged firms only. The Fideicomiso para la Cultura Mexico-Estados Unidos, the artists in residency exchange program of the Consejo Nacional para la Cultura y las Artes (CNCA), and, of course, the Consejo Nacional de Ciencia y Tecnología (CONACYT) scholarships for foreigners point in a direction that needs to be expanded. There is a need for greater initiative on the part of the CNCA in cultural and communication studies, particularly in the most advanced fields. But above and beyond what ought to be done at the national level, a megalopolis like Mexico City should have international policies of its own. Experiences of exchanges among European cities and in the intercity networks of Mercosur (for example, between Porto Alegre and Buenos Aires) demonstrate the sorts of initiatives that cities can undertake in order to strengthen themselves reciprocally.

Defending the Multiculturalism of the Future

It is to be expected that sometime before the Free Trade Agreement of the Americas (FTAA) is signed in 2005, one or another of the negotiation meetings will take place in Mexico. I doubt that the transnational businessmen and government officials who come to such gatherings—like squatters occupying empty spaces—will choose to hold their events in the Mexican capital: the problems that have arisen in places like Seattle, Davos, and Geneva will probably discourage any such possibility.

Yet even if none of FTAA's meetings take place in Mexico City, its agreements will have profound effects on the city. From what we know about NAFTA and the World Trade Organization, we can anticipate that the accords will enable transnational investors to appropriate the lion's share of the tangible and intangible cultural heritage of Mexico and Latin America. We already know that the banks they have purchased no longer belong to us, and that in the process we have also lost historic buildings, paintings, and information that is vital to the country. The appropriation of movie theaters by the same corporations that produce and distribute films from Hollywood not only privatizes urban spaces, but also reduces opportunities to see Mexican, European, Latin American, and Asian films. In so doing, it privatizes decisions about our multicultural future. In this context, the city government's decision to sell four cinemas it had purchased at the end of the 1990s, precisely in order to help reverse the trend toward a narrowing of cinematic voices and imagination, testifies to the improvised manner with which we confront our subordination and to the short-term character of our gestures to defend our independence. We hear little about the fact that at the national level as well the budgets for Imcine and the Cineteca are insufficient either to support broader diffusion of Mexican films or to show them in the hundreds of municipalities in which theaters have closed since the early 1990s, when 197 million spectators attended the movies each year, compared to 130 million now.

One of the few strategies available to us to combat the effects of the FTAA is to begin to study and to document our tangible and intangible cultural heritage now and to protect these resources through legislation before the small advances that have been made are negated by such transnational practices as dumping and other forms of unfair competition.

Without a doubt, one of the better ideas from Alejandro Aura's administration in the Ministry of Culture, subsequently continued under Enrique Semo, is that we need to appropriate the Zócalo, culturally and multiculturally, so that one can go there to hear the voices of, for example, Eugenia León, Madredeus, Rubén Blades, Manú Chao, and Charly García. But in addition to ensuring that the world's music can be heard in our main plaza, in our most visible space, this music should also be transmitted through the invisible networks that link us electronically on an everyday level and through which we maintain our relations with the rest of the planet.

In addition to using the Museo de la Ciudad to document our distinct culture, we could place this information—and much more than could ever fit in the museum—in digital format and make computer terminals available in every cultural center, library, and university in the city, across the country, and in cities around the world that are connected by historical or potential relationships with the Mexican capital. Our social memory, our artistic innovations, and the culture that we offer day in and day out would be made available to both physical and virtual visitors. This is much more than a widening of cultural diffusion. Given that in a globalized world we have physical neighbors and neighbors linked to us through networks, these exchanges will enable us to grow as fellow citizens with people who inhabit those places in the world with which we choose to connect ourselves.

A central question of cultural policy, especially in megacities with a strong presence of radio, television, and information, concerns how we should manage the electromagnetic spectrum through which ever-increasing volumes of communication and trade take place. The most valuable property that one can possess in the information era, as Jeremy Rifkin recently wrote, is the system of radio frequencies through which messages are received by our computers, radios, televisions, and Internet servers. Many large cities have begun to abandon the principle that the maintenance of these systems is solely the responsibility of national entities. It is necessary to increase local capacity to regulate the management of these vital and socially valuable resources, engaging in the process both private and public sector actors.

Some cities have globalized through the investments they attract in strategic areas such as recent technologies; others have done so through the construction of emblematic buildings that celebrate the work of famous architects, like the Guggenheim Museum in Bilbao, designed by Frank Gehry; others appear in newspapers and on television around the world for a few weeks because of violent clashes between the globalized and the globalizers. Porto Alegre has entered the global urban iconography through its sponsorship of the World Social Forum, an event that has enabled protest to move beyond disruptions of the assemblies of governmental and corporate leaders and toward reasoned discussion about the conditions which can bring growth not just to the volume of investment, but to societies as well.

A history as rich in social, intellectual, and artistic movements as that which is condensed in Mexico City leads me to propose that the megalopolis should become the site of a World Forum for Innovations in Cultural Policies. I envision a forum that will focus reflection on experiences that renew articulations of culture with social movements and with communication industries and that will seek to expand these linkages. This event would not be simply another political spectacle designed to seduce voters; neither would it become a party space for the nostalgic Left seeking to return to a time before the advent of cultural industries or of the technologies that facilitate the emergence of global markets. Rather, the goal is to try to imagine what to do with communication resources that have globalized not only markets and their vicissitudes, but also the mass media, the arts, critical thinking, and the international human rights movement. Globalization is much more than what neoliberalism wants it to be.

To be serious, a forum along the lines I have proposed should not be disconnected from what the city is already doing. The Social Forum of Porto Alegre had its core backing from a Workers Party government that for fourteen years had been supporting social participation and democratic budgetary management in the city. So that a Forum of Cultural Policy does not become just one more meeting of nongovernmental organizations or of writers and filmmakers who protest globalization without being heard by those who administer it, two conditions have to be met. First, it must facilitate dialogue among the diverse organizations, artists and writers, musicians and filmmakers, mass media institutions, and social scientists studying art, culture, and communication. The second condition is that, as in Porto Alegre, the forum should be founded on the commitment of a city to make use of its resources through new policies of investment, communication, artistic experimentation, and social innovation. This commitment should begin immediately.

Mexico City can bring this forum to reality and use it to propel its own reflection about what it means to be a metropolis in the process of globalization as well as to establish alliances with other cities. We can take advantage of our location at the crossroads of diverse cultures and use it as a foundation for policies of growth and solidarity. In order to accomplish this, however, we must also have the resolve to find solutions to the problems that make the city a chaotic, dangerous place that shies away from shaping its present and its future. Despite insufficient investments, cultural inequalities, and social disintegration, we have what it takes to create our own globalization.

2 Maneuvers

The Cultural Agency of Wounded Bodies Politic: Ethnicity and Gender as Prosthetic Support in Postwar Guatemala

DIANE M. NELSON

> pros-the-sis (präs'the sis) *n.* 1. [NL. fr. Gr. addition, fr. *prostithenai* to add to, fr. *pros*, in addition to +*tithenai*, to place, DO] *Med.* a) the replacement of a missing part of the body, as a limb, eye, or tooth, by an artificial substitute *Corp.* b) tool, support, phantasmatic structures *Cyb.* c) Hooked on technology, able to send a whole part of myself out, an extension of my will, of my instrumentality *Fem.* d) overcoming a lack of presence, the site of pleasure and pain—**n. prosthetic relationality** (medium of connection)—*Websters* 1980, Gray et al. 1995, Stone 1995

Culture—as tradition, timeless practices, identity—is often associated with women. It is the mother who passes culture down through the generations; the woman who maintains traditional clothing, language, practices. This *idea* of the Traditional Woman is a fantasy, a powerful ideological construct, if sometimes also real. In discussions of ethnic and nationalist movements (powerful sites of agency or activism), this idea of Woman has been described as the ground of culture *on* which politics is based.

In this essay I explore the role of this fantastical Traditional Woman in Guatemala, where she is Maya. I call this figure or idea *La Mujer Maya* (italicized and capitalized, following the format that differentiates Woman as idea from real women) to differentiate it from actually existing Mayan women. I explore attempts to deploy agency—*actuario* as the term is translated in Guatemala—in an unequal world through the way the Guatemalan nation, Ladinos (nonindigenous people, who comprise between 40 and 60 percent of the population), and the revolutionary project rely on the cultural image of the Maya, and especially *La Mujer Maya*, as prosthetic. I then explore how the burgeoning Mayan cultural rights movement, bearing the weight of this dependency while seeking representation and agency within the nation-state and beyond, itself depends on the prosthetic support of *La Mujer Maya* (as does "Américan" scholarship, of which this essay is a part).[1]

I suggest that these identifications, nation, ethnicity, gender, vocation, are like wounded bodies and rely on supports like the imagined *Maya* and *Mayan woman* in order to exist.

The prosthetic makes up for something missing, covers over an opening, overcomes a lack of presence (Stone 1995). National, ethnic (Maya and nonindigenous), gender, and trans-Américan identities are stumped, in the sense of being incomplete, wounded, and rudimentary as well as being baffled and unsure. "To stump" also means to make political speeches or support a cause, to deploy active agency, and I argue that, similarly, these identities are always political, the result of process and work. These images of the *Maya* and *La Mujer Maya* also affect actually existing indigenous people who, like nationalists, policymakers, revolutionaries, and intellectuals, are also attempting to stump, or make political impact, that is, deploy some agency, on postwar Guatemala as it is buffeted by changes in national and global capital. This chapter looks at the conditions of possibility for Mayan people's expression and cultural agency, even as they are leaned on and themselves in turn lean on *La Mujer Maya* for support.[2]

In a language different from the one I have decided to use here, this prosthetic support might be called a fetish. A fetish, with its congealed labor and mystical properties, appears to have agency, to act in the world. But it gains this power prosthetically or vampirically, hiding its reliance on human work and creativity. It seems crucial to explore this confusing fissure in attempting to understand cultural agency and to work with the tensions Martín Barbero identifies between difference and inequality. Of course, our entire Cultural Agency project—of which this book is just one effect—is concerned with overcoming distance and connecting through and via difference, without denying differentials. The connections we are making in the form and content of this project across various borders—disciplinary, national, global, linguistic, and even understandings of the keywords *culture* and *agency*—blossom out into the productive stumping (confusion *and* politics) of prosthetic relationality. The authors gathered here, like people in Guatemala and throughout the Américas, are actually existing and struggling for agency, yet also are stumped, limited, constrained. I suggest these are the contradictory, prosthetic conditions of possibility for cultural agency. I hope the prosthetic metaphor aids us in thinking about agency / action as always already an interaction, an articulation—between the wounded, stumped body and the supports it relies on.

Wounded Bodies Politic

Guatemalans often speak of their nation as a wounded body. When asked about Mayan cultural rights activism, both Ladinos and Maya say that such activism is a "finger in the wound" (*un dedo en la llaga*), suggesting that the addressing of ethnic difference is a painful prodding into a constitutively open field—that identities are stumped. Until recently a human rights pariah, Guatemala is split open by an apartheid-like divide between indigenous peoples and Ladinos, wracked by civil war (a peace treaty was signed in 1996, but much of it remains unimplemented), and suffering stunningly high rates of infant mortality, poverty, and illiteracy. Similarly, five hundred years of colonization and the recent massive violence of the civil war have fractured indigenous identity, never a unified thing, in a process the pan-Mayan movement seeks to remedy. In utopian imaginings of an actively promoted healing of these bodies, culture, via ethnicity and gender, figures prominently. At a time of increasing economic stress and structural adjustment, images of indigenous people, especially women, serve as potent tropes in efforts to construct not only Guatemalan national identity, but Mayan identifications as well as that ambivalent cyborg connection of *gringa* (Adams 1998) and "Américan" scholarly solidarity. To understand these stumped identities, one needs to think of them all together, paying special attention to the idea of the *Maya* and *La Mujer Maya*, who, as prosthetics, make these wounded bodies able to function. How, in turn, do actually existing Mayan men and women, as opposed to the fantasmatic construct of *La Mujer Maya*, achieve cultural agency?

Saving

I began thinking about the metaphor of *La Mujer Maya* as prosthetic because of one of the more macabre jokes I've heard in the seventeen years I've been working in Guatemala. I relate it as a symptom, not because I think it is funny.[3] It goes something like this: an anthropologist had lived in a high-land Mayan village for several years but left when the civil war got bad in the early 1980s. When he returned in the early nineties he noticed a remarkable change and mentioned it to an informant: "You know," he said, "when I lived here before, the women always walked ten steps behind the men. No matter what I would say, they wouldn't change. But now they walk ten steps in front! It seems like you are finally catching up with the times. Before, women would never walk in front of the men." The informant said, "Before there were no land mines."

I suggest that this awful joke does several things in post-Quincentennial Guatemala. This is a moment in which the struggles over the meanings of 1492 and the recent peace treaty have highlighted the many ways ethnic and national identities are stumped, bewildered. When Ladinos tell it, the joke may function as an artificial limb, taking the place of the more overt discourses of racism, amputated by the increasing strength of Mayan activism. For them, the joke may also function as the colonial discourse of *sati*, or widow burning, did for the British in India, as discussed by the postcolonial critics Gayatri Spivak and Lata Mani. It allows Ladinos to feel superior and may legitimate allegedly protective intrusion into Mayan life. Like British intervention into *sati*, the joke allows, in Spivak's formula, for "white[r] men saving brown women from brown men" (1988:297), with saving a potent form of agency.

Notice, too, the irruption of a discourse of progress in the joke ("you are finally catching up with the times"), in which the treatment of women becomes a mark of modernity. Progress discourse, of course, has legitimated assimilationist policies from the British outlawing of *sati* in India to the civil war and structural adjustment in Guatemala. However, there is clearly ambivalence here. What looks modern (like women's rights) is something shockingly different—the grim surprise of the joke. When Mayan men tell this joke, it may express their terror at living in the aftermath of genocidal civil war, which has killed over two hundred thousand primarily but not only indigenous people since the early 1960s (CEH 1999). It may suggest the hope that brown women will save brown men from white counterinsurgency—or even from invisible (hand) counterinsurgency. When a gringa recounts this joke, the audience may laugh guiltily and grimace in horror. But I hope that, offensive as it is, it captures something of the continuing power of patriarchy.

It may also justify an intervention, like this essay, in which I hope to be an agency-full white woman saving brown women from dark humor.

Ground vs. Agency

Spivak, with her "white men saving . . ." calculus, suggests that colonial discourse on *sati* reduces colonized women to an object in order for imperialism to imagine itself as good—as a modern body politic. Mani argues that women are not even objects in this colonial discourse. It is not about them. "I would argue that women are neither subjects nor objects but rather the ground of the discourse on *sati*. . . . In the course of the debates, women came to represent 'tradition' for all participants. Women became the site on which tradition was debated and reformulated" (Mani 1990:117–18). The trope, parallel to what Doris Sommer (1991) calls a "foundational fiction," serves in part to explain why actually existing Maya and women remain largely excluded from postcolonial nationalism and from many ethnic rights movements. Mani suggests we "attempt to reconstruct woman as subject" (Mani 1992:403), but this move from ground/foundation to subject or cultural agent, seems troubled by Spivak's (1988) persistent question: "Can the subaltern speak?"

What Spivak is asking of intellectuals who presume to save the cultural agency of brown women and other disempowered people, of course, is "Can you hear her?" The transparency of access to subjectivity, the very category of subaltern, indigenous, or woman, and the move to "speak for" the other have been stumped (bewildered *and* made political) for some time now. Many of the essays here and the discussions in Cuzco problematize the ways that speaking for someone—crossing fissures of class, race or ethnicity, language, nation, global power, gender, and so forth—can simultaneously drain them of agency while also dialectically, prosthetically supporting and energizing particular bodies politic. The response to these challenges cannot be, of course, to give up on these attempts. But is there a more productive way to engage the desire to save women from being the ground, that is, agency-less? to keep these contradictions surrounding speaking, subjectivity, and cultural agency alive? How are we to investigate the *formation* of identity and the often overwhelming constraints on agency created by enormous power inequalities? I find I am stumped, in fact, by the very metaphor of women as ground because I find it does not encompass the very processes by which national, ethnic, and modern identities and senses of agency-fullness are established. The metaphor assumes already constituted national or colonial and ethnic identities that meet to do battle on the ground of indigenous people or woman—a site, in turn, always already constituted. I chose to tell the land mine joke because its content foreshadows an alternative metaphor: that *La Mujer Maya* functions as a prosthesis. In the joke, imagined as minesweepers, they serve as tools, as bodily extensions in desperate attempts to survive. Fittingly, the ground in the joke is a space of violent fragmentation.

Prosthetics

Asked to explore agency, I try to understand how the *Maya* and *La Mujer Maya* as prosthetic sustain and move nation, ethnicity, modernity, tradition, revolution, and scholarship, while they are simultaneously moved by them. Mark Wigley describes a prosthesis as "a foreign element that reconstructs that which cannot stand up on its own, at once propping up and extending its host. The prosthesis is always structural, establishing the place it appears to be added to" (quoted in González 1995:135).[4] In seeking to understand the multiple interchanges among these identifications or sites of apparent agency in Guatemala and the Américas, I want to describe the deployment of the *Maya* as this active connection, this articulation that changes and constitutes the elements involved through their joining. This is no passive ground. The metaphor insists on culture and agency as always being in process, as a recombinant relation.

The prosthetic metaphor is drawn from recent work in cyborg anthropology, feminist studies of science, philosophy, political economy, disability studies, and neurophysiology (see Davis 1997; Grosz 1994; Jain 1999; Kurzman 2001; Sobchack 1995; Willis 1995). Prosthetics mediate a whole series of those binaries we know we need to think beyond, but which still tend to ground our politics and our theory: self/other, body/technology, actor/ground, first world/third world, culture in the humanities sense of art, theater, literature/culture in the social sciences sense of that great whole which encompasses rules, ritual, organization, meaning systems.

For many of the people we work with and who are reading this book, prosthetics are not metaphoric, as their bodies have been disabled through connections with transnational power—weaponry, assembly lines, toxic pollutants, computer keyboards—or by illness, congenital difference, or the riskiness of everyday life. Like disability studies, attention to prostheses helps us question liberal notions of the individual and agency, the sovereign subject that disavows interdependence. This is because I do not take prosthetics to be lifeless things, "pegs" stuck on to stumped bodies. Instead, like any technology, prosthetics are animated by congealed human labor and emotional investments, inhabited by phantom limbs, the result of actor networks. In turn, in what might be called prosthetic relationality, the body changes through its articulation with the prosthetic, which must be incorporated by the body via what neurophysiology and psychoanalysis call the body image.

Elizabeth Grosz (1994:62–85) describes the body image as a concept mediating mind and body, self and other. It is necessary for posture, movement, and tactility and is a spatiotemporally structured and structuring model of the subject (66). The dimensions and functioning of the body image are apparent in cases of the phantom limb, the abiding sense that an amputated body part is still present. Artificial limbs are made to work through the phantom because amputees learn to manipulate their phantom limb so that it flows into a strapped-on prosthesis, allowing them to maneuver in the world (71). The neuroscientist Paul Schilder calls the phantom limb "a model of how psychic life in general is going on" (in Grosz 73). The body image extends to include external objects and implements with which the subject interacts, "anything that comes into contact with the surface of the body and remains there long enough will be incorporated into the body image— clothing, jewelry, *other bodies* . . . It is only insofar as the object ceases to remain an object and becomes a medium, a vehicle for impressions and expressions, that it can be used as an instrument or tool" (80, emphasis added).

Grosz suggests that this site of interaction, made up of physical perceptions, sensations, and movements of the organic body as well as the fantasmatic dimensions, may be as close as we can get to a self or, for our uses, agency. This self that swells through the phantom limb, that extends the body image to flood, embrace, and make its own any prosthetic brought into use is not untouched by these experiences. The body image is a third term between mind and body that "attests to the necessary interconstituency of each for the other" (85).

I discuss the intersections of material bodies, particularly gendered and racialized or ethnicized bodies, with larger bodies politic as sites of prosthetic relationality precisely because there are huge power differentials at work (imagine all the weight of a body bearing down on the peg leg). Unlike liberal models which want to see two equal bodies meeting on a perhaps uneven playing field, I do not suggest that those bodies leaned on as prosthetics can easily challenge the bodies politic that deploy them. However, I also invoke the notions of body image and prosthetic relationality to resist seeing this power as unidirectional, always moving one way from center to periphery, metropole to margin, body politic to individual body, male to female, white to brown. The prosthetic metaphor does not offer transcendence or even hope of steady ground to stand on, but instead extends what Gray and Mentor playfully describe as the cyborg dialectic—thesis, antithesis, synthesis, pros-thesis. This dialectic is "different than a synthesizing [process] . . . enhance-ments and replacements are never fully integrated into a new synthesis, rather they remain lumpy and semi-autonomous" (1995:466). Allucquere Rosanne Stone describes falling in love with prostheses, writing of such interactions as "couplings" with all the affect that term implies, and she insists that "the structure of pleasure and play . . . is the heart and soul of prosthetic sociality" (Stone 1995:397).

I tender the metaphor of prosthetic rather than ground because it evokes the active and deeply affecting possibilities in these relations. This is a com-plex relationality with a somewhat active participant—not fully synthesiz-able, not a passive ground, and also not the rational free agent of liberal humanism, but a semiautonomous prosthetic in intimate connection with the self. So, without assuming access to the subjectivity of the actually exist-ing indigenous people, I think that the notion of the *Maya* and *La Mujer Maya* as prosthetic can disrupt traditional categories, like actor vs. ground, and get one closer to a theory of cultural agency. Even Lévi-Strauss acknowl-edges this special affect, reminding us that it exists even at that quintessential site of men forming a relation with each other through the exchange of women: "Even in a man's world she is still a person, and in so far as she is defined as a sign she must be recognized as a generator of signs. . . . This explains why the relations between the sexes have preserved that affective richness, ardour, and mystery" (1969:496).

National Prosthetic

That richness and ardor animate the immediately identifiable image of indigenous people, and especially *La Mujer Maya*, in Guatemala. They are constantly troped performing supposedly traditional rituals, providing local color, situated in nature (near a mountain shrine) and/or the past (pre-Colombian ruins). *La Mujer Maya*, dressed in traditional handwoven clothes such as a *huipil* or *traje* with her long hair, is a primary mode for representing the Guatemalan nation in newspapers, postcards, international beauty pageants, business literature, museums, advertisements, and tourism brochures (Otzoy 1996; Hendrickson 1995; Nelson 1994). The nation needs the presence of the image of the *Maya* in public places to suggest the incorporation of the indigenous population, rather than the open wounds of ethnic exclusion. In turn, the *Maya*, especially *La Mujer*, distinguishes Guatemala in the transnational realm. Coverage produced by and about Guatemala often includes the *Maya* for their immediate identifiability.

But modernity and tradition are in complex relation. Partha Chatterjee describes the difficulties facing nationalists in India, which necessitated "rationalizing and reforming the 'traditional' culture of their people," including "science, technology, rational forms of economic organization, modern methods of statecraft," and so on. But this "could not mean the imitation of the west in every aspect of life . . . the self-identification of national culture would itself be threatened" (1990:237).

If the West stands for modernity, with its science and rationality, this national culture also needs tradition—historic depth, origins, a proud link to an ancient Golden Age which may return again. The deep, affecting bond of an imagined community needs more support than military parades and shopping trips to Miami. The national body image needs a relation with sincerity, with moral rectitude, and with the ardor and mystery of home. The Mayan past, represented both by pre-Colombian ruins *and* by contemporary indigenous rural life, serves as this prop for Guatemala, an extension that overcomes the distances between glorious past, degraded present, and hoped-for future. A case in point: while working in a small indigenous village near Lake Atitlán during a recent presidential campaign, I was sitting in on a Catholic Mass when a candidate on a flesh-pressing tour pulled into town with his entourage and tried to enter the church. After waving from the back the candidate withdrew, under the dour gaze of the priest, but several of his Ladino aides remained, and I overheard one say, "My God! This is just like ancient times! See the women all on one side of the church, their heads covered? It's like going back in time!" His companion concurred, saying, "They're all in costume! We really should get out here more often. This is the real Guatemala."

Here it seems that rural village life of the past and the nation itself get condensed into the figure of the *Maya* and *La Mujer*, gender-segregated in public, respectfully worshiping, clad in their traditional finery. While in some towns Mayan men wear *traje*, in most places—especially the capital city—all but the most elder men wear Western clothing, making the significa-tion of traditional clothing almost isomorphic with *La Mujer Maya* who weaves it and wears it. And *traje* brings with it the weight of tradition in general, condensing a whole range of signifieds about spirituality, commu-nity, food, language, children, and the past onto *La Mujer Maya*. This is why she works so well as a prosthetic extension, joining the modern nation's contradictory need to be simultaneously traditional.

Prosperity

The *Maya* are vital for the production of Guatemalan national identity in scenes where, without them, it wouldn't have a leg to stand on. Just as the landmine joke posits *La Mujer Maya* as prosthetic, bearing the brunt of historic violence, so indigenous people have been deployed to face the toxic conditions of Guatemala's frontlines in its articulations with transnational capital. Forced indigenous labor, of course, supported first the colonial and then the incipient national economy. Land expropriation, vagrancy laws, *fincas de mozos* (youth farms) (Oglesby 2002), and other political economic ethnic organizations have made indigenous workers central to Guatemalan development. This dependence is powerfully expressed in the ferocity of state terror unleashed on anyone trying to organize labor unions, especially those that unite indigenous and Ladino (Levenson 1994, CEH). The wry comment of a Ladino friend put it succinctly: "In the civil war they couldn't kill all the Indians. Then who would do the work?"

In the mid-1980s, under conditions of war, debt crisis, rampant corruption, and the historic effects of underdevelopment, Guatemala entered a severe economic crisis that proved to be long lasting. The response negotiated with international lenders (in which, like the peace treaty signed in 1996, only white men were present at the table) has been termed "structural adjustment," and its aims are to lower inflation, drastically reduce public spending, and increase foreign reserves (AID 1982; AVANCSO 1998; Barry 1987; Poitevin 1993). These processes emphasize the image of Guatemala as being wounded, ill, stumped. As Willy Zapata, former president of Guatemala's Central Bank, says, "the medicine must be taken" (quoted in Forster 1996). In Guatemala, the medicine is nontraditional exports, including new crops like snow peas and flowers, maquila production (primarily of textiles), and tourism. The medicine has serious side effects, including increasing poverty caused by the privatization and its accompanying price increases of various basic services and the cutting of government subsidies.

These therapies are supported by particular ethnic and gender power structures. When white men agree to take this medicine so that Guatemala can function in the transnational world, they are leaning on the prosthetic of the *Maya* and of the *Mujer*. Throughout the world, the cheap rural labor that supports urban life and industrialization is often done by ethnically marked people (the terms *peasant* and *indigenous* are frequently confused [Kearney 1996]). These markings are also gendered (Ong 1987; Mies 1991; Enloe 1990). Women's labor makes this new international division of labor possible, in part through what Mies calls their "housewifization." Because women's work is supposedly supplemental to family income—she is "helping out" a father or husband—her wages are much lower than men's: "They see it as a complementary support, they do not value it as vital for the family's survival" (AVANCSO 1995:32). Similarly, the UN Mission to Guatemala (MINUGUA) denounces the fact that "it has become habitual in the agrarian sector that women are not recognized as workers, rather they are seen as collaborating on their husband's tasks and, due to this, they do not receive the wage due for their labors" (2000:16).

Nations pull in foreign investment with what is called an attractive labor pool, and indigenous people and Mayan women, many displaced by war and willing to work for four dollars a day (Green 1999:35) or less, are extremely attractive. Studies of the maquila and new crops in Guatemala have found that many employers prefer to hire young, unmarried women and insist on intrusive, violent means to ensure that they remain productive (and not reproductive). Kurt Peterson, working in Guatemala, reports that "owners almost unanimously desire young, unmarried women in order to capitalize on their availability, youthfulness, and endurance" (Peterson 1992:42). He quotes the personnel manager at a Korean maquila saying, "My ideal worker is young, unmarried, healthy, thin and delicate, single, and does not have previous experience. If they have experience they come with many vices. They do not like to follow orders" (Peterson 1992:43). Over four-fifths of the workers in Guatemala's maquila factories are women, and many of them are indigenous.

Women are also understood to be naturally docile, dexterous, nimble, and genetically programmed to sew and process food—unlike men, whose labor requires strength and effort (Pérez Sáinz et al. 1992; Castellanos de Ponciano and Poitevin 1992). In fieldwork, Claudia Dary (1991:69) and the AVANCSO (1995) research team separately found that most men and women working in the new industries in Chimaltenango, Guatemala—both workers and employers—accept these stereotypes and the resulting wage differentials.

Jane Collier suggests that the division between private—the home as space of leisure and desire—and public—the world of labor and alienation—that defines enlightenment, and the ideals and institutions of citizenship and bourgeois law which facilitate Guatemala's incorporation into transnational markets, depend on this idea of women's natural predilections. The *Maya* in general and especially *La Mujer Maya* function as prosthetic housewife—theirs is the unpaid and underpaid labor of providing food, care, clothing, and so forth. The understanding of indigenous people's so-called natural predilections for this type of work stems both from raciological stereotypes (Gilroy 2000) that they are brutish and best suited to manual labor, and also "genderological." As Hendrickson (1995) has argued, Mayan men are feminized in the gender/ethnic power matrix in Guatemala. Some Ladinos, commenting on the Mayan movement, said to me, "But this is like a wife leaving her husband! She can't just leave, they have a contract, a relation!"

thereby feminizing Mayan men as the wife. Many analysts of state terror in Guatemala and the Americas make a similar claim—that part of the goal of the macho state is to feminize and thereby control men through counter-insurgency violence (Bunster-Burroto 1986). Indigenous men were the primary victims of the Guatemalan army.

Enlightenment's national institutions require people to have natural characteristics, to obey inner voices. "The ideal of a free market for jobs and commodities—that accompanied, and was made possible by, the spread of bourgeois legal concepts and institutions—required competitors for employment and sales to have inner capacities and desires that distinguished them from rivals" (Collier 1997:206–7). The "inner capacities" Mayans and indigenous women deploy in export processing are linked to the home and to women's incarceration there as housewife—an unpaid laborer because she does it for love. In women's "hearts and homes rational men can seek the 'inner voice' that speaks their cultural heritage" (Collier 1997:210). In turn, since this is a modern nation and home and no one is forcing men to labor on plantations and in factories for a pittance, and no one is forcing women to cook and clean, they must do it because they want to. Working in textile manufacturing maquilas and with new crops, Mayan men and women are seen to be doing what comes naturally in the home—weaving, food preparation, and gardening—while simultaneously participating in modern production methods and the production of modern selves. Their reasons for taking on this work are complex, responding to economic and familial pressures as well as hopes and dreams of their own, which often include both pride in their Mayan identity and the desire to be modern. So, while the Mayan home may seem vestigial to the national political economy and transnational markets, I argue that these new industries lean on the interplay of modernity, tradition, nature, and home which coalesce in *La Mujer Maya* at work on the assembly line.[5]

Ladino men may imagine themselves as white men saving brown women through "structural adjustment" and "national development," but that's a joke. Through agro-export development, tourism, maquila production, the new crops, and indigenous men and women's underpaid labor on plantations and in the service industries, actually, brown people are saving white people from red ink.

Revolution

Guatemala's civil war was a struggle to save the nation. The revolutionary movement sought to save Guatemala from these very processes of imperial capitalism and the ensuing red ink. The army and government saw themselves as saving it from the "red scourge" of Communism.[6] The impossible demands of being both modern and traditional also play out in warring salvation narratives.

The rebels were influenced by underdevelopment theory, which argues that advanced or first world countries became that way by vampirizing resources and capital from their (neo)colonial holdings, actively underdeveloping or "stumping" countries like Guatemala (Gunder Frank 1970). The more tightly such countries are tied to this world system, the less likely they are to develop themselves, becoming, instead, wounded bodies politic. As long as Guatemala simply exports a limited number of primary crops and a few value-added manufacturing goods it will always remain a traditional banana republic rather than a modern sovereign nation wielding political, economic, and cultural agency. The structural adjustment medicine agreed on by white men seeking to save the wounded Guatemalan nation is diagnosed by the Left as a poison. It further weakens the (increasingly less) patient, draining the very resources needed for recovery. The revolutionary movement that, in various forms, took up arms from the early 1960s to 1997 was struggling to modernize on a different model of the nation, one based on political and economic sovereignty, and thereby save the patient from this so-called cure.

The first Rebel Armed Forces (FAR), partly inspired by the Cuban revolution of 1959, were primarily Ladino and focused their organizing in the eastern regions of Guatemala, which are not heavily indigenous. A terrible counterinsurgency campaign that included the deployment of U.S. Green Berets destroyed most of the FAR's columns by 1969. As a number of works (CEH 1999; Falla 1992; Frank and Wheaton 1984; Jonas 1991) have described, the 1970s were a transformative period in Guatemala (as elsewhere). A ferment of grassroots organizing—imbricated with liberation theology, struggles for indigenous rights, new social movements like students, migrant workers, women, and the formation of the CUC, or Campesino Unity Committee, which linked rural and urban, Ladino and indigenous workers—created the conditions of possibility for a massive popular movement by the mid-1970s as well as for increasingly repressive countermeasures by a succession of military governments. As U.S.-backed governments fell in Vietnam, Iran, and Nicaragua, and legal means of social change were ruthlessly cut off in Guatemala, increasing numbers of young people began to see armed insurgency as a viable option. "You can't imagine what it was like," a Ladino friend said to me in 2000. "All of your friends were going to the mountain, taking up arms. You didn't know from one day to the next if you might just up and go!"

Two new guerrilla organizations, the Guerrilla Army of the Poor (EGP) and Revolutionary Organization of the People in Arms (ORPA), convinced of the error of working only with Ladinos, who make up less than half the population, concentrated on organizing in the primarily indigenous highlands. According to numerous testimonials (Harbury 1994; Jonas et al. 1984; McAllister 2002; Menchú Tum 1984), thousands of people joined or became unarmed supporters. The army's scorched earth counterinsurgency campaigns killed some seventy thousand people between 1978 and 1984, displaced over one million people, and sent at least one hundred thousand people into exile; several thousand people formed communities of the population in resistance, or CPR, living inside Guatemala but outside army control. The URNG or Unidad Revolucionaria Nacional Guatemalteca (National Revolutionary Unity of Guatemala) lost the war in part because no one foresaw the ferocity of the army's campaign, which destroyed some four hundred villages and was clearly raciological and genocidal (CEH 1999).

The guerrilla forces, including many of the refugee camps in Mexico and the CPR, formed a site of intensive, sometimes violent, and perhaps transformative intimacy between Ladinos and indigenous people, an effect of modernity and nationalism which also complexly joined ethnicity, class, and gender. I don't have space to describe this dense and rich site but want to explore briefly the way the *Maya* and *La Mujer Maya* function as prosthetics to Ladino and revolutionary bodies politic. A returned exile said in October 1992, "The worst part of all this 500 Years stuff is the Maya saying that the Ladinos have no culture. How ignorant! I am Ladino, petit bourgeois, and they tell me I have no culture! We have our literary tradition and a history of resistance! Without us there would have been no 1944,[7] or the resistance of the 1960s. We have a valiant history. We have our own Nobel prize winner in Miguel Angel Asturias!"[8]

These comments reflect a shift in the previous hegemonic reading. Before, culture was a mark of powerlessness, but Mayan organizing, much of it having detoured through the guerrilla movement (Bastos and Camus 2003) is rearticulating culture as a sign of power, throwing previously unproblematic Ladino and progressive identifications into question. Although the Democratic Spring of the 1940s was primarily an urban, Ladino process, it also depended on indigenous support (Smith 1990). Even more dependent, the guerrilla movements of the 1970s that became the URNG incorporated large numbers of indigenous peoples, sometimes entire communities at a time. The guerrilla organizations created transformative alliances, and the resulting changes in consciousness are documented in the two most famous testimonials about the organizing, those by Rigoberta Menchú Tum (1984) and Mario Payeras (1983).[9] The guerrilla organizations worked to theorize the relations among class, ethnicity, and nationalism and attempted to create equal relations among indigenous people and Ladino, men and women, on the ground. They supported indigenous customs as much as possible given their mobility, drew on the heritage of the Conquest-era Maya-K'iche' hero Tecún Umán, and attacked racism in self-criticism sessions (Simon 1988; Díaz-Polanco 1987; author interviews).

There are mixed feelings on how well they succeeded, and public discussion has been, of course, sharply limited and highly overdetermined by the government's ferocious counterinsurgency attacks. (Until 1996 few people were willing even to say the names of the revolutionary organizations out loud!) Clearly, many of the combatants now returned to their communities are indigenous and identify strongly with the revolutionary struggle. But many other indigenous peoples left the organizations, some as part of larger splits, some simply fed up with what they perceived as ongoing racist discrimination, which sometimes turned violent. Despite the large numbers of indigenous combatants and lower-level officers, there were no indigenous *comandantes* representing the guerrillas in the peace talks and few ranking Maya officials (although several Maya have been elected to Congress on the left ticket).

Just as for the Guatemalan nation, the *Maya*—here primarily in the form of the *mujer*, Rigoberta Menchú Tum—functions as a prosthetic to overcome this lack of presence. Although she has distanced herself from them, Menchú Tum is popularly understood to be, if not part of, then quite sympathetic to the URNG.[10] She was the only indigenous person in the United Representation of the Guatemalan Opposition (RUOG), an exile group which spoke during the 1980s for a range of Guatemalan opposition organizations before the UN, foreign governments, and solidarity groups. Her testimonial *I, Rigoberta Menchú* (1984), which makes clear her family's connections to the guerrillas, was produced in collaboration with them and Elizabeth Burgos-Debray as part of a public relations campaign. Her powerful and poignant story, chosen from many others, was deployed prosthetically to explain to world opinion why a people would justly rebel against their government. Menchú Tum is an extraordinary woman whose personal skill, grace, and gravitas have all contributed to the position she holds today, but many Mayan men, Ladino men, and Ladina women have similarly powerful and poignant experiences, many of which are published and available. I argue that the condensations that create *La Mujer Maya*, who prosthetically supports national identity, have also combined to make this particular story known worldwide and to make Menchú Tum an international symbol of resistance and survival. She is both a Mayan woman, acting on the national and transnational stage, and *La Mujer Maya* propping up the wounded body politic of a revolutionary movement that was militarily defeated.

Menchú, as UN goodwill ambassador, also prosthetically supported the peace process, shuttling among the various participants (representatives of the URNG, the Guatemalan government, the UN, and international supporters like the United States), several times jump-starting stalled negotiations. Her presence also helped forestall increasingly bitter critiques from the popular and Mayan movements about their lack of access to the process. While her incorporation was semiautonomous, she was also a brown woman saving white men from red-faced embarrassment at these exclusions. But prosthetic relationality also helps us understand the *Maya* and *Mujer* as a medium of connection among all these sites. She props up stumped bodies politic—Ladino, revolutionary, international solidarity—which could not exist on their own. She extends their scope of operation through international representation; but she is incorporated in intimate, complex ways into these body images. She is lumpy, semiautonomous. Menchú Tum's story may be an ideal prop for extending revolutionary consciousness, which, like national identity, must be both modern and traditional, but in turn she has extended herself in surprising, transformative ways. Some of these changes have been due to her prosthetic, active, recombinant, connection with a variety of bodies, including the guerrillas, the national and international indigenous rights movement, and the UN.

Mayan Prosthetic

While Mayan men have been important prosthetics in supporting the Guatemalan nation, the economic system, and the guerrillas, the pan–Mayan rights movement also depends on *La Mujer Maya* as a prosthetic. In ways strikingly parallel to the wounded bodies politic of the nation-state and state pretenders (the guerrillas) that lean on the Maya to extend their scope of operation, many Mayan activists struggling for cultural agency also prop up their wounded body politic on *La Mujer Maya*, who, of course, is also incorporated in intimate and lumpy ways. Just as Guatemala is imaged as wounded, so the Maya image themselves as stumped, broken. The Guatemalan Mayan Language Academy (ALMG) says, "The Spanish invasion broke the process of our *own* evolution . . . because of the huge differences between one world and another, this experience was highly traumatic for the *pueblo Maya*. . . . we are not only oppressed, but mutilated and atomized" (ALMG 1990:26).

Pan-Mayan organizing for cultural agency and empowerment and against internalized colonialism entails the formation of a body politic from the stumps and wounded body images left by conquest and civil war. This emerging identity must also prove itself appropriate to modernity, which entails appropriating Chatterjee's (1990) markers like science, rationality, technology, and organization as well as speaking Spanish, dressing "professionally," and living in the city. As Collier (1997) suggests, a major marker of modernity required by bourgeois law is following one's inner voice, making rational choices, rather than blindly and mindlessly following tradition. At the same time the Maya must show that they are inappropriate(d) by modernity (Trinh 1986; Nelson 1996). Otherwise they would just be Ladinos, without a valid claim for a separate cultural existence. As Collier says, "Modern nationalists have to find traditions that distinguish them from other nations without marking them as traditional or backward. This task is ultimately impossible . . . but the impossibility does not relieve [them] from the obligation to attempt it" (1997:207).

Struggles for agency are seriously constrained by the unequal power relations that weigh on them with all the force of the national body politic. I argue that owing in part to these very constraints, Mayan cultural rights activists deploy *La Mujer Maya* as prosthetic to overcome this impossibility. Mayan men can take on the signs of modernity necessary for successful activism *because La Mujer Maya* represents tradition. Mayan women are almost completely absent from the upper echelons of the urban-based Mayan organizations, where it is most essential to look modern, but *La Mujer Maya* seems essential to their body image.

Many male activists commute weekly or monthly to highland villages and towns to be with their families. They can have Mayan children—who speak a Mayan language, grow up in a community with ties to the earth, and know their elder family members—because their wives or sisters or mothers remain in the villages and raise the children there. *La Mujer Maya*, who lives in the rural villages, raises children, is monolingual and illiterate, weaves her own clothing, retains the Mayan calendar, pats out tortillas by hand, and maintains the *milpa* (corn crop) while her husband or brother is in the city agitating for indigenous rights, represents the living link to the past, to the Classic Maya. She is the prosthetic that extends across historical distance, making the past present, and thus she legitimizes the urban-based, Mayan activist claim that they are both appropriate to the modern nation and inappropriated by the corruption of current events. Some Mayan activists claim that because Mayan women stayed in the villages and in their homes during the Conquest and Colony they did not interact with the damaging effects of Spanish rule. Thus, they claim, she has never been conquered, and so retains a direct link with the cultural past.

The Mayan movement leans on *La Mujer Maya*, who is produced through the same phantasmic split between public and private that supports the maquila and Guatemalan nation-building. *La Mujer Maya* provides the support necessary for the inappropriated Mayan activist to be both traditional and modern. A symptomatic example of this is an issue of the magazine *Iximulew* produced by the Center for the Study of Mayan Culture (CECMA) and Cholsamaj, staunch members of the urban Mayan movement, and published in *Siglo XXI*, a major daily newspaper. Their issue of August 9, 1996, was dedicated to "Mujeres Mayas," and it repeats tropes I heard over and over in interviews with Mayan male activists. The opening editorial states, "As we reach the millennium we must remember and recognize the decisive and fundamental role played by *La Mujer Maya* throughout time, as the guardian of life, wisdom, knowledge, and the reproduction of our ancestral culture. Especially now when feminist movements from other cultures, foreign to our own, attempt to divide indigenous peoples, as if the divisions promoted by the Protestant sects, the Catholics, the army, the guerrilla movement, and the political parties were not enough, to mention just a few" (CECMA 1996:1). When Mayan women like Francisca Alvarez try to discuss gender issues in the Mayan movement, some Mayan men call them "ethnocidal" (Alvarez 1996:8).

Similarly, one leader of the ALMG said, "A Mayan woman is not a woman unless she makes tortillas. Some women say they don't have time, but this is part of a woman, she cannot leave it behind." Richard Wilson suggests that the Qawa Quk'a movement in Alta Verapaz, which seeks to boycott national and international products in favor of traditional local goods, will lean most heavily on women's labor. "Men's clothes and agricultural tools (especially machetes) are two types of goods that involve participation in the market, yet they are excluded from the boycott. . . . The boycotting of foodstuffs, manufactured soap, and plastic vases is likely to affect women's labor more than men's" (Wilson 1995:287). Women's labor is once again naturalized. Performed in the private space, and because she wants to perform it (since, as Collier reminds us, the home is a place of freedom, so no one is making her do it), it becomes part of her essence. The fact that most Mayan women are monolingual is similarly naturalized as *La Mujer Maya*'s valiant commitment to maintain her language and heritage, rather than an effect of gendered schooling practices which more frequently pull girls than boys out of school to work at home or for wages (Pérez Sáinz et al. 1992). Also naturalized is the hard work of saving money and preparing for and cleaning up after festivals and *cofradía* rituals—all signs of tradition, culture, community, and identity—which naturally falls to *La Mujer Maya* (Stephen 1991; Collier 1997).

Discussion of the genocide suffered by the Maya and emphasis on the natural role of women in passing on the culture to their children have resulted in a marked pronatalist stance among the Mayan rights movement—

another way this body politic leans on *La Mujer Maya*. This discourse leans on *La Mujer Maya*'s naturalized reproductive capacities and domestic role and also suggests the spiritual superiority of the Mayan home, so essential to establishing the Mayan body politic. Similarly, in an almost universal trope, both male and female organizers, when asked about women in the Mayan movement, claim that gender relations are equal among the Maya. This discourse of gender complementarity, central to the paeans in *Iximulew*, separates the Mayan home, represented by *La Mujer Maya*, from the outside world and legitimates the demands of the Mayan body politic. In turn, attempts to inoculate indigenous women against the divisive effects of foreign feminism (which in the *Iximulew* editorial is linked to Protestant sects and the Guatemalan army as threats to the integrity of the Mayan community) suggest an awareness that the prosthetic is lumpy, semiautonomous, and may have a mind of her own.

In turn, detailing this *production* of *La Mujer Maya* as traditional is not to say, as Collier (1997), Paul (1974), Stephen (1991), and others point out, that women do not enjoy a great deal of satisfaction from performing this work well. Clearly, these discourses of ethnic pride move them powerfully and allow them to articulate a range of meanings to their labor. As a prosthetic, *La Mujer Maya* is always more than an exploited victim.

Mayan Women

Intriguingly, in the intimate connection between body politic and prosthesis, sandwiched in the *Iximulew* supplement between the editorial and Mayan men musing about her new awakening to modernity, is a centerfold of notable Mayan women, where a different voice momentarily breaks through. Here are professionals, congresswomen, linguists, professors, journalists, engineers, and researchers—educated, sophisticated, and articulate. This different voice suggests Mayan women find themselves in an ambivalent position, incorporated and essential to Mayan body politics, but also leaned on, and only semiautonomous, deploying cultural agency but also deeply constrained, weighted down. Many Mayan women are active in the movement and find that it incorporates quite nicely with their body image. As Sangari and Vaid (1990) and others have suggested, the figure of Woman that supports national identity formation also holds "ardour and mystery" for that elusive actually existing woman. The home as a place free of colonial disfiguration, ancient stories of gender complementarity, the spiritual power of *La Mujer Maya*—these are empowering discourses for real Mayan women. Mayan women may also lean on *La Mujer Maya* to construct their own visions of the Mayan body politic, although for them she is a less wieldy prosthetic.

For example, a Mayan woman activist said, "Indigenous women use only natural methods of birth control. They would never abort a child! You have the children God gives you and you accept it. Using contraceptives causes birth defects and in the Maya cosmology it is viewed as a sin." In another interview several weeks later, however, she asked me what kind of contraception I used and if I could supply her with information. She said that her husband had left her five years ago with one child and that abstinence was her form of birth control: "If I had stayed with him I would have had many more children and I would not be involved the way I am now, in the Mayan organizations, and going to school. It would have been impossible!"

Many women I interviewed would admit there were problems connected to alcohol consumption, violence, and abandonment in their communities, but would also insist that "among the Maya the man respects the woman. Men are our support, we must walk together." Such statements are *both* about the heterogeneity of body images (see Moraga 1983; Mohanty et al. 1991) *and* a strategic leaning on *La Mujer Maya*. Just as the Maya movement as a whole appropriates modernity and nationalist and sometimes revolutionary discourses of unity along with the glorious Mayan past for their own body politic, Mayan women are leaning on stories of gender equality in the *Pop Wuj*, the traditional Maya book of creation, to struggle over how that body image will look and feel.

Olga Xicox, a Mayan activist, said, "We have to fight against cultural patterns for women to participate. In the communities women worked in the home. Also, before, if a woman began to emerge as a leader and the government noticed, she would suffer government repression, violence. Women are still afraid of participating." In addition to women's own reluctance, they have encountered problems with financing and with the suspicions of Mayan men: "At first the men questioned our work. They were afraid we would tend towards feminism. Only women participate, but we are not feminist. We do not want a westernized organization. . . . Women are the ones who have participated the least, who receive the least support. To be full partners for men and partners in the struggle to maintain our culture, we need to develop ourselves, create new ways of participating."[11]

Mayan women began organizing as women by 1987, and many were energized by the Quincentennial counterdemonstrations and by Menchú's Nobel Peace Prize. By 1994, Mayan women were organizing within the aegis of the peace accords. In the Civil Society Assembly (ASC) they are active in the multiethnic Women's Forum and are working in Guatemalan Coordinator of Organizations of the Pueblo Maya (COPMAGUA) and the Permanent Commission for the Rights of the Indigenous Woman. The commission mobilized twenty-seven thousand indigenous women and helped found the state-supported Mayan Women's Legal Aid Office (*Defensoría de La Mujer Maya*) mandated in the peace accords. In addition, more autonomous groups like Kaq'la and Kichin Konojel have formed.

The sorts of pressures that Xicox suggests above, based in the naturalization of *La Mujer Maya*, influence the conditions of possibility for Mayan women. The Mayan activist Delia Tujab says she has found it impossible to work in the Mayan cultural rights movement: "When you look at the Executive Councils and Boards you see there are not any women participating. Some men are worse than others, but many can't stand for anyone else to be in charge—especially not when it is a woman." Other women trying to be active in the movement complain of intense teasing and sexually tinged harassment from Mayan men, often on the theme that they need to produce more Mayan babies to make up for the genocide. They also suffer subtle exclusions like the drain of having to struggle constantly to be listened to and last-minute changes in meeting times or places which, given their dependence on child care arrangements, make it difficult for them to attend.

Mayan women—like Guatemalan nationalists, Ladinos, revolutionaries, and Mayan men—are caught between the simultaneous modernity and tradition demanded for cultural agency by nationalist politics, bourgeois law, and their male companions in struggle. Just as "tradition is not modernity's opposite, it is modern as well" (Collier 1997:215), the Mayan woman is not opposed to modernity, she is part of it, produced by it. As a lumpy, semi-autonomous prosthesis she sustains modernity and is in turn changed by it, made problematic. The conditions of possibility for Mayan organizing also mean that more Mayan women are pursuing education rather than staying in their villages, and many do not have time to weave or make tortillas. Women are also losing the financial autonomy that allowed them to buy thread, contribute to festivals, and participate in tradition, as their vegetable plots (for which they controlled the earnings) are now devoted to export crops whose earnings tend to be controlled by the husband or father (Dary 1991). In addition, many indigenous communities are now both disrupted and sustained by the emigration of young women and men to the capital, the maquila, or the United States. Thus more of these professional Mayan women lean on the labor of other Mayan women to be both modern and traditional (Menchú, for example, certainly does not have the time or energy to weave all of her beautiful *huipiles*). The body image of Mayan women who identify themselves with *La Mujer Maya*—as the ones who uphold tradition in a culture where "gender relations have always been equal"—is in complex relation with a body politic in which Mayan women are deeply engaged in modern forms of production and in which many activist women are divorced or widowed and excluded from positions of power.

On a late afternoon in July 2000, with the rainy season downpour darkening the room, I sat with two Mayan women, Emma and Adela, talking about the business of Kaq'la, their new nongovernmental organization (NGO), created by and for Mayan women. They had recently inaugurated a series of seminars designed to put indigenous women into contact with each other and to help them organize to defend their rights. We were discussing the boring bureaucratic work it takes to put such ideals into practice: Did they invite everyone they should have? Were enough invitations sent? Did they need to offer day care? Adela asked why a mutual acquaintance of ours, Anastasia, had not come? Emma asked, "Is that the Anastasia from the town of Sololá?" "No," Adela, said, "she's from Joyabaj." Then Emma, trying to remember her face, asked, "What does she wear? Is it the Joyabaj *huipil* [traditional shirt]? or Chichi?" "No," said Adela, "she's K'iche' but she dresses like us, it's pan-, it's cosmovis . . . no . . . ," she searched for the right word. "Pancosmo?" asked Emma, laughing. " No, it's cosmo-política," said Adela. After a little more joking and talking they figured out which Anastasia it was and went on to other matters.

I was struck by this conversation. First, by the clever pun Adela had made joining the words for cosmopolitan and political. Second, because it was

interesting to me that a woman dedicating her life to Mayan cultural revitalization would describe something as traditional as the *huipil*, usually a handwoven shirt distinctive to each Mayan community, as cosmopolitan, that is,
not bound by local or national habits, at home in all places. The Mayan
woman struggles to overcome the distance between tradition, or cosmo-
vision—a people's belief system, origins, sense of place in the world or cosmos, all condensed into the figure of *La Mujer Maya*—and the millennial
cosmopolitanism of full-on globalization in the speeded-up world of techno-
science and cyberspace. Adela and many others are working to politicize
their cosmos (which includes their prosthetic relation to the image of *La
Mujer Maya*) and to be simultaneously cosmopolitan. Like the women in the
Iximulew supplement, the prosthetic of *La Mujer Maya* as tradition rubs in
both irritating and exciting ways with images of Mayan women as engineers
and lawyers. *La Mujer Maya* is always more than passive ground, even as she
struggles with limited cultural agency.

Cultural Agency, "Américan" Scholarship, and Prosthetic Relationality

There is a danger that this analysis is one more instance of Spivak's "white
women saving brown women," an analysis that does not acknowledge that
brown people, and especially women, support the wounded body image of
U.S. anthropology and much "Américan" intellectual production, whether
raising our children, cooking our food, or producing the culture we study.
Academics in the Américas can seem very agency-full, especially to those we
work "on," as we cross the multiple fissures of class, race, vocation, nation,
discipline, language, and culture that bring us together even as they separate
us. Yet we are also, in our own small ways, a part of a wounded body politic. We
are often afraid of becoming unemployed and, especially in Latin America, of
violence and repression aimed at us, our students, and our interlocutors. Like
all of the bodies politic examined here, scholars in América are in a seemingly
impossible situation, a situation in which we must simultaneously respond to
the modern demand to think for ourselves by performing critical analysis
(objectivity) *and* hold on to the tradition of being in solidarity with the people
we work with. Like the nation and other bodies politic examined here, we are
simultaneously leaned on—by the institutions, funding agencies, theoretical

frameworks, teaching loads, and research requirements that simultaneously support and limit us—and must, in turn, lean on others for support.

The authors represented in this book point out the colonizing nature of salvation discourses, and the transnational, raciological, and gender privileges that allow easy mobility for some and incarceration for others. These critiques may feel like "a finger in the wound" for intellectuals—paralleling Guatemalan Ladino reaction to Mayan organizing or Mayan men reacting to feminism. Maybe that's because the wound is the place where these stumped identifications meet the lumpy, semiautonomous other of prosthetic relationality. Scholars, of course, lean on the Maya as subjects of analysis and supports for our careers. But to depict them solely as victims returns us to the already constituted "Américan" scholar who produces her professional and political subjectivity over the ground of Mayan organizing and *La Mujer Maya*. I have been arguing that these prostheses are more lumpy, semiautonomous, in intimate, irritating, and exhilarating prosthetic contact. Gender, class, nation, revolutionary mobilization, ethnicity, and scholarship are media of connection, the straps that hold body to prosthesis. This is prosthetic relationality, in which the Maya, or women, or any of the people discussed in these pages, are not *only* victim or ground for the formation of the "Américan" scholarly body politic. These are stumped identities—open, wounded, bewildered, and political. They are shot through with power differentials but are never so simple as actor versus ground. To approach our desire to understand and enact cultural agency in the Américas, I suggest that we must always think of inter / actions—among the imagined and lived body of the bleeding nation, between indigenous rights and the project of nation building, among class war, race war, and utopian imaginings, of the simultaneity of modernity and tradition, and between real bodies and social fantasy, solidarity and critique. We need to think in all of these sites of both the manipulation and violence involved in using actually existing indigenous men and women as well as the *Maya* and *La Mujer Maya* as prosthetic devices, and the ambivalence and affect involved in the intimate joins of that relation with an active, thinking tool (a sign and generatrix of signs). Cultural agency is not an easy project. But disconnecting from these complex relationalities is not an option, especially after September 11, as we must increasingly struggle to be cosmo-political.

Notes

Acknowledgments: Fieldwork for this paper was made possible through the generous support of Stanford University, the National Science Foundation, and Lewis and Clark College. My greatest debt is to everyone in Guatemala who shared time, experience, and analysis so generously. I also want to thank Jane Collier, Marcia Klotz, Scott Mobley, and Christa Little-Siebold as well as Crystal Hables Gray, Deborah Heath, Stephen Kurzman, Sarah Jain, Bill Maurer, Dan Segal, Suzanna Sawyer, and Netta van Vliet. Special thanks to José Fernando Lara and Paula Worby, and especially to my main support, Mark Driscoll. Special thanks to Doris Sommer, Marcial Godoy Anativia, the SSRC, and conference participants, and for postconference reflections from Martín Barbero, Doris Sommer, and Charlie Hale.

1. *Américan* refers to all of us seeking to describe and deploy cultural agency in the Américas—hopefully thereby accenting, making visible, and de/colonizing the U.S. monolingual geographically stunted purloining of the term.

2. This work is part of a larger project on the relations between the Guatemalan state and the Mayan cultural rights movement. Unless otherwise indicated, all quotes are from author interviews conducted during a year of fieldwork (October 1992 to October 1993) supplemented by stays of one to three months in 1996, and every year from 1998 to 2003.

3. It turns out this is a widely told joke: Chris Gray says it was told in Italy after World War II, and Maya Procell e-mailed me a version set in Iraq.

4. Here I would like to acknowledge Steven Kurzman's work on prosthetics, which takes issue with a number of the tropes I am deploying here (2001).

5. Similarly, tourism in Guatemala is deeply dependent on the ardor and mystery of *La Mujer Maya*—as condensation of indigenous culture as well as on her underpaid labor.

6. With a brief cosmetic exception in the mid-1960s, the Guatemalan government was run by the military from 1954 to 1985.

7. This was the beginning of Guatemala's Democratic Spring—ten years of elected governments—which was amputated by the CIA-backed coup of 1954.

8. While living in France, Asturias began to write modernist prose (to distinguish himself from the "backwardness" of his Guatemalan origins) but distinguished himself in turn from the rest of the modernists by turning to Mayan traditions. The resisting indigenous hero of *Men of Corn* (1983) is named Gaspar Ilom, the *nom de guerre* chosen by Asturias's son, Rodrigo, when he became a guerrilla.

9. Payeras's book *Days of the Jungle* is virtually unknown outside Guatemala,

especially compared to Menchú's book. However, Peace Corps volunteers have told me that it is part of their preparatory curriculum for starting work in Guatemala. Through this training one young gringo learned that "the guerrillas really didn't care anything about the Indians, unlike the Peace Corps, which addresses their real needs." This is, of course, a highly interested reading. Payeras, also a poet and novelist, was deeply concerned with complexly thinking ethnic, national, and class identities as interrelated and always in process. This commitment led him to break with the EGP, which he had cofounded (1997).

10. Criticized for inviting Rodrigo Asturias (Gaspar Ilom), one of the three commanders of the URNG, to the Nobel Prize ceremonies in Oslo, she said her invitation was extended because of his relationship to Guatemala's other Nobel Prize winner, not to the revolution. A popular joke at the time of the Nobel asked, "What is Rigoberta's blood type? URNG-positive."

11. The 1996 yearly report of the National Indigenous and Peasant Coordination (CONIC), an organization situated on the cusp of Mayan activism and popular organizing, admits that "despite our efforts we continue to fail in our work with women. We continue to suffer deficiencies in terms of the remarks made at last year's assembly, which argued that men are refusing to allow women to increase their participation."

Tradition, Transnationalism, and Gender in the Afro-Brazilian Candomblé

J. LORAND MATORY

Candomblé is an Afro-Brazilian religion of divination, blood sacrifice, spirit possession, and healing. Believers attribute miraculous powers and exemplary flaws to gods known as *orixas*, *voduns*, *inquices*, and *caboclos*, depending upon the Candomblé denomination. The adventures, personalities, and kinship relations of these beings are described in an extensive mythology and body of oracular wisdom, which divines the personalities and fates of worshipers, including the worldly relations among them. Through blood sacrifice and lavish ceremonies of spirit possession, the gods are persuaded to intervene beneficently in the lives of their worshipers and to keep their foes away. Priests and practitioners, no less than the social scientists and politicians who seek to speak for them, tend to emphasize the ancientness of Candomblé and its constituent traditions.

In this essay, however, I document a series of international dialogues involving Afro-Brazilian priests alongside state officials and an international community of scholars with the aim of tracing fundamental changes in the gendered leadership of this religion during the twentieth century. I will argue that Candomblé owes much of its international fame and also the internal transformation of its leadership to Ruth Landes's *City of Women* (1947), in which the religion becomes a living, time-honored example of matriarchy that should inspire the opponents of sexism back home in the United States.

But Candomblé has also been a convenient template for very different political agendas that depend on the opposite, manly character of the cult. From Gilberto Freyre's "Regionalist" nationalism, to Melville J. Herskovits's effort to redeem African Americans from the "myth" that they are cultureless, to Oyeronke Oyewumi's diasporic Yoruba nationalism, women hardly count. Both scholars and political leaders have presented Candomblé as a metonym of the imagined communities they would invoke and lead.[1]

The realities of Candomblé resist these agendas and normative dispositions. For example, a silent touchstone in the transnational debates over the meaning of Candomblé and the communities it authenticates is a cultural persona, as normal in the Candomblé priesthood as he is anathema to the modern nation-state. He is the *ade*, or "passive homosexual." The Brazilian *adé* priest, like his counterparts in the African-inspired religions of Cuba and Haiti, is eminently respectable for most devotees but has, since the 1930s, been summarily dismissed both by nationalist and feminist scholars as either untraditional or nonexistent. I offer this essay to correct what I believe is wrongheaded scholarship and also to observe the role of national and international scholars in canonizing imaginaries of geographically bounded and historically inert folk traditions.

The City of Women

Ruth Landes became a foremother of feminist anthropology when she celebrated the unique status of women in Candomblé. Her book *The City of Women* claimed that, by tradition, women were uniquely suited to serve the African gods. In particular, she found the Quêto/Nagô denomination of Candomblé inspiring as both an example of African cultural survival in the Americas and a real-world matriarchy honored by time and tradition—hence the book's title. Her research embarrassed Euro-Brazilian nationalists for two reasons: First, it publicized Brazil's blackness. Second, in order to prove the antiquity of this matriarchy, she revealed the open secret that male priests were widely believed to be homosexuals.

As a student of the cultural relativist Franz Boas, Landes studied Afro-Brazilian religion as a rich transnational legacy, not a racial embarrassment. Even more important for Landes, it was an inspiration for women's equality elsewhere in the world. Her book ends like this: "When I left Rio for the United States, Brazilian friends escorted me to the boat, and one of them said, half teasing but with a certain defiant patriotism, 'Now you can tell them that no tigers walk in our streets.'

I nodded, and added: 'I'll tell them also about the women. . . . Will Americans believe that there is a country where women like men, feel secure and at ease with them, and do not fear them?'"[2]

Though she knew Brazil to be a sexist country, Landes seemed to find evidence of a "cult matriarchate" in which women ruled in the religious affairs, the most important affairs, of blacks in the Brazilian state of Bahia.[3] But she tampered with the evidence and assumed her audience was far enough away not to notice. She had invoked the male priests' reputation for homosexuality in order to establish that the male presence was a recent pathology rather than a contradiction to Landes's own construction of Candomblé tradition. Mark Alan Healey would later call her portrait of ancient matriarchy a primitivist cliché.[4] Perhaps wishful thinking encouraged her to write, "I know by now that women are [in Bahia] the chosen sex. . . . I take it for granted just as I know in our world that men are the chosen sex."[5] Like Margaret Mead, Landes had silenced or distorted the evidence.[6] For example, she dismissed the significant number of men leading Candomblé temples during her visit as violating "African tradition," allegedly suffering from psychological problems, and admissible only because of the ritual laxity of the women.

Candomblé is divided into various nations, or denominations, which reflect what worshipers regard as the African origin of each nation's ritual protocols. Besides the Yoruba-related Nagô nation (called Quêto today), there were also, in Landes's day, the Fon-inspired Jeje nation, the Angola nation, and the expanding clergy that worships the Brazilian Indian, or *caboclo*, spirits. Landes joined the line of scholars who privileged the Quêto/Nagô nation for its alleged African purity and authenticity.

Landes associated the "laxity" of the priestesses who admitted men with a variant of the Nagô religion in which the *caboclo* spirit predominated. But given the fact that a priestess of the Nagô nation is credited with having founded the *caboclo* cult,[7] that the Nagô *orixás* remained preeminent even in the *caboclo*-worshiping houses,[8] and that virtually every Nagô temple also worshiped *caboclos*,[9] the line that Landes drew between the female-dominated Nagô temples and the male-dominated *caboclo* temples does not hold, as temple leaders make evident in their declarations about practices.[10]

In fact, male leadership is an old phenomenon in all nations that practice Candomblé. Throughout the nineteenth century, men outnumbered women generally in the Bahian priesthood, and they were common even in the supposedly all-female priesthood of the Nagô and Jeje nations. It was the increase in *female* leadership that was news for the cult.[11] Kim Butler believes that a tradition of exclusively female temple leadership began in the Casa Branca, or the Ile Iya Naso, temple, in the mid–nineteenth century (relatively late in the documented history of the Jeje and Nagô in Brazil) and spread with the growing prestige of that temple among scholars and elite sponsors.[12] Yet even here the evidence—statistically or in principle—of an exclusively female leadership is ambiguous before the 1930s.

In the 1930s, male priests still significantly outnumbered females.[13] Nonetheless, since the publication of Landes's work,[14] the scholarly advocates of Jeje and Nagô superiority have come to speak with one voice on the matter, agreeing that for the priesthood, "women are the chosen sex." Fortunately for students of Candomblé, Landes and her companion Édison Carneiro recorded, albeit dismissively, copious evidence against their own interpretation. Yet Landes's conclusions clearly changed the minds and conduct of Candomblé's leading bourgeois advocates, and, consequently, they changed the conditions of the religion's reproduction in Brazilian society.

Grounds for Dismissal: The Nation-State vs. the Adé

In the just cause of women's liberation, Landes played with the facts and constructed a unique status for women. Yet her erasure of the historically male majority in the Candomblé priesthood played into the cause of male-centered nationalism because, as George Mosse shows, it depends on homophobia.[15] Landes's appeal to a counterfactual nostalgia, equally typical of nationalisms, dismissed the male presence in Candomblé as a recent corruption. As if to confirm the nonnormative character of male possession priests, Landes reported the widespread view that they were all *adés*, "passive homosexuals" in Landes's medico-pathological terms. Making no reference to indigenous discourse, Landes diagnosed these men as diseased and thereby alienated from any legitimate *cultural* tradition, though she reports that their sexual orientation did not bother other priests or adherents.[16] As priests, Landes observed, *adés* were "supported and even adored by those normal men of whom they were before the butt and object of derision."[17]

Landes's revelation of these sexual matters discomfited her Brazilian colleagues, even those who welcomed her work on the demographic and cultural importance of Afro-Brazilians. These scholars were more sensitive to international standards of national respectability, more concerned to guard Brazil's open secrets, than were the priests and subjects of trans-Atlantic sacred nations. The state functionary and culture-broker Arthur Ramos flatly denied Landes's claims about a "cult matriarchate" and about a significant homosexual presence. In retaliation, he cooperated with Herskovits in foreclosing future professional opportunities for Landes. She later blamed her professional undoing on Ramos's anger over her outing homosexuality in Brazil.[18]

Édison Carneiro, the journalist who became Landes's guide in Bahia, published *Candomblés da Bahia* (1948) after her two books had come out in 1940 and 1947. During their acquaintance, Landes apparently changed Carneiro's mind, or at least his public posture. Whereas in the late 1930s she had quoted Carneiro's words of admiration for the beauty of the male homosexual priests and the liveliness of *caboclo*-worship, Carneiro's own subsequent publications were frankly hostile.[19] By 1948, he was denouncing the male priesthood:

> Of the 67 temples registered in the Union, 37 were directed by priests and 30 by priestesses.
>
> It seems, however, that there were not always priests and priestesses and that, in the past, Candomblé was, distinctly, the domain of women. . . . Only the Congo temples can be seen as an exception. . . . In contrast to the inner strength that emanates naturally from the Nago and Jeje priestesses, the male priests of the Angola nation, of the Congo nation or the *caboclos* are almost all improvised, self-made, "learning one song here and another song there," as the Nago and Jeje leaders say.[20]

Fully aware that male chief priests outnumbered their female counterparts in the 1930s, Carneiro attempted to rescue the reputation of the *authentic* Candomblé with an unsubstantiated claim that the Candomblé priesthood of all nations had once been exclusively female. Following Landes, he now dismissed the male priesthood as a recent deviation. Carneiro added that they belonged to what he considered the least representative and respectable of Candomblé nations—the Angola, Congo, and Caboclo nations. Like Landes (esp. 1940), he went on to argue that almost all male priests were uninitiated charlatans, commercializers, tyrannical leaders, poor administrators, and practitioners of evil magic. They were said to gossip like women and to be sexually confused. Not even the most contorted argument was scorned in efforts to construct a legitimate tradition. Male chief priests were said not to believe in the evil magic they allegedly practiced, while female chief priests were credited with rather naïve faith in the innocent magic they practiced.[21]

Carneiro had a special stake in dignifying the West African Nagô and Jeje nations. He was a mulatto himself and belonged to a school of Northeastern Regionalist writers who sought to rescue the Northeast from its reputation of inferiority on account of its black and mulatto majority. At the turn of the century, Brazilian officials inspired by eugenics had invested enormous resources in recruiting European immigrants to whiten the population of the southeastern state of São Paulo, which had industrialized with the profits of initially slave-based plantations. Advocates of the relatively underdeveloped Northeast argued that, although their region was poorer and blacker, its blacks and mulattoes were superior (on account of their disproportionately West African Nagô and Jeje origins) to those of the Southeast (whose origins were mainly West-Central African—for example, Congo and Angola).[22] Thus, nostalgia for the Jeje-Nagô-centered, allegedly matriarchal, and innocent prehistory of Candomblé came to unite the spokespersons of two imagined communities: the northeastern regionalist Carneiro and the transnational feminist Landes.

In the cultural logic of the nation-state, Michael Herzfeld describes a "structural nostalgia," or "the longing for an age before the state, for the primordial and self-regulating birthright that the state continually invokes."[23] Such invocations of the nation-state are regularly fictional and apologetic. I am suggesting that similar forms of nostalgia are invoked by the leaders of alternative, non-state-based communities with the intent to naturalize their authority along with the conventions, boundaries, and hierarchies that keep them in power. Such naturalizations rest similarly upon highly selective and sentimentalized constructions of the past.

Carneiro, however, remains more ambiguous and ambivalent than Landes. If he reproduces the ideology of primordial female leadership in Afro-Bahian religion, his familiarity with the material makes him unable to ignore the facts supporting other constructions of tradition. For example, he details evidence of male leadership at the heart of the reputedly most traditional and orthodox lineage of Nagô temples—the line of Casa Branca. He credits the nineteenth-century African-born male priest Bambuxê (Bamgbose) with initiating Aninha, a member of Casa Branca and the future chief priestess of the Opo Afonja temple. Aninha's disappointment that another man, Joaquim

Vieira, did not succeed the recently deceased chief priestess of Casa Branca is adduced as the reason for Aninha's secession from that temple and for her efforts to found the Opo Afonja temple. Even though the histories recounted nowadays at Opo Afonja leave little doubt that Aninha founded the house as its first chief priest, Carneiro reports that the male priest Joaquim had been that temple's first chief.[24] He is among numerous male priests of the Jeje and Nagô nations whom Carneiro mentions as eminences during his time.[25] They defy his own post-Landean synopsis of the tradition.

In sum, Landes and Carneiro shared a dirty secret. Yet a comparison of Carneiro's early remarks to Landes suggests that Candomblé's "passives" were neither dirty nor secret before 1938. The *adés* became a subject of tabu amid the conflict between the North American feminist and the Brazilian academic gatekeeper Arthur Ramos. Faced with the powerful international gaze, Ramos simply denied the embarrassing reality and, with the help of Herskovits, defamed Landes. A close observer of Bahia and a close friend of Landes, Carneiro could hardly deny the homosexuality, but he did try to mitigate its relevance to the local tradition.

The Mãe Preta and the Mãe-de-Santo:
The Candomblé Priestess in the Nationalist Narrative

Light-colored Bahian elites have tried to downplay local homosexuality to save face in the eyes of richer regions of Brazil and of more "advanced" nations. The efforts have almost certainly been among the motives behind Brazilian scholars' disproportionate attention to female-headed Candomblé temples. The Northeastern Regionalists therefore shared with Landes a desire to dignify Candomblé's female leadership. Once an embarrassment to the bourgeois nation-state, the priestess eventually attained a pride of place in Northeastern Regionalism and its close ally, Brazilian nationalism. She gained ground from her superficial likeness to the Mammy (*Mãe Preta*, literally "Black Mother") that, a few years earlier, had become an object of nostalgic adulation in Gilberto Freyre's influential narrative of *mestiço* nationalism, *The Masters and the Slaves* (1933).[26] Freyre had sought to demonstrate that the slave plantations of his native Northeast were sites of such sensual interaction between white men and their black nursemaids, pals, and mistresses that Brazil evaded the kind of racial purism and segregation that created the infamy of U.S. racism and German Nazism.

Hence, far from being a land of racial inferiority, as Brazilians feared they were seen from the outside, the country was a paragon of racial and cultural hybridity, or *mestiçagem*, and of "racial democracy," or interracial equality and conviviality. Variants of this historical and cultural revisionism were common in Latin America and the Caribbean in the 1930s. Neither in Freyre's narrative nor in the popular cultural images that multiplied in its wake did the implicit logic of racial and sexual inequality disappear—it was simply surrounded by a halo of nostalgic innocence, in which the dignity of the Black Mother is guaranteed by her personal relations with the lord of the manor. Today's journalistic descriptions of Candomblé's black priestess seem similarly tinged with nostalgia for this innocent past, in which the Black Mother is gentle and generous to her white children, but also stern enough to control her black children.[27] These are the terms of her ongoing incorporation into the narrative of *mestiço* nationalism, and they appear to explain to a large extent why, since the 1960s, the city government of Salvador, the Bahian state, the Brazilian federal state, businesses, and the national media outlets have lent disproportionate moral support and funding to the female-headed temples.

Some female-headed temples have certainly benefited, but most Afro-Brazilian women get little from their inclusion in the Freyrean romance. In 1980, for example, the average white woman earned 69 percent of the average white man's salary, while the average black man (*preto*) earned only 63 percent, the average black woman (*preta*) only 38 percent, and the average mulatto woman (*parda*) only 36 percent of the average white man's earnings. Any casual visitor to Brazil notes immediately that black and mulatto women are cruelly overrepresented among domestic servants, accounting for over 80 percent in a society that is only 45 percent black and mulatto.[28] Despite the omnipresent public affirmation in Brazil of the Freyrean nonracist vision of the country, 60 percent of black and mulatto men surveyed say that whites are racist; black and mulatto women are even *more* likely (69 percent) to say so.[29] Thus, the available statistics offer little evidence to support Landes's view of gender equality in black Brazil or her sense of a general white male preference for Afro-Brazilian *women* generally over Afro-Brazilian men.[30]

My intention is not to minimize the accomplishments of Candomblé's priestesses since the nineteenth century (their triumphs over racism and sexism have been impressive), but to underline precisely the historicity of a constructed tradition that has served several recent ideologies. The conditions of the female triumph in the Candomblé priesthood have been recent in genesis, unique in the Yoruba-Atlantic world, and explicable only in terms of an ongoing transnational cultural politics.

Priestesses have always been important leaders in Candomblé, in its West African antecedents and its contemporary Yoruba counterparts. But I have argued that the current *preeminence* of priestesses results from a convergence between nationalist and transnational forces. These forces have created a few irresistible opportunities since the 1930s for an otherwise underprivileged class of people. Since the 1930s, a few priestesses have acquired mighty advocates in the overlapping imagined communities of the Brazilian nation and transnational feminism. To the same degree, all the male priests of the Candomblé have acquired a powerful set of enemies.

Priestesses, Too, Question the Matriarchate

Notwithstanding the harmony of black female religious authority with white sentimentality about the Black Mother and with the Ur-matriarchy imagined by some transnational feminists, leading priestesses talk about gender and authority in ways that complicate any description of Candomblé as matriarchal. Mãe Stella and other mothers of the great so-called traditional temples *do* tend to avow publicly that women possess a special acumen for priestly duties, such as culinary artistry and the capacity for motherly warmth (*aconchego*) as well as a unique legitimacy to rule. But the gender of sacred agency often contrasts with the priestesses' personal sexual identity. For example, in response to one of the numerous journalists seeking an explanation for "the cult matriarchate," Mãe Stella of the prestigious Opo Afonja temple made it clear that, for her, for her predecessor Mãe Senhora, and in the "African tradition," the consummately macho god Xangô has always been the real boss (*chefe*).[31] The late Mãe Nicinha of the preeminent Jeje temple, Bogum, explained, "In our nation, the only person who can occupy this post [chief priest] is a woman who has a male saint [that is, who is consecrated to and possessed by a male god]."[32]

Leão Teixeira argues that the very image of divine authority in the Candomblé is masculine.[33] Thus, in a further example, the sequence in which the gods are saluted during sacred festivals implies an association between maleness and superior rank among the gods. Older or male gods tend to be saluted earlier in the liturgical song sequence, or *xirê*, while younger and female gods tend to be saluted later. The unique ritual prerogatives of men, the servility expected of the daughters of goddesses, and the restrictions placed on menstruating women and on the daughters of goddesses all suggest that priestly ritual competency and leadership themselves are also coded male.[34] In indigenous terms, Candomblé hardly invites description as a cult matriarchate.

The Cultural Logic of Passivity

Years ago, I publicly proposed an explanation for the locally perceived normalcy of "passive homosexuals," or *adés*, as possession priests and therefore as the heads of Candomblé temples. The debate it engendered demonstrates that, like regionalist, nationalist, and international feminist communities, the African diaspora is also constituted by certain open secrets and can be reconstituted by reselections and rereadings of what secrets need to be defended.

There are no reliable statistics on how many Candomblé priests engage in what Landes called "passive homosexuality." Thus my thesis did not concern their actual numbers. Rather, I asked why so many members and cognoscenti of Candomblé assume—with or without statistical accuracy—that male initiates in the possession priesthood are normally *adés* and why many Afro-Brazilian men who love men feel at home in Candomblé.

Today, there are numerous explanations for the alleged prominence of *adés* among possession priests. In order to understand them, one must grasp where they fit in a set of semantic contrasts in Brazilian gender categories. English-speaking North Americans tend to distinguish sharply between those men who engage in sex with other men (homosexuals) and those who don't (heterosexuals). But Brazilians are far more likely to distinguish men who penetrate others during sexual intercourse (*homens*, or "[real] men") from those who are penetrated (*bichas*, *viados*, or, in Candomblé language, *adés*).[35] They share this pattern of classification with many peoples around the Mediterranean, as well as much of premodern Europe, precolonial Native America, and most of the rest of the world.[36] Modern European and Anglo-American prison populations and sailors seem no exception. The contrast between penetrators and penetrated is not the only idiom of sexual classification in Brazil, particularly in recent decades.[37] However, this particular difference remains central to most working-class Brazilians' vocabulary of social classification and to men's and boy's daily negotiation of respect. Even when the Bahians I know use the term *homosexual*, most mean only the party who is habitually penetrated, or passive. Of course, the real behavior of both *homens* and *bichas*, or *adés*, is usually more varied than one word will allow, and the normative assumption that the sexually "active" party is dominant outside of bed is not necessarily true.[38] However, local *ideological* assumptions and expectations tend to link habitual male passivity with transvestism, feminine gestures, feminine occupations, and the social subordination of the penetrated party.

So why do many Brazilians think there is a connection between the possession priesthood and men who love men?[39] Peter Fry suggests that the shared classification of male passives and possession cults as deviant makes the priesthood an appropriate niche for homosexuals. Following Victor Turner and Mary Douglas, Fry argues that the homosexuals' *liminal* status in Brazilian national society suits them symbolically, in the Brazilian popular imagination, to professions dealing with "magical power."[40] Délcio Monteiro de Lima moves in the direction of acknowledging what is normal about homosexuality in Candomblé ideology: both Afro-Brazilian religions and Brazilian Kardecist Spiritism, he argues, have shown themselves more generally tolerant than the Roman Catholic Church.[41] More to the point, Patricia Birman reports that men whose heads are governed by female divinities—like Iança, Oxum, and so forth—are expected to share in the female dispositions and desires of the goddesses.[42] Thus, according to Candomblé's indigenous personality theory, the homosexuality of male priests is in their natures (*naturezas*), is derived from nature (*natureza*), and is authorized by the sacred—hence their attraction to and social acceptance in Candomblé.

Fry also notes the advantageous flexibility enjoyed by *bichas*, or passives, in the performance of social roles normally reserved, in the wider society, primarily for one sex or the other. That is, they can acceptably do the cooking and embroidering necessary for the temple and yet, in a similar religion in Belém do Pará (where Fry conducted his research), retain the social advantages of men in transactions with the "world of men"—of police, judges, doctors, lawyers, and politicians, "whose services they themselves may use or broker to clients for their own advantage."[43] In the Bahian case, men's advantages over the great Nagô mothers in this regard are not so evident. What is more evident, and is observed by Leão Teixeira, is that homosexual men bring to the Candomblé three other advantages over women: (1) higher average earnings; (2) license as men to perform all the ritual duties normally restricted to men, such as the sacrifice of four-legged animals, the care of the gods Exú (of sex, mischief, and communication) and Ossaim (of herbal medicine) and of the Eguns, or spirits of the dead; and (3) immunity from restrictions on menstruating women, such as exclusion from shrine rooms.[44] A woman consecrated to a male god is eligible to receive a further initiation (*mão de faca*) that entitles her to sacrifice birds, but, while menstruating, she cannot even do that.[45]

The cult matriarchy, then, is not a fact given simply by tradition, but a plausible interested and contested *construction* of tradition based on a cosmopolitan repertoire of precedents and interpretive logics. And despite the pronounced homophobia of many contemporary third world bourgeois nationalists (including a number of prominent Anglophone African elites), one would be hard-pressed to locate the precolonial, traditional Yoruba precedents for the homophobia that Landes, Ribeiro, and Roger Bastide have presented as psychoanalytic proof of male priests' inferiority and as defiance of African tradition. The homophobia that denormalizes the prominence of *adés* in the Candomblé priesthood has its roots in a nationalism and a transnational feminism of the mid–twentieth century.

The proliferation of latter-day explanations of the prominence of *adés* in the Brazilian Candomblé (not to mention the Cuban Ocha priesthoods) and the well-documented history of Candomblé adherents' comfort with *adés* in this role appear to have a common root. That root is evident between the lines of Landes's informants' testimony in the 1930s and most clearly implied by my comparative field research between Brazilian Candomblé and what most adherents regard as its West African homeland.

James H. Sweet is one scholar who argues that transvestites, including homosexual transvestites, were once common in southern and West Central Africa and that some of these homosexual transvestites were important ritual experts.[46] They embodied a set of African "core beliefs" that, as a result of the slave trade, appeared among captives from that region in sixteenth- and seventeenth-century Portugal and Brazil as well. Sweet's argument inverts the third world nationalist diagnosis that homosexuality is a white man's disease. Instead, the lapse of homosexuality and transvestism among West Central African male ritual experts in the postcolonial period is blamed on Western missionary and colonial influence.

Having no knowledge of these traditions, Carneiro had argued that male priests, who he assumed were passive homosexuals, were virtually restricted to the West Central, African-identified Angola and Congo nations and to the worshipers of the *caboclo* Indian spirits.[47] He did not suggest that male priests were any less vile for participating in such alternative traditions; rather, he emphasized their nonconformity to the uniquely African and uniquely dignified standard of the West African–inspired Jeje and Nagô nations. The sixteenth- and seventeenth-century records analyzed by Sweet leave unexplained the cultural logic by which West Central Africans and their descendants believed ritual expertise to be connected to transvestism and homosexuality and the degree to which practitioners believed the connection to be a strong or necessary one. Historical and ethnographic records from the twentieth century have, however, left evidence of a strong connection precisely in the trans-Atlantic nations connecting the Brazilian Nagô to the Nigerian Yoruba and the Brazilian Jejes to the Ewe, Gen, Aja, and Fon peoples of West Africa. Today at least, the shared West African Yoruba, West African Fon, and Brazilian Candomblé imagery of marriage to the divinity, who episodically displaces his bride's personality and consciousness, is in fact foreign to West Central African religions (Wyatt MacGaffey, p.c., 8 August 1996). But in Landes's and Carneiro's research, all of the nations of Brazilian Candomblé appeared to share this West African imagery.

Mounted Men: What Nigerian Male *Elegun* and New World Passive Priests Do and Don't Have in Common[48]

Oyo-Yoruba people formed a plurality not only of the African captives taken to Bahia in the nineteenth century but also of the founding priests and priestesses of Bahia's most influential temples, including Casa Branca. No African ethnic group has influenced Candomblé more than this Yoruba subgroup. In West Africa, Oyo-Yoruba worshipers employ multiple metaphors to evoke people's relationships with the gods. Like Brazilian *candomblécistas*, Oyo-Yoruba worshipers of the *orisa* gods might call any devotee of a god the child (*omo* [Yoruba]; *filho* [Portuguese]) of that god. In both traditions, motherhood and fatherhood are used as metaphors of leadership in the worship and activation of the gods. For example, a senior male West African Yoruba priest of, say, Sango might be addressed as *Baba Onisango* ("Father Owner-of-Sango"); a senior priestess would be addressed as *Iya Onisango* ("Mother Owner-of-Sango"). In Brazil, the male head of a Candomblé temple is called a *pai-de-santo* ("father-in-divinity"), while a chief priestess is called a *mãe-de-santo* ("mother-of-divinity").

Yet the Yoruba terms that mark out the priest's competency to embody the god through possession-trance and to act as his or her worldly delegate rely, above all, upon allied metaphors of marriage and sexuality. According to Carneiro, as we shall see, these metaphors were very much alive in the Brazilian Candomblé of the 1930s, and they were present in local understandings of male and female participation in the priesthood. In the speech of many twenty-first-century Brazilian *orixá* worshipers these metaphors are now dead or dying. Yet, the death of a metaphor seldom means that it has lost its effectiveness in communicative acts; instead, it has often become naturalized, implicit, and pervasive. In present-day Brazilian Candomblé, metaphors of marriage and sexuality stand powerfully alongside metaphors of parenthood and birth in the often-contested representation of tradition and reproduction of the priesthood.

Most Oyo-Yoruba possession priests in West Africa are women. The numerous male possession priests cross-dress. But their cross-dressing requires a culture-specific reading. They dress not as women but as wives or brides (*iyawo*)—a term that otherwise refers only to women married to worldly men. Novices to the priesthood, whether male or female, are designated metaphorically as *iyawo*, meaning "brides" or "wives." The degree to which Bahians understand the word *iaô* to mean "wife" or "bride" has declined since the 1930s, but the implications of its Yoruba meaning upon the logic of priestly recruitment have echoed into the third millennium.

The overlapping implications of West African Ewe-Gen-Aja-Fon (E.G.A.F.) vocabulary of spirit possession have faded a bit more since the eighteenth-century era when these captives predominated in the slave trade to Bahia. Also in that West African cultural zone, which believers regard as the homeland of the Afro-Brazilian Jeje nation, most possession priests are women, but there are also numerous men. As in Yorubaland, male and female possession priests are generically called wives (*sì* in Fon) of their divinities. However, chief priests in the E.G.A.F. region are called mothers (*no*) of the god, regardless of their sex. This latter term is foreign to both Yorubaland and Brazil.

For months after initiation, male and female novices among the Oyo-Yoruba wear women's clothes: *iro* (wrap skirts), *buba* (blouses), and *oja* (baby-carrying slings); on ceremonial occasions, they also wear *tiro* (antimony eyeliner), *laali* (henna for the hands and feet), delicate bracelets, earrings, and so forth. As mature priests, or *elegun*, women and men braid their hair and follow the latest styles in women's coiffures, but on ceremonial occasions they also continue to don *tiro* eyeliner, henna, and delicate jewelry. Many uninitiated Yoruba women do these things, but male possession priests are virtually the only men who do so. In the Oyo-Yoruba town where I conducted my principal West African field research, both the strip-weaving of cloth and barkeeping are considered female professions. So, almost predictably, the only male strip-weaver and the only male barkeeper in the town are ango possession priests.

Yet the most pervasive and dramatic gendered symbol in the representation of the priests' symbolic role—from the initiation onward—is the complex web of metaphors implicit in the verb *gun*, meaning "to mount." The very term for possession priest (*êlêgun*) means "the mounted one." It refers to what a rider does when astride a horse (hence, possession priests are sometimes called horses of the gods [*êin oria*]). The term *gun* also refers to what an animal or a brutal man does sexually to his female partner (and possession by Sango is often spoken of as a brutal act).[49] The term *gun* also refers to what a god, especially Sango, does to his possession priests. And Sango's is the most influential possession priesthood not only on the Bight of Benin but, to an even greater extent, among the *oria* worshipers of Brazil, Cuba, Trinidad, and the United States.[50] However one translates the verb *gun* into English, the term *montar* in Caribbean Spanish and Brazilian Portuguese and the Haitian Kweyòl term *monte* (all cognates of the English verb "to mount") encode the same three referents and have a long history of usage by worshipers in Cuba, Brazil, and Haiti.

Carneiro illustrates how Afro-Latin Americans, such as the priests and cognoscenti of the Bahian Candomblé, still consciously construed these West African Yoruba metaphors in the 1930s:

> Sometimes they call a priestess the *wife* of a god, and sometimes she is his *horse*. The god gives advice and places demands, but often he just *mounts* and plays.
>
> So you can see why the priestesses develop great influence among the people. They are the pathway to the gods. But no *upright* man will allow himself to be *ridden* by a god, unless he does not care about *losing his manhood*. . . .
>
> Now here's the loophole. Some men do *let themselves be ridden*, and they become priests with the women; but they are known to be *homosexuals*. In the temple they *put on skirts and mannerisms of the women*. . . . Sometimes *they are much better-looking than the women*.[51]

This language is largely consistent with the West African, Oyo-Yoruba symbolism of spirit possession I observed among Nigerian Sango priests of both sexes in the 1980s, but for one detail: the reluctance of "real men" to be possessed in the Brazilian Candomblé. Sex was not an infrequent topic of conversation among male friends of my age group in Igboho, and the Sango priests in the town were vocal and ribald in their humor about the matter. Yet I never became aware of any commonly used vocabulary in Oyo-Yoruba language to distinguish upright men from a category of men who are homosexual or somehow like women. I have never heard any West African *orisa* priest speak of himself or his fellow priests as anything like a homosexual or as engaging in same-sex intercourse. I argue simply that Afro-Brazilians have reinterpreted West African metaphors of spirit possession in the light of Brazilian gender categories. For many Brazilians in the 1930s and now, submission to a god's agency has seemed analogous to sexual passivity. In other words, a physically mountable man seems highly qualified, in a symbolic sense, to be mounted spiritually. The metaphor-ridden "loophole" by which Carneiro and his priestly friends understood men to have recently entered the Yoruba/Queto/Nagô possession priesthood in the 1930s was virtually identical—in both its terms and its emphases—to the hegemonic logic of the Oyo-Yoruba Sango priesthood that I observed in the 1980s and that others had observed in that West African priesthood since the nineteenth century.[52]

Dozens of Yoruba scholars have written cogently about gender and gender relations in Yoruba religion and culture generally.[53] Their work acquires new dimensions with the increase in the numbers of Yoruba scholars in the diaspora and in interactions with New World priests of the Cuban *orichas*, Brazilian *orixás*, and African-American *orishas*. In this context, my argument has recently sparked controversy in a new diasporic community—that of Yoruba scholars and African-American priestesses of Yoruba religion in the United States.

One Yoruba scholar in the United States, the sociologist Oyeronke Oyewumi, read my argument and then published an accusation: I had described the West African possession priests as "drag queens" and "actual if not symbolic homosexuals."[54] The purpose of this denunciation was to affirm the author's argument that there is no gender in authentic Yoruba culture. Like Freyre, Oyewumi attempts to turn the tables on North American and West European cultural and racial chauvinism by arguing the superiority of her own allegedly nondiscriminatory culture.

In evidence, the author cites the extensive gender coding of pronouns, names, kinship terms, and occupational terms in English, in contrast to the numerous Yoruba pronouns, kinship terms, and occupational terms that, in her opinion, do not encode gender—terms such as *oun* ("s/he"), *omo* ("child"), *egbon* ("senior sibling or cousin"), and *oba* ("monarch"). Although gender concepts and gender inequality are important elements of contemporary Yoruba society, Oyewumi argues that these terms evince a time before the slave trade or before colonialism when Yoruba culture had no gender at all. Thus, in its essence, even today's Yoruba culture is gender-free. Oyewumi must then explain away the gender coding that actually does appear in much well-established Yoruba terminology and social practice. There are clearly words in Yoruba for "male" (*ako*), "female" (*abo*), "man" (*okunrin*), and "woman" (*obinrin*). The terms of address and reference for parents, senior relatives, senior strangers, and people of almost every occupation indicate the referent's gender—for example, *Baba* ("father," "senior male," or, rarely, "senior patrilateral relative"), *Iya* ("mother," "senior female," or, rarely, "senior matrilateral relative"), *Baba Ayo* (the teknonymic "Father of Ayo"), *Baba Eleran* ("male butcher"), and *Iya Alaso* ("female clothier"). In Yoruba society, practitioners of most professions have long been vastly more of one sex than the other: for example, virtually all social clubs (*egbé*) are segregated according to sex, and certain religious and political titles are strongly gender marked, despite their infrequent adoption by a person of the other sex, such as *babalawo* (a type of divination priest [lit., "senior-male-who-owns-the-mystery"]), *baalè* (nonroyal quarter or town chief [lit., "father of the land"]), *iyale* (eldest wife of the house [lit., "mother of the house"]), and *baalé* (head of residential compound [lit., "father of the house"]). The last two terms are etymologically distinguished only by the gender of the referent. Yet in real social life the persons described as fathers of the house rank far higher in the house than do the people called mothers of the house.

How Nationalist Scholars Shape "Folk" Culture

Since Gilberto Freyre organized the First Afro-Brazilian Congress in 1934, dozens of such conferences have brought together priests and scholars to rethink and reorganize *orisa* religion and to reflect on its significance for the imagined communities of the region, the nation, and the African diaspora. Several of these conferences have had momentous effects. For example, the congress organized by Édison Carneiro in Bahia in 1937 culminated in the organization of the Union of Afro-Brazilian Sects, the first organization to unite the Bahian temples and their supporters against police repression. In 1983, Wande Abimbola and Marta Moreno Vega organized at the University of Ife, Nigeria, the first World Conference of Orisha Tradition and Culture. For the first time a conference brought together scholars and priests of *orisa* religion from Brazil, Cuba, Puerto Rico, Trinidad, the United States, and Nigeria. A dozen such conferences have followed, albeit under an increasingly factionalized leadership. As the leader of one series of conferences, Abimbola has, in the opinion of some groups, become the leader of the global *orisa*-worshiping community.

It is against this backdrop that events at a conference at Florida International University in 1999 acquire their significance. Titled "Orisa Devotion as a World Religion: The Globalization of Yoruba Religious Culture," the conference brought together dozens of U.S.-based Nigerian, Cuban, Puerto Rican, native North American, and Brazilian scholars with priests of equally diverse geographical and national origins. Despite its logical and empirical errors, Oyewumi's argument received a standing ovation from two Trinidadian priestesses and an African-American priestess. The nostalgic reconstruction of an ideal Yoruba past and essence appealed both to New World priestesses who would resist the sexism of U.S. society (including its local forms of *orisa* worship) and to diasporic Yoruba people offended by North American disregard for Africa and its cultures. The African-American priestess who applauded told me years later that she appreciated Oyewumi's assertiveness. Supportive senior Yoruba scholars added even more examples of gender neutrality, such as the Yoruba practice of calling one's paternal relatives of either sex *baba* (normally meaning "father" or "senior man") and maternal relatives of either sex *iya* (normally meaning "mother" or "senior woman") in certain contexts.

Other scholars in attendance restricted their comments to private conversations. One Yoruba professor of philosophy was first taken with the gender-free argument but then reconsidered when I asked him to consider the implications of viri-patrilocal postmarital residence, whereby a woman is normally expected to spend most of her life in a household in which she automatically becomes junior to everyone else in the house. There, she will always be expected to defer to those male and female in-laws born before her marriage and to the earlier-married wives. Another Yoruba scholar told me that Oyewumi's argument was not significant enough to challenge.

Oyewumi's *Invention of Women* was awarded the Distinguished Book Award of 1998 by the Sex and Gender Section of the American Sociological Association (Judith Howard [selection committee member], p.c., 19 November 2001). Africanists, much less Yorubanists, were not consulted. Thus, a new structural nostalgia has reunited transnational feminism with nationalism, just as such movements combined in the 1930s and 1940s to cover up the "scandal" of *adé* priests of the Candomblé. The alliance is new in some details but remains logically similar to the union of Brazilian Regionalism and nationalism with Landes's transnational feminism. It is not clear how fast, how commonly, or how deeply this new alliance of ideological forces will affect the practice of *oria* worship, but every subsequent conference of scholars and priests is likely to add authority to these motivated representations of the shared past.

Notes

1. The term "imagined communities" alludes to Anderson's thesis that monolingual, vernacular print capitalism allowed the citizens of the nation-state to "imagine" sharing the same communal experience as fellow citizens whom they might never have met (Benedict Anderson, *Imagined Communities*, rev. ed. [1983; London and New York: Verso, 1991]). However, I broaden Anderson's reference by suggesting that nation-states are not the only communities so united by machine-reproduced texts and that the rituals shared by dispersed populations (including those recommended by texts that are distributed fast or over long distances) also enable powerful "imaginations" of communally shared experience among unacquainted parties.

2. Ruth Landes, *The City of Women* (New York: Macmillan, 1947), 248.

3. Ruth Landes, "A Cult Matriarchate and Male Homosexuality," *Journal of Abnormal and Social Psychology* 35 (1940): 386–97.

4. Mark Alan Healey, " 'The Sweet Matriarchy of Bahia': Ruth Landes' Ethnography of Race and Gender," *Dispositio / n* 23, no. 50: 87–116.

5. Landes, *City of Women*, 202.

6. On Mead, see Derek Freeman, *Margaret Mead and Samoa: The Making and Unmaking of an Anthropological Myth* (Cambridge: Harvard University Press,1983).

7. Landes, "A Cult Matriarchate and Male Homosexuality," 391.

8. Ibid., 391–92.

9. Édison Carneiro, *Candomblés da Bahia*, 7th ed. (1948; repr. Rio de Janeiro: Civilização Brasileira, 1986), 54.

10. Compare Landes, "A Cult Matriarchate and Male Homosexuality," 393, with Carneiro, *Candomblés da Bahia*, 52.

11. See esp. Rachel E. Harding, *A Refuge in Thunder: Candomblé and Alternative Spaces of Blackness* (Bloomington: University of Indiana Press, 2000), 71–74, 77, 103; Carneiro, *Candomblés da Bahia*, 57, 104–9; Kim D. Butler, *Freedoms Given, Freedoms Won: Afro-Brazilians in Post-Abolition São Paulo and Salvador* (New Brunswick, N.J.: Rutgers University Press, 1998), 193, 195; Fayette Wimberly, "The Expansion of Afro-Bahian Religious Practices in Nineteenth-Century Cachoeira," in *Afro-Brazilian Culture and Politics: Bahia, 1790s to 1990s*, ed. Hendrik Kraay, 74–89 (Armonk, N.Y.: M. E. Sharpe, 1998), 82–85.

12. Butler, *Freedoms Given, Freedoms Won*,193–209; Butler, p.c., 12 / 3 / 02.

13. Mariza Corrêa, "O Mistério dos Orixás e das Bonecas: Raça e Gênero na Antropologia Brasileira," *Etnográfica* 4, no. 2 (2000): 245; Carneiro, *Candomblés da Bahia*, 104.

14. Landes, *The City of Women*; Landes, "A Cult Matriarchate and Male Homosexuality."

15. George Mosse, *Nationalism and Sexuality* (Madison: University of Wisconsin Press, 1985).

16. Corrêa, "O Mistério dos Orixás e das Bonecas," 246–48, esp. 246nn24, 25; Healey, "The Sweet Matriarchy of Bahia," 88. See also Roger Bastide, *O Candomblé da Bahia* (São Paulo: Editora Nacional, 1961), 309; René Ribeiro, "Personality and the Psychosexual Adjustment of Afro-Brazilian Cult Members," *Journal de la Société des Américanistes* 58 (1969): 122.

17. Landes, *The City of Women*, 37; Landes, "A Cult Matriarchate and Male Homosexuality," 393.

18. Indeed, Landes's "A Cult Matriarchate and Male Homosexuality" not only asserts the numerical importance of "passive homosexuals" in the Candomblé, but also identifies a dozen such men by name and describes them in the most demeaning terms possible. However, Ramos's offense did not seem to derive from her violation of these men's privacy and good name.

19. For Carneiro's admiring quotes, see Landes, *The City of Women*, 37. Also see quote below.

20. Carneiro, *Candomblés da Bahia*, 104–5.

21. Ibid., 103–9.

22. J. Lorand Matory, "The English Professors of Brazil: On the Diasporic Roots of the Yoruba Nation," *Comparative Studies in Society and History* 41, no. 1 (1999): 72–103, and J. Lorand Matory, *Afro-Atlantic Religion: Tradition, Transnationalism and Matriarchy in the Afro-Brazilian Candomblé* (Princeton: Princeton University Press, forthcoming).

23. Michael Herzfeld, *Cultural Intimacy: The Social Poetics of the Nation-State* (New York: Routledge, 1997), 22.

24. Carneiro, *Candomblés da Bahia*, 57; also Butler, *Freedoms Given, Freedoms Won*, 195.

25. Carneiro, *Candomblés da Bahia*, 119–23.

26. Gilberto Freyre, *The Masters and the Slaves*, trans. Samuel Putnam (1933; repr. Berkeley: University of California Press, 1986).

27. See also Leni M. Silverstein, "Mãe de Todo Mundo: Modos de Sobrevivência nas Comunidades de Candomblé da Bahia," *Religião e Sociedade* 4 (1979):143–69; Matory, *Afro-Atlantic Religion*.

28. Agentes de Pastoral Negros, *Mulher Negra: Resistência e Soberania de uma Raça* (Petrópolis: Vozes and Quilombo Central—Agentes de Pastoral Negros, 1990), 26, based on the Brazilian Census of 1980 [IBGE].

29. Paul Singer, "Radiografia da 'Democracia Racial' Brasileira," in *Racismo cordial, A mais completa análise sobre o preconceito de cor no Brasil*, ed. Cleusa Turra and Gustavo Venturi (São Paulo: Editora Ática S. A., 1995), 70.

30. Ruth Landes, "Negro Slavery and Female Status," *Mémoires de l'Institut Français d'Afrique Noire* 27 (1953): 265–68.

31. See Hamilton Vieira, "A história do Axé Opô Afonjá na homenagem a Mãe Stella," *A Tarde*, 14 September 1989, 20 Caderno (Pasta 324, *AT* archives); "Mãe Stella: 'Se nós não preservamos a natureza viva, termina tudo,'" *A Tarde*, 30 April 1995, 20 Caderno, p. 1, Recorte de Jornais, Bahiatursa office, Salvador.

32. "'Cirrum' começou no Bogum e 'Gamo' e' a nova yalorixá," *A Tarde*, 30 December 1975, 3.

33. Maria Lina Leão Teixeira, "Lorogun—Identidades sexuais e poder no candomblé," in *Candomblé: Desvendando Identidades*, ed. Carlos Eugênio Marcondes de Moura (São Paulo: EMW Editores, 1987), 33–52.

34. Ibid., 43–44, 48.

35. Peter Fry, "Male Homosexuality and Spirit Possession in Brazil," *Journal of Homosexuality* 11, no. 3–4 (1986): 137–53.

36. Richard C. Trexler, *Sex and Conquest: Gendered Violence, Political Order, and the European Conquest of the Americas* (Ithaca: Cornell University Press, 1995).

37. See, e.g., Peter A. Jackson, "Reading Rio from Bangkok: A Southeast Asianist Perspective on Brazil's Male Homosexual Cultures" (review article), *American Ethnologist* 27, no. 4 (2000): 950–60; Don Kulick, *Travestí: Sex, Gender and Culture among Brazilian Transgendered Prostitutes* (Chicago: University of Chicago Press, 1998); Richard G. Parker, *Beneath the Equator: Cultures of Desire, Male Homosexuality, and Emerging Gay Communities in Brazil* (New York: Routledge, 1998); James N. Green, *Beyond Carnival: Male Homosexuality in Twentieth-Century Brazil* (Chicago: University of Chicago Press, 1999).

38. See, for example, Kulick, *Travestí*.

39. Many Cuban and Puerto Rican adherents of similar traditions think so too. A category of men known as *maricas* or Addodis has for decades been identified as common in the Yoruba-affiliated denomination of Afro-Cuban religion called Regla de Ocha or Lucumí. They are said to be protected by the goddesses Yemayá and Ochún, who love them dearly. See Lydia Cabrera, *El Monte* (1954; repr. Miami: Colección del Chichirekú, 1983), 56; Rómulo Lachatañeré, *El Sistema Religioso de los Afrocubanos* (1939; repr. Havana: Editorial de Ciencias Sociales, 1992), 223–24. The earlier of these written accounts dates from the same period as Landes's observations about homosexuals in the Brazilian Candomblé, the late 1930s.

40. Fry, "Male Homosexuality and Spirit Possession in Brazil," 138; Victor

Turner, *The Ritual Process* (Chicago: Aldine, 1969); Mary Douglas, *Purity and Danger* (London: Routledge and Kegan Paul, 1966). It must be acknowledged that Fry's analysis is far removed from the psychological framework and pathologizing conclusions of Landes, Carneiro, and their successors Bastide (e.g., 1961:309) and Ribeiro (1969:109–20). Fry's is a symbolic analysis of local images of "magical power" and the role of *inversion* within them. I remain concerned, however, that all of the analyses focusing on the abnormality or invertedness of Afro-Brazilian cultural phenomena implicitly use Eurocentric readings of *Carnaval* as the model of all Afro-Brazilian culture. Despite the best of intentions, this model prioritizes nationalist logics of respectability and normalcy over the distinctly Afro-Brazilian forms of symbolism, logic, hierarchy, and planning that shape these religions. Afro-Brazilian culture ends up looking like a form of "letting-loose," a sort of compartmentalized abandon. Indeed, the Europeanist model of even the *Carnaval* as social inversion has limited applicability to the Brazilian case—*pace*, for example, Victor Turner, "Carnival in Rio: Dionysian Drama in an Industrializing Society," in *The Celebration of Society: Perspectives on Contemporary Cultural Performance*, ed. Frank Manning, 103–24 (Bowling Green, Ohio: Bowling Green University; London, Canada: Congress of Social and Humanistic Studies, University of Western Ontario, 1983).

41. Délcio Monteiro de Lima, *Os Homoeróticos* (Rio de Janeiro: F. Alves, 1983), 167ff.

42. Patricia Birman, "Identidade social e homossexualismo no Candomblé," *Religião e Sociedad* 12, no. 1 (1985): 2–21; also Leão Teixeira, "Lorogun—Identidades sexuais e poder no candomblé," 48, and Landes, "A Cult Matriarchate and Male Homosexuality," 395. A number of sex-*changing*, or ambisexual, divinities—like Logunedé and Oxumaré—are also said to inspire and legitimize their male worshipers' men's same-sex desires. Birman also observes the cultural controversy over whether men start out homosexual, even if their natal relationship to a given divinity made them so, or are turned into homosexuals during the initiation process. Though Birman attributes the former view to priests and the latter to outsiders, some priests have told me that an unscrupulous priest could indeed change the sexual preference of an initiand by placing a certain leaf under his or her sleeping mat in the initiation room.

43. Fry, "Male Homosexuality and Spirit Possession in Brazil," 147–49.

44. As Andrews shows, men of any given social race earn more on average than the women of that social race (George Reid Andrews, "Racial Inequality in Brazil and the United States: A Statistical Comparison," *Journal of Social History* 26 [1992]: 252). It has also been observed that, in contexts in which light-skinned gay men successfully conceal their sexuality, they possess considerable economic and political

advantages over women as a group and blacks as a group (*Veja*, 12 May 1993, 52–59). For an explanation of the term "social race," which I use in the absence of an alternative generic term for the Brazilian color and status categories, see Charles Wagley, "Introduction," in *Race and Class in Rural Brazil*, ed. Charles Wagley, 14 (1952; repr. New York: U.N.E.S.C.O./International Documents Service, Columbia University Press, 1963); Carl N. Degler, *Neither Black Nor White: Slavery and Race Relations in Brazil and the United States* (Madison: University of Wisconsin Press, 1971), 105.

45. Leão Teixeira, "Lorogun—Identidades sexuais e poder no candomblé," 44–45; see also Maria Stella de Azevedo Santos, *Meu Tempo É Agora* (São Paulo: Editora Oduduwa, 1993), 52–54, on the servile status of women consecrated to female *orixás*.

46. James H. Sweet, "Male Homosexuality and Spiritism in the African Diaspora: The Legacies of a Link," *Journal of the History of Sexuality* 7, no. 21 (1996): 184–202.

47. Carneiro, *Candomblés da Bahia*, 265.

48. I have previously presented the main body of this argument in J. Lorand Matory, *Sex and the Empire That Is No More: Gender and the Politics of Metaphor in Oyó Yorùbá Religion* (Minneapolis: University of Minnesota Press, 1994); "Sex and the Empire That Is No More" (Ph.D. diss., University of Chicago, 1991); and "Homens montados: Homossexualidade e simbolismo da possessão nas religioes afro-brasileiras," in *Escravidão e Invenção da Liberdade*, ed. João José Reis, 215–31 (São Paulo: Brasiliense, 1988).

49. In a probative contrast, the term *mágùn* (lit. "don't mount") refers to a "medicine," or magical application, that kills the paramour of a married woman at the moment he attempts to penetrate her.

50. Duly warned by my colleague Wande Abimbola, I acknowledge that the English gloss "to climb" better captures the fact that many *orisa* (though not Sango) are regarded as rising from the ground rather than descending from above (Wande Abimbola, *Ifa Will Mend Our Broken World: Thoughts on Yoruba Religion and Culture in Africa and the Diaspora [Interviews with an introduction by Ivor Miller]* [Roxbury, Mass.: Aim Books, 1997], 152–54). But this gloss fails to encode the equestrian and sexual implications implicit in the terms *esin* ("horse"), *iyawo* ("bride" or "wife"), and *gun*. It also unintentionally deemphasizes the fact that the divine agent is understood to end up *on top*—that is, in a position symbolizing his or her control over the priestly medium. The main virtue of the gloss "to climb" is not its greater semantic precision as a translation but in its sublimation of the equestrian and sexual implications of the folk terminology, which might otherwise appear to stigmatize the religion in the eyes of mightier religions and nations. Hence, it is not my aim (nor is it within

my competency) to contradict Abimbola, a widely traveled *babalawo* diviner, spokesperson of the priesthood at its Ife heartland, and university professor. Rather, it is to examine both the historical roots of cultural reinterpretations like his own and the cosmopolitan cultural politics that shape them.

51. Landes, *The City of Women*, 37.

52. Matory, *Sex and the Empire That Is No More*, 171. This priestly cross-dressing has been documented at least since 1910, and there is no reason to believe that it was new at that time.

53. E.g., Rowland Abiodun, "Women in Yoruba Religious Images," *African Languages and Cultures* 2, no. 1 (1989): 1–18; Bolanle Awe, "The Iyalode in the Traditional Yoruba Political System," in *Sexual Stratification*, ed. Alice Schlegel, 144–60 (New York: Columbia University Press, 1997); N.A. Fadipe, *The Sociology of the Yorùbá* (1939; repr. Ibàdàn, Nigeria: Ibàdàn University Press, 1970); O. O. Okediji and F. O. Okediji, "Marital Stability and Social Structure in an African City," *Nigerian Journal of Economic and Social Studies* 8, no. 1 (1966): 151–63; 'Molara Ogundipe-Leslie, "Women in Nigeria," in *Women in Nigeria Today*, ed. S. Bappa, J. Ibrahim, A. M. Imam, F. J. A. Kamara, H. Mahdi, M. A. Modibbo, A. S. Mohammed, H. Mohammed, A. R.Mustapha, N. Perchonock, and R. I. Pittin, 119–31 (London: Zed Books, 1985); etc. Consider also the important work of the non-Yoruba scholars Niara Sudarkasa (*Where Women Work* [Ann Arbor: University of Michigan, 1973]), and Judith Hoch-Smith ("Radical Yoruba Female Sexuality," in *Women in Ritual and Symbolic Roles*, ed. Judith Hoch-Smith and Anita Spring [New York: Plenum, 1978]). All of these scholars have made the reasonable point that Yoruba gender arrangements differ from Western ones, without reaching Oyewumi's extreme conclusion that Yoruba culture is without gender.

54. Oyeronke Oyewumi, *The Invention of Women: Making an African Sense of Western Gender Discourses* (Minneapolis: University of Minnesota Press, 1997), 117.

The Discourses of Diversity: Language, Ethnicity, and Interculturality in Latin America

JUAN CARLOS GODENZZI

Within the space of today's multiple communicational circuits—be they rural, urban, or digital—there are important economic, political, and cultural flows of global proportions that are reshaping the place and functions of states. In multicultural societies, these transformations are weakening the homogenizing impact of orthodox policies that have often been based on notions of a single culture and a single language, and they are allowing for the emergence of a number of discourses that, although perhaps perceived as strange, dissonant, fragmentary, hybrid, or unintelligible, are acquiring a growing legitimacy among increasingly expanding audiences.

These are subaltern discourses because they are coming from those who lack power and who are subject to social and cultural forms of discrimination. I am referring here to the discourses of indigenous populations, migrants, the popular classes, women, and children. These same discourses, however, constitute a new and radical constellation of voices and demands that are waiting for responses that may inaugurate intercultural dialogue. A deeper recognition and understanding of these discourses may serve as the basis from which we can undertake a project of reflection, social knowledge, and democratic renovation.

Following a brief characterization of Latin American cultural diversity, I will focus on specific narratives produced within nonhegemonic spaces which give new meanings to the world, to life, love, and suffering, and that seek to create a culture that is open to dialogue and diversity. These are discourses that propose new ways of thinking about and communicating cultural realities. Later in the essay, with a view toward establishing a link between this new discursive horizon and the task of education, I will discuss efforts currently being made in Peru to develop intercultural and bilingual education. I will conclude with some remarks regarding the rethinking of social and cultural studies.

Plurilingual and Multicultural Realities

Cultures are battlegrounds defined by ideological struggles and conflicting social interests:

> Culture—in other words, the ideal self-image of the capitalist world economy—is the product of our collective efforts over time to manage the socio-political contradictions, ambiguities and complexities of this particular system. . . . At the heart of the debate are, in my opinion, the ways in which the established antinomies (unity and diversity, universalism and particularism, humanity and race, world and nation, person and man / woman) have been manipulated. I have pointed out before that the two main ideological doctrines that have emerged during the history of the capitalist world economy—universalism on one hand, and racism-sexism on the other—are not antithetical, but rather part of one symbiotic pair. I have also suggested that their *adequate dosage* has enabled the functioning of the system as a whole, which takes on the shape of an ideological zigzag (Wallerstein 1999:171).

Within the tension between universalism and particularism, there are individual and collective subjects that are struggling to construct or redefine their identities. The indigenous populations of Latin America, which total close to fifty million people and speak over four hundred different languages, are among the most disempowered of these subjects. In certain countries, like Mexico, Guatemala, Ecuador, Bolivia, and Peru, indigenous people constitute a significant percentage of the total population, whereas in others, like Chile and Colombia, for example, this figure is significantly lower (see table).

In the case of Peru, there are two important Andean languages—Quechua and Aymara. There are also forty other languages belonging to sixteen linguistic families: Arabela, Arahuaca, Bora, Cahuapana, Candoshi-Shapra, Harakmbut, Huitoto, Jibaro, Pano, Peba-Yagua, Simaco, Tacana, Ticuna, Tucano, Tupi-Guarani, and Zaparo. A good number of these languages extend across the national borders with Ecuador, Colombia, Brazil, and Bolivia.

Yet, Latin America's cultural and linguistic diversity does not exist outside of history. A first important historical frame is the Amerindian diversity that existed before European colonization; another is the diversity that emerged during the colonial period; and a third is the currently exist-

TABLE. Percentage of indigenous population by country

Latin American Countries	Percentage of Indigenous Population
Argentina	1.5
Bolivia	59.2
Brazil	0.2
Chile	5.7
Colombia	2.2
Costa Rica	0.8
Ecuador	33.9
El Salvador	2.3
Guatemala	59.7
Honduras	3.2
Mexico	7.5
Nicaragua	8.0
Panama	6.8
Paraguay	2.3
Peru	36.8
Venezuela	1.5

Sources: Zimmerman 1995: 68–69; Gleich 1989; Adelaar 1991.

ing postcolonial diversity in which the matrix of the coloniality of power still persists, alongside the forces of globalization. Throughout this process, Amerindian languages have suffered a gradual process of subordination and have become the basis for social and political discrimination against those who speak them.

Latin America's wars of independence during the late eighteenth century and early nineteenth secured decolonization vis-à-vis Spain, Portugal, and other European powers, yet coloniality served as the foundation upon which these nascent nations were built, engendering an "internal colonialism" within each and every one (Quijano 1999). An understanding of cultural process and its diverse agents in the Americas must begin with an understanding of colonization and of the different ways in which it is reflected in the linguistic, ethnic, and social diversity that exists today: "The fact that globalization is today undermining the sovereignty of nation-states and that transnational corporations are moving across national borders does not mean that internal colonialism has ceased to exist. First, it is important to make a distinction between the concept of the nation-state in Europe and in the

Third World, and second, this concept should be redefined taking into account the new forms of coloniality in the transnational world" (Mignolo 2000b:112).

Heterogeneous Discursive Practices

Cultures are constructed and transformed through the discursive exchanges and flows of their participants. As Bruce Mannheim and Denis Tedlock (1995:2) suggest, "cultural 'facts' are not simply the sums of the actions of individual participants, with each of them expressing a preexisting pattern. They, in fact, constitute the arenas within which a shared culture emerges as the result of interaction." Cultures are thus dialogic in nature, understanding dialogue in the manner suggested by Octavio Paz—as the direct contact of two identities, which is more frequently a struggle than an embrace (Paz 1979:222). Cultures, in sum, inhabit the intersubjective world of the diverse discourses generated by their members and are never beyond the mechanisms through which power is exercised. This is what explains the existence of both official, canonical, and socially legitimated discourses and discourses which are marginalized, silenced, and subordinated.

A graffito that appeared recently on a wall in the city of Cochabamba read, "Official history is not written by memory; it is written by what is forgotten." The memories of subaltern peoples and nations are neither recognized nor recorded and thus are not incorporated into the treasure chest of national traditions. The fact that the vanquished tend to forget their own history further weakens them, explaining why forgetting is such an effective mechanism in the reproduction of the inherited colonial asymmetry of power. Official history is in conflict with the histories and oral traditions of indigenous peoples.

Discourses also enter into conflict in the realm of knowledge production. As Enrique Dussel (1995) and Walter Mignolo (2000a) suggest, the postmodern critique of modernity has maintained an "epistemic silence" about the particular ways of knowing which have been denied recognition as epistemologies within the canons of modernity. These include religion, folklore, and nonacademic ways of knowing. The great wealth of knowledge of indigenous peoples is thus subordinated and denied recognition as theory. It is perhaps necessary to ask, "Where has knowledge been produced over the past 500 years and what have been the criteria used to justify a certain kind of rationality that has its own local history and geo-historical position as epistemology?" (Mignolo 2000a: 6).

Such conflicts in the discursive realm, moreover, become visible in struggles over participation and political exclusion. Javier Prado (1871–1921), a distinguished representative of Peruvian officialdom, expressed his views regarding the place of indigenous populations within social and political structures in the following manner: "The main obstacle has necessarily come from race—the foremost social factor in the equation. . . . I cannot put enough emphasis on the pernicious influence of inferior races in Peru" (cf. Niño-Murcia 1995:266).

In order to expand the narrow limits of the discursive construction of history, of theory, and of politics, it is necessary to enable channels of contact and communication with the world of the "others"—indigenous populations, migrants, women, children, popular cultures—and to apprehend other discourses and establish new, interdiscursive relationships.

Our Blood Boils With Anger

Rufino Chuquimamani is a Quechua teacher, originally from Sollocota in the Azángaro province of Puno in the southern Peruvian Andes. When asked about his identity, he answers as follows:

> Who am I? Well, I was engendered by a Quechua man and birthed by a Quechua woman from whose Quechua breasts I took nourishment. My parents, and their parents, had always worked for and lived on the land of a *misti* [a *mestizo* or *criollo*; someone nonindigenous]. This *misti* would herd us around as if we were his property. My parents are blind, although they have beautiful eyes; they are deaf, although they have good ears; and they are mute, although they have a healthy tongue. My generation has also been born into a world full of suffering. Our lives consist of work and more work. From the moment we wake up, we work all day; work never ends. And who reaps the fruit of all this work? . . . Yet just as everything eventually comes to an end, these sources of suffering are also condemned to passing. The time has come to awaken. The ideas are maturing in our heads and our hearts; our eyes are slowly opening. Both the village priest as well as

all the *mistis*, including the judge and the other authorities, are cut from the same cloth. They tell us, "Do not steal!" but they steal. Everything is prohibited to us except work. We observe all of this patiently, and as a result, our blood boils with anger. What a great law! Some benefit and the rest suffer. The outsiders arrived as the great landowners, while the real owners are without land. I myself am Quechua; but this territory called Peru does not have a big place in my heart, because this Peru is the property of the big authorities, it is the feudal domain of those who control economic power. We the Indians are not part of it; we do not participate in this Peru. This is why we are forgotten and marginalized as if we were not part of this territory. (Chuquimamani 1988:37–39)

This testimonial constitutes a critical discourse about history, knowledge, and power and is enunciated from the flip side of history, from a subaltern location. It reveals the mechanism of exploitation and evinces the arbitrary nature of postcolonial power and of the social and political organization of contemporary Peruvian society. The narrative also provides some keys for understanding the country's internal fragmentation. As in all discourse, subjectivity is present, and this particular discourse does not attempt to obscure it. In fact, it highlights its power affective charge, its passion and anger in the face of oppression, and its hope for social change. And although this manifesto is not part of any officially sanctioned political agenda, it carries a powerful message capable of interpellating intellectuals as well as indigenous and popular organizations for the task of constructing new historical, political, and theoretical horizons.

A New Discursive Power

A bilingual Aymara–Spanish text edited by Denise Arnold and Juan de Dios Yapita (1994) tells the story of Elvira Espejo Ayka, a young Bolivian girl from the Bolivian Andes. The narrative gives an account of a particular mode of perception and a unique consciousness of cultural identity from an intercultural perspective. It also contains a pedagogical dimension—the school as a place where different kinds of knowledge are interwoven, multiple dialogues and subjectivities are interpellated, where those who learn are also capable of teaching, and where those who teach are also capable of learning. Elvira says, "I like school and I also like to knit. I want to know both so I can teach afterwards. I could teach the birds, the condors, the lizards, the llamas, the eyes and *tipa* leaves. Now I am knowing the birds and the *tipa* leaves, and I am knitting the condors and the llamas." The tenderness and hope inherent in this discourse are constructed on a long history of cultural exclusion, an exclusion that has left indigenous children and adults, men and women, without a quality education. This is also suggested by Asunta, a Quechua woman from the southern Peruvian Andes. "Kunanpas wawiypa rikusqanta deletreayta atichaniraqmi, aunque manna hayk'aqpas letrakuna leesqayta entenderanichu" (Now I can spell what my eyes can see, although I have never understood the letters that I see) (Valderrama and Escalante, eds., 1981:97).

Much like Asunta, a large part of the rural, vernacular-speaking population does not understand what they read and cannot write. Insecurity in the use and writing of the Spanish language among these populations, along with scarce access to media and communication technologies, reinforces the asymmetries of power in the construction and interpretation of discourses.

The cases of Elvira and Asunta raise a number of questions. What meaning might globalization have for indigenous populations? What importance might the existence of indigenous populations have for globalization processes? These questions reveal some extreme tensions, but it is precisely such questions that may enable critical reflection. On the one hand, people who have been placed in subaltern positions need to expand the flows and circuits to which they have access through the media and through the language of the new information technologies. Much as they need literacy to write, they need access to these new languages. Such instruments and competencies will help them demand and exercise their citizenship. On the other hand, it is also necessary to develop a critical discourse—both among subaltern populations and in society as a whole—regarding the intolerance and exclusion which that process itself may generate. These realities thrust us fully into the great challenge of the new century, the construction of an ethic of respect and solidarity. In the face of a kind of globalization that flattens everything in its path, we may thus propose intercultural practice and democratization as alternatives.

Gender and Discrimination

Irene Collahua Juarez is a Quechua-speaking domestic worker and migrant from Apurimac in the southern Peruvian Andes. She tells the story of how she was denied an education because of her gender, and at the same time she reaffirms her loyalty toward the Quechua language:

> I didn't go to school. I was not taken. According to custom during that time, boys had more courage for going to school. Women didn't. This is what my parents thought—that women who went to school would be wasting their time there, writing letters to boys who were perceived as more entitled to education. In spite of this, some girls did go. Even boys had a hard time going to school sometimes, because they had to help their parents working the land and this took all of their time. The parents also had a hard time because they lacked the money to buy the notebooks and all the other things that are required. I started school when I was fifteen thanks to a family for whom I was working at the time. They were very good people. They took an interest in my education, and I did as well.
>
> My children do not have much regard (for Quechua). They are not interested in it because they were born here, in the city. Not like us, who take much interest because we consider it our own, something we cannot negate. But our children are not very interested because they have not been there. That is why they don't take interest, at least for now. The language is the origin of our race. The Quechua language is equal to other languages and it is necessary that they learn it because it will allow them to go anywhere and communicate with anyone that they come across (Collahua 2000).

This narrative reveals how the unequal distribution of rights between men and women as well as the ways in which a social imaginary that justifies such inequalities is constructed. It also raises another common and very painful problem—the cultural, conceptual, affective, and aesthetic fragmentation within families, between parents and their children, between migrants and the children of migrants. What passions, conflicts, and political projects are brewing in contemporary urban multicultural spaces?

The Words That Do Not Exist in My Language

Arturo Alvarado is Quichua and a bilingual teacher in the Bilingual Education Program of Alto Napo in the Peruvian Amazon, where he has worked for eleven years. He is aware that the advancement of indigenous peoples depends on a quality education, which besides being rigorous needs to be imparted "in the context of people's values and in the context of their own language":

AA [ARTURO ALVARADO]: Indigenous cultures must not disappear because they are a source of wealth both inside and outside the country. What do you think attracts the researchers, linguists, and sociologists? They come because they are a part of life, part of the economy, a very important part of cultural wealth, because in our communities we are the authorities, because we communicate through our own language. . . . I believe that indigenous peoples have the right to learn like any other citizens. Like any other person, they have the right to a quality education. . . . I have worked hard so that my students can acquire knowledge. Today, indigenous teachers go into their communities with greater confidence. They are closer to their communities. Students approach them more easily and vice versa because they are of the same race. As a result, there is a quality education being imparted—one that is being taught within the framework of people's own values and in their own language. . . .

[INTERVIEWER:] *Do you consider yourself a modern Quichua?*

AA: Yes, because as I learn I am becoming more modernized, because I am using words that do not exist in my language and sometime using neologisms in my writing. As time passes, these will be appropriated by science, technology, and pedagogy. When I began this program, my language skills were poor, and as I have learned, I have taken on the task of recuperating certain values in order to communicate them through books and other texts. There are instruments that are waiting to be utilized. I am looking at a diskette and using the computer now. (Alvarado 2000:35)

Alvarado's narrative adds complexity to human experience. It is not enough to simply "get" knowledge. Knowledge must be accompanied by values that strengthen identity and community. The dialogue between languages will enable these to enrich each other. Quechua needs to be able to name the new technological objects. The creation of neologisms grows as idiomatic contacts multiply and linguistic borrowing increases. Quechua speakers do not want to be excluded from history and do not want to be discarded from the modern world, and they should not be forced to give up their culture and their values in order to be a part of it. Here are the seeds of a new politics of indigenous languages and cultures. Decisions need to be made so that these are not lost and so that they can develop in ways that will enable them to enrich the meanings of the worlds and lives of those who speak them.

Lerner Guimaraes Vásquez is a Shipibo teacher and promoter of bilingual education. In the following interview, he constructs a discourse that is motivated by strong intercultural feelings:

> [INTERVIEWER:] *You also have a Shipibo name, Satun Sina. What does your name mean in Spanish? Did you give yourself this name? Have you registered it with official institutions?*
>
> LGV [LERNER GUIMARAES VÁSQUEZ]: It means "a furious person whose fury is controlled." It could be registered, although the official registries do not allow it. I am only known by that name in the community and among my family, but my other friends, my *mestizo* friends, do not know it. The name was given to me by my grandmother, my father's mother.
>
> [INTERVIEWER:] *Would you say that there is a greater acceptance and understanding of bilingual education among [indigenous] communities in general?*
>
> LGV: I think so. . . . Now we are focusing on how to develop an intercultural bilingual education in the face of a dominant non-indigenous society that controls the economic and political arenas. We are now concerned about how to position ourselves vis-à-vis such a dominant society, and about how to create more equality throughout society with respect to education. Many parents have taken their children to the cities in search of better educational opportunities, so that they can become good professionals. Yet the children coming out of schools in urban areas do not do well because they are taught how to live in a society which is not their own. They acquire other values and lose their love for their own indigenous culture. They also lose their motivation to work for the development of their own communities. They come out with another mind set.
>
> [INTERVIEWER:] *What are your expectations with respect to the education of the children in your town? What is needed in order to offer them a high-quality education, above and beyond the things we have already mentioned?*
>
> LGV: I think everything we are doing is focused on today's children, those who are in their first years of school. For me it is also thinking about the future, because I would like to see these children, these youth, reconnected with their own identity. I would like to see them think of themselves as full citizens, like any other person, with equal life opportunities in economic and social terms. I would also like to see every community be able to benefit from sustainable forms of development so that there will no longer be conditions in which we are per-

ceived as "those in need." At this particular moment, we want solid, forward-looking policies that will last into the future. I want these children to someday have strong leaders, to defend their rights, to demand respect, to be able to work and apply their knowledge in their own communities.

[INTERVIEWER:] *Do you think it is possible that you will receive some technical infrastructure, like computers, in the near future?*

LGV: I think it is possible. We need to take these new technologies into homes, into the communities themselves, so they can be used to open minds and so that people will understand that there is more out there than our own culture and traditions—that these exist in a broader social context. We do not have that much further to go, but we need help with the final steps, particularly with respect to information technology. We need people who are trained to operate these things so that they can be installed in communities where they can help people become informed; to provide a place where a child can learn how the world works. (Guimaraes 2000:139–42 passim)

As part of an Amazonian community, the speaker here knows that his discourse comes from the "angle" in which he has been placed by the dominant society. It is from this location that social change must be approached in order for indigenous communities to achieve full citizenship. This makes educational work meaningful insofar as one is "working to develop a particular kind of intercultural bilingual education in the face of such a dominant society." Education is not outside the fields of social relations and power, and it must be an integral part of the construction of an intercultural society.

Guimaraes's text suggests that we rethink education, keeping in mind the postcolonial character of our countries. It also helps us understand that interculturality is deeply tied to the construction of citizenship, which seeks to create individuals with rights guaranteed by the state and with responsibilities toward the political community. Supposing the existence of an even playing field, citizenship requires respect for ethnic, cultural, and linguistic differences.

It Is All Here, in My Organization

In Latin America, there are countless indigenous migrants from rural areas living in the region's big cities. What changes do they experience in this new urban environment, and what happens to their cultural practices? What happens with their children? Consider the case of Malenray, who was born in Santiago, Chile, and whose parents are Mapuche:

> I am Mapuche, and here in Santiago I have learned to play Mapuche musical instruments and have learned the traditional dances. Everything I know about my culture I have learned here, in my organization, because although my parents are Mapuche, they never really taught me any of this. Everything I know I owe to my organization, *Inchiñ Mapu*, which is here in Santiago. (cf. Abarca 2000)

As Abarca's narrative suggests, organized Mapuches in Santiago, Chile, have created close to seventy associations, each of which has around thirty active members (2000). These organizations reach out to countless other Mapuches in the city on a variety of occasions, such as celebrations and cultural events like the *Nguillatun*, the *We Tripantu*, and the *Palin*. The land is no longer the place where everyday life takes place, but rather the city and the organization. Increasingly, the city constitutes the spaces which indigenous people inhabit, and it is in the city that most Mapuches live their lives. Their organizations are the place where cultural identities are reproduced and transformed. They are the space in which culture is reinvented and in which emancipation is imagined in terms of history, knowledge, and political action.

The Semiotics of Voices in Conflict

Bruce Mannheim pays close attention to the heterogeneous and transcultural discursive practices in the southern Peruvian Andes during different historical periods. Among the practices he examines are a Christian hymn composed before 1622, a vernacular song collected around 1960, and a particular textile design from the Cusco region that was made in the early 1980s following the country's agrarian reform (1999). Mannheim's objective is to develop a semiotics of discourse—*semiotics* because it goes beyond verbal language and *of discourse* because it reconstructs the moment and circumstances in which the text or the object becomes meaningful and reveals its intentionality.

Each of the set of discourses Mannheim explores is located within a space of conflict that is transected by an ambiguity that allows for the emergence of voices in conflict that are interwoven within a specific set of discursive forms. This is the key to understanding the diverse discursive practices in the Andes from colonial times to the present. More than just mere juxtaposition of diverse cultural elements or syncretism, discourses constitute the space of negotiation and compromise between diverse ethnic, cultural, and linguistic groups within which diverse interests and passions, survival strategies, utopias, and rebellions are forged.

A semiotics of discourse allows one to identify the more or less recurring discursive schemes in these different texts, based on a reading of their multiple signifying effects. In the framework, the "model" found in the vernacular song can also be detected in the textiles. This generates modes of analysis that can be extended to other discursive fields.

What is particularly interesting here is the way in which an Andean framework for dealing with diversity can be used—the acceptance, use, and promotion of variability. Both the colonial and republican projects in the region were much more interested in homogeneity, tending to erase diversity from their discursive universes. Today, however, there is a growing consciousness about the need to rediscover and revalorize the hidden treasures of diversity. This can create the circumstances in which a new intercultural education can be developed, and perhaps a more equitable society as well.

Osip Mandelstan's epigraph, which Mannheim cites (1999:15), refers to poetic discourses: "Poetry is the plow of time, that digs up its deep layers, its black subsoil, so that they may rise to the surface." Cultures such as those found in the Andes, in which metadiscursive functions have not been greatly developed, invest all their richness in the poetics of their texts, textiles, dances, and other practices. An adequate analysis and interpretation of these discourses allows one into the heart of these indigenous cultures—the patterns and mechanisms of their models of and for behavior. Discourse carries with it the density of tradition and envelops the relationships of the present. There are no neutral discourses.

A Bilingual and Intercultural Education

A quality bilingual education for indigenous peoples—one that could lead to the effective exercise of citizenship—requires a diversity of strategies that can incorporate the ethnic, cultural, and linguistic particularities of those toward whom it is directed. All real learning takes place within highly contextualized settings. The strategic importance of such an education lies precisely in its ability to generate the human resources necessary for the formation of new cultural agents which are grounded in their own tradition and at the same time open new ways of inhabiting and intervening in society and in the world. Many Latin American countries have bilingual and intercultural education programs of different scopes and orientations, but I will limit my discussion here to the Peruvian case.

Bilingual Intercultural Education (BIE) in Peru

As a response to the educational needs and demands of indigenous peoples and communities in Peru, the Ministry of Education has designed and implemented—through the Unit of Bilingual Intercultural Education, which is part of the National Directorate for Preprimary and Primary Education—a Plan for Intercultural Bilingual Education (1997–2000). Below I list the plan's objectives, coverage, strategies, and interventions.

Objectives

1. To provide educational services to the majority of the vernacular-speaking population in rural areas at the pre-primary and primary level according to the framework of bilingual intercultural education.
2. To achieve an accumulative and coordinated bilingualism in the students to elevate their learning capacities and their self-esteem.
3. To contribute to changing discriminatory behaviors and attitudes at all levels within the educational system with the objective of creating equal opportunities for the full exercise of citizenship rights.

Coverage

At the moment, educational services are provided to vernacular-speaking children in thirteen departments: Ancash, Apurimac, Arequipa, Ayacucho, Cusco, Huancavelica, Moquegua, Puno, Amazonia, Lambayeque, Loreto, San Martin, and Ucayali. In some of these departments, the vernacular-speaking population over the age of five represents a significant percentage of the total population: Apurimac and Puno, 77 percent; Ayacucho, 71 percent; Huancavelica, 67 percent; Cusco, 63 percent; Ancash, 36 percent (National Population Census 1993).

In 1998, educational services were provided to approximately seventy thousand children, and between 1999 and 2000, some one hundred thousand children received these services each year. Nevertheless, there are still many children who are not receiving services that are within the framework of bilingual intercultural education. Partial services are being provided to children who speak Quechua (in the distinct varieties found in Cusco, Ayacucho, Ancash, Ferreñafe, and San Martin), Aymara, Aguaruna, Huambisa, Achuar, Shipibo, Ashaninca, Chayahuita, Cocama, Bora, Matsiguenga, and Huitoto. Yet there are other linguistic groups that also need this kind of education. The majority of current demands for bilingual intercultural education are being made by indigenous groups from the Amazonian region through their organizations.

Strategies

1. *The pedagogical treatment of languages.* Depending on the languages spoken by children, one finds a number of linguistic scenarios in rural and semi-urban environments: (a) The first language is a vernacular language, and children do not have much exposure to Spanish. (b) The first language is a vernacular language, and Spanish is the second, although incipient, language. (c) A vernacular language and Spanish are the first languages, and children have equal command over both. (d) Spanish is the first language, and the second language is the vernacular language, which is incipient. Scenarios *a* and *b* are a priority insofar as students need to be educated in a language other than Spanish. This necessitates the elaboration of pedagogical and methodological frameworks that allow for the development of academic and cognitive capacities in a vernacular first language, and the treatment of Spanish as a second language. Scenario *c* differs from the first two in terms of the scheduling and curricular distribution between one language and another, while scenario *d* has only been experimented with in pilot projects, such as the one in the Tupe district where people speak Jaqaru. Other such cases have been taken up through specific projects or other institutions. In the last scenario, one of

the essential criteria is the desire and will of the population to reaffirm and revalorize their local language and culture.

2. *The pedagogical treatment of interculturality.* Efforts are currently under way to recuperate and revalorize indigenous knowledge and to articulate it with others in order to strengthen cultural pride and self-esteem. Advances in this arena can be found in the educational materials elaborated by indigenous teachers in their own languages and in reference to their own experiences and cultural referents. These advances can also be seen in the curricular arena. With respect to more systematic analysis, workshops and colloquia have been organized with the objective of defining both the conceptual and the operative aspects of intercultural education. A document entitled "Proposal for the Treatment of Interculturality in Education" summarizes the state of these discussions. It names seven pedagogical criteria for intercultural education: (a) self-esteem and knowledge of one's culture; (b) local knowledge and local social practices; (c) the identification and recognition of difference and otherness; (d) the knowledge and social practices of others; (e) the issues of cultural conflict, racism, and negative cultural relations; (f) unity and diversity; (g) communication, interrelatedness, and cooperation. It also contains a matrix of pedagogical criteria, organized according to competencies and capacities along cognitive, procedural, and attitudinal axes.

Major Activities Undertaken

1. *Training.* Training for BIE teachers has the support of a number of institutions within civil society and the state, including universities, teaching institutes, nongovernmental organizations, indigenous federations, and others. Following an open call for proposals, the selected institutions receive training and funds from the Ministry of Education to train teachers in various Andean and Amazonian regions. Teacher training is carried out through workshops and training seminars that emphasize the following kinds of themes: (a) the use and pedagogical treatment of languages; (b) methods for dealing with both first and second languages; (c) how to use BIE materials. These workshops tend to be decentralized and usually incorporate the life experiences of the teachers into their discussions. Between 1997 and 2001, approximately ten thousand rural teachers from

bilingual areas of Peru received training. Although coverage has not yet reached 100 percent of the national vernacular-speaking population, there are plans to institute a permanent self-training program designed to maximize human resources within indigenous communities themselves.

2. *Educational materials.* A number of stages are involved in the elaboration of educational materials. Among these are (a) definition of the specific products and the languages; (b) reaching a consensus regarding the written standardization of the language; (c) the selection of indigenous specialists to perform these tasks; (d) organization of workshops for the production of workbooks for the areas of mathematics and integral communications. Ninety-four such workbooks in five varieties of Quechua, Aymara, and nine languages from the Amazonian regions have been published to date. Additionally, each classroom has its own library. Besides Spanish language educational materials, bilingual classrooms also have (i) Occasions to Learn, a series of fifty cards, each with a suggestion for classroom activities; (ii) reading texts in indigenous languages; (iii) materials for ethnomathematics—such as Yupana, Taptana, and Khipu—which are mathematical resources that have been recuperated from historical indigenous traditions. Soon, moreover, there will also be dictionaries in Ashaninka, Matsiguenka, three varieties of Quechua, and Aymara.

Some Accomplishments and Difficulties

This process, which began in 1997, has yielded a number of accomplishments:

— Users of these services feel like they are receiving quality materials that are comparable to those used in urban monolingual schools. The reactions of parents tend to be favorable.

— A good number of the teachers involved assume that BIE can work. Initial reservations about the use of vernacular languages in school instruction tend to give way, and teachers, as they work within the framework, increasingly feel it is the best approach for the places in which they teach.

— The programs have established institutional links with other offices and units within the Ministry of Education as well as with indigenous and international organizations.

—It has been verified that students learn more and in better ways, despite the fact that the levels of performance achieved continue to fall short of the established expectations.

—Advances have been made in the standardization of indigenous languages, particularly in the case of the Amazonian languages that have the largest numbers of speakers.

—There have been advances in educating and changing perceptions among diverse sectors of society about issues of bilingualism and interculturality—among communities, parents, organizations, teachers, and public servants. One indicator that points to this is the growing demand for training and materials. Teaching institutes and universities have begun to express interest in creating programs that offer certification in bilingual education, such as masters programs, specialization courses, and others.

There have also been difficulties along the way:

—There is still strong resistance to and prejudice against BIE. There is much work to be done to raise awareness and create the social conditions that will favor the development of diverse experiences and educational innovation in the country's diverse sociolinguistic contexts.

—The efforts made in the field of BIE are not accompanied by explicit, critical, and coherent linguistic and intercultural policies tailored to local realities.

—Existing research on certain issues of great importance is insufficient. Among these issues are (a) frameworks of parenting and socialization in contemporary indigenous communities; (b) worldviews and the conceptual organization of space, time, and social interaction; (c) indigenous knowledge and practices related to the environment; (d) grammar and the discursive structures of diverse indigenous languages from the Andean and Amazonian regions; (e) ethnomathematics; (f) indigenous knowledge and practices related to health and the body.

—The workbooks were designed to divide knowledge into different grades or levels, yet in most of the centers where bilingual education takes place, instruction is not structured this way. One teacher teaches multiple levels simultaneously. Materials that reflect the organization of pedagogy in these centers are not yet available.

—Teacher training is still insufficient, given the scale of the needs and demands that require attention and considering that teachers, in their initial schooling, were not trained to deal with linguistic and cultural diversity among their students.

—The production and publication of diverse kinds of creative texts in indigenous languages is still insufficient and requires sustained support.

New Perspectives

1. *Rethinking the program.* On April 5, 2001, the National Directorate for Bilingual Intercultural Education (DINEBI) was created via Supreme Decree # 018–2001-ED under the rubric of the Vice Ministry of Pedagogical Programs. As a result, the Unit for Bilingual and Intercultural Education (UNEBI), which fell under the authority of the National Directorate of Preprimary and Primary Education, was dismantled. An examination of DINEBI's mandate reveals that the scope of its programmatic activity will be broader than that of UNEBI. Among its objectives are (a) to design a national policy of bilingual and intercultural education; (b) to guide and regulate the implementation of the national policy of BIE at all levels of the national educational system and establish the necessary links with other institutions; (c) to standardize the educational use of indigenous languages in conjunction with researchers, native speakers, and organizations from civil society; (d) to identify and promote research on ethnocultural, sociolinguistic, and pedagogical issues relating to Andean and Amazonian indigenous languages; (e) to implement programs for the development and evaluation of educationally, culturally, and linguistically relevant materials in the various languages used in BIE.

2. *Forming a National Consultative Committee for BIE.* A National Consultative Committee for BIE has been convened with nine indigenous and six nonindigenous members. The committee establishes a permanent conduit capable of guaranteeing the participation of civil society, the academic community, and popular organizations in the development of BIE.

3. *Elaborating a document about a national policy for languages and cultures in education.* As a result of a consultation process and two national workshops within the framework of the recently implemented dialogue for a National Accord on Education, there is now a document that offers policy guidelines for intercultural education as well as for BIE.

Final Remarks

The Analysis of Discourses

All language is characterized by a dialogic or conversational quality. In other words, it is discursive. In fact, the very act of comprehension is structured around the call and response relationship that characterizes discourse: "Comprehension itself is fundamentally related to the characteristics of language" (Gadamer 1991:475). The narratives and testimonials studied by historians and social scientists should also be considered discourses. As Joseph Moingt argues, "A specific event would not become part of a historian's knowledge were it not for testimonies, and all testimony is discursive—it narrates, interprets and frames. This is particularly true in the case of a non-ocular witness, who does not simply repeat what he or she has heard, but narrates what he or she has been taught in a particular manner" (1993:44). History and the social sciences share the task of adequately identifying and analyzing discourses, understanding from the outset that these are reasoned constructions with precise intentions that are strongly related to the impulses of social life (Bakhtin 1981:293).

The Body, Perception, and Knowledge

We know that the history of theories of signification has revolved around the theories of the sign and of systems of signs. Nevertheless, contemporary semiotics is oriented toward a theory of discourse that focuses its analytics on sets of signifiers. The unit of analysis is the text, be it verbal or nonverbal. As Jacques Fontanille points out, the semiotics of discourse supposes the coexistence of two worlds, the internal world of signifieds and the external world of signifiers; value systems; the point of view that structures intentionality (sense). Instead of examining the two "faces" of the sign, however, it is necessary to look at the two planes of language which "are separated by a sentient body that takes a position in the world of meaning, and that defines, as a result of taking a position, the boundary between the domain of expression (the exterior world) and the domain of content (the interior world). It is also that body that brings together those two planes in one language. In this manner, what is *sensible* and what is *intelligible* become inexorably united in the act that bridges these two planes within a single language. The semiotics of discourse, much like cognitive sciences, cannot ignore the interaction between the sensible and the intelligible" (Fontanille 1998:20) The semiotics of discourse take on a special relevance because it offers a common ground for interdisciplinarity by insisting on the importance of perception in the construction and production of knowledge.

The Formation of Intercultural Agents

The plurality of discourses and the role these play in the construction of knowledge and in cultural creativity pose an important challenge for cultural studies and the social sciences with respect to education. This challenge is to communicate research results, discourse analysis, and critical reflections with the agents of that education so that these may enrich curricula and pedagogical interactions. In this way, these disciplines will be contributing to the formation of intercultural agents capable of reinventing our life in society.

Conspiracy on the Sidelines:
How the Maya Won the War

ARTURO ARIAS

Cultural agency is a term that calls attention to the ways that subjects, often peripheral or subaltern, empower themselves through cultural practices. Scholars have developed valuable research and theory on the ways in which ethnic and linguistic diversity present opportunities as well as challenges for the construction of a democratic citizenry. But the focus is especially important now, and also especially challenging, since the rapid flows of capital, information, and populations across national borders render the very concept of identity too narrow to describe contemporary subjects. Today, individuals and even groups adopt multiple identities to survive and to empower themselves. Attention to cultural agency, therefore, often identifies projects that establish legitimacy in the public sphere through the various cultural practices—including alternative politics, transfer, use and acquisition of new technologies—that construct subjects with more than one identity.

These alternative interventions suggest, as Doris Sommer points out, how humanist scholars can assume more responsibility for the asymmetries of rights and resources.[1] She adds that, although one might be skeptical about any possible escape from globalized power, one can recognize the significance of the *jogo de cintura*; that is, the sidestep ordinary people in Latin America take to avoid big hurdles and to cope creatively with everyday life in ordinary—meaning difficult—circumstances. In this essay I will illustrate how the *jogo de cintura* has worked in the concrete situation of Guatemalan Mayas in recent history. Over the past twenty-five years in Guatemala, creative sidesteps around powerful government and also antigovernment forces have led not only to cultural empowerment, but also to the radical transformation of the social landscape of their country, the Mesoamerican region as a whole, and the cultural corridors which connect them with indigenous populations in the United States and Canada.

Guatemala has approximately eleven million people. Of that total, approximately 60 percent are indigenous, mostly Maya. The mestizo population is called Ladino, a word originating in colonial times to designate someone who spoke Latin, meaning that he worked in the service of the local priest, as a translator for the Spanish-speaking community. Mayas were forbidden from learning Spanish during colonial times for fear they might acquire useful knowledge along with their linguistic skills. Mayas are divided into twenty-three ethnic groups, with approximately sixteen Maya languages. Of those, four are dominant: k'iche', kaqchikel, mam, and q'echi'. Of the approximately six million Mayas, at least four million speak one of those dominant languages.

The Mayas' situation changed rapidly beginning in the 1960s, when the progressive wing of the Catholic Church helped to prepare them for primary and secondary school. Mayas took advantage of this opportunity to better serve their community in the future. Many were able to enter San Carlos University by the 1970s. These Mayas became the first truly organic Maya community leaders with liberal professions and technical qualifications beyond traditional village roles.

As Gustavo Porras has pointed out, the Guatemalan revolutionary crisis resulted from the modernization efforts initiated by the Ladino state.[2] The state simultaneously fulfilled the role of agent for development and inhibitor of the predominantly Maya population in order to keep the modernizing features from bringing about changes in the power structure. Those attempts at modernization, nevertheless, created expectations in the Maya population and unsettled the traditional order of things, generating rapid changes in Maya social structure. The worldview that legitimated only tradition no longer made sense in light of the new, emerging conditions. The congruence between people's daily lives and their identity had been broken, precipitating a revolutionary crisis of personal and collective purpose. One result is that many Maya joined the armed revolution against Guatemala's government.

Given that their leadership had been built patiently through the sixties and seventies, however, the Mayas who joined the revolution were not passive subjects who followed marching orders from the Ladino Left. Mayas joined the war for reasons different from the issues affecting Ladinos. Their motivation was primarily racism, not class conflict, and the Mayas' goal was to create their own nation to affirm precisely the ethnic attributes that the government despised.

The traditional Marxist, Ladino-led Left saw themselves as the intellectual architects of the revolution, so they monopolized the leadership posts, while Mayas apparently provided most of the cannon fodder as combatants and logistical support. The Mayas saw the roles differently. They had joined the movement for their own self-empowerment, so for some combatants the Left was more a vehicle for a culture war than the representative of a collective will. But Mayas generally kept their alternative hierarchy a secret, even from most Ladino revolutionaries. They called this strategy of working through the war *la conspiración dentro de la conspiración* (the conspiracy within the conspiracy). As articulated by the Maya Ixil leader Pablo Ceto in 1981, it consisted of trying to move up the revolutionary ladder as far as they could, not necessarily to promote all the revolution's goals, but rather to advance the Mayas' own secret goals of cultural agency.[3] Internal debates developed between those who thought the Ladino state had to perish before the Maya could be empowered and those who agreed on the need for agency and empowerment but disagreed on the need to violently confront the Ladino state. Many of the moderate militants were studying in Europe and the United States to qualify for professions that would enable them, in the future, to contribute to the Maya nation-building process. Thus, the Ladino-led revolutionary process became a means of striving toward another goal: the defense of Maya identity as the ground for the future constitution of the Maya nation.

According to the official history of Guatemala as told by Ladino political scientists, there was, from 1979 to 1982, a spontaneous insurrection in the Maya highlands within a broader revolutionary effort that had begun in 1974, when the Guerrilla Army of the Poor (EGP) was founded. The Ladino revolutionary organizations, however, were unable to bring those undisciplined masses under their control. As a result, the movement as a whole was neutralized politically by 1982 and defeated militarily the following year; after lingering in the jungle for over a dozen more years as a means to gain leverage, the leaders of the movement signed a peace treaty in December 1996 that enabled it to save face by becoming a legal political party. It is clear that, in this narrative, which has become the standard not only for the Guatemalan state, but also for most surviving members of the Guatemalan Left who now operate in various legal political parties, the revolutionaries lost the war.

The Maya tell a different story. Most people outside of Guatemala think the Maya were the war's greatest victims, the people most devastated by the violence. This is true, in statistical terms. Of the quarter of a million war dead and the hundreds of thousands of refugees, most were Mayas. The army itself admitted wiping out at least 450 Maya villages. And yet, the attitude of the present-day Maya leadership is surprisingly positive. They would never be so facile as to claim they won the war, and to this day they mourn their victims and search unmarked graves to exhume the bones of loved ones. But present-day Mayas walk with a quiet confidence and self-assurance they did not have twenty-five years ago. How did they regain this sense of agency?

By exercising agency inside the war, despite being recruited as canon fodder. Simply put, Mayas took advantage of the war for their own con-structions of future histories. When that effort stalled with the end of the guerrilla, they poured their newly energized collective will into reviving their cultural heritage through peaceful, often institutional, means. During the late eighties, while most of the fighting subsided, a fragile democracy began to take shape and to replace military dictatorship. Peace negotiations were initiated at that juncture. A social and political effervescence drew most self-exiled Mayas back home. Cadres who were studying in Europe and the United States returned to organize various *cultural* movements. Activism, in other words, was almost synonymous with cultural agency.

In 1985, the linguist Demetrio Cojtí Cuxil began to publish articles on the need to expand the use of Maya languages.[4] This led to the creation of the Círculo Lingüístico Francisco Marroquín, an independent NGO aided by the Centro de Investigaciones Regionales Mesoamericanas (CIRMA) that became the model for the governmental Academy of Maya Languages created in the nineties. Through the efforts, first, of the Círculo and then of the academy, all surviving Maya languages were submitted to systematic presentations through codified writing conventions and published dictionaries. This had never happened before: Maya languages had belonged to the oral tradition at least since the Spanish Conquest, and virtually nothing had been written in them since the *Popol Vuh* in the middle of the sixteenth century. Nora England, who collaborated in all of Cojtí's projects, explains: "Maya are concerned with language maintenance in the face of increasing signs of language shift, they are concerned with expanding the domains of usage of Mayan languages, especially written language, and they are concerned with achieving a balance between language as a marker of local identity" (Fischer and McKenna Brown 1996:178).

Maya literature began to appear for the first time written in Maya languages. There were bilingual editions with Spanish, not only because readership in Maya languages was much smaller, but also to exercise cultural influence over Ladinos. These Maya texts include a range of genres. One might think initially of *testimonios*, such as those of Rigoberta Menchú and Víctor Montejo, which were a first attempt to frame a rhetoric of being and to name agency for Mayas, to state the right to be themselves. Yet the output includes novels, too, such as those written by Luis de Lión, Gaspar Pedro González, and Montejo, short stories by Luis Enrique Sam Colop, and poetry by Humberto Ak'abal, Santos Alfredo García Domingo, and Calixta Gabriel Xiquín, among others. In all of these works there is a discursive performativity that explores the contours of a collective identity, representing the construction of a subjective and moral "imagined community." The emergence of these writers has led to the formation of an Association of Maya Writers.

During the period leading up to the peace process in 1996, various institutions that facilitated Maya agency were created both inside and outside governmental structures. A Secretariat for the Maya Woman was created as a cabinet position and occupied for the first time by a Christian Democrat Maya leader, Gloria Tujab, in 1986. In 1993, Alfredo Tay was appointed minister of education, the country's first Maya cabinet member.

At the same time, following the strategy of parallel campaigns that characterized the war years, the Maya movement also created its own organizations at the grassroots level as well as practices for cultural reappropriation. They began to study and bring back to the community the hieroglyphic writing of their ancestors as an expression of Maya revitalization. Maya clothing also became a source of critical creativity and a means for mobilizing widows and Maya women in general around the problematic of their identity, transforming their dress into an issue of being (Fischer and McKenna Brown 1996:154). Finally, some Maya public intellectuals appeared on the scene for the first time: from academically trained intellectuals like Cojtí Cuxil, to diplomatic figures such as Otilia Lux de Cotí, to organic intellectuals in the Gramscian sense, such as Menchú and Catalina Tuyuc. They all began community building from their respective positions, Cojtí Cuxil providing the blueprint for the politics of Maya rights. In 1990, Cojtí Cuxil published clear territorial, political, and jurisdictional demands that articulated territorial rights for the Maya nation, including the following: control and utilization of natural resources, political autonomy, Maya representation in Congress, Maya participation in public planning, the appointment of public functionaries based on ethnicity, the preeminence of international law, a politics of bilingualism, the codification and implementation of Maya law, the reorientation of the cultural policies of the Guatemalan state, the abolishment of military solutions to social and ethnic conflicts, and a reduction of the discrepancy in material development between the nations. Some of these items were incorporated into the peace agreement, albeit under different terms. And, even more surprisingly, most of them are being implemented at this juncture, even if some, such as political autonomy and utilization of natural resources, are still in the gestation stage.

After Rigoberta Menchú won the Nobel Peace Prize in 1992, tilting the balance of intellectual power in the country, she argued for and endorsed the UN proclamation of the decade of indigenous peoples in 1994. She also advocated congressional approval of the International Labor Organization (ILO) Convention 169 on indigenous rights. Menchú first created the Vicente Menchú Foundation in Mexico in 1993, then dissolved it to recreate it as the Rigoberta Menchú Tum Foundation in Guatemala in 1995. One of the first efforts of the foundation was to mobilize Mayas to vote. This was part of the process of local empowerment, allowing Mayas to gradually gain control of their own town halls, as the XEL-HUH Coalition did in Quetzaltenango— Guatemala's second-largest city—by helping Rigoberto K'emé Chay to win a surprising victory in the mayoral election. K'emé Chay became the first Maya presidential candidate ever in the elections of 2003.

As a document of the Hemisphere Initiates states, the Maya movement emerged as the one distinctive, rising social movement during the peace accords: "Mayan organizations in the ASC fought vigorously for the Accord on Indigenous Rights and Identity (AIDPI), and grew in strength and stature during the negotiations. Forming COPMAGUA, the largest umbrella group of Mayan organizations, was considered a crucial step for Mayan unity. The peace accords recognized COPMAGUA as an official counterpart of the government in peace implementation. These developments made many feel that the time of the Maya had finally arrived" (21). The peace accords of 1996 established bilingual education for the entire Maya population. However, problems emerged almost immediately and have continued. Six years later, the commissions created by AIDPI survive as official organs created by the peace agreements, but their power has been severely curtailed. Alfonso Portillo (2001–04), elected president of the country in 2000, opted for a policy of greater visibility but, apparently, less substance. He named Maya k'iche' leader Otilia Lux de Cotí as minister of culture. On her own, she named the Maya novelist Gaspar Pedro González as literature director of the ministry, with the objective of promoting bilingual publications. Portillo also named the well-known Maya k'iche' intellectual Demetrio Cojtí as vice minister for education. Cojtí, in turn, ensured that the AIDPI Commission on Education Reform retained its seat on the National Consultative Commission on Education, turning its members into his advisors and allies. Cojtí has used this support, and his own position, to quietly push for bilingual education while keeping himself out of the spotlight. Three years later, Maya educators are in charge of managing all bilingual education programs in the ministry, despite the fact that both economic and political support are lacking. Cojtí, however, has also run into problems. Non-Maya teachers and their union oppose bilingual education because they regard it as a threat to their status and hierarchy, and they claim that the meager budget of the Ministry of Education has prioritized it. As a result, a two-month-long strike paralyzed public schools throughout the country in January and February 2003.

In unobtrusive ways similar to those pursued by Cojtí, other institutions have made significant gains for the Maya in the past few years. Since 2001 Maya organizations have seemed to be absent from the national scene. In part, this is because international funding has dried up. But it is also part of a new strategy to quietly take concrete steps to further their goals, although this has created a certain sense of frustration among most activists because there appear to be only partial, localized gains. These can be important, however. For example, the Land Commission successfully established the Fondo de Tierras, or Land Fund, which provides credit for land purchases and technical assistance to landless peasants.

In March 2003, I had dinner in Pasadena with Otilia Lux de Cotí, the culture minister, who was on her way to Tokyo to inaugurate an exhibit on Maya art. She gave me a copy of all the bilingual books, manuals, and compilations of Maya culture that the ministry has published during the previous three years. Cotí had been publicly accused of selling out because she collaborated with the corrupt Portillo government after she had been one of the leading members of the Truth Commission that unearthed the military's human rights abuses in the late nineties. As I expressed my amazement at the enormous amount of work she had quietly done as minister, she looked me straight in the eye, laughed, and said, "La conspiración dentro de la conspiración."

Soon afterward, Rigoberta Menchú shared her plans for a Maya University with me and then with the entire LASA 24th International Congress in Dallas, also in March 2003. She explained how this would not be a conventional university. It would be located in rural areas instead of in the capital, and it would be built by the entire community. The community would contribute bricks, as many as each family could afford or wanted to contribute, as well as steel frames or any other construction material, so that the university would rise as a communal effort and not as a result of a rich donation or a national fund. What is more, she told us that, per agreements between the Guatemalan and Cuban governments, three hundred Mayas had gone to Cuba to study medicine; when they returned to the country some would open up community clinics, thus radically transforming health care in Maya areas, while others would work in creating the School of Medicine within the Maya University.

The transnational relations and cultural corridors that Menchú has created to connect the Maya with indigenous populations in the United States and Canada have allowed her to seek support for these efforts outside of Guatemala itself. For example, Menchú mentioned that the Maya University would work together with the University of Saskatchewan, Canada, noted for being a university that has empowered "first peoples" in that country, and with the Circumpolar University, which groups native peoples living across the Arctic regions of Canada, Scandinavia, Russia, and elsewhere. Their experiences and exchanges would not only be profitable for the Maya University, but would also enable Guatemalan Mayas to build a new model of transnational spaces in which Mayas from other countries—for example, from the states of Chiapas, Tabasco, and Yucatan in Mexico as well as the United States—could work organically with their institution, study there, and even house new campuses in the future. After Menchú left, Doris

Sommer commented that just as the community was building the university brick by brick, Menchú herself was building the Maya nation brick by brick, not to displace the Guatemalan state but to revive the premodern and (for postmoderns) very useful difference between (cultural) nation and state as an administrative structure. The old Guatemalan state was dysfunctional and despotic, to a great extent because it denied the difference and imposed one Ladino culture on a heterogeneous population.

It goes without saying that this nation-building process is far from perfect. In addition to the high cost of transforming Guatemalan society in the 1980s—in terms of the dead, the disappeared, and the immeasurable psychological trauma of hundreds of thousands of survivors—the movement has experienced infighting and periods of inaction. Additionally, it has failed at times to develop necessary technical and political skills. Sometimes, a lack of clear, prioritized goals is evident, which shows not only the newness of renewal after centuries of exploitation, oppression, and racism, but also the high, unrealistic short-term expectations that the "conspiración" has set for itself (and that the world set for it, as well).

Even on the narrowly cultural front, gains in flexibility go hand in hand with essentializing habits that are hard to shake. Pedro González has written the first book of literary criticism, *Kotz'ib': Nuestra literatura maya*, in which he defends Mayas' conceptual space, arguing that the Maya oral tradition has now become a written expression. This, in turn, has allowed the Maya to constitute an alternative identity in the country (125). He adds:

Kotz'ib' abarca las distintas maneras de expresar el pensamiento mediante signos, símbolos, colores, tejidos y líneas. La literatura maya como producto cultural de una sociedad, que tiene un particular punto de vista filosófico sobre el mundo y la vida, no siempre debe ser sometida al análisis bajo los cánones de la cultura occidental. Pues los ojos y los sentimientos de sus autores, se enmarcan dentro de esa cosmovisión que les permite la cultura.

[*Kotz'ib'* covers the different ways of expressing knowledge through signs, symbols, colors, weavings, and lines. Maya literature, as a cultural product of a society, and with a particular philosophical point of view about the world and about life, should not always be subjected to analysis according to the norms of Western culture. This is because the eyes and the feelings of their authors are framed within the worldview of their own culture.]

We cannot ignore the conceptual problems in this defense of essential cultural differences. Nevertheless, it has the virtue of enacting the critic's positionality and taking stock of his privileged relation with his object of study. From this perspective, González restates the goals of interpretation in relation to Maya languages as well as their philosophical worldview, with the goal of establishing a new literary history at the service of emerging Maya subjectivity. That is also why he adds, "Metodológicamente, se presenta el trabajo en tres momentos históricos: período prehispánico, período colonial y período contemporáneo" [Methodologically, the present work is organized in three historical moments: the prehispanic period, the colonial period, and the contemporary period]. That is, by articulating dissimilar historical periods to those of the Ladino world, but in relation to their oppression, he generates a foundational discourse for Maya subjectivity, with all the risks involved in such a metanarrative process.

"Cosmovisión" signals a will toward collective subjectivity through the agency of the community's culture, whether or not these cultural supports are liminal to Western values or a hybrid of both. The strategic combination of cultural references is different from the notions of both transculturation and heterogeneity, because what matters is neither the transposition of cultural values from one culture to the other, nor the emergence of an alternative "Mestizaje" that creates new heterogeneous cultural traits. Rather, what matters is who exercises the power/knowledge relations in this process. In other words, Mayas have no problem being neither Mestizo nor Western, as long as this comes out organically from their own initiative and agency process, one that includes a revaluation of their own culture and languages. They also know that the Westernized state can be a useful vehicle for an indigenous nation.

Despite the challenges of this national "work in progress," the Maya examples recounted here are concrete, positive evidence of cultural agency. They are also clear examples of how, when a resolute community multiplies the points of entry through which they can insert themselves into history, they can indeed exercise agency and build autonomous parallel spaces within foreign bodies. Mayas have succeeded in finding those open spaces from which they can profit to gain power and construct the bases for their nation, proving that small emancipations are indeed possible and that there are multiple ways both to engage in political activities and to fortify civil society. Maya cultural agency is living proof of a transculturation process from below.

Notes

1. Personal communication. Panel on "Cultural Agency." 24th LASA International Congress. March 29, 2003.

2. Quoted in Arturo Arias, "Changing Indian Identity: Guatemala's Violent Transition to Modernity," in *Guatemalan Indians and the State, 1521–1988*, ed. Carol Smith, 230–57. Austin: University of Texas Press.

3. Personal communication. Mexico City. Avenida Universidad 1900, Spring 1981.

4. See "Introduction," Edward F. Fischer and R. McKenna Brown, eds., *Maya Cultural Activism in Guatemala* (Austin: University of Texas Press, 1996).

Radio Taino and the Cuban Quest for *Identi . . . qué?*

ARIANA HERNÁNDEZ-REGUANT

Amo esta isla, soy del Caribe (I love this island, I am from the Caribbean)
—Pablo Milanés, 1981

Malcolm Equis (Malcolm X)
Me honraría ser un negro igual que tú. (I'd be honored to be a black like you.)
Igual que tú, nigger. A nigger like you. (Just like you, nigger. Un negro como tú.)
—Primera Base, 1997

En el aire, yo quiero ser Bob Marley (On the air, I want to be Bob Marley)
—La Charanga Habanera, 2000

In 1999, Cuban identity was the object of a propaganda campaign at Radio
Rebelde. Like other nationwide campaigns produced by Rebelde's Propaganda Department, this one featured a series of spots that were broadcast
many times a day. One featured the following dialogue over a background of
early twentieth-century Cuban classical music:

MAN: On our unique culture. . . .
WOMAN: On the legacy of our forefathers . . .
MAN: On the education we all have the right to . . .
WOMAN: There is our imprint, what makes us different.
MAN: National Identity: Five centuries of development. Enrichment. Endur-
ance.[1]

The spots informed listeners all over the island that their community was
unique, different from all others. Unlike typical propaganda messages, they
did not emphasize the need for political action but merely stated the uncon-
testable "facts" of being Cuban—which resulted from culture, historical
legacy, and collective rights. Radio Rebelde's campaign was only one sign of
the country's identity crisis. In fact, the station joined the widespread debate
on Cuban identity quite late. In the Cuba of the Special Period (from 1991,

when the Russians pulled out and Cuba's government appealed to patriotism in the face of economic crisis), the issue of national identity arose as a salient question to confront the incoming globalization threat.

By 1995, when I began my fieldwork in Havana, imagining life without the tutelage of the state had become a daily preoccupation. After the demise of its European socialist trading partners, the state's inability to provide for people's material needs required greater individual self-reliance, while at the same time, the introduction of foreign products and mass culture offered a glimpse of more seductive lifestyles elsewhere. In this context of material need and consumptive attraction, the nationalist discourse emphasizing citizenship and political participation that had been prevalent in media campaigns and in educational programs rang hollow to many people, especially the young. If, under the Revolution, Cuban identity had been linked to allegiance to the state, the resonant question became, What will hold society together in a post-Communist future?

The strategy followed by both intellectuals and state officials was to emphasize traditional culture rather than political community as the key element of Cuban social unity. As Jürgen Habermas (1989) has pointed out, under conditions of economic globalization nation-states often respond to a loss of social control by making local culture the scene for symbolic politics as well as a source of governmental legitimacy. A discourse of cultural nationalism is thus used to rally the population behind the state to face the challenges posed by globalization to the state's hegemony. These types of discourses polarize the social universe into two mutually exclusive categories: the global and the local. The local conflates state with society in the resistance against the global. Social inequalities are obscured under the category of the local, in a move that precludes debates on new governmental possibilities (García Canclini 1999). In Néstor García Canclini's own words, "Political debates consider identity as the core of culture. Culture is assimilated to local identities, and therefore imagined as the antithesis of globalization: the option, then, is whether to go global, or whether to defend identity" (García Canclini 1999:84).

For the Cuban government, going global was not an option. Instead, conferences, speeches, shows, plays, and publications variously addressed the issue of identity, signaling a helplessness in the face of global crosscurrents of capital and culture and a preoccupation with the survival of

Cuban socialism and "its accomplishments"—often reduced to free access to health care and education.

This emphasis on culture as the locus of national identity marked an appreciable change from the early days of the Revolution, when the victorious Cuban government put forth a nationalist ideology based on allegiance to the revolutionary project. Then, national sentiment capitalized on the construction of the future—now, it capitalized on the experience of the past. That does not mean that political nationalism disappeared. As Lenin and more recently Stuart Hall (1977) pointed out, ideological constructs do not immediately substitute for one another but coexist over a period of time and are alternately deployed in different contexts.

I will outline here the shifts in official Cuban nationalist discourses from the 1970s onward, initially in the context of relations with the exile community; and more recently within the context of economic globalization. I will turn the lens on Radio Taino, a station originally intended to broadcast to Cuban expatriates in Florida; since 1993, Radio Taino (whose name comes from the original inhabitants of Cuba, the Tainos) has been the only electronic media in the island to feature a commercial-like format. Finally, I will point toward the popular indifference to grand narratives of belonging, as they exclude alternative representations and nonnational allegiances.

Cultural Nationalism and International Politics

After 1959, the victorious Cuban government presented the revolutionary triumph as the culmination of an ongoing war of independence that had begun in the mid–nineteenth century—first against Spain and then, since 1898, against the United States (Hart 1983; Medin 1990). Nationalism was based on political community, and the idea of *patria* was firmly based on the national territory. Abandonment of the island was unlawful; it was considered an act of treason, as it implied joining the enemy abroad. But the war against the enemy—namely, the United States—was also a battle to be waged at home against the way of life represented by that enemy; against such values of capitalism as individualism, consumerism, and inequality. Education and the media were used to further socialist ethics and a nationalism that legitimized the political regime.

A new possibility for belonging emerged in 1978 during the first official meetings between the Cuban government and exiles. As a result of warming in U.S.-Cuban relations under the Carter administration, moderate exile groups were able to negotiate with the Cuban government the release of political prisoners as well as return visits by expatriates—those who, for almost two decades, had been regarded as traitors to the fatherland and were characterized as *worms*. Seeking to gloss over ideological differences, Fidel Castro admitted for the first time during these meetings that not all émigrés shared anti-Communist ideas or took part in antirevolutionary activities. He made clear that they, too, regardless of their ideology, also belonged to the nation—especially those constituting a second generation raised in exile and who had had no part in their parents' decision to abandon the island. Castro referred to Cuban emigrants simply as "the Cuban community," an expression that is used to this day, meaning the Cuban community *abroad*. In a display of relativism, he referred to the island's residents as "the Cuban community *here*," "our people on this side," and "the community that is residing on the island" (Aguirrechu and Madan 1994). He went so far as to label Miami "Cuba's second city" and to praise exiles for their efforts in maintaining their Cuban identity under adverse conditions in a foreign land. In his own words: "It seems to me that the Cuban community tries to maintain its national identity. . . . And that, of course, merits our solidarity and our sympathy. It does not matter that they do not sympathize with our Revolution. We are happy to see that the Cuban community seeks to keep its language, its ways, its Cuban national identity" (quoted in Aguirrechu and Madan 1994:51). Hence, the Cuban government sought to establish a common ground for negotiations, partly through opening, discursively, the possibility of a broad Cuban national identity that would encompass both island residents and exiles.

Subsequently, the Castro government allowed exiles to return to Cuba for two-week visits beginning in 1979. In the short run, this was a public relations coup for the government, affording both a source of foreign currency and an opportunity to improve its human rights image. About 100,000 exiles returned, spending somewhere between $10 and $150 million over the course of little more than a year, according to various sources (Bach 1985; Boswell and Curtis 1983; Garcia 1996). But the exiles' display of wealth in the eyes of the local population as well as their narratives of economic and professional success in the United States captured the popular imagination and compounded people's frustrated consumption desires (Bach 1985). The exiles' return ended up fostering social upheaval—what some scholars have called "the blue jean revolution"—and indirectly precipitated a new crisis in U.S.-Cuba relations that culminated in the Mariel boatlift in the summer of 1980, in which over the course of a few months 125,000 Cubans made their way by boat to the Florida coasts (Garcia 1996).

Just as the Cuban government was coming to terms with the first wave of exiles, this new mass exodus abruptly ended the honeymoon. Would-be emigrants were once again labeled as thugs, criminals, lumpen, scum, worms, sociopaths, traitors, déclassé, and enemies of the nation—Castro even said they were born in Cuba "by mistake" (Castro 1980; Medin 1990). The reconciliatory discourse inaugurated in 1978 in the spirit of dialogue had lasted little more than a year.

More than fifteen years elapsed before new conversations between the Cuban government and exile groups were attempted, but many of the themes of the 1978 *Diálogo* were to reappear in a new guise. In 1985, the Cuban government launched a new radio station, Radio Taino, broadcasting to Cuban expatriates in Florida with a sound and programming designed to convey a Cuban cultural identity.

Radio Taino, Part One: 1985–93

In the complex and tense relations between the United States and Cuba since the Revolution, radio has been one of the main ideological battlefields.[2] Cuba has repeatedly objected in international forums to the intrusion of U.S.-operated propaganda stations and has frequently resorted to jamming them (Frederick 1986; Nichols 1996). When the Reagan administration inaugurated Radio Martí in May 1985, broadcasting to Cuba, Cuba proceeded to scramble its signal, as usual, with noise. But when yet another anti-Castro station, Radio Mambi, appeared on the Havana airwaves half a year later, the Cuban government responded swiftly with its own transmission. Two days later, on November 20, 1985, Radio Taino was on the AM band, using the same frequency as Martí and broadcasting toward the north through powerful transmitters that allowed it to reach Florida, while jamming Martí in Havana.

Radio Taino was launched as a "tour station," that is, a station dedicated to the foreign tourists who had begun to visit the island. This appeal to tourism was "a kind of camouflage," according to a Taino official, to avoid criticism from the public, the Communist Party, and, possibly, the United States. Its programming was designed on Communist Party Central Committee guidelines to compete with Radio Martí. Both stations emulated 1950s radio as they sought to reach older Cubans who were politically ambivalent, but they had very different communication styles. While Martí used obviously anti-Communist rhetoric and relied on political talk, Radio Taino maintained a depoliticized language, featured cultural programming with mostly music and light talk. Even Martí's name, honoring the independence leader José Martí, contrasted with Taino's, which recalled cultural roots rather than political symbolism. And whereas Martí sought to instill political dissidence in Cuba, Taino appealed to the exiles' nostalgia for a bygone era and an inaccessible place.

To this effect, Taino's announcers were chosen from among old glories of prerevolutionary times who were familiar to older audiences, people like Margarita Balboa and José Antonio Cepero Brito. The music was also from earlier in the century and included performers who had vanished from the Cuban media, either because they were in exile (for example, the bolero singers Blanca Rosa Gil and Orlando Contreras) or had fallen out of fashion or favor (for example, Benny Moré, Rita Montaner, Bola de Nieve, and the Trio Matamoros). Even the station's announcement ("Radio Taino, broadcasting from Radio Centro, in Havana") sought to situate the listener in the 1950s, as it mimicked CMQ, the most popular station before the Revolution. Taino's programs sought to "safeguard" a national identity "free of adulteration" (Tabares 1987:60), while "working with the elements that would make us connect with the Cuban community in the United States," according to the then-director of programming. At Taino, popular culture was the uncontested receptacle of a de-ideologized Cuban national identity with which every person of Cuban origin, islanders and expatriates, revolutionaries and dissidents, could identify.

Music shows, light newscasts, and bilingual talk (in Spanish and English) aimed to create a communicative space that transcended ideological differences. Programs like *Hablando de Cuba* (Speaking of Cuba), *Pueblos y Ciudades* (Villages and towns), and *Mapa del Viajero* (Traveler's map) presented themes of popular culture and local history described as being "of a non-epical variant,"[3] while music shows such as *Cuba Canta Para Tí* (Cuba sings for you), *Al Son del Danzón* (To the beat of danzón), *Esta es Mi Música* (This is my music), *Memorias* (Memories), and *Cantos de Cuba* (Songs of Cuba) specialized in various traditional musical genres (Rozada 1987). These one- and two-hour programs were punctuated by three-minute spots promoting the island's beauties and describing traditions, proverbs, and speech forms, the origins of national symbols such as the flag, cooking recipes, the history of street names, and biographies of rural characters—all to convey the idea that the authentic Cuban identity was only to be found in Cuba itself. Similarly, the station's identification spot, a song by Pablo Milanés, stated, "Amo esta isla, soy del Caribe" (I love this island, I am from the Caribbean), stressing the geographical anchoring of national emotions.

This image of Cuba as the depository of tradition was combined with one of modernity, a place in which "authentic culture" had been preserved intact but which included all the modern amenities required by Western tourists, such as, said one spot, "Eurocard, Diners, Visa, and Mastercard." Furthermore, in striving for a nonideological tone, Radio Taino was the only Cuban station that did not broadcast either speeches by Castro and government officials or the one o'clock national news. Light news shows like the dailies *Temprano* (Early) and *En 89 Minutos* (In 89 minutes) reported on sports, travel, entertainment, and the arts, carefully avoiding political issues as well as bad news such as disasters and crimes. If need be, Castro was referred to as prime minister, rather than as the usual commander-in-chief, Cuba's National Assembly of the Popular Power became the Cuban Parliament, and party militants, the Cuban communists. This script was the design of Orlando Castellanos, a popular radio host at Radio Habana-Cuba, Cuba's international shortwave station. Castellanos imported to Taino a news language designed to appeal to listeners worldwide and instructed his staff "to abandon their old ways at the door" and strive for both a Cuban sound and a cosmopolitan flair that would appeal to audiences in Florida. During weather reports, Havana' s warm temperatures were favorably compared with those of other world capitals, thus situating Cuba within the universe experienced by an overseas audience. This unusual style often confused Cuban listeners, who would call the Institute of Radio and Television to inquire if Taino was indeed a Cuban station.

Radio Taino kept this format until the end of 1993, when the economic crisis forced a rationalization of resources and a restructuring of the radio system. By then, Taino's goals were no longer a priority and its audience was uncertain at best, owing to both poor reception and increasing competition from other stations. In Havana, in particular, radio stations now featured live, dynamic broadcasts, call-in shows, improvisational communication, investigative journalism, and timely musical programming. Between 1986 and 1991, Radio Ciudad in particular emerged as the voice of Havana's youth with shows like *Melomania* (specializing in classic rock) and *El Programa de Ramón*, which with biting political humor and music by underground local bands reached an audience of 300,000 in the city of Havana alone, while pirated tapes of the show circulated throughout the island (Teillagorry and Leon 1990). Taino, by contrast, had skirted the journalistic glasnost of the Rectification Period (1986–91), when the mass media sought to appeal to young people, whose interest in foreign radio stations had become a central political concern (Alonso 1988). Taino's atemporal *Cubanidad* was attractive only to older people—its taped, scripted shows and traditional music had become soporific, presenting an image of Cuban culture as having ended in 1959.[4]

In 1993, while all other stations returned to ideological orthodoxy as a reaction to the demise of East European state socialism, Radio Taino acquired a unique commercial-like format and a fresh, dynamic deejay style. Its stress on leisure and entertainment and a cosmopolitan image of Cubanness launched the station to the top of the ratings in the island's urban centers. The earlier cultural identity discourse disappeared from the airwaves but went on to become the Ministry of Culture's official view, guiding cultural policies as well as academic research agendas throughout the decade.

The Limits of the Nation

A wide cultural shift in Cuban nationalist discourse occurred in the early 1990s, when the disappearance of the European socialist bloc and the ensuing economic crisis caused widespread preoccupation over the future of socialism and a philosophical turn inward in search of a unique Cuban path. In 1992, revisions to the Constitution proclaimed the independence thinker

José Martí the ideological forebear of the nation and eliminated all references to international socialism. In addition, the amendments established the state's duty to "defend the identity of Cuban culture and look after the preservation of the cultural patrimony" (Art. 39). By 1995, October the twentieth, called Cuban Culture Day, had become an annual celebration of the nation's cultural melting pot (Bueno 1995)—even though the holiday had been established in 1980 to commemorate the birth of the nation as a political project during the First War of Independence.[5]

In this climate, works by early-twentieth-century cultural nationalist thinkers like Fernando Ortiz and Jorge Mañach were reprinted, and in 1994, the writer and senator Miguel Barnet formed a foundation to further Ortiz's legacy.[6] Subsequently, a number of research projects in areas like folklore and immigration history attempted to prove the existence of a single Cuban national identity linked to cultural traits (Martin 1995; Martinez Heredia 1995). For instance, Jesús Guanche, an anthropologist trained in the former Soviet Union and recipient of the 1997 National Social Sciences Award, followed Ortiz in claiming the unity of Cuban culture as the main attribute of Cuban ethnicity (Guanche 1996a). According to Guanche (1996b), this Cuban ethnic group was multiracial and shared a culture as well as a language, a psychosocial personality, national sentiment, territory, mode of production, and an aspiration for political and economic self-determination.[7] For the psychologist Carolina de la Torre (1995), who investigated the consciousness of national identity among children, Cubans shared, above all, mental representations both of themselves—as a people—and of others. Hence, for these scholars, national sentiment was anchored not just on the existence of a homeland, but on common culture, understood both as cultural production and as forms of social interaction. This emphasis on culture and ethnicity, rather than on territory and political community, allowed these authors to redefine the limits of the nation and include those who rejected the revolutionary project and resided outside the national territory.[8]

This discursive move first occurred, once again, in the context of a dialogue between the Cuban government and exiled intellectuals—the first of its kind since 1978. At a conference called "La Nación y la Emigración" (The nation and emigration), held in 1995, Abel Prieto, then-president of the Union of Writers and Artists, gave a lecture entitled "Cultura, Cubanidad y Cubanía" (Culture, Cubanicity, and Cubanness) that established the official position on the issue. Prieto did not completely disengage nation and state, but he did disengage nation from territory. He saw the state as the culmination of the national form and still linked national identity to a political project and nationalism to patriotism. However, he located the formation of identity *before* the creation of the state: in the act of collective resistance during the battles for independence, in which people from "multiple and diverse ethnic and cultural groups" were able to bond in the struggle against the colony. Hence, the current revolutionary government, as the first truly independent government, was the utmost embodiment of Cubanidad. For Prieto, a Cubanidad not committed to the political project of the state would either be "faked" or "castrated"—the kind of Cubanidad often found in those supportive of U.S. policies and those "who stopped participating in the collective national project" (Prieto 1994:47). He conceded that such castrated Cubanidad could be found anywhere: there could be true Cubans residing abroad, just as there could be castrated Cubans on the island. What was common to all Cubans without exception, in Prieto's scheme, was culture, both in the sense of psychosocial traits and cultural production. (Cultural production by Cuban émigrés was, he said, a part of the Cuban national patrimony.) Prieto concluded that it was precisely in the arena of culture where the nation met its emigrants.

The official acknowledgment of a Cuban culture and its concomitant identity beyond the national territory inspired intellectual thought. In 1995, a University of Havana conference on Cuban identity brought together Cuban intellectuals from both sides of the Florida Straits. They agreed that national identity transcended national borders and ideological boundaries and was based on a shared culture (Garcia 1995).[9] As the Cuban literary critic Ambrosio Fornet (1997) remarked, the unity of Cuban culture became the most widely discussed topic at all meetings between Cuban intellectuals from inside and outside the island. Subsequently, Prieto, who has been minister of culture since 1997, has called for the dissemination of exile literature on the island (Hernandez Valdes 1997), and important Cuban journals like *Gaceta de Cuba* and *Temas* have published debates on Cuban emigration, Cuban American literature, the role of gender in diasporic identities, and the limits of the nation.

Contrary to Jorge Duany's (2000) contention that Cuban revolutionary nationalism has ignored the diaspora, that discourse has been configured precisely in relation (whether opposition or inclusion) to the exile community. A discourse of cultural identity including Cuban exiles in the national imaginary has been framed by the dynamics of U.S.-Cuban relations (both of confrontation and rapprochement) as well as by the need, at certain moments, to seek allies among sectors of the exile community. Such discourse was embraced by certain agencies within the Cuban state and not by others, and it permeated institutional intellectual production—as long as its focus was a remote common past or a hypothetical future in which transnational "ethnic" solidarity could foster economic ties.

A discourse including expatriates in the national imaginary has been strategically deployed not only by a sector of the Cuban government at different times, but also in productions by the Cuban Film Institute (ICAIC), productions that highlight the ties between families across borders (Jesús Díaz's film *Parting the Ways* [1985], and Pastor Vega's *Parallel Lives* [1993] come to mind). Popular expressions of pan-Cuban solidarity, however, have been repressed, and more conservative institutions such as the Cuban Institute of Radio and Television (ICRT), responding directly to the Communist Party's Department of Ideology, have not allowed broadcasts sympathetic to the issue. Rigoberto Lopez's documentary *Yo Soy, del Son y de la Salsa* (I belong to Son and to Salsa) is emblematic of these internal disagreements. While the film won the Coral Prize at the Havana Film Festival in 1996, its soundtrack was not aired on Cuban radio because it highlighted the contributions of the exiled singer Celia Cruz to the history of Cuban music. Likewise, on the possibility of playing the Miami star Gloria Estefan on Radio Taino, the station's director of programming responded,

> Gloria Estefan? That's impossible! Here we follow the music policies issued by the Director of Music for all Cuban radio. In this case, that Gloria Estefan you just mentioned cannot be played. That is, it is not in the interest of Cuban radio to promote that actress—I mean, that singer. Like her, there are four or five other people that should not be broadcast; first of all, because we feel that their Cubanness is not to our liking. That does not mean that people cannot listen to her at home if they have her albums. But not on Radio Taino. . . . Radio cannot become a vehicle to disseminate that. Such is the case of Celia Cruz too. People like to listen to her a lot, but her music cannot be played on the radio for political reasons: because of all the things she has said against the government. It is the same

everywhere. In other countries too. Every radio station has an owner, and the owner decides what should be played, and what should not.[10]

Cuban officials at the ICRT have argued that the primary cause for exclusion is not so much residency as political opinion. Lucrecia, for instance, a salsa singer who legally migrated to Spain, received airplay until she criticized Cuban migratory policies and went to Miami to record a song about a Cuban rafter whose life improved only after he made it to Florida.[11] Songs by popular Cuba-based singers, for example, Pablo Milanés's *Exodo* and Carlos Varela's *Foto de Familia*, received no airplay since they depict the dramas of family separation and exile. This is not to say such songs are unknown to audiences. On the contrary, they are occasionally performed live, and home-made taped versions of them circulate widely. Such was also the case of a song by the *timba* star Manolín, El Médico de la Salsa. Called *Yo tengo amigos en Miami* (I have friends in Miami), the song is a reaffirmation of common identity and solidarity between Cubans on the island and Cubans in Miami:

Ya está quedando atrás	We are leaving behind
la vieja mentalidad . . .	the old mentality . . .
cubanos de aquí y de allá	Cubans from here and there
no importa donde estás	It does not matter where
dejemos los rencores . . .	Leave grudges behind . . .
Hay que vivir para ver	*Live and learn*
Los tiempos cambian,	Times are changing
tu va a ver	You will see
Yo tengo amigos en Miami . . .	*I have friends in Miami . . .*
Y que mas da	What's the fuss
Si todos somos hermanos . . .	if we are all brothers . . .
Viva mi Cubita Linda	Long life to my beautiful Cuba
Y que vivan los cubanos	and long life to the Cuban people
Donde quiera!	Wherever they may be![12]

The song's release on CD was not publicized, and it effectively marked the beginning of a decline in Manolín's career. Soon after, he sought residency in Miami—only to move back to Havana, then back to Miami, and then back to Havana again. His repertoire was shunned by the Cuban media. A few years later, in a rare public appearance in Havana, Manolín was forcibly removed from the stage for singing *Yo tengo amigos en Miami*. The next day, the Communist Party daily, *Granma*, rejected his "extramusical" agenda: "We do not have any reason to put up with his explicit allusions—in his ominous chorus—to a rosy path between Miami and Havana, when he knows very well how muggy and tense is the relationship, and all because of those there who attack our identity and our culture. The Beny Moré Dance Hall is in Havana, and not in Dade County" (de la Hoz 2001).[13]

This official discourse of inclusion was not designed for a local audience, and calls for action by individual artists were obviously not welcome. In addition, cultural nationalism failed to connect with important sectors of the population, most notably the young, who were more concerned with concrete policy outcomes regarding migration and U.S. relations than with nostalgic narratives of belonging. Part of the problem was that the discourse of cultural identity had much in common with the earlier one on political community. Both were deployed as ideological arguments against foreign cultural flows, whether from the United States or disguised under the banner of globalization. But most important, they both construed their constituency as the masses, rejecting alternative identities as both the products of market capitalism and a subversion of the national borders. The extension of Cuban identity to the Cuban diaspora was thus not paralleled by an acknowledgment of racial, generational, educational, sexual, and gendered experiences of belonging, perhaps because it was precisely race, generation, education, sexuality, and gender that brought officials and intellectuals on both sides together in ways that ideological differences would not permit.

Take the Test of Cubanidad that the Communist Party's school used around 1998 to stimulate discussions on national identity among students.[14] My neighbor in Havana, Gustavo, got a hold of the test. One spring day in 1998 when I was visiting with other neighbors, Hilda, Aida, and Aida's daughter Sailin, he walked in, and, delighted to find an audience, he proceeded to test us all. "What time is the daily cannon blast in Havana?" "What do people sing when they die?" "At what time was Lola killed?" "What happens to the shrimp that falls asleep?" "Where are singers from?" "Where is 'the sinful corner'?" As soon as Gustavo had read all the questions, Aida and Hilda, who are both in their sixties, competed to see who could answer the most questions. Aida answered all of the 300 plus questions correctly, closely followed by Hilda. Gustavo, in his early forties, scored third. Young

Sailin and I did not fare very well. Gustavo defended his disappointing defeat by asking who could possibly know the songs that were in the hit parades forty years ago. My neighbors suspected that the authors of the test had to be old people.

They were older people indeed. A group of white, Cuban-born men residing in North America since the early 1960s had formed an Internet newsgroup on Cuban affairs in 1994 and had put together this test to assess their own degree of Cubanidad. What they came up with were questions on Cuban popular culture and music of their time, including song lyrics, names of band leaders, proverbs, and the like—there were no questions on social or political issues.[15] For these exiles, identity was located in pre-1959 Cuba and was not related to political allegiances, residence in the national territory, or language, but on the everyday experience of popular culture. The only trace of the exile experience in the test was precisely its generational quality.

A couple of months later, I attended a conference on identity for Latin American psychologists at the University of Havana. Abel Prieto, minister of culture, Roberto Fernandez Retamar, a famous writer and literary critic, and Ambrosio Fornet, a leading intellectual, chaired the closing session on Cuban cultural identity. To illustrate a point about the uniqueness of Cuban culture, Fornet told the following story. In the early 1990s, on the border of Texas and Mexico, thousands of "wetbacks" trying to cross were caught and sent back. One of these returnees came up with a brilliant idea. What they had to do was say they were Cuban instead of Mexican. Not only would they not be deported, but they would be given a home, health care, and a monthly stipend. And, as the story goes, it worked. That is, until the U.S. Border Patrol figured out what was going on and decided to make things a bit harder. To all those claiming Cuban citizenship, they now required them to sing the Cuban national anthem, to describe the Cuban flag, to tell the year of the country's independence, and to name the Cuban president (all symbols of political community). As the word spread, Mexican migrants got Cuban schoolbooks, memorized them, and then successfully crossed the border. The U.S. patrol held a meeting. It was of utmost importance to differentiate Cubans from Mexicans, since Cubans could be allowed in while Mexicans were to be sent back. What could they do? They decided to hire a Cuban to devise a test that non-Cubans would always flunk, a test with questions that nobody could memorize, that only Cubans could possibly know the answers to. This was called a Test of Cubanidad, continued Fornet. He went on to describe the test in detail—as we know it—and acknowledged that young people would probably not score very high. He went on to note that most questions were related to popular music, and that indeed Cubans were very musical people.

Fornet did not know that this was in fact a test devised by Cuban exiles on the Internet to assess their own Cubanness, and, although obviously apocryphal, his story was not far-fetched. Certainly, the Test of Cubanidad meant to distinguish Cubans from Mexicans and from other immigrants. But it was a test meant to be put to use *within* the United States itself, to establish other borders and border crossings aside from that of "the Border" (that is, the U.S.-Mexico border). As envisioned by its authors, it was to confirm the identity of Cuban migrants as *truly* Cuban, despite their extended residency outside the island. The truth of this Cuban identity—because the answers could not be learned at school or memorized—lay in the truth of lived realities, in the way that the test's answers could only have been imbibed through the everyday experience of a Cuban environment, of being exposed to forms of Cuban popular culture. The test, then, presumed that the central consensual marker of Cuban identity was participation in a popular culture shared by an "imagined community" in spite of other social differences.

As recognized by both Fornet and my neighbors, however, this was a popular culture of which young people had not partaken. The test was grounded in the experience of an earlier generation of both Revolution and exile, a generation divided by migration and political cleavages, yet united in other ways by their race, education, and urban upbringing. But that generation had little knowledge and understanding of contemporary youth culture on the island—of the contemporary forms of Cubanidad. Their identity in exile had been defined by their opposition to the Castro government, just as the Cuban government defined Cuban identity as the commitment to the socialist project. This is why the Test of Cubanidad could be appropriated by Communist Party officials as their own, without suspicion of its diaspora origins, precisely because there was little difference between them and exiles of the same generation in terms of ideas about popular culture. This is also why it was unclear to many listeners whether pre-1994 Radio Taino was broadcast from Cuba or from Florida, and why it appealed—if to anyone—to older people on both sides.

Young Cubans would most likely flunk the Test of Cubanidad. They have accrued other characteristics of a transnational sort—traits and tastes that mark them as members of a cosmopolitan youth culture beyond the surveillance of the U.S. Border Patrol. The Cuban country music singer Albita and her band stand as an emblematic example. During a visit to Mexico in 1993 they decided to migrate to the United States in search of better prospects. The *New York Times* reported as follows: "In the spring of 1993, for two long days in the Mexican border town of Ciudad Juarez, Albita and her band had debated strategy in a Chinese restaurant. They were among Cuba's top-earning performers; how best to defect? Finally, they decided to be brazen.

"White, black and Chinese Cuban, with shaved heads and buzz cuts, they simply sauntered over the bridge into El Paso, Texas, seemingly invisible to the Border Patrol in their ethnic diversity and funkiness" (Sontag 1997). Style and looks set these Cubans apart from Mexicans, but not because of their Cuban appearance; precisely the opposite: because of their cosmopolitan urban style and embodiment of transnational fashions, apparently not a look identified with migrants by the *migra*. With Cuba's opening to transnational culture, youth identities are increasingly expressed through appearance, aesthetics, leisure habits, and consumption tastes expressing membership in like-minded communities that cross nationalities. To the generation of both the Revolution and exile, this contemporary popular culture appears to be departing from an ideal of cultural authenticity. From the perspective of the Cuban government, if national identity seems to be fragmenting and if political struggle is no longer a force that binds society together, how can the revolutionary state foster national pride, while ensuring its own survival?

A young contemporary dance ensemble addressed the dilemma in November 1998, at a downtown Havana theater.[16] In one skit, six dancers in military outfits marched in line behind a female officer. At one point, the officer blew her whistle and shouted: "IDENTITY. What is identity?" The dancers stood firm. "Identi . . . qué?" asked one. "Identi . . . quoi?" asked another one. "What is that thing, identity?" asked a third. The officer repeated slowly: "What is identity?" After a long pause, a dancer hesitantly shouted an eleven-digit number. The others followed, each shouting what appeared to be the number on their national identification card. That was, however, not the answer she was looking for. Confused, they walked in circles under a dim light, searching for clues, until one of them began singing and dancing to Los Van Van's timba hit *Se Me Pone la Cabeza Mala*. Another dancer proceeded to do the same with Amenaza's rap song *No*, followed by another one who did *La Macarena*. Their dance moves freed them from their uniforms, which slipped off, showing colorful outfits underneath. Each then proceeded to do his or her own thing. One actor played a video game, another listened to music on his headphones, another typed on a computer, and two others talked simultaneously on their cell phones. But this was still unsatisfying. The actors removed some of their clothes and, half-dressed, danced with each other. The play ended with all of them cheerfully lying down together.

The play sought to resolve the contradiction between community and individuality, as posed by socialist ideology, and attempted to formulate a happy medium. Yet the issue of identity was both raised and defined by the powers-that-be, not by the individuals themselves. Accordingly, their response was their assigned identity as citizens, which was in fact a non-identity, as the national identification card number is the antithesis of self-expression, merely identifying the individual vis-à-vis the state bureaucracy. The needs of the modernist state for order and control clashed with those of individual expression. Neither egalitarianism nor individualism were solutions either, and the actors finally opted to express themselves as if the state did not exist.

This dilemma also eased tensions at Radio Taino, as in 1993, in the midst of the worse economic crisis in recent Cuban history, it sought to raise its audience ratings and attract advertising revenue. While all other stations had their airtime curtailed because of lack of resources, Taino's was increased to twenty-four hours using both the AM and FM bands for better quality sound. This move disassociated the station from Radio Martí and sought to attract an audience of urban dwellers on the island—namely, young people, upcoming entrepreneurs, and those with access to foreign currency. That is, people with the ability to enjoy the entertainment options publicized and to purchase the goods and services advertised. For the first time in three decades, advertisements were to run on a Cuban station, but they required a new approach to broadcasting. Fast-paced shows with the latest hits from both Cuba and abroad and entertainment programs in Spanish and English supplanted the old programs dedicated to Cuba's cultural roots, which were either eliminated or confined to low-audience times, since it was impossible to secure commercial sponsorship for them. Taino featured more foreign music than any other station on the island, which confused listeners, who sometimes, again, assumed they were listening to an overseas transmission.

Radio Taino's star show was *From Five to Seven*, a daily program dedicated to the hottest Latin dance music. The latest Cuban dance music (mostly timba) was played along with foreign salsa, presenting a community of Latin music producers and fans that extended through the whole hemisphere.[17] Similarly, entertainment news situated Havana in a network of world metropolises that included Madrid, Miami, and New York. The show featured a commercial segment every fifteen minutes, and its announcers spoke in both Spanish and English. Other programs with wide appeal included the daily talk shows *De Mañana* (In the morning) and *A Buena Hora* (At the right time) and the nightly classical rock program *Cuba Tonight*, which presented the latest hits from both the U.S. *Billboard* charts and Spain's *Los 40 Principales*, thanks to agreements with the shows' sponsors. *Cuba Tonight*'s host, Jose Luis Bergantiño, along with his colleagues at *De Mañana* (the director Yvonne Leantó and conductor Camilo Egaña), were hired by Radio Taino to cash in on their popularity among Havana's youth, having established their names on the most popular shows at Radio Ciudad de La Habana during the late eighties.[18] These shows could be heard blasting from house windows and cafeteria loudspeakers and in virtually every public space in Havana.

Radio Taino's distinctive sound—of cosmopolitan optimism during the day and sultry intimacy at night—entwined various interests: the Cuban Communist Party (PCC), the ICRT, the needs of advertisers, the transnational music industry, the station's executive personnel, audience desires, and the creativity of the station's staff. Deejays and program directors needed to interpret official ideology broadly, while satisfying both the institute's guidelines and their mode of expression as members of an emerging urban middle class with access to information and foreign currency. Their popular success resided in their ability to situate Cuban music hand-in-hand with the latest hits in the world's urban centers and, accordingly, in their representation of audiences not as politicized workers, but as cosmopolitan individual consumers and vacationers—thus tapping into their desires for travel and consumption fostered by the state's market reforms.

Conclusion: Globalization or the Nation?

Radio Taino's commercial success and its high ratings caused tremendous insecurity among executive personnel at the ICRT. The station successfully addressed the institute's pressing need for cash, but, as a state institution, it also needed to endorse socialist ethics that were at odds with its newly adopted business approach and its dissemination of mass consumer culture. Taino's alleged appeal to a tourist audience was an attempt to reconcile these antagonistic needs in the eyes of Communist Party officials. That is, the station adhered to a commercial style but rationalized it by its hypothetical non-Cuban audience. But the station's "double consciousness" (it designed its programming according to what the station imagined that foreign ears would fancy) resulted in a paradox: The station did not attract tourists but was instead, according to annual audience surveys, most popular among urban youth (Jara and Diaz 1996). The fiction of a foreign audience was publicly maintained to protect the station from institutional criticism by government sectors opposed to the economic opening and hence to ensure the influx of payments from commercial spots as well as the perpetuation of jobs that the staff enjoyed and, in some cases, profited from.

The government's endorsement of a nationalist discourse based on cultural identity put the station in a bind. Radio Taino's director commissioned annual workshops, reports, and a survey to demonstrate the station's commitment to the promotion of Cuban culture. An in-house report in 1996 established guidelines to align Taino's commercial format with the discourse of cultural nationalism. The report's recommendations included interspersing ads with spots about traditions and folklore, covering topics of popular culture within regular programs, playing more Cuban music, and having announcers reflect "the Cuban character" in their communication style (Jara and Diaz 1996). As a result, a collaboration was established in 1998 with the Fernando Ortiz Foundation to coproduce a weekly show called *Arte y Folklor* exploring Cuba's cultural roots. In addition, program directors were instructed to increase the percentage of Cuban music and limit their coverage of issues related to North American pop culture. In addition, commercial campaigns—not only at Taino—began emphasizing Cubanidad (a very visible campaign was that of Popular Cigarettes, whose slogan was, "I am Cuban, I am *Popular*"). Also in 1998, a survey sought to elucidate popular opinions on the station's Cubanness.[19] In relation to other stations, Taino was rated lowest as a source of Cubanness, but highest as a source of entertainment. Most respondents expressed a wish for even more foreign music and entertainment news and more shows like *From Five to Seven* (which commanded the highest ratings, as opposed to *Arte y Folklor*, which had no known listeners). These results were ignored in order to highlight, instead, the total number of people who did think the station sounded Cuban. The survey was not intended to change programming, but rather to serve as a proactive measure that could allow the station to demonstrate its Cubanness.

As the station had learned a few years earlier, the goals of commanding large audiences while stressing cultural roots were irreconcilable. Shows on folklore and traditions appealed neither to audiences nor to advertisers—that had been the reason for their elimination in the first place. Cubans with buying power and a lifestyle in which leisure was a prominent marker of social identity were not as concerned with their cultural roots—nor with their political allegiances, for that matter—as they were with accessing a transnational world of mass culture, products, services, and styles. Pablo Milanes's song *Amo esta isla* from 1981 had lost its currency.

Young people's quest was not to discover "who we are," but "who we want to be like." A hit from 1998, repeatedly played on *From Five to Seven*, was La Charanga Habanera's *El Charanguero Mayor*, a fast timba/reggae version of *No Woman No Cry* with English and Spanish lyrics. The song's catchy chorus, "En el aire, yo quiero ser Bob Marley" (On the air, I want to be Bob Marley), invoked a desire to belong to a transnational community larger than Cuba, and it obviously reflected the increasing popularity of reggae music and rasta aesthetics among Havana and Santiago's black youth. Similarly, at the Havana Rap Festival in 1998, an award went to Primera Base's song *Igual que Tú* (Just like you), a homage to Malcolm x:

Malcolm Equis,	Malcolm x
Me honraría ser un Negro igual que tú,	I'd be honored to be a black man like you
Igual que tú nigger: a nigger like you.	Just like you, nigger: Un negro como tú.

The same Cuban youth that as schoolchildren pledged to emulate el Ché (Ernesto "Ché" Guevara) now sung to the symbols of a transnational black consciousness. As opposed to Radio Rebelde's version of national identity, these youth identities were neither immutable nor incompatible with other cultural tastes and practices. In broadcasting these music styles, Radio Taino was tapping into more fluid youth identities that expressed a desire of being as well as a philosophical outlook on life that, by and large, was unconcerned with national political struggles.

Timba music, which constituted the bulk of Taino's most popular shows, was a different case. Unlike rap, timba received institutional support because of its international demand. Precisely because of its international popularity, the music was always presented by the Cuban media and the Ministry of Culture as quintessentially Cuban—as the latest development in Cuban music history (for example, in *Yo Soy del Son y de la Salsa*), even though timba bands mostly attracted Afro-Cuban youth to their concerts. Not only was timba heavily influenced by Afro-Cuban rumba and African American jazz and hip hop, but it featured lyrics on Afro-Cuban religion and the urban experience of love, sex, and survival during the Special Period, in which the men were often referred to as *niches* (blacks) and the women as *mami* or *negra*. In these lyrics timba musicians proudly identified themselves as black. For instance, Los Van Van's opening song in live performances, *Llegó Van Van*, includes the chorus, "Van Van son negros Lucumí, cuidao, ten cuidao" (Van Van are *Lucumi* blacks, watch out, you watch out) as well as the following segment: "Y no te metas con mi negrito, porque esos negros están preparaos y volaos. Y como si fuera poco, ahora yo en la orquesta tengo dos babalaos" (And don't mess with my little black guy, because these blacks are ready and crazy. And if this is not enough, now in the orchestra I have two *babalawos* [priests of santería]). Similarly, one of La Charanga Habanera's most popular songs refers to the band members' popularity among women: "Estos niches estan acabando con las mujeres de La Habana" (These blacks are getting all the women in Havana).

These were very different expressions of Afro-Cuban identity from the one that was pegged to national heritage early in the twentieth century to allow Cubans to differentiate themselves from Spaniards and other Latin Americans. These were also very different from the folklorized version of music and religion presented by cultural institutions during the revolutionary period, after Afro-Cuban cultural expressions such as the rumba were moved from the streets and patios into classrooms, performance halls, heritage festivals, and dance folkloric ensembles (Daniel 1995; Kutzinski 1993; Moore 1997). The mere possibility of racial identities has been dismissed by Cuban officials as a U.S. import, and an open debate on race has been avoided in the name of national unity, despite Afro-Cuban intellectuals' demands for higher visibility (Kinght 2000).[20]

Young people see no contradiction between their Cubanness and their participation in youth movements expressed through music (Pacini and Garofalo 1999). Timba, rap, reggae, and rock exemplify the hybridity of contemporary youth cultures, challenging the stress on purity and authenticity in cultural identity discourse. They evidence the existence of communities across borders that are based not on ideology, but on taste, artistic expression, generation, race, and class. Rock, for instance, banned during the first two and a half decades of the Revolution as a product of U.S. imperialism, was accepted as Cuban only in 1999, when Abel Prieto, a self-proclaimed Bob Dylan fan, conceded that it could be a Cuban music form too and discussed the possibility of giving professional status to rock musicians, which would allow them to get paid and tour abroad (Cantor 1999). This occurred only when the argument was presented to him in terms of cultural identity, that is, when the case was made that Cuban rock was not a North American replica. Rather, it was *rock en español*, a true Cuban musical expression that linked Cuban youth to their Latin American (rather than North American) counterparts.

As the state's "hegemony of representation"—to borrow Alexei Yurchak's (1997) term—is fading out, propaganda campaigns, mass organizations, school education, and state rituals such as the May First Parade continue to seek citizens' allegiance to the Revolution. At the same time, a discourse on cultural identity also seeks to foster national community by stressing cultural roots and psychosocial traits and rejecting globalization and its culture of consumerism as alien to the Cuban spirit (Hart 1998). Even though such nationalism allows for the inclusion of expatriates in the national imaginary, it does not provide a voice to alternative identities, particularly—on the Cuban case—those claimed by Afro-Cubans and the young, among others. And that is because extending the geography of the local maintains a dual view of the cultural universe in which the global may be plural, but the local is one.

With the advent of consumer culture and global trends one thing is clear: in Cuba, state legitimacy will be upheld not by propaganda alone or by the memory of past achievements, but by its ability to insert the island into global networks of production, circulation, and consumption, while providing for its citizens within the national borders.

Notes

1. MAN: En nuestra cultura única . . .

WOMAN: En el legado de los proceres . . .

MAN: A la instrucción a la que todos tenemos derecho . . .

WOMAN: Ese es nuestro sello, lo que nos hace diferentes.

MAN: Identidad Nacional: Cinco siglos de formación. Enriqueci-
miento. Permanencia. (my translation)

2. This section is based on analysis of historical recordings and other archival materials and on interviews with Ilse and Frank Bulit (Bohemia), Leo Bueno (Soc.Culture.Cuba), Frank Donikian (Radio Rebelde), February 1999, Orlando Castellanos (Radio Habana Cuba), Mercedes Hernandez (Radio Taino), Elisabel Diaz (Radio Taino), Angela Oramas (ICRT), Ismael Rensoli (Radio Rebelde), Pedro Perez (Radio Taino), Jose Luis Bergantiño (formerly Radio Taino), Yvonne Leanto (Radio Taino), Reinaldo Muñoz (formerly Radio Taino).

3. Elisabel Diaz, Radio Taino's program consultant, personal interview (September 6, 1996).

4. Elisabel Diaz.

5. Cuban Culture Day has been celebrated on October 20 every year since 1980. It was established by Decree Law 74 on August 22, 1980, to commemorate the day (October 20, 1868) when the troops of Carlos Manuel de Céspedes liberated the town of Bayamo during the War of Independence. As they occupied the city, they sang a local song, "La Bayamesa," which subsequently became the Cuban national anthem.

6. The anthropological writings of Fernando Ortiz, for instance, unpublished since the 1940s, were reissued beginning in 1991 by the state social science publisher (Editora de Ciencias Sociales). Jorge Dominguez pointed out that his extensive political commentaries were, in contrast, omitted, as they expressed his liberal and democratic thinking (Jorge Dominguez, personal communication, 2000). In 1994, a special issue of the Union of Writers and Artists' magazine, *Gaceta de Cuba*, was dedicated to the culturalist works of Jorge Mañach, a conservative thinker who in 1928 outlined the psychosocial traits that were part of the Cuban character (no. 4 / 1994).

7. Fernando Ortiz, considered the father of Cuban cultural nationalism, questioned the validity of racial constructs and proposed cultural heritage as the cornerstone of a cultural identity common to all Cubans: "To understand the Cuban soul, we should understand cultures rather than races," he announced (Ortiz 1939 [1996]:20). For Ortiz (1940 [1996]), Cuba was an "ajiaco," a stew of ethnicities and cultures to which new ingredients were constantly being added; these new ingredients transformed the stew's taste and texture as they transformed themselves in a process called transculturation. Cuban culture, according to this view, was the sum of all immigrants' cultural baggage and the strategies they develop to master the new natural environment. Cultural differences were attributed to regional variations as much as to different national origins. A consciousness of insularity, the experience of migration and adaptation, and the constant contact with foreign elements resulted in a spiritual bond as well as the development of both a national culture and a national character, whose ultimate expression was the drive for self-government (Ortiz 1939 [1996]; Suarez 1996).

8. The same thing happened in China when Deng Xiaoping opened the country to global capitalism, attracting the Chinese expatriate community to new business opportunities in the homeland. A new nationalist discourse developed, as a result, among mainland intellectuals, highlighting common values such as Confucianism rather than political community (Ong 1997; Zhang 1998).

9. It was sponsored by the University of Havana's Center for the Study of Political Alternatives (a think tank dedicated to studying "the Cuban community abroad") and the Union of Writers and Artists (UNEAC).

10. Reinaldo Muñoz, director of programming at Radio Taino, August 8, 1996.

11. *Un carro, una casa y una buena mujer* (CD Pronósticos, 1997).

12. Author's translation. CD De Buena Fe, Caribe 1996.

13. His brief appearance took place at the popular dance hall La Tropical, during the thirteenth anniversary concert of NG La Banda, on April 7, 2001.

14. One of these workshops was attended by Radio Rebelde's propaganda producer, Frank Donikian, who designed the spots initially as a class exercise.

15. I am a cofounder of that newsgroup and a witness to the test's development and dissemination.

16. Teatro Mella. Compañía Danza Abierta. "El Arbol y el Camino" (Dir: Marianela Boan), November 29, 1998.

17. Timba was a form of Cuban salsa that was characterized by its intense rhythmic base drawn from Afro-Cuban rumba and influenced by jazz and hip hop. Timba musicians such as the aforementioned Manolín, El Médico de la Salsa, expressed in their lyrics the everyday hardships of young urban people during the Special Period.

18. Eventually, they all encountered problems at Taino as well and ended up either temporarily sanctioned, again unemployed, or in the United States.

19. Two sociologists affiliated with the Center for Social Research of the ICRT interviewed six hundred people in Havana and Santiago during May 1998. The survey asked each respondent to give five adjectives to describe "how we Cubans are." With this in mind, it asked to rank radio stations according to their degree of Cubanness. If the respondent listened to Radio Taino, specific questions followed on the station's treatment of Cuban culture, national identity, information, and entertainment.

20. At the 1999 UNEAC's Caracol meetings, the issue of racial discrimination was hotly debated.

Olodum's Transcultural Spaces: Community and Difference in Afro-Brazilian Contemporary Performance

DENISE CORTE

Until recently, Brazil was seen as a country with a comparatively benign pattern of race relations.[1] In postcolonial Brazil, there has never been an institutional or legal distinction among the races. Quite the contrary: both the state and popular wisdom have denied the legitimacy of color prejudice. The unique capacity of Brazilian society to combine political repression and co-optation with a culturally sophisticated denial of racial conflict has always made the development of black oppositional currents very difficult. Brazilian elites, both of the Right and the Left, continue to dismiss the significance of race in political and cultural life. The long-standing tendency to subordinate racial dynamics to those of class remains in play across the entire political spectrum. Because Brazilian segregation was never absolute, its existence could always be denied, and several attempts to sustain a national black movement have proven unsuccessful.

The late 1970s, however, witnessed a proliferation of popular movements, as the political project of the Brazilian military regime began to stagnate. Brazil's *abertura* (the "opening" to democracy) saw radical democratic themes take on greater prominence, as social movements articulated demands around such issues as amnesty for political exiles, direct elections, and state redemocratization. Afro-Brazilians were intimately involved in these events, and although they did not organize *qua* blacks, the quest for citizenship emphasized by these movements placed a new focus on racial themes.[2] In this context, various black organizations emerged, deeply influenced by anticolonial mobilizations in Africa, particularly in Lusophone African countries. Probably the most significant were the *Movimento Negro Unificado* (Unified Black Movement) and the *Grupos Afro* (Afro Groups).[3]

The first Afro Group was created in Salvador, Bahia, in 1974. The *Ilê Aiyê* (literally, house of life in Yoruba) was soon to be followed by a multitude of similar associations which for the past twenty years have not only guaranteed the participation of blacks in carnival but have become crucial to the revalorization of black culture in general and of African-derived practices in particular. Presently, these groups have become central in black organizational efforts, serving as informal nationalist institutions, performing educational and consciousness-raising activities, and structuring community associations. One of the most important organizations to grow out of this movement and to transcend its local character was the *Grupo Afro Olodum* (Olodum Afro Group).

Founded in 1979, the Olodum was created as a recreational option for the inhabitants of Pelourinho during the carnival period and to give the community the right to participate in the festivities in an organized form, through the creation of a *bloco de carnaval*.[4] In the late 1980s, as part of its decision to expand its activities beyond carnival, the Olodum became the *Grupo Cultural Olodum* (Olodum Cultural Group) and launched a new cultural project for the association.[5] The project included the creation of theater and dance companies, workshops on photography and the visual arts, and an after-hours school aimed at complementing traditional education with the teaching of fundamental concepts such as citizenship and Afrobrazilian history.[6]

Impelled by the rise of the Ilê Aiyê and the transformation of the Olodum into a cultural holding, a number of grassroots and popular theater groups that sought to redress questions of Afro-Brazilian representation were launched in Salvador.[7] Despite the initial momentum, however, a variety of factors rendered most of these theaters notably short-lived, and most of the initial groups and more recent ensembles were unable to sustain production by the late 1990s.[8] Given this bleak trajectory, the *Bando de Teatro Olodum* (BTO, Olodum Theater Group) stands out as a uniquely successful and enduring Afro-Brazilian theater company.[9] The broader reception of the BTO has confirmed its status as the most powerful and influential voice of the contemporary Afro-Brazilian stage. Since its inception in 1990, the BTO has been extremely prolific, producing not only a trilogy of plays created entirely by the group's performers but also adaptations and "transgressions" of such major dramatic works as Bertold Brecht's *Threepenny Opera*, Georg Büchner's *Woyzeck*, and Heiner Müller's *Medeamaterial*. Recently, the company was invited to perform at the Black Theatre Cooperative and the LIFT festival in London.

This essay examines the BTO's trilogy as part of a larger project of analyzing the group's trajectory up to the present and conceptualizes the impact of the BTO and theatrical production more generally on the current transformation of racial dynamics in Brazil.[10] It will do so, in part, by looking at the interplay between a transcultural imaginary and the ways in which the BTO challenges the fixity of cultural systems—those of identity formation and social signification—through its conscious appropriation of spatial metaphors as trope for cultural interaction and negotiation.[11]

The *Trilogia do Pelô* includes *Essa é a nossa praia*, *Ó paí, ó*, and *Bai, bai Pelô*. All three plays are collective creations based on the experiences of the actors themselves, and all center on the Pelourinho (Pelô) community located at the Historical Center of Salvador. Since 1992, its residents have been gradually displaced by the state government to allot space for the restoration of the area's colonial buildings and its transformation into a tourist district. On one level, the *Trilogia* conveys the community's struggle against displacement and its frustrated efforts to be integrated into the new project for the region. On another level, it transcends local boundaries, offering different methods of participation to its audiences.

The plays constitute three separate, independent representations of reality. Taken together, however, they form a continuous whole. The interplay between fragmentation and continuity, combined with the *Trilogia*'s increasing emphasis on transcultural encounters, diffuses the notion of identity as a fixed tradition and allows for a remapping of the terrain of social interaction. At the same time, the plays move from a notion of community based on geographic occupation (*Essa é a nossa praia*, *Ó paí, ó*) toward a political redefinition of community not limited by spatial boundaries (*Bai, bai Pelô*). At the end, "community" figures as a reaction or even a resistance to the vicissitudes of (dis)placement.

This redefinition is concomitant with the BTO's objectives and self-representation as a popular theater group.[12] In other words, the transformation of community and culture in the *Trilogia* and its positing of the boundaries and limitations of the concept of identity (especially black identity) parallel the group's redefined educational objective as being above art. If its early connection with Pelourinho was primarily ideological—that is, situating the Historical Center and the emerging Afro-Bahian cultural signifiers in the context of the movement initiated by Afro Groups—the BTO gradually abandoned instrumental stances and embraced an intermediate position, whereby its work encompassed both artistic and social priorities.[13] This reconfiguration was extremely important because it allowed the group to enter regional and national media outlets commercially and to transform the social stratification underlying the process of theater production in Salvador.

At the same time, the *process* of the *Trilogia* constitutes a kind of "liminal" or "liminoid" space betwixt and between one context of meaning and action and another; concerning both the BTO's formation and development and the work's reconfiguration of identity and reenactment of community. Taken diachronically, the play's structure is similar to the phases of a social drama, each representing, in part, the phases described in Victor Turner's model— that is, breach, crisis, redress, and *either* reintegration *or* recognition of schism (Turner's emphasis).[14]

Turner's ethnography signifies in part the notion of the mimetic as a theoretical tool to understand the BTO's processes of creation and performance. As Michael Taussig argues, the practice of imitation or mimesis is as important as the experience of or insistence upon difference in cross-cultural encounters. As I hope to demonstrate later in this essay, the BTO's productions' emphasis on mirroring (sameness/imitation/borrowing) has profound contextual implications for its transcultural project.[15] Moreover, the ethnographic conceptualization of liminal spaces seems especially appropriate to the *Trilogia*, because of its stronger connections to popular theater and the interactions between actors/characters and spectators *in* performance. Turner does not conflate ritual with theater; nonetheless, he notes the theatrical properties of ritual, especially as it negotiates conflict through the enactment of social drama. In such reenactment, the tension between actual transformed states of consciousness and mimetic performance is constant. Examining the *Trilogia* in these terms expands the production's liminality, establishing it as a potential space within Brazilian society where creativity is unleashed, norms are questioned, and different futures are imagined.[16]

The first play, *Essa é a nossa praia*, introduces the characters who are part of the everyday life of Pelourinho and who "are still very present in the audiences' imagination as a fundamental symbolic representation of Afrobahian culture." The characters take the stage as the residents take to the streets of the Historical Center: with "their singular language, their expressive gestures, and their sensuous dance and rhythms."[17] They are rogues, corrupt policemen, prostitutes, devout women, mothers, domestic servants, mulattas, priests, transvestites, independent artists and artisans, women from

Bahia, black movement militants, Candomblé disciples, Pentecostals. All characters participate in actions and relate among themselves according to the Pelô lifestyle. Their problems, conflicts, intrigues, and complicities always refer to this specific place: to move within Pelourinho's several spaces (undulating streets, swarming bars, gold-filled churches, encircled squares) signifies a constitutive factor of identity in the interweaving of the characters' experiences. Its title, *Essa é a nossa praia* ("That's our thing"), conveys the Pelourinho residents' claim to their community as well as their resistance to the state government's maneuvering to displace them. Ironically (Pelourinho is not located on the beach), the title also conveys a sense of exclusion (the city's best residential neighborhoods *are* on the coast and predominantly white) while signifying cultural affirmation of other forms of social interaction, or "beach fun." Thus, on the one hand, the play and its performance reiterate the cultural and socioeconomic significance of Pelourinho to its residents, who, in turn, affirm their right to that space by marking their difference from other segments of Bahian society. On the other hand, the breach caused by the state's plans for the area translates into a crisis that displays a set of intraracial divisions within Pelourinho's supposedly unified Afrobrazilian cultural formation. Although *Essa é a nossa praia* ends with the characters declaring themselves a collectivity established on the basis of geographic and cultural location, the numerous confrontations among the residents in the play—deriving from the conflict between ideology and identification—already signal the final impossibility (in *Bai, bai Pelô*) of building community around such static notions of identity politics.

Ó paí, ó, which opened in 1992 (a year after *Essa é a nossa praia*), was considered one of the season's best plays in Salvador and earned the BTO a formal invitation to present its new play at the closing ceremony of the prestigious Shell Theater Award Ceremony in Rio de Janeiro.[18] The play's title conveys a typical Bahian expression used to call attention to something. *Ó paí, ó* ("Look at that, look") calls attention to the urgent social reality of the characters introduced in the previous play through the lenses of two important current events in Pelourinho: the dramatic acceleration of the displacement of its native population and the extermination of the community's children.[19] This time, the action does not unfold entirely on the streets; it also takes place in one of the community's *cortiços*, whose occupants are facing imminent eviction.[20] In contrast to *Essa é a nossa praia*, *Ó paí, ó* ends with the characters coming together around the discovery of the missing children's tragic fate. In part, the introduction of a climactic closure in an otherwise episodic structure (the scenes in all three plays follow what the BTO calls "*estrutura de bloco*") appeals to some sort of *redressive action*.[21] Such action, however, necessarily involves a problematic, "possibility of agency, social transformation, representability, and recognizability," which, as Judith Butler points out, are some of the burdens of the notion of identity and its correlation to cultural specificity.[22] Taken in its entirety, the production is definitively ambivalent. The BTO came to understand these burdens through the radical transfiguration of Pelourinho and the intensive research the group undertook to create the *Trilogia*'s last play.

The paucity of public debate and information about the restoration of the Historical Center and its effects on the area's former residents is today a topic for research by many academic institutions, scholars, and civil organizations in Salvador. "Meanwhile, the BTO decided to stage its own version of the facts."[23] *Bai, bai Pelô* (Bye, Bye Pelô) opened in 1994 and marked the conclusion of the architectural renewal.[24] The performance emerged from research and close contact with residents (the ones who remained and the ones who left), community leaders, and cultural organizations as well as through debates with various segments of organized civil society, the university, and businesses.[25] Adding some new personalities to the previous set of characters, the BTO attempts in part to portray the broadest range of changes that have occurred in the area. Hence, the old *cortiço*'s landlady loses not only her house but also her power over the tenants; the bar's owner adapts to new times and modernizes her business; the *baiana* now caters to a more sophisticated clientele who eat her treats in portions; the vagrant loses his freedom to wander the Pelourinho streets because of the massive police presence in the region. All suffer profound transformations in their lives. In the end, it is a new, sanitized Pelourinho that emerges in *Bai, bai Pelô*.

As the play demonstrates, however, not everybody has to leave; those who are able to adapt to the new times receive financial incentives from the local government to relocate back to the area. These are, of course, the residents who in one way or another can turn their informal means of production (and survival) into commodities (ethnic food, crafts, art, etc.) amenable to the tourism industry's project for Pelourinho.[26] Not surprisingly, this differential treatment by the state government further divides the community and seals the fate of a concerted resistance based on racial and/or cultural loyalties. In *Bai, bai Pelô*, black movement militants—who had initially (*Essa é a nossa praia*) mobilized the residents around an oppositional movement that achieved a certain degree of dominance in the area (*Ó paí, ô*)—turn completely ineffective by the end of the play. The political response to this latent power of the community's "mobilization in place" was not only renewed restoration and eviction but, more important, the priority assigned to the building of commercial space. In short, the state's quick response was "to locate power in the spaces which the bourgeoisie controls." As David Harvey argues, this strategy, with the concomitant "disempowering [of] those spaces which oppositional movements have the greatest potentiality to command," constitutes "the principal task of the capitalist state."[27] In view of the state's maneuver to empower local businesses to move into the Historical Center, *Bai, bai Pelô* proposes—and the BTO effectively puts into practice—a differentiated sense of community. This new mode of imagining community is intimately connected to the recasting of culture and tradition.

Despite the community's effective displacement at the end of the play, *Bai, bai Pelô* still corresponds to the third structural phase of the processional form as Turner defines it: "The social drama concludes, if ever it may be said to have had a 'last act,' either in the reconciliation of the contending parties or their agreement to differ."[28] Considered as part of the *Trilogia*'s long process of creation, dialogue, and reflection, *Bai, bai Pelô* demonstrates the community's failure to organize black solidarity and, consequently, the impossibility of taking racial or cultural identity as a valid concept. It gestures instead toward building coalitions around an understanding of identity as dynamic—"simultaneously formed and formative."[29] At the end, it poses questions instead of offering converging answers to its audiences. As the play's open-ended last *bloco* suggests, consensus can only be provisional.

Since its inception, the BTO has grappled with the notion of particularism. Although the group's members have always identified themselves as blacks, the *Trilogia* never embraces a clear-cut concept of black culture as resistant against oppression or the category of black as a *place* toward which all the varieties of racial classification should converge.[30] Against racially exclusive or culturally inclusive (multicultural) strategies, the plays oppose a multitude of situations in which issues of color as well as phenotype shape intraracial relationships among characters.[31] Already in *Essa é a nossa praia* discrimination along the color line is pervasive, and the interplay of race, marginalization, and poverty further complicates possibilities of effective friendship. Moreover, as Gomes da Cunha points out, the valorization of particular cultural aspects deemed black by Afro-Brazilian activists and intellectuals in the 1980s constituted a strategy of politicization in which the idea of resistance entailed a distancing from and negation of the nationalistic dogma reflected by the myth of racial democracy. This redefinition shifted the perspective away from a construct that awarded miscegenation the highest praise and therefore recharted the map of identity in black and white terms. In the *Trilogia*, however, the fragmentation suggested by intraracial confrontations and the persistence of the ideology of whitening denounce the limitations and boundaries of this new cartography.[32] More important, the BTO exposes the complex implications of efforts to characterize the myth of racial democracy as the country's official ideology. The plays not only question the hierarchical ways in which myth and reality are used in the discourses of activists and intellectuals, but also distinguish racial democracy as an ideal from attempts to prove its nonexistence at the concrete level of race relations in Brazil. In this sense, it seems contradictory that the BTO seeks recourse to exotic stereotyping as a means of exposing the ways in which the existing racism has similarly pernicious effects on blacks, *mestiças*, and *mulatas*.

Interestingly, the BTO's appropriation of racial stereotypes became a source of great discomfort to middle-class audiences and reviewers as well as a major obstacle to their appraisals of the plays. Some reviewers, apparently unable to get beyond the superficial shallowness of stereotypical representation, dismissed its pervasiveness in the *Trilogia* on the basis of the actors' "amateur condition." Others even referred to the characters as "reminiscent of *Comedia del' Arte* types," thus avoiding the need to confront the implications of their embodiment by Afro-Brazilian actors.[33] Given the visceral reactions of white spectators, the reviewers' insistence on locating the *Trilogia*'s performance choices solely within a theatrical tradition effaced the political import of the BTO's appropriation of stereotypes. Moreover, even when stirred by the works' unexpected national projection, reviewers still ignored the very central question of why, despite their negative reviews, the productions reached such a broad public and became so successful among black audiences.

These reactions, in conjunction with other instances of media (mis)representation of Afro-Brazilians (and within the political context of the state's attempt to erase discourses about race), indicate the intricate centrality of race relations in Brazilian society. In part, the crucial issue is that the BTO's performers embody sensibilities and attitudes so completely in their performances that they simultaneously become these sensibilities and attitudes and offer a transgressive commentary on them. Their embodiment of marginalization in the *Trilogia*—through the use of offensive language and the constant degrading of morals, social class, intelligence, lack of education, and racialized appearance—becomes so intense that it brings up disturbing questions. Such extreme self-dramatization reflects a disconcerting autonomy that estranges white audiences and reviewers alike. More important, in a radical autoethnographic move, the BTO's actors/characters superimpose this alienation onto another aspect of marginalization: they turn themselves into exotic objects of pleasure and fascination in the most extreme formulation of Orientalism. By marking their otherness, they play into the stereotypes set forth by dominant society in a way that explodes mass-media clichés and defuses normalizations of the cultural around them.

At the same time, insisting on the humor of its appropriation of stereotypes, the *Trilogia* presents a series of characters, each one carrying cultural matters to their illogical extreme in order to expose the limits of the stereotyping process. For example, in *Essa é a nossa praia* one of the mothers prohibits her sons from participating in the Olodum's Youth Band.[34] Because the band welcomes street kids, Dona Joana viscerally resists the idea and creates absurd situations to sabotage the whole project.[35] In the first two plays, the character of Lucia (a *mulata* whose dream is to trap a *gringo* into marriage in order to get out of the country) becomes involved in hilarious contentions over the correct classification of her skin color—"*quase branca*" (almost white), as she loudly insists. Throughout the *Trilogia*, the actors/characters' extravagant self-definitions defy normalizations of race, class, gender, and nationality by pointing to their constructedness. The juxtaposition of race and gender generates stereotypical representations of black women as sexual objects (*mulatas*, prostitutes) or mothers (single, abandoned, devout, superstitious). Notwithstanding their social predicament, however, these women prove to be independent and capable of challenging their male counterparts. In all three plays, the fallacy of the stereotype of the Brazilian system as indiscriminate with regard to race is debunked when the very act of marginalization implies that Afrobrazilians are nonproductive or illicitly productive. Most of the *Trilogia*'s characters fall into one of these two categories according to the authorities responsible for enforcing the evictions from Pelourinho.

Finally, the phenomenon of blacks enacting racial stereotypes has too often been interpreted as a form of misguided internalization of cultural oppression. Although the excess that marks the site of the Other seeks to elude this binary logic, it can be argued that the desire of minorities to function effectively within the institutional limits dominant society dictates constantly harnesses transgressive representations of this excess. Hence, not only does individual assertion depend on a negation of collective action, but also the very *survival* of minority groups rests on a violent othering of themselves. Such assertions become even more problematic within an ideological rhetoric that conceives discourse about race to be a threat to the nationalist agenda. The *Trilogia*, however, carries the destructive potential of stereotyping to its tragic consequences and exposes the inherent pitfalls of this type of representation as resistance. In *Ó paí, ó*, for example, the children of Dona Joana are the ones murdered by the corrupt police. In the same play, the beautiful, pretentious Pissilene realizes Lucia's dream, only to discover that once abroad her *gringo* husband quickly abandons her; in order to survive and eventually return to Pelourinho, she has to prostitute herself. Confronted with these violent occurrences, the actors/characters gradually begin to scrutinize the gaps, "the telling spaces" that emerge in the contradictions between "the rhetoric of nation and the grammar of the nation."[36]

At the same time, and despite the stranglehold of the whitening ideology over both Brazilian and Afro-Brazilian culture, the concept of self-imposed alterity accounts only partially for the complexity of responses to the BTO actors' articulated ambivalence about the desire felt for the body-as-stereotype. Stressing the idea that rather than passing as white, one should become an "alternative fantasy," the *Trilogia* offers a different vision of stereotyping; one that exposes what is inherently violent in its *performance*. In *Bai, bai Pelô*, for example, rather than arguing that it is possible to escape racial identity, the characters relapse into their former selves. By becoming whites' fantasies, rather than white, they expose the paradoxes of this fantasy life with all its own failures and inconsistencies. Thus, the *mulatas* have no desire to leave the community anymore. The Historical Center has become "international" and "crowded with *gringos*" strolling through its streets accompanied by black women. Pelourinho has turned into a "cultural ghetto, totally stylized," Lucia rejoices.[37]

As the plot of *Bai, bai Pelô* unfolds, however, the renovation excludes more and more residents who are not only forced toward the city's outskirts but who are arrested for mingling with tourists by the police occupying every street corner. On the one hand, the BTO's performances set out to destabilize normative notions of cultural identity by exaggerating markings of difference so as to expose the workings of nostalgia and desire to consume and/or contain otherness. On the other hand, the saturation of media stereotypes on stage produces a dangerous double movement in which the truth that could form the core of the nonpejorative typing becomes a way of creating an enabling cultural space that serves to strengthen the stereotype based on perceived behavior rather than assumption. Clearly, what is at stake is by no means a simple condemnation of reductive stereotypes; rather, stereotypical constructions are consciously deployed in the *Trilogia* as tools to activate a process of reflection on the part of its audiences. Nevertheless, the question of whether the performances ultimately reinforce rather than subvert dominant practices must be posed. As deterritorialized artists seeking to break down the dominant social structures that support the myth of Brazil as a racial paradise, the BTO's actors are forced to engage the naturalization and presumed centrality of this myth. Examined diachronically, however, the process of the *Trilogia* (which entails the trajectory of the BTO as well) moves beyond an argument over the success or failure of stereotypical representation and moves toward an explicit negotiation between essentialist and constructivist notions of racial identity. Although the BTO's actors identify themselves as blacks, the community reflected in the mirror their productions hold up—populated with marginalized Afro-Brazilians—is most recognizably the nightmare vision of the dominant culture. Blacks, *mestiças*, and *mulatas* have long been assigned these roles in Brazil, as blank surfaces on which white Brazilians contemplate their own images by reflecting on what they are not. The BTO acknowledges this historical legacy, placing these dynamics of power at the center of the groups' works, yet the whole project is motivated by the performers' attempt to take control of this mirroring in order to reconfigure it for their own ends.

Judging by the class and racial differences separating those critics who responded positively to the *Trilogia* and those who responded negatively, it can be argued that if the BTO's performances did not transform the reality of the Pelourinho community, they at least contributed to making its dehumanizing process more visible.[38] Many reviewers expressed great discomfort over the actors' identities and, unsurprisingly, understood the proximity between the social and artistic limits and contradictions—given the "productions' exploitation of popular segments and stereotyping."[39] Critics' emphasis on the plays' blurring of distinctions and on middle-class spectators' protests over their offensive content confirmed that white audiences were literally unprepared to confront the harsh realities of Pelourinho represented on stage; and even less prepared to consider the BTO's appropriation of stereotypes. Oddly, stereotypical Afro-Brazilian characters populate mainstream theater, film, and the country's popular mainstay (and major cultural export), the soap opera. Because most Brazilians seem so oblivious to the pervasiveness of black stereotypes in mainstream forms, the fact that many white spectators were so unsettled by the BTO's incorporation of these same conventions in the context of the *Trilogia* speaks to the marginalization of Afro-Brazilian cultural spaces as instances of local eccentricities.

In a complementary vein, criticism of the BTO's aesthetic choices did not confine itself to the plays' incorporation of stereotypes. Equally crucial was the impact of the productions' transculturation of local and foreign genres. The critics' call on the BTO to reproduce cultural traditions with accuracy also tells a great deal about the persistent sterilization of Afrobrazilian culture and its relegation to the status of folklore by Brazilian elites. If the representation of black characters through a fixed and uniform set of cultural and racial features means dangerous stereotyping, so does the claim to authenticity. As Julie Stone Peters puts it, "Those who insist on the radical nature of difference feel uncomfortable with the mixing of cultures and forms." Moreover, "such an insistence on authenticity (an insistence on orthodoxy) shows little recognition of the conditions of theater or, for that matter, of cultural pluralism (indeed culture's only condition) as a whole."[40] Most metropolitan critics, however, centered their criticisms on the productions' failure to preserve cultural specificity. According to one reviewer, the performances suffered because they were "more concerned with the picturesque than with the most authentic or traditional traits of Afro–Bahian culture."[41] Ironically, although this critic did not define "authentic . . . Afro-

Bahian," one of the play's features she excluded from this line of criticism—Afro-Bahian music—is the transcultured mix of such diverse influences as Caribbean, African, and Brazilian rhythms.

These views not only suggest a misperception of culture as fixed but also claim that cultural manifestations emanate from a national patrimony secured by the transcendental authority of the state. In addition, such claims also expose the persistence (within the current discourse on globalization) of an apparently colonized mentality among the country's elites. In Brazil, as in many countries which are considered or consider themselves peripheral for historical and economic-scientific reasons, there has always existed a problematic relationship with the notion of borrowing. Since the avant-garde movement of the 1920s and 1930s (*modernismo brasileiro*), Brazilian intellectuals have, in one way or another, confronted the question of aesthetic imitation in literature, theater, and the arts in general.[42] In an insightful analysis of the problem, Roberto Schwarz takes up the phenomenon of the seemingly "imitative nature" of Brazilian culture, arguing that "the very *perception* of foreign imitation as a *problem* is ideological, reflecting the Brazilian elite's historical alienation from the culture of the masses it exploits." Therefore, the problem of imitation, he points out, is a false one because it "concentrates its fire on the relationship between elite and model whereas the real crux is the exclusion of the poor from the universe of contemporary culture."[43]

As previously mentioned, the BTO never embraced the concept of Afro-Brazilian culture. On the contrary, since its first production, the group has drawn upon such heterogeneous influences as African-derived rituals, popular music, mass culture, the avant-garde, Western dramatic forms, and carnival to structure its performances. Throughout the *Trilogia*'s creative process the BTO's conscious transculturation of these forms stood in opposition to the limits encased in tradition. More important, the notion of transculturation became crucial to the plays' rendition of the characters' identities as spatially situated and formed in relation to one another.

Three levels of the notion of transculturation, as conceptualized by Fernando Ortiz, are relevant here.[44] First, as Diana Taylor asserts, the concept of transculturation "points to long-term reciprocities, to the degree that the dominant groups that define, acquire, and impose culture are themselves transculturated sooner or later, whether they want it or not."[45] Second, contrary to notions of interculturalism and multiculturalism, the transfor-

mative, local process of transculturation necessarily involves (and emphasizes) the element of loss in *all* the cultures involved in the transcultural
encounter. Finally, Ortiz's concept is more than an analytic instrument aim-
ing to correct some inadequacies of contemporary North American accul-
turation research. On the one hand, like Gilberto Freyre's *lusotropicalismo*
and José Vasconcelos's *mestizaje*—and, indeed, José Martí's famous dictum
that to be Cuban is to be "more than white, more than black"—it is also a
proposal for a self-consciously modernist New World nationalism transcending the racial *and* cultural prescriptions imposed upon Latin American nations by European and North American intellectuals. On the other hand,
there is an important sense in which Ortiz supersedes earlier formulations.
For him, "hybridity" is neither a conservative, nor a radical utopia—a state of
being prefigured in a colonial past or expectable in a national future. As Ortiz
makes clear several times, *cubanidad* is not the endpoint, but the kernel of the
processes he subsumes under the label *transculturación*. In short, these processes cannot be equated with hybridity in the sense of a consummated
synthesis; instead, they stress the ways in which cultural formations are
always in flux, sharing in a condition of instability with *all* cultures, always on
their ways to novel (unstable) predications.

   This concept finds its most characteristic elaboration in two less well
known essays in which Ortiz conjugated the notion of transculturation
through a series of culinary metaphors. According to him, Cuba is an *ajiaco*,
the stew most typical of Cuba and most complex (*más complejo*).[46] There is
more to Ortiz's choice of the image of the metaphorical *ajiaco* over the
melting pot than its rhetorical function as a jibe at North American conceptual imperialism and its subtle play with the trope of local knowledge. It also
contains an analytic dimension whose implications have not been adequately
explored. By the 1940s, Ortiz had come to reject not only the essentialist
discourses that had earlier enabled him to perceive and differentiate the
constituent elements of both *lo cubano* and *lo afrocubano*. He had also broken
with a kind of rhetoric which essentialized hybridity by either projecting it
backward onto preadapted identity formations affecting colonizing men-
talities, or forward into the quasi-eschatological consummation of difference
in a yet-to-be achieved future of national synthetic conformity. Ortiz privileges not *fusión*, but the more *ajiaco*-like, processual *cocedura* as a representational device that enables one to imagine culture becoming something that

looks and tastes differently depending upon which level of the pot one takes her/his sample from and at what point in time. Ortiz's *ajiaco* is not just a more appropriate metaphor; it is an epistemological project, encompassing a distinct vision of *temporal and spatial variables* in the analysis of culture(s).[47]

Within the *Trilogia*'s matrix of intersecting cultures, transculturation between distinct formations as well as between members of the same community involves the meeting of manifold differences and identifications which are not only transformed through time (the moment one takes the sample) but, more significantly, through space (where the sampling takes place).[48] In other words, although time continues to be contemplated in the *Trilogia*, the plays' plots, based as they are on transcultural encounters, function as spatial practices foregrounding space and movement through space. Theatrical space often functions as trope for cultural location—for identities and knowledge as produced through location as well as history. Concomitantly, setting functions as symbolic geography may signal or mark the specific cultural locations of the community within the larger society.

Throughout the *Trilogia*, character transformation is produced by changing cultural interactions and locations. For example, the eviction of the Pelourinho residents in *Bai, bai Pelô* results in the shrinking of their psychological horizons structured around a succession of dislocations within transcultural encounters. Hence, performance movement is not so much developmental, subject to psychoanalytic probing, as it is locational. The plot moves from space to space, each location delineating an identity for the characters: the streets of the Historical Center as the sites of bitter racial and class collisions (*Essa é a nossa praia*); the crowded interiors of the decaying colonial houses and their precarious living conditions (*Ó paí, ó*); the bars and small establishments allowed to operate after the renovation as the new "native" digs; the stylized tourist shops to which the community is denied access; the constant state repression of emerging informal businesses; the heavily policed streets of the new, sanitized Pelourinho. All of these spaces are constructed simultaneously as tourist havens and as sites of extreme brutality against the wandering population (*Bai, bai Pelô*).

Despite the obvious power imbalances in these exchanges and the apparent unilateral character of loss in them, the playful and sarcastic tone of the BTO's actors and their conscious exploitation of transcultural devices in performance make white middle-class spectators grow nervous about their hybrid identities exposed on stage. White audiences also become uncomfortably aware of their own decentralization and cultural losses. As Taylor puts it, "Transculturation is not inherently or necessarily a minority or oppositional theory," but it does allow the " 'minor' culture (in the sense of the positionally marginalized) an impact on the dominant one, although the interactions are not strictly speaking 'dialogic' or 'dialectical.' Transculturation suggests a shifting or circulating pattern of cultural transference."[49]

In the BTO's performances, it is primarily the event of self-other encounters, spatially located and articulated, that provides the plays with the momentum that propels this circulating movement. At the same time, the *Trilogia* questions the notion of self/other confrontation as a meeting based solely on difference. Their conscious assertion of transculturation undermines ethnographic assumptions that pure and distinctly different cultures exist prior to transcultural interactions. The construction of ethnic, racial, gender, national, and other affinities is posited as an effect, rather than the cause, of cultural transactions that emerge in an increasingly globalized world in which identities constantly overlap and change as transcultural processes and production. In their performances, the actors/characters' identities become more or less racialized according to the complicities they establish with the new (local *and* global) cultural influences being transposed into Pelourinho.

The patterns of interaction in the *Trilogia*'s performances do arise out of a dialogical oscillation between sameness and difference through the cross-cultural encounters between and among actors and spectators. These interactions occur in a liminal space, materially and culturally in-between. Such a space involves a further movement back and forth between alterity and mimesis, between difference and sameness. This oscillation—what Homi Bhabha calls "the back and forth of the interstitial spaces"[50]—serves as the engine that drives the action forward in the BTO's plays. The division of scenes in *blocos* fosters the significance of movement within a spatial configuration that has the potential to become the site of connection through transitive transculturation. Carnival in Salvador includes the spectators. The passage of the *bloco de carnaval* does not constitute a parade-like event (as with the *Samba Schools* in Rio de Janeiro and other metropolitan centers) that presupposes spectators watching. Rather, the Bahian *blocos* call for participants, for engagement in the contact zones they establish. Together, the

Trilogia's *blocos* constitute the unending construction and deconstruction of racial and cultural borders followed by their momentary dissolution in the affirmation of possible, if ephemeral, coalitions. This takes place, for example, in the recognition of a provisional bond rooted in shared economic marginalization. However much the BTO's performances underline the impossibility of friendship across boundaries of difference, they also more covertly chart the space of transcultural interaction as changing both sides of subject to subject contact.

At the end of the *Trilogia do Pelô*, the community is indeed displaced, and its members no longer rule the streets of Pelourinho as in *Essa é a nossa praia*. Preventing this from happening, I would argue, was never the objective of the BTO's actors in performing their stories. The BTO's performances do much more: they recuperate a command of space that is not confined to place. The *Trilogia* departs from the notion of community that occupied a prominent *place* in activists' efforts to redirect the significance and roles of most black associations in the 1980s, to inscribe the struggle of the Pelourinho's residents as a *space* from which a new vision of community as a political reference can be articulated; a vision no longer *grounded* in racial or cultural identity but one that is instead congenial to the relational / fluid kernel of all identities.

Notes

1. Only in the 1950s, when UNESCO sponsored a series of studies on racial dynamics, did traditional theoretical approaches, which focused on the concept of racial democracy, come under sustained attack. Briefly, the concept of racial democracy was developed by Gilberto Freyre when, in a series of talks given in the United States in the early 1940s and later published under the title *Brazil: An Interpretation*, he advanced the notion that it was precisely in the process of miscegenation that Brazilians had found a way of avoiding the racial problems that tormented North Americans. In Emilia Viotti da Costa, *Da Senzala à Colonia* 3rd ed. (São Paulo: Editora Brasiliense, 1989). As Howard Winant points out in "The Other Side of the Process," in *On Edge: The Crisis of Contemporary Latin American Culture*, ed. George Yúdice, Jean Franco, and Juan Flores (Minneapolis: University of Minnesota Press, 1992), the work of the UNESCO researchers "documented as never before the prevalence of racial discrimination and the persistence of the supposedly discredited ideology of 'whitening.'" Despite setting new terms for debate and constituting a new racial

"revisionism," the UNESCO research also had significant limitations. "Chief among these was a tendency to reduce race to class, depriving racial dynamics of their own, autonomous significance" (88).

2. I am consciously using the words *black* and *Afrobrazilian* interchangeably throughout this essay. However, the classification of race in Brazil entails much more than skin color. One very strong finding of those applying multiracialist constructs to Brazil, for example, has been the ascriptive nature of racial categorization. The terms by which individuals identify themselves (and are identified by others) focus on phenotype rather than ancestry and / or imply "lighter" skin color as Afro-Brazilians achieve social and economic success. In Brazil, multiracialism results in an infinitely divisible continuum of racial categories. In the national census of 1980, the *Instituto Brasileiro de Geografia e Estatísticas* (the federal statistics bureau) identified 136 terms used within Brazil to identify racial and / or color categories. See Hasenblag, *Discriminação e Desigualdades Raciais no Brasil* (Rio de Janeiro: Graal, 1979).

3. The Unified Black Movement Against Racial Discrimination (MNU) was established in 1978 in response to the forms of violence that most greatly affected the black population. The MNU emerged at a time when many black associations (cultural, recreational, and entertainment) were promoting a variety of activities that lacked explicit (antiracist) political organizational objectives. On the MNU, see Leila González, "The Unified Black Movement: A New Stage in Black Political Mobilization," in *Race, Class and Power in Brazil*, ed. Pierre Michel Fontaine (Los Angeles: UCLA, Afro-American Studies Center, 1985). See also Pierre-Michel Fontaine, "Transnational Relations and Racial Mobilization: Emerging Black Movements in Brazil," in *Ethnic Identities in a Transnational World*, ed. John. F. Stack Jr. (Westport, Conn.: Greenwood Press, 1981). The process through which the Afro Groups developed has its roots in the city of Salvador, Bahia. The novelty produced by the growth of these groups in the political and cultural atmosphere of Salvador was replicated in other cities and contexts, and thus the trend became more than a localized phenomenon. For a more detailed description of this process, see Antônio Risério, *Carnaval Ijexá* (Salvador, Brazil: Corrupio, 1981).

4. Pelourinho and Maciel (hereafter referred to only as Pelourinho) are two contiguous (poor and predominantly black) neighborhoods located at the Historical Center of Salvador, Bahia. The area was designated a Historical and Architectural Preservation World Monument by the UN in 1959. *Bloco de Carnaval* is the name given to the organized form that groups take in order to parade through the city streets during carnival. Because the initial aim of the Afro Groups was to guarantee the participation of Afro-Bahians in carnival, these associations are also referred to as *Blocos Afro*. During carnival, their membership money is used to build costumes for

the dancers and provide instruments for the percussionists who will play the song composed especially for the occasion.

5. As Olivia Maria Gomes da Cunha puts it, "Aware of the power of the market for goods categorized as 'afro,' Olodum and Araketu were the first groups to signal the gradual expansion of their areas of activity to exploit this commercial opportunity by selling records and tapes. They also promoted themselves in media outlets by emphasizing their cultural roots. These groups invested in local solidarity networks that stimulated voluntary participation and professionalization. . . . This practice of 'reterritorializing' the music in specific localities implied a re-evaluation of the purposes and objectives of the *blocos*, and, as a consequence, of the black movement in Salvador." "Black Movements and the 'Politics of Identity' in Brazil," in *Cultures of Politics, Politics of Cultures: Revisioning Latin American Social Movements*, ed. Sonia E. Alvarez, Evelina Dagnino, and Arturo Escobar (Boulder: Westview Press, 1998), 234.

6. Marcelo Dantas, *Olodum: De bloco afro a holding cultural* (Salvador, Bahia: Grupo Cultural Olodum, Fundação Casa de Jorge Amado, 1994), 15.

7. For example, the Palmares Group developed popular performances centered on the contributions of Afro-Brazilian and indigenous cultural segments to Brazilian culture; the SESI Group produced highly participatory street theater events performed in peripheral (mostly black) neighborhoods to promote Afro-Brazilian traditions; the Avatar Group attempted to train black actors and to research alternative acting methods based on Afro-Brazilian ritual techniques.

8. Information on such groups is extremely scarce. Most of my knowledge of their activities was acquired through interviews with directors and actors who have been involved in sporadic performances. Since 1998, the anthropologist Christine Douxami has been tracing black theater groups throughout the country. Douxami told me that a major obstacle to her attempt at building a coherent account of their activities has been the dearth of documentation; most of the companies do not maintain any sort of record about their work, and many formed and disbanded around a single production.

9. To structure its theater company the Olodum announced that actors would be selected through an open workshop guided by one of the best directors of Salvador. The first workshop attracted some eighty participants from several communities. After a month of classes on acting, improvisation, dance, and voice, twenty-two participants were selected to form the new theater group which received the suggestive name *Bando de Teatro Olodum* (during slavery in colonial Brazil, *bando* designated a group of runaway slaves). The original company was thus formed entirely of nonprofessional actors; although a few participants had some previous theatrical

experience, the majority had never taken part in a theater production before the workshop.

10. Recently, many authors have argued that racial dynamics are indeed being transformed in Brazil. This is the central argument of Howard Winant, for example. Employing "racial-formation theory," Winant argues that "over the past decade, traditional racial patterns have been deeply, perhaps irrevocably transformed. A politicization of race is beginning—a far-reaching chain of events that has the potential to reshape Brazilian politics" (98). See also Gomes da Cunha, and Gail D. Triner, "Race, With or Without Color? Reconciling Brazilian Historiography," *Educación y Política en América Latina* 10, no. 1 (1999): 1–23.

11. I borrow the phrase from the title of Johannes Birringer's chapter in *Performance on the Edge: Transformations of Culture* (London: Athlone Press, 2000).

12. As Michel de Certeau points out, popular culture is not only impossible to define but also the result of a repression: "studies of popular culture take as their object *their own* origin." In *Heterologies: Discourse on the Other*, trans. Brian Massumi, foreword by Wlad Godzich (Minneapolis: University of Minnesota Press, 1986), 128. My usage of the term reflects the BTO's self-description as a "popular theater group." By "popular" the group meant a theater linked by its practice and themes to the immediate interests of economically or socially marginalized peoples, using resources of the traditional popular theater, and addressing a popular audience. In 1992, the headline of a major newspaper article on the BTO's participation in the Belo Horizonte festival suggestively read: "The Theater of Citizenship by Olodum." The article's opening paragraph introduced the group and welcomed its noncommercial stance: "There is an emergent theater being produced in Brazil . . . which has everything to threaten the overt commercialism practiced in the sector—especially in major centers—in the near future." It concluded by pointing out that the BTO had already been highly praised in cities throughout the country for its "political commitment of developing the practice of citizenship through the valorization of culture." In Ailton Magioli, "O Teatro da Cidadania pelo Olodum," *Diário da Tarde*, 15 July 1992.

13. In 1994, as the BTO's success and visibility were fueling great interest in their performances, the group decided to launch a campaign to restore an old theater (the Vila Velha Theater outside Pelourinho); it would become the company's permanent space. The "New Vila Project" was devised to transform the old, decayed theater into a multipurpose facility designed to accommodate the BTO and three other groups, including a children's theater and a dance ensemble. As the BTO's director explained, the idea was to rebuild the space and provide for its maintenance through a system of

quotas. In exchange for buying these quotas, investing institutions would receive "cultural products" provided by the resident groups. In Edson Rodrigues, "Márcio Meirelles explica proposta do Novo Vila," *A Tarde*, 6 November 1994, 13–14.

14. Victor Turner, *From Ritual to Theater: The Human Seriousness of Play* (New York: PAJ Publications, 1992), 113, 69. Turner makes a distinction between liminal and liminoid: the former is an obligatory state that every social participant must pass through to attain a place within the established norms of traditional societies, while the latter occurs in modern societies and is optative. In both cases, the phase is characterized by the appearance of marked ambiguity. The "ambiguous figures" formed during this phase "mediate between alternative or oppositional contexts, and thus are important in bringing about their transformation" (113).

15. Michael Taussig, *Mimesis and Alterity: A Particular History of the Senses* (London: Routledge, 1993).

16. This is not to say that a practical state of liminality could actually be maintained and thus create a sustained political space. As Turner puts it, "Clearly, the liminal space-time 'pod' created by ritual action, or today by certain kinds of reflexively ritualized theatre [he is referring to Grotowski] is a potential perilous" (*From Ritual to Theater*, 84).

17. Marcelo Dantas, "Baiano teatro da vida," in *Trilogia do Pelô* (Salvador, Bahia: Edições olodum, 1995), 50.

18. While in Rio de Janeiro, the group also performed both plays at several alternative and community spaces in peripheral neighborhoods and even at the *favela da Mangueira*. The Mangueira community, located on one of the hills surrounding Rio de Janeiro, houses one of the city's most important *Escolas de Samba* (the name given to the ensembles that participate in the carnival parade in Rio, São Paulo, and other major centers).

19. Taken as street thieves, the community's children were being murdered by corrupt policemen who received bribes from the new businesses moving into the area to "protect" their commercial establishments from theft. By the time the BTO was creating *Ó pai, ó*, the police similarly murdered seven children in downtown Rio de Janeiro. The incident attracted international attention and forced the federal government to investigate the case and punish the murderers. The media repercussion of the police violence against street children in the country certainly contributed to the play's sudden visibility and the invitation to perform at the theater award ceremony.

20. *Cortiço* is a pejorative name given to the collective residences of the poor in Brazil. Here the term refers to Pelourinho's colonial houses, in which several families divide the space, each family occupying one of the rooms. Almost all of the houses in

Pelourinho were originally occupied by homeless people many years ago. In general, the family or person who arrived first "rented" rooms to the others and acted as a kind of landlord, assuming responsibility for maintaining the property.

21. According to Turner, redressive action involves "the widest recognized cultural and moral community, transcending the divisions of the local group" (*From Ritual to Theater*, 10).

22. Judith Butler, "Collected and Fractured: Response to *Identities*," in *Identities*, ed. Kwame Anthony Appiah and Henry Louis Gates, Jr. (Chicago: University of Chicago Press, 1995), 440.

23. Dantas, "Baiano teatro."

24. The title is again ironic in its choice of language. It not only refers to the many foreign tourists flocking to the Historical Center but also to the transcultural character of the area and its visitors. According to V. Kahrsch, "Twenty years ago, there were very few foreign tourists found in the Northeast region of Brazil. Only during the dictatorship (1964–85) was this region transformed into the El Dorado of mass tourism. The military needed foreign currency and a new image. The country of terror and torture should transform itself on the outside into the paradise of the tropics. The big campaign for 'everybody's tourism' in the Northeast counts on two clichés: beautiful beaches with palms, and exotic, hot-blooded, beautiful *mulatas* in provocative tangas." In "*Sextourismus in Brasilien*," quoted in Angela Gilliam, "The Brazilian *Mulata*: Images in the Global Economy," *Race and Class* 40, no. 1 (1998): 66.

25. According to Judith Weiss, et al., in *Latin American Popular Theater: The First Five Centuries* (Albuquerque: University of New Mexico Press, 1993), popular theater groups in Latin America establish "the basis for dialogue by reaching out to learn more about the community and understand it. A considerable majority of groups research among their audiences . . . both to determine the priorities among issues of general concern or the level of interest in different topics and to establish how best to develop the production, what artistic methods are most suited to it, and what elements of communication can be adopted from different sectors of the community" (163, 168).

26. For an examination of the role of informal economies in Brazil, see George Yúdice, "Postmodernity and Transnational Capitalism in Latin America," in *On Edge*, 1–28. Yúdice examines the phenomenon and suggests that these economies can "pose alternatives to the *grand récit* of postmodernity as it has been constructed by Lyotard, Jameson, and their predecessors." Although the example of Pelourinho in the *Trilogia* exposes the limitations of such theorization, it is interesting to note that after the restoration many "new" informal modes of production / consumption have

emerged around the Historical Center, despite constant efforts by state authorities to repress and eradicate them.

27. David Harvey, *The Condition of Postmodernity: An Enquiry into the Origins of Cultural Change* (Cambridge, Mass., and Oxford: Blackwell, 1990), 236–37. Following Henri Lefebvre, Harvey points out several examples to illustrate the crucial power relations between the domination of place and the command of space: "[While] simultaneity of revolutionary upsurges in different locations, as in 1848 or 1968, strikes fear into any ruling class precisely because its superior command over space is threatened," the "various revolutions that broke out in Paris in the nineteenth century foundered on the inability to consolidate national power through a spatial strategy that would command the national space" (ibid).

28. Turner, *From Ritual to Theater*, 10. The play's lack of closure, refusing to represent the "last act," not only documents the failure to produce a unified Afrobrazilian subject but also the capacity to move beyond racialism. Curiously, many reviewers faulted *Bai, bai Pelô* exactly because of its open-endedness.

29. Butler, "Collected and Fractured," 446.

30. In her account of the different positions intellectuals and activists associated with the black movement advocated during the 1970s and 1980s in Brazil, Gomes da Cunha describes how the concepts of cultural diversity and black culture articulated the notion of difference as an artifact demarcating distinct historical, cultural, and ethnic attributes: "At the time, the idea of 'difference' assumed an ontological status that could be explained by a mixture of cultural and historical elements determined by the origins and vicissitudes of the black presence in the Americas. If there was a privileged place within this debate, it was in the sphere of culture. *Cultural diversity* . . . could be perceived and exemplified in the *quilombos*, in religious brotherhoods and samba schools. *Difference* and *diversity* were attributes used to configure other possible 'unified wholes' to be incorporated under the polymorphous notion of 'black culture.' This was an effort to create collective references capable of capturing, embracing, and reconfiguring the disparate ways in which the presence of blacks was felt in Brazilian society" ("Black Movements and the 'Politics of Identity,' " 224).

31. Paul Gilroy refers to strategies of convergence as "culturally inclusive" and shows how the construction of an ethnonationalist discourse, in the English context, avoids references to the categories of hybrids and Creoles. In "The End of Antiracism," in *Race, Culture, and Difference*, ed. A. Rattansi and J. Donald (London: Sage, 1993).

32. In other words, the plays demonstrate that the conceptualization of black identity has a delimiting role. According to Gomes da Cunha, the interventions of the black movement into poor and black communities based on racial identification

were much less effective than among those who considered themselves free from hegemonic culture, that is, among black intellectuals.

33. "A arte negra do Olodum no Festival de Inverno," *Estado de Minas*, July 16 1992.

34. The play comments on the community's reaction to a program designed to involve street kids in artistic activities. Many of the community's mothers strongly opposed the initiative and prohibited their children from participating in the band, fearing they would be viewed (and judged) by society as criminals.

35. In one *bloco*, she becomes hysterical before an Evangelical priest. The scene—which also remarks on the rivalry between Pentecostals and black organizations in Brazil—is very funny, as the priest, claiming that Dona Joana is possessed by the devil, decides to perform an exorcism. Dona Joana attempts to "play the role" (and take advantage of the attention she gathers to blame the Olodum band for contributing to the community's bad image) only to have her farce revealed when, to the priest's dismay, she invokes her Candomblé *orixá* in the middle of his Christian ritual.

36. Mary Layoun develops the notion of "telling spaces" to explain the role of "Third World" women in the engendering of national narratives. Quoted in Sangueeta Ray, "Rethinking Migrancy: Nationalism, Ethnicity, and Identity in *Jasmine* and *The Buddha of Suburbia*," in *Reading the Shape of the World: Toward an International Cultural Studies*, ed. Henry Schwarz and Richard Dienst, 195 (Boulder: Westview Press, 1996).

37. *Bai, bai Pelô*, in *Trilogia do Pelô*, 157.

38. Clearly, the BTO's productions deeply destabilized conservative theater critics and middle-class audiences alike. Reviewers, who oscillated between elitist and patronizing stances in their appraisals, were in fact in the difficult position of juggling their personal dislike for the *Trilogia* and its appeal to popular audiences. Particularly in Salvador, the reviewers' dilemma corroborated views that mainstream theater paradoxically remains an elite event, considered suitable to educated audiences only. It also demonstrated that critics were baffled by the productions' full houses, standing ovations, and levels of participation they witnessed during the performances. See, for example, Jacques de Beauvoir, *Tribuna da Bahia*, February 22 1991; Isabela Larangeira, "*Essa é a nossa praia* revela a força da emoção sobre o academicismo," *Correio da Bahia*, February 22, 1991; "Bando de Teatro mostra o Pelourinho," *Diário Oficial*, March 29 1991; Edson Rodrigues, "*Ó Paí, Ó* revela toda a alegria do Bando do Olodum," *Correio da Bahia*, February 13, 1993; Jacques de Beauvoir, "Um bando chamado sucesso," *Tribuna da Bahia*, May 23, 1992; "Bando Olodum traz 'Ó Paí, Ó' de volta ao palco do ACBEU," *Tribuna da Bahia*, May 6, 1992; Clodoaldo Lôbo,

"Achado Antropológico," *A Tarde*, November 24, 1994; and Cláudia Pereira, "A difícil arte de ser simples," *Correio da Bahia*, November 5, 1994.

39. Macksen Luiz, "No compasso contagiante do Olodum," *Jornal do Brasil*, March 13, 1992. Luiz, for example, faults the episodic structure of *Ó paí, ó* for contributing to the exacerbation of stereotypical characterization. He does not attempt to hide his condescending attitude toward popular audiences when he remarks that, despite confining the play's scope, this kind of structure does "increase the performance's communicability, especially for less demanding audiences."

40. Julie Stone Peters, "Intercultural Performance, Theatre Anthropology, and the Imperialist Critique: Identities, Inheritances, and Neo-Orthodoxies," in *Imperialism and Theatre: Essays on World Theatre, Drama and Performance 1795–1995*, ed. J. Ellen Gainor (London: Routledge, 1995), 207–8.

41. Barbara Heliodora, "Monotonia em montagem oca e um show de percussão: *Brida* e *Ó Paí, Ó*," *O Globo*, March 13, 1992. For Heliodora, the only authentic features of the play were the "passionate rhythm of the percussion" and the characters' language, which, admittedly, she could not understand.

42. As Diana Taylor points out, there is another dimension to the problem as well: "While certain dramatic forms were forcefully imposed during the colonial period, since then Latin American dramatists have tended to 'borrow' models. (Commentators generally speak of *influence* on First World authors; Third World writers seem to borrow)." "Transculturating Transculturation," in *Interculturalism and Performance*, ed. Bonnie Marranca and Gautam Dasgupta (New York: PAJ Publications, 1991), 67.

43. Quoted in Neil Larsen, "Brazilian Critical Theory and the Question of 'Cultural Studies,'" in *Reading the Shape of the World*, 137–38. The thrust of Schwarz's critique, Larsen points out, is that "*both* cultural nationalism *and* a postnationalist cultural studies rest on a common ideological ground insofar as *both* think culture, whether 'patrimonial' and fixed or 'transcultural' and decentered, in isolation from its economic basis in labor and class relations" (138).

44. The concept of transculturation was developed by Fernando Ortiz in the 1940s in one of his most important historical and sociological ethnographies on Cuban life and culture, *Contrapunteo cubano del tobacco y el azúcar* (Havana: Editorial Ciencias Sociales, 1991 [1940]). Since then, many authors have expanded on his theory. See José María Arguedas, *Formación de una cultura nacional indoamericana* (Mexico City: Siglo Veintiuno Editores SA, 1975); Angel Rama, *Transculturación narrativa en América Latina* (Mexico City: Siglo Veintiuno Editores SA, 1982); and Antonio Cornejo Polar, *Literatura y sociedad en Perú: La novela indigenista* (Lima: Lasontay, 1980). Also, many works use transculturation as a theoretical framework—

for example, Mary Louise Pratt, *Imperial Eyes: Travel, Writing and Transculturation*; Silvia Spitta, *Between Two Waters: Narratives of Transculturation in Latin America*; and Phyllis Peres, *Transculturation and Resistance in Lusophone African Narrative*.

45. Taylor, "Transculturating Transculturation," 73.

46. Fernando Ortiz, *Estudios etnosociológicos* (Havana: Editorial Ciencias Sociales, 1991), 14. The other work is *Un catauro de cubanismos* (Havana: Editorial de Ciencias Sociales, 1975).

47. Gustavo Pérez Firmat, in *The Cuban Condition: Translation and Identity in Modern Cuban Literature* (Cambridge: Cambridge University Press, 1989), refers to Ortiz's *ajiaco* as a metaphor for the complexity and diversity of elements that compose Cuban culture.

48. The endless multiplicity of stories that such transcultural interactions generate in the performances and the marketability of this generative power are well known to the television and film industries in Brazil. They are well known to the BTO as well. As the interactions between and among residents, state authorities, and tourists in the *Trilogia* make clear, these are far from being reciprocal in power.

49. Taylor, "Transculturating Transculturation," 63.

50. Homi K. Bhabha theorizes these in-between spaces and their potential for transgression in his examination of the function of ethnic stereotyping in colonial discourse. See "The Other Question: Stereotype, Discrimination, and the Discourse of Colonialism," in *The Location of Culture* (London: Routledge, 1994).

Political Construction and Cultural Instrumentalities of Indigenism in Brazil, with Echoes from Latin America

ALCIDA RITA RAMOS

My purpose here is to explore some distinctions between Brazil and other Latin American countries against the background of the events that took place during the five hundredth anniversary of Brazil's discovery in April 2000. The descriptive mode of the essay aims at highlighting both the unexpected twists and turns of what should have been a straightforward civic festival and the implications of those events for indigenism both in Brazil and in Hispanic America.

State and People at Cross-Purposes

It would be fair to say that the recent history of Brazil is a history of public indifference toward events that turned out to be decisive for the country. Even Brazil's change of status from colony to independent nation went largely unnoticed by the population as independence from Portugal was solitarily proclaimed by the Portuguese Regent Prince Pedro I on September 7, 1822, under pressure from Brazilian elites and after negotiations that cost Portugal two million British pounds (Carvalho 2000:69). Pedro I's son, Pedro II, Brazil's second and last emperor, was ousted on November 15, 1889, by a military coup in Rio de Janeiro that installed the republican regime. The nonparticipating populace observed the military's maneuvers under the impression they were watching a festive parade (Carvalho 1990). On April Fool's Day, 1964, again the baffled inhabitants of Rio witnessed a military coup d'état unaware that a long and cruel dictatorship was beginning.

In turn, state indifference is often the response to public demands. One of the most glaring examples of the mismatch of wills between the public and state authorities was the massive popular engagement in the campaign for direct elections in 1984. While thousands of citizens filled urban squares all over the country demanding a definitive stop to the twenty-year-long military regime, the majority of national congressmen ignored the roaring shouts of *diretas já* (direct elections now) and voted for a compromise solution, U.S.-style: the first civilian to become president in two decades would be chosen by an electoral college. The civic disappointment that ensued enlarged the chasm between the demands of the people and the decisions of state powers. A short respite in this public retreat was the uproar against President Fernando Collor de Mello, whose hyperbolic corruption led to his impeachment in 1992 after two of the stipulated four years in office.

The quincentennial of Brazil's discovery, celebrated on April 22, 2000, would have been yet another occasion for popular indifference had it not been for the extraordinary overreaction by state officials to the organized protests of minority groups, especially indigenous ones. This essay explores the implications and surreptitious meanings of the rituals of rebellion, so to speak, or rather the social dramas, into which the country's five hundredth anniversary was transformed. What happened at the site of the commemorations not only confirmed the love-hate relationship the Brazilian state has maintained with its indigenous minorities (Ramos 1998:284–92) but reaffirmed Brazil's position as an odd fellow in Latin America. It is common knowledge that the country's oversized territory and official language, Portuguese, sharply distinguish it from its Spanish-speaking neighbors. But what fewer people realize is that Brazil has a birth date of its own that has become a symbol of its individuality, as distinct from Hispanic nations. Is Columbus, the generic discoverer of the Americas, revered in Brazil for having unveiled the future Brazilian nation to the Old World? Not in the least. Brazil has its own exclusive discoverer in the figure of the Portuguese admiral Pedro Álvares Cabral, who anchored his caravels ten days after Easter Sunday in 1500 (Galvani 2000; Schüler 2001) at Porto Seguro on the coast of today's state of Bahia.[1] Whether Cabral, like Columbus, came upon the massive new continent on purpose or by accident is a matter of interest to historians but is virtually irrelevant as far as national identity is concerned. What matters is that, for better or worse, Brazil has its own discovery calendar, its own style of colonization, its own way of treating its minorities, and its own ideological script about cultural diversity. For sure, there are in this respect certain family resemblances between Brazil and its neighbors, but both their linguistic and political idioms are so different as to be often mutually unintelligible. Hence, comparing the Brazilian situation to that of other countries in Latin

America is frequently an exercise in deciphering contrasts. Obviously, the full implications of such a comparison cannot be undertaken here, for they would require intensive research and voluminous writings.[2]

Differences and Similarities

Unlike South American countries such as Ecuador, Peru, and Bolivia, whose indigenous populations are very large, if not demographically predominant, Brazil holds the dubious record of having the smallest Indian population in the Americas and perhaps in the Caribbean as well. Even in Argentina, after the brutal warfare against indigenous peoples euphemistically known as the Conquista del Desierto, there are perhaps more Indians than in Brazil in absolute terms and certainly more in proportion to the national population. Whereas in Brazil the Indians represent 0.25 percent (about 350,000 of a total of nearly 170 million people), in Argentina they are estimated to be 1 percent of the country's population (Hernández 1995:267n.14; see also Hernández 1992).

In 2001, the Brazilian Institute of Geography and Statistics published partial results of its census of 2000. It reported the surprising total of 701,462 Brazilians who identify themselves as Indians. This extraordinary increase might be partly due to the question of ethnic identification in the 1991 census that served as suggestions for rethinking one's identity. Along with the natural growth during the intervening years of the Indians living on their own lands, and the growth of Indian populations in towns and cities, more Brazilians were calling themselves Indians. A process of ethnic resurgence developed, and a growing number of groups of people have come to identify themselves as Indians in various parts of the country. Even so, this sudden increase raises the percentage of indigenous peoples to a mere 0.5 percent of the national population.

Although there has been a steady demographic increase since the 1950s, when Indians numbered fewer than one hundred thousand, the indigenous population in Brazil is far from representing a serious political or geopolitical threat to the state. There are over 200 different ethnic groups speaking about 170 different languages and living in highly dispersed communities that occupy approximately 11 percent of the national territory. Their formal education is extremely deficient, and very few complete higher education: "Recently . . . over 200 Indians were admitted to Brazilian universities. . . . Most of the time they have to leave their villages to study in town . . . without a job and nowhere to live. . . . Sometimes they manage to complete one semester and have to interrupt, abandon [the university]" (Terena 2000). For all these reasons, Brazil's indigenous peoples have no significant demographic, intellectual, or political impact on the nation's affairs. Whereas in countries like Ecuador the strength of indigenous protests can depose presidents, and in Bolivia the majority Indian population cannot be ignored by the state, in Brazil the effect of indigenous political pressures is practically limited to its symbolic power, in itself a kind of political power, but in the restricted field of interethnic relations. It is a power that affects the country's image rather than its realpolitik.

Nevertheless, small as this minority is, its symbolic presence has populated the minds of the majority society with rare potency. If it were not for exceptions such as Argentina, one might even risk a sweeping statement: the smaller the indigenous population, the larger its place in the national imagination. Consider, for instance, a statement like this: "In a country like Colombia where all the people classified by government censuses as Indian would fit into a few city blocks, the enormity of the magic attributed to those Indians is striking" (Taussig 1987:171).

Part of the mental resources that feed the national imagination regarding internal minorities is the country's creation myth, according to which nationality has been the result of the happy mixture of three races: Indian, Black, and white. But neither the Brazilian *mito das três raças* nor, for instance, the Colombian *tres potencias* was created to accommodate legitimate racial and ethnic differences. What the bricoleurs of these myths expected was that the genetic vigor of the whites would overwhelm that of the others in a process that has been described as *branqueamento* (whitening) (in Portuguese) or *blanqueamiento* (in Spanish). The very fact of the demographic imbalance, when, during the process of colonization, the Indians were outnumbered by Portuguese and Spanish colonizers and to a lesser extent by Black slaves, has helped the national intelligentsia maintain this fantasy. But again Argentina emerges as a sobering exception: while rendering generalizations inadequate, the Argentine case provides a useful contrast for the analysis of nationality formation. Whereas Brazil, Colombia, and Venezuela, among other countries on the continent, admit to having obvious ethnic differences, albeit regarding them as raw material for the development of a uniform and unique national population, Argentina has been reported as having established as a dominant policy the outright denial of differences of any kind. Its model might be comparable to the French republican principle of uncompromising national equality were it not for the missing aspect of state-protected universal rights to citizenship. The problem with minorities in Argentina is that before they aspire to having their alterity legitimated, they must make it visible (Briones 1998; Grosso 1999; Segato 1991).

The apparently benign way in which the Brazilian state has treated its Indians in the twentieth century by approaching uncontacted peoples with gifts rather than guns (Ramos 1998, chapter 5), by drafting protective legislation according to which the Indians are its official wards, and by assigning them often generous amounts of land may deceive an outside observer. These protective measures have cost the Indians their autonomy, their right to proper health and education, and, perhaps worst of all, their civil and political agency. The infantilization that goes with the condition of being "relatively incapable," as defined in the Civil Code of 1916 (finally revoked in 2001), and the attendant legal device of the *tutela*, or tutelage, have been colossal barriers to indigenous empowerment. Faced with having to overcome such tremendous obstacles to achieve citizenship without losing their ethnic identity, many indigenous peoples have resorted to instrumentalizing cultural traditions, whether long established, recently invented, or simply borrowed, to impress upon the national consciousness their right to ethnic dignity (Ramos 2003). In short, Brazil's style of conquest conceals a devastatingly effective control mechanism behind the façade of a humanitarian state policy. The fact that Brazilian Indians now number close to the fewest of any country in the continent belies the benevolence that public figures such as the Villas Bôas brothers have spent decades proclaiming to the world.

Outros 500

Most Brazilians, including myself, cannot trace the origin of the prosaic expression *isso são outros 500* (equivalent to "that's another story"). An example of the usage of this expression might be the following hypothetical dialogue:

—Os políticos do país estão afundando na lama da corrupção. Até quando vão continuar impunes? (The politicians in this country are drowning in the mud of corruption. How much longer will they go on unpunished?)

—É verdade, mas daí a serem punidos, isso são outros 500! (It's true, but whether or not they will be punished, well, that's another story!)

The proximity of the quincentennial gave this saying new depth, as the double entendre added an ironic dimension to the event. In preparation for repudiating the commemoration of Brazil's five hundredth aniversary, a group was organized in 1999 under the name *Movimento de Resistência Indígena, Negra e Popular—Brasil Outros 500*. Part of their activities was the *Marcha Indígena 2000*, a massive rally and march by Indians from various parts of the country with stops and protests in Manaus, Brasília, Salvador, and finally in Porto Seguro, where President Fernando Henrique Cardoso was to meet Portugal's President Jorge Sampaio for the official ceremonies.

While in Brasília, a group of Indians, mainly Pataxó from the state of Bahia, went to the National Congress seeking support. They ended up in the Senate, where they met with the Senate's all-powerful president at the time, Antonio Carlos Magalhães (also known as ACM), the strongman from the state of Bahia and the official most responsible for the armed repression that confronted Indians and non-Indians in Porto Seguro a few days later. In the mounting emotion of the scene, a Suruí leader from the western state of Rondônia confronted ACM, blaming him for the suffering of the Pataxó. He was shown on television and in print pointing an arrow at Magalhães's face. Magalhães was furious and responded with shouts of "*Exijo respeito!*" (I demand respect!). Other protests occurred in several state capitals but nothing as dramatic as the military riots of Porto Seguro.[3]

Before the official ceremonies began on a hill overlooking the ocean, police barriers had stopped all traffic into the area around Porto Seguro. But thousands of demonstrators, including the resident Pataxó, were already in the area preparing for a peaceful march converging on the site of the commemorations. According to one estimate (*Caros Amigos*, May 2000:14–15), there were about three thousand Indians, two thousand members of the Black movement, and approximately five thousand members of the militant *Movimento dos Sem Terra* (MST, Movement of the Landless). Most of the protestors never made it beyond the police barriers.

The *Conselho Indigenista Missionário* (CIMI, Missionary Indigenist Council), a Catholic Church affiliate with a thirty-year record of activism in indigenous rights, had apparently intended to bring MST members and Indian militants to the same march, but the police barriers frustrated that plan. Accusing officials of co-optation, CIMI successfully halted an indigenous delegation in charge of meeting President Cardoso with a letter of demands. There was, then, no encounter of Indians and authorities at the site of the ceremonies on April 22. Only the fifteen-kilometer march began as planned.

The march of Indians, some Blacks, journalists, and a few leftist congresspersons came to an abrupt halt as five thousand armed military police advanced on the marchers with strict orders from ACM, as their commander later revealed (*Caros Amigos*, May 2000:14), to stop anyone who attempted to get near the Brazilian and Portuguese presidents and the envoy from the Vatican. The police action lasted the long hours that took the official ceremonies to come to an end. Tear gas, rubber bullets, billy clubs, and much pushing and shoving resulted in the arrest of 140 people, some of whom were slightly wounded, and the powerful image of a Terena youth kneeling on the wet asphalt with arms wide open in supplication at the feet of the battalion. As he lay on the road, military boots stepped over him and kept on. Gildo Terena made most of the following day's headlines in a symbolic remembrance of yet another intrepid, but anonymous, youth who one day faced Chinese tanks at yet another sacred site of nationality. Granted that the degree of violence represented by each of these pictures is incomparable, nevertheless, the evocative imagery they portray is quite disturbing.

Meanwhile, members of the Brazilian Catholic Church, according to the latest fad, were piously expressing their apologies and requests for pardon for the genocide the Church had perpetrated centuries earlier against the Indians. An especially solemn mass took place two days later with high dignitaries of Brazil and the Vatican. Amidst the Christian pomp and circumstance, a young Pataxó man, no longer under police harassment, interrupted the rites and issued forth with a fiery speech denouncing the destruction by the Bahia military police of a monument the Indians had erected a few days earlier, the metal cross the government had planted nearby, and the shock troops, the shooting, and the tear gas. "With our blood," he continued, "once more you've commemorated the discovery," and added: "Aren't you ashamed of this memory [of genocide] that is in our soul and in our heart? We shall recount it for justice, land, and freedom" (http://www.cimi.org.br/jerry.htm). Referring to the appeals for pardon from members of the Brazilian Catholic Church, he insisted, "I don't forgive this massacre" (*Jornal do Brasil*, April 27, 2000:6). The 500 years episode had been predictably foretold in a popular phrase: *Comemorar o que, Cara Pálida?* (Commemorate what, Pale Face?).

At home, in front of their TV sets, most Brazilians placidly watched groups of Indians in various parts of the country, true to popular folkloric expectations, engaged in "Indian dances" in a whirl of feathers, straw skirts, bead and tooth necklaces, body paint, and bows and arrows. To enhance the native spectacle, or fearing the Indians might show up in the nude, the then-minister of Sports and Tourism, Rafael Greca, had the spirited but aborted idea of supplying the dancers with skin-color tights! (*Veja*: 44).

The repercussions of the Porto Seguro fiasco were immediate. Headlines from abroad fired away (*Veja*: 47): "Brazilians shrug off discovery festivities" (*Washington Post*); "Indians lead protests as Brazil parties" (*Observer*); "Police under fire after Brazil celebrations" (*Boston Globe*); "Brazil celebrates its 500 years repressing its Indians" (*Libération*); "Amargo V Centenario en Brasil" (Bitter 5th centennial in Brazil) (*El Pais*). At home, President Cardoso was said to have associated the Porto Seguro protests with fascism, denied that the federal government was responsible for the violence, and added, "Provocation is repelled by democracy because it opens the door to fascism, and I come from struggles against autoritarianism" (*Folha de S. Paulo*, April 23, 2000:1–10; Herschmann and Pereira 2000:208–9). An old foe of indigenous alterity, the political scientist Hélio Jaguaribe complained about the "insolent interruption of the mass celebrated by the papal delegate Angelo Solena, in Cabrália, on April 24th, in celebration of the first mass of Brazil" (*Jornal do Brasil*, May 4, 2000:3). The minister of culture at the time, Francisco Weffort, also a political scientist, condemned the protest by declaring, "It was as though someone invited to a wedding party spat on the floor" (*Veja*, May 3, 2000:42). In short, Brazilian authorities took the five hundredth anniversary to be a private party from which subversive and uncouth trespassers should be banned.

The official pantomime that celebrated the five hundred years of discovery reached its deceitful climax with the most spectacular government failure of all in this turn-of-the-century extravaganza, namely, the replica of Cabral's flagship. Costing the federal treasury and private firms nearly two million dollars, the copy of Cabral's fifteenth-century *Nau Capitânia* never sailed anywhere because of technical incompetence. Barely kept afloat, the period piece had to be lined with fourteen tons of lead and, when the lead ran out, an additional four tons of cement (*Veja*: 45). In case the fifteenth-century winds failed to reappear or the crew bungled the sailing, the ship was equipped with two engines. Even so, it never got offshore and became an instant national joke.

Porto Seguro turned into the scene and symbol of a huge imposture: a fake battlefield, fake Indian skin, the fake period garments of Cardoso's entourage, fake pardons, and a fake ship that never showed up as planned. It was a superlative farce, that is, a farcical Carnival. Put in a nutshell, "of the whole spectacle set up by the government to celebrate the discovery of Brazil, what will remain are the pictures of Indians and *sem-terra* being forcibly stopped by shock troops and the solemn requests for pardon by Catholic bishops— and promptly rebuffed by Indian leaders" (*Veja*: 48).

The most serious casualties were not, however, the few lightly injured Indians and other protestors, but government officials: Minister Greca was fired, and the president of the National Indian Foundation (FUNAI), the lawyer Carlos Marés, resigned after the aborted meeting with President Cardoso. Having counted on accompanying the Indian delegation to the official site, Marés ended up at the Porto Seguro melee amidst the demonstrators and the tear gas.

President Cardoso's remark on fascism and his declaration to the press just before the ceremonies at Porto Seguro that he was not willing to put up with offenses from the MST (*Jornal do Brasil*, April 22, 2000:5) imply that the nervousness of both federal and state of Bahia officials was caused by the significant attendance of MST militants, who represent the most tangible challenge to today's power in Brazil. But, true to form, it was the Indians in their hyperreality (Ramos 1984) who stole the show. Landless peasants on the other side of the barriers could not compete with feathers and bright body paint for the hundreds of cameras that recorded the unforgettable civic parody. It was the indianization of the quincentennial.

While an echo does not reproduce the original sound literally, it retains and amplifies the initial message despite a certain warp caused by distance. One might say that the quincentennial in Brazil was a delayed and intensified echo of the Latin American version eight years earlier. The ingredients were the same: five hundred years of ethnic injustice, loss of indigenous territory, religious defilement, severe impoverishment, and nation-states on the defensive. Like Spanish America, Brazil was the satiating spring at which Europe could quench its thirst for space and for utopia (Fuentes 1990). Like Brazil, Spanish America created the "celebrations of the 'Meeting of Two Worlds' " as a utopian fantasy of their elites. But unlike Brazil, the other Americas reacted with indignation in the form of popular protests. Where they converged was in the angry response of the original nations "that challenged the celebration by converting it into a 'commemoration' of the 500 years" (Delgado 1996:34).

The distinction between commemoration and celebration is worth noticing. Although in popular and academic contexts alike the two terms seem to be freely interchangeable (see, for instance, Trouillot 1995:132), for purposes of analyses like this one, it is useful to differentiate them: official celebrations emphasized the joyous, festive aspect of the occasion, whereas the people's commemoration stressed the component of grief in the comemory, the remembrance of miseries past . . . and present. However, the outcomes of these ceremonies were distinct in many ways. Hispanic America took the events of October 12, 1992 (which, incidentally, were preceded by widely publicized indigenous demonstrations during the Rio Earth Summit), as a direct reflection of the frank antagonism that exists in normal interethnic coexistence. A plethora of books before and after the American quincentennary marked the long season of cathartic analyses and accusations of interethnic justice over five hundred years. Yet news items of October 12, 1992, from various Latin American countries report nothing exceptional in terms of political demonstrations against Western domination. In turn, Brazil, as though intent on establishing its distinctness in the continent, lived its 2000 discovery date as a dramatization of its hidden, hence unresolved, ambivalences.

To begin with, the rather vacuous intercourse of President Cardoso with

Portugal's President Sampaio, epitomized by the trite pictures of the pair, shovels in hand, planting a tree together while surrounded by an indulging court, contrasted with the less than idyllic relations between the two countries after Portugal entered the European Union and created embarrassing problems regarding Brazilian immigrants. The irony with which the press treated the tree-planting scene is notable. The daily *Jornal do Brasil*, for instance, juxtaposed the photograph of the smiling presidents holding their shovels with the headline "Violence explodes in Porto Seguro" (April 23, 2000:10A). The subtle use of irony by the press (Brait 1996) has been analyzed as a major trope for disclosing contradictions, deception, and fraudulent attitudes of power holders. Hence, it is not surprising to see how irony marked its potent presence as a rhetorical whip at the quincentennary just as it does nearly everyday in the country's public life.

Perhaps unique in the Americas is the self-ascribed image of the Brazilian as a "cordial man" (Buarque de Holanda 1989). It represents a veritable Bakhtinean chronotope of the national character and refers not to gentleness of manners, as the word might indicate, but to the compulsive inclination to mix private and public spheres, to praise the law so long as it is applied only to one's enemies (DaMatta 1979, chapter 4), and, as a consequence, to engender an uncomfortable double bind among the citizenry. Indians are legally declared minors and wards of the state, their official protector, but in full view of the nation's and the world's cameras the very same state unleashes armed police on the peaceful indigenous marchers in perhaps one of the most spectacular cases of social transference, if the main target was indeed the MST. Throughout Brazil's history numerous violent rebellions and uprisings have marked the extreme discontent of the people in various parts of the country. Yet official history has taken great pains to conceal these facts and encourage the popular illusion that Brazil is a peaceful and harmonious society, as placid as its nature, free as it is of the earthquakes, tornadoes, blazing volcanoes, and other calamities that periodically afflict our Latin American neighbors. However, like Freudian slips of the tongue, bursts of violence such as the crass police action in Porto Seguro belie the cordiality of the Brazilian archetype. It is true that one should not take government deeds as representing the people's will (which is seldom the case), but a large number of Brazilians overtly express their anti-indigenous feelings, notwithstanding the surprising results of a recent poll in which 78 percent of a sample of two thousand men and women around the country indicated a sympathetic bent toward the Indians (ISA 2000; Santilli 2000:51–85).

Whereas some, if not most (Trouillot 1995:136n.55), Hispanic American countries have elected October 12 as the celebration of nationality under the name *Día de la Raza*, mostly dedicated to praise New World ethnicity, Brazil has diluted its civic mementoes by routinely celebrating its independence rather than its discovery.[4] The social irrelevance of the official date was reaffirmed by the absolute silence that surrounded April 22, 2001. In contrast, the widely celebrated national days are April 21 for the execution of Tiradentes, an eighteenth-century fighter for independence (and, in 1960, the foundation of Brasília), and September 7, for the actual Declaration of Independence in 1822. The Indians have been allotted a *Dia do Índio* on April 19, and, almost as a footnote on the nation's celebratory calendar, Blacks are mutely honored on May 13 for the termination of slavery in 1888. *Raza*, or rather *raça*, is thus an ungrammatical term in Brazil's idiom of nationality. In the Brazilian version of the "myth of the three races," it is not the idea of race that is exalted, as the Porto Seguro disaster made quite clear, but the idea of society, a hybrid by all means, but docile, "cordial" community imagined by its governors to be under the wardship of the state, like the Indians themselves. What the ideal Brazilian nation-state needs is not real Indians, real Blacks, or real poor, but a palatable, hyperreal image of the Indian, the Black, and the stoic humble populace, whose combination might elevate the country to an enviable racial and social democracy. When hyperreality threatens to become real, the state reacts violently as though against an enemy. As long as ethnicization remains within the bounds of folkore, everything is fine and dandy, but when it becomes a political instrument, it activates the state's antibodies, whether in the form of police repression or of subtler disempowering mechanisms such as discriminatory policies and actions, among which is the state's tenacious negligence regarding proper education.

This issue unveils yet another set of differences in Latin America. Although it would be thoughtless to attempt an analysis of the concept of race without meticulous research on the subject, it is possible to read some signs of how various countries elaborate their own conceptions. For instance, Mexico commemorates its Día de la Raza in praise of *mestizaje* and to the detriment of the Indians, or what Guillermo Bonfil Batalla called *México profundo* (Bonfil Batalla 1990). In Peru, in turn, national pride does not hinge on idealized *mestizaje*, but on the morality of *gente decente*, that is, people with access to higher education and all the other benefits of full citizenship (Cadena 1998, 2000). It is thus not entirely surprising that the Peruvian national holiday is not October 12 but October 9, in celebration not of race but of National Dignity (Trouillot 1995: 136n.55). In either case, the concept of race is not built on postulates of natural, biological differences. Unlike these two countries, where racism is based on sociocultural differences, Brazil, despite various sorts of metaphorical usages, has basically taken the concept of race to be closely associated with racism. More recently, perhaps influenced by the revival of the race concept among Blacks in the United States, the Brazilian Black movement has recuperated the notion of race as a political emblem.

Politicized minorities are anything but passive puppets in the nation's power games. One path indigenous peoples have taken to mobilize their political energy is to appropriate the anthropological concept of culture as a platform in what academics have called essentialism, itself a conceptual battlefield. Essentialization is a widespread political device among indigenous peoples in Brazil and elsewhere (Ramos 2003):

> El esencialismo cultural indio, se concentraría en la reposición de la espiritualidad nativa, la manutención de las religiones nativas o de sus formas de concebir lo sagrado, la reinstauración de las lenguas nativas, la territorialidad, la utilización de sistemas tradicionales de producción agrícola, y el sentido de "nación india" al interior de las sociedades "nacionales" (Delgado 1996:56–57).

> Indigenous cultural essentialism would be concentrated in the recovery of native spirituality, in the maintenance of native religions or in their ways of conceiving sacredness, in the use of traditional systems of agricultural production, and in the sense of an "Indian nation" within "national" societies.

The events at Porto Seguro provided splendid examples of essentialization on the part of all participants. State power was displayed in such exuberant details as the joint venture of tree cultivation by the two presidents, the period attire of their escorts, and, above all, the disconcertingly crippled flagship. On the Indian side, cultural diacritics were visible all the way from the profusion of bright red body paint and feather and bead ornaments to the monument the police destroyed and the Indians reconstructed before the fateful day.

While much of the display of cultural alterity was based on longstanding traditions, there were some interesting cases of invented history. For instance, the Pataxó, who have lived in the Porto Seguro region for less than a century, emerged on the quincentennial scene as those who first met Cabral and his seamen. By a feat of prestidigitation around comemory, the Pataxó replaced the extinct Tupinambá and acted as if they had themselves been there for the past five hundred years. Whether accepted as original inhabitants or not, the Pataxó played historical hosts, even though Tupinambá ancestry is now being claimed by a group of people in south Bahia (Marmelo 2000). Núbia, a "Tupinambá" spokeswoman, has thus been described as having the "physical type of the Indian woman—who in hair and nose equals that [depicted] in the letter by Caminha [Cabral's scribe]" (Viegas 2000).

But the quincentennial moment was not limited to the rather predictable demonstration of the political force of cultural essentialism. It also created the conditions for an Indian cry of independence from the historically powerful influence of the Catholic Church. In the aftermath of the Porto Seguro events, representatives of twenty-five indigenous organizations from all over the country circulated via the Internet a document sent from Brasília, dated May 17, in response to another electronically disseminated text by CIMI titled "The many faces of a war." It was in this text that CIMI accused a number of unnamed Indians, presumably Pataxó, of having been co-opted into playing a progovernment role during the official ceremonies in Porto Seguro—the planned meeting of an Indian delegation with the president. The document signed by the Indians, entitled "The dark faces of missionary indigenism," addresses several issues. It describes the preparatory activities of the Indigenous Conference steered by the *Conselho de Articulação dos Povos e Organizações Indígenas do Brasil* (CAPOIB; Organizing Council of Peoples and Indigenous Groups of Brazil), repudiates CIMI's accusations of co-optation, and, most important, denounces the missionary council for imposing exclusive rights over the Indians' initiatives, particularly regarding agreements with government bodies such as the National Health Foundation. Under the heading "CIMI's identity crisis," the undersigned expose what they regard as the missionaries' severe paternalism and gradual loss of power:

Little by little CIMI has seen its prominent role as defenders of indigenous rights die out without having defined clear strategies for a new relationship with the indigenous movement, and desperately clinging to a practice that, unfortunately, is not so very different from the state wardship of the National Indian Foundation—FUNAI—it so intensely criticizes. CIMI continues to insist on speaking for indigenous peoples and deciding on the Indians' destiny. This is inadmissible. It is each Indian, [whether] belonging to some organization or not, who has the legitimacy to speak for himself/herself or for his/her people.

This is a far cry from the 1970s, when the contemporary indigenous movement took its first steps guided by CIMI.

The deep involvement of the Catholic Church with indigenous movements in Brazil has parallels in other countries. Suffice it to evoke the crucial role of the Salesians in the first phases of political organizing among the Shuar in Ecuador, which culminated in the influential Shuar Federation in the early 1960s (Salazar 1977; Hendricks 1991). In a pattern that has notable similarities with the CIMI experience, the initial thrust that propelled the Shuar on to Ecuador's political scene was followed by an affirmative cry of independence on the part of the Indians.

Over and above the instrumentalization of culture, Brazilian Indians have learned the political and economic value of organizing in formal associations for the purpose of dialoguing with the state, confronting it, and supplying the services the state should but often fails to provide, such as education, health, and economic projects. In just over a decade, about two hundred indigenous organizations emerged on the scene of Brazilian indigenism (Albert 2000; Ramos 2003). As the number of their partners increased, particularly with the advent of nongovernmental organizations, the political options of indigenous peoples in Brazil have diversified, and they are no longer the helpless pawns of either state or Church—or both.

Echoes from Afar

The events described here demonstrate the extent to which the instrumentalization of indigenous culture can create the conditions of possibility for the emergence of a power field in which indigenous peoples can engage in a political conversation, tense and nondialogical though it may be, with the national society and, more specifically, with the national state. As recent contentions over the concept of culture have amply demonstrated (Abu-Lughod 1991; Fitzpatrick 1995; Hannerz 1995; Stolke 1995), culture is far from being a neutral invention safely kept within the walls of academia. In contexts as explosive as Brazil's quincentennial feast, cultural diversity was most forcefully instrumentalized both by Indians and non-Indians as each party unfolded its political agenda. The colossal overreaction by state authorities dramatically revealed this point and greatly reinforced the public's awareness that Indians and Blacks, *qua* political agents, like MST militants, are here to stay. At the exact moment when the expression of cultural and ethnic diversity was being exaggeratedly repressed—and perhaps for this very reason—the visibility and legitimacy of that diversity were being impressed upon the population at large via the images that television brought into Brazilian homes. On account of the quincentennial fiasco, which resulted in a general sense of indignation, the cause of ethnic justice won a few points. In the dialectical spiral of the state thesis of uniform obedience and the ethnic antithesis of defiant plurality, one more turn toward a new synthesis was made as the double bind, in which the state attempts to trap indigenous peoples, was painfully exposed.

What comes to my mind as inspiration to unravel the meaning of the misfired quincentennial festivities is a modern classic of the ethnographic tradition, namely, Victor Turner's analysis of ritual symbolism among the African Ndembu (Turner 1957). Among the Ndembu, social unrest is usually interpreted as the revenge and punishment of ancestors who feel insulted by unsocial behavior on the part of the living. In order to appease their forebears' anger, the people need to perform certain placating rituals during which social conflicts are, as it were, exorcised. By means of what Turner called drama analysis, it is possible to identify contending actors and actions against the background of the society's structure and history.

Following Turner, I find in the fields of drama analysis a fitting thread to untangle the Porto Seguro occurrences. Indeed, in good Turnerian fashion, the nationality ritual as acted out during Brazil's five-hundredth anniversary appears as a New World version of those African dramas of affliction. Porto Seguro echoes Turner's "community of suffering" (Turner 1957), complete with farcical ancestor *wor-ship* (the pun notwithstanding), theatrical wars, religious performances, and a great deal of civil resentment. As many times before in the history of the country, in exposing its troubled identity, the Brazilian state selected the Indians as scapegoats for its seemingly perpetual malaise regarding internal differences. The "marvelous fiasco" (*Veja* 2000) of the fervently anticipated five hundred years only confirms how disturbing indigenous proximity is to the nation's self-consciousness. Reminiscent of Ndembu rituals for soothing the wrath of the ancestors, the Indians seem to represent, no matter how unconsciously, the irate ancestors of Brazilianness who emerged on the civic scene to claim redress for five centuries of disrespect. But here the Ndembu analogy stops. In reenacting a long tradition of tense coexistence with social contradictions (generated primarily by the juxtaposition of rules of matrilineality and patrilocality), the Ndembu transfer to their dead foreparents both the source of discord and its remedy by means of certain powerful rites of conviviality. But what makes the ancestors angry? It is precisely the misbehavior of their living offspring, whose misfortunes and illnesses are no more than the ancestors' signal that there is something very wrong in the realm of social affairs and in need of repair. It is the profound respect the Ndembu people have for their forebears that drives them to correct the course of their social life.

In the case of the relationship between Brazil and its indigenous peoples, it is as though the living posterity of the ancestral Indian, now metamorphosed as Brazilian citizens, rebels against this ancestry and punishes the flesh-and-blood Indians for reminding them of a social origin they would rather not have. In creating the myth of the three races, the Brazilian imagination, as acted out in state praxis, fell into its own trap: it engendered an ideal Indian ancestor only to repel him. It is against the background of this profound ambivalence that Brazil has forged its national ethos and branded its type of indigenism. The twisted history of obedience to the state and defiance by ethnic groups took one more turn toward a new synthesis. In so painfully exposing the double bind in which it attempts to trap indigenous peoples, the Brazilian state unveiled a little more of its ambivalence toward its internal differences. At the same time, it is precisely in the context of this ambivalent ethnoscape that the Indians impress their political agency upon the nation and upon the world.

Acknowledgments

My thanks to Dominique Buchillet, Roque Laraia, Wilson Trajano, and Nelly Arvelo-Jiménez for having read and commented on previous versions of this paper. I am especially grateful to Roberto Cardoso de Oliveira for his critique and information about Mexico, to Wilson Hargreaves and Doris Sommer for their important comments and bibliographical suggestions.

Notes

1. The letter addressed to the king of Portugal by Pero Vaz de Caminha, Cabral's scribe, was dated May 1. In his letter, Caminha reported his impressions during the short week Cabral spent offshore. This means that the landing occurred after April 22. In the absence of a precise logging of Cabral's arrival on the coast of Bahia, the date of discovery has been the object of historical controversy and represents yet another example of how history is reinvented according to political interests. The Gregorian Reform of the Christian calendar in 1582 was the reason for a lively dispute in the late nineteenth century between the Fourth Centennary Association and the Brazilian Historical and Geographical Institute over the effects of the sixteenth-century correction of the Brazilian discovery date. While the association favored May 3, the institute insisted on April 22, which, in 1900, coincided with Easter Sunday, a propitious coincidence that certainly contributed to the final decision (Oliveira 2000:188–89).

2. Indeed, my current research interests aim at a careful analysis of the genesis of indigenism in South American countries where indigenous populations are demographic minorities. A timid beginning to this long-term project can be found in Ramos 2002.

3. The flow of political events in Brazil has introduced an overdose of irony to ACM's indignation. In April-May 2001, ACM was entangled in a massive scandal involving breach of parliamentary decorum in the Senate. Accused of tampering with the electronic system of secret voting, he was under severe scrutiny by his peers. Public opinion demanded the cessation of his mandate precisely for his lack of that respect he had commanded from the Pataxó Indian a year earlier. He ended up resigning his senatorial mandate.

4. Much as this theme calls for full attention, this is not the appropriate moment

to address it. In fact, the various conceptions of race in Latin America represent an extremely fertile field of research in their own right. As Trouillot perceptibly points out, "*La Raza* has in Mérida or Cartagena accents unknown in San Juan or in Santiago de Chile, and Columbus wears a different hat in each of these places" (1995:136).

Questioning State Geographies of Inclusion in Argentina: The Cultural Politics of Organizations with Mapuche Leadership and Philosophy

CLAUDIA BRIONES

When examined through the lens of diversity-based rights, the 1990s appear to have been a decade of transcendental changes in Argentina. For the first time in history, the federal government and some provincial governments seem to be willing to rethink their monocultural conceptions of citizenship so that its diverse inhabitants and citizens may find more equitable spaces of expression within the public sphere. At the same time, the condemnation of discriminatory practices based on gender, religion, and physical disabilities led to the adoption of selective affirmative action measures in an effort to neutralize social inequalities.

In the specific case of indigenous rights, the National Constitutional Reform of 1994 included the explicit recognition of "the ethnic and cultural preexistence of Argentina's indigenous peoples." One of the most notable changes of this phase of the judicialization of "the indigenous question" is that for the first time the indigenous population is recognized as peoples rather than simply as dispersed communities constituted by members of one or another broad collectivity. Also for the first time, the law speaks of providing guarantees and recognizing certain rights, rather than simply of extending specific privileges. The National Congress, moreover, is instructed to "ensure" indigenous participation "in matters related to their natural resources and other interests that may affect them."

In terms of the diverse struggles of Mapuche communities, this recognition has been accompanied by a paradoxical political development. The vigorous and highly visible attempts to create an organization that could represent the entire Originary Mapuche People and Nation, which characterized the years immediately before and after the constitutional reforms, are giving way to more localized strategies and demands. Since the late 1990s, what has predominated have been the initiatives of organizations and coalitions whose claims to political representation have been limited to the specific provinces in which Mapuches are a significant percentage of the population—Neuquen, Rio Negro, and Chubut.

A closer analysis of the changing scenarios, modalities, and strategies of political demands requires an exhaustive examination of factors that I will not attempt here.[1] Although a recently formed research team is now pursuing this objective, my aims in this essay are much more circumscribed.[2] I will attempt to make some initial contributions from an anthropological perspective to an understanding of the paradox articulated above, beginning by identifying and describing the contours of its emergence.

In order to provide context, and drawing upon existing analyses, I intend to summarize the genesis and some of the characteristics of the juridical framework within which Mapuche demands are currently inscribed. I describe the organizing principles around which Mapuche organizations have articulated their demands and their all-encompassing arguments about the Originary People-Nation of Pwelmapu ("land of the east"; Argentina) during the first half of the decade—a process which was the subject of my doctoral dissertation (Briones 1999). Within this introductory framework, I will pursue an exploratory evaluation of the forms that Mapuche reflection is taking within the three provinces mentioned, identifying toward the end a number of problematic axes that emerge from the ways in which these transformations are currently being conceptualized.

Along these lines, I am interested in putting the dilemmas and critiques facing Mapuche cultural activism in perspective, particularly with regard to the ways in which it conceives and constructs its political base and to the ways it speaks on its behalf. Following Gayatri Spivak (1998), I am interested in the manner in which this activism deploys with two distinct yet interconnected meanings of representation—*Darstellung*, denoting the recognition of the Mapuche People as the unequivocal subject/agent of the process, and *Vertretung*, which points to a process of political representation that involves the substitution of that political constituency. In any case, such exegesis will also require an equally critical examination of the hegemonic demands and anthropological politics of representation through which Mapuche activism is "judged," while ignoring the paradoxical nature of the Law (*el Derecho*) as a recognition granted to "social bodies" with coherent intentions, but which must also create democratic spaces for a diversity of positions demanding representation.

Reforms and Foundational Tropes

From a regional and subnational perspective, the reform of the Argentine Constitution in 1994 is not an isolated event. Besides the fact that Argentina's constitutional reform is part of a broader regional process in which a number of Latin American countries incorporated indigenous rights to their constitutions, Argentina's reform at the federal level was both preceded and followed by equivalent reforms in a number of the country's provinces.[3] In this context, it is interesting to examine the degree to which the reform of the juridical framework was the result of a real interest in changing the practices and policies directed at indigenous peoples or more the result of a superficial accommodation to the rhetoric that has dominated international forums since 1982, when the United Nations Working Group on Indigenous Peoples was created, and more specifically since 1989, when the ILO Article on Indigenous and Tribal Peoples in Independent Nations was drafted.

As an initial attempt to point out the ambiguities surrounding this local turn, two related events need to be mentioned. Just as it is not insignificant that in 1992 the National Congress ratified ILO Article 169 as National Law N 24071, it is also not insignificant that it was not until July 2000 that the Ministry of the Exterior returned and ratified the accord before this international body.

In any case, indications that the constitutional reform of 1994 was intended to be a profound transformation of the existing political economy of diversity are minimal.[4] In fact, there is plenty of evidence to suggest that the central objective of the reform—much as in other Latin American countries—was to reform (read: reduce) the state in order to accommodate it to new processes of making capital flexibile and restructuring the international system (Iturralde 1997).[5] Even under these circumstances, however, indigenous struggles and mobilization played an important role; one important enough to have the constituent process include as one of its objectives the rewriting of the anachronistic article which assigned the task of "maintaining peaceful treatment of the Indians and promoting their conversion to Catholicism" to the National Congress.

Indigenous mobilization for constitutional reform dates back to March 1990, when the Undersecretariat for Human Rights and numerous nongovernmental organizations sponsored a symposium, the first of its kind, entitled "Indigenous Peoples in the Reform of the National Constitution" (Carrasco 2000). Yet this initiative must itself be seen as a product of the development of indigenous activism that began with the return to democratic rule in the early 1980s. It was during this period that various indigenous demands disarticulated or silenced by state terror since the 1970s began opening spaces from which they could be enunciated and resolved within the public sphere. Sometimes with the support of human rights organizations and other times without it, spaces from which indigenous demands could be articulated began to multiply after 1983. Public opinion and political pressures thus generated circumstances favorable for the passing of National Law N 23302 in 1985 and for its implementation, albeit delayed, in 1989, as well as for the mobilization in favor of indigenous legislation in the provinces. These developments, moreover, slowly began to shape not only the reorganization of indigenous activists with long trajectories of struggle, but also the emergence of a new leadership that would slowly become national in scope.[6] If the predominant "structure of feeling" during that time was anchored in an all-encompassing demand for human rights, which had been so egregiously violated by the military regime, the claims of indigenous peoples to such rights were based on the idea that civil and political society needed to redress their "historical debt" to indigenous peoples—the practices and policies that had made them "the poorest of the poor," "the most discriminated among the discriminated," and at the same time, "the richest and most distinctive among the culturally distinctive."

In this sense, the legislative agenda of 1983–84 was pioneering. It identified indigenous people as the explicit beneficiaries of legislative action in a country that until then had lacked any comprehensive indigenous legislation. In contrast with a previous history of assimilation, the new indigenous laws institutionalized notions of reparation, incorporation, insertion, and integration and established that it was neither appropriate nor sufficient in these cases for public policies of the provincial governments or the national state to operate as mere extensions of general socioeconomic rights. The spirit of these norms, however, reveals the paradoxes that exist in a country in which the very welfare state that serves as the guarantor of the rights of free citizens acts as a paternalistic guardian where its indigenous citizens are concerned.

Thus, the rhetoric about distinctive cultural identities tends to materialize as an extension of a kind of state assistance in which the uses and customs of indigenous communities are considered epiphenomenal.[7]

It is precisely in its recognition of a different "juridical personhood" that the 1994 constitution represents a substantial discursive and political shift. Yet a comparison between this new juridical rhetoric and the policies implemented by the national state and by provincial governments—which, depending on convenience, either embrace or distance themselves from laws and constitutional reforms—raises two important issues. First, the predominant attitudes and behaviors in Argentine civil and political society continue to be grounded in a neo-indigenist framework that promotes extremely limited and paternalistic modes of indigenous consultation and participation (Briones and Carrasco 2000). Second, the rethinking of notions and modes of citizenship that should have accompanied the recognition of a distinctive indigenous juridical personhood has also been limited in scope (GELIND 2000b).

The limited character of both of these processes is not surprising. Pressure from indigenous organizations as well as a regional context favorable to the recognition of indigenous rights influenced conventional wisdom in favor of the ratification of the amended legislation. Yet the constituent debates themselves, along with the declarations and policies that followed, suggest that the new juridical construction of aboriginality has had only a relative impact on what have been and continue to be the foundational tropes of the Argentine nation.

Numerous analytical works have documented these tropes in their historical and contemporary dimensions. I will thus raise only two issues here.[8] First, in the Latin American context, Argentina has been one of the countries that has most explicitly and systematically sought to negate any indigenous contribution to the constitution of a national being, which is imagined as deeply Europeanized in appearance, aspirations, and lifestyle. In this environment, indigenous people have emerged time and time again either as anachronistic testimonial subjects or as evidence of an extinction that is as imminent as it is definitive. Second, the notion of uniform whiteness has emerged from the construction of cultural hegemonies which have persuaded a large majority of the population that their "distinctiveness" is the direct result of a melting pot that was as "open to all the men of the world" as it is closed to native populations. This story has also cemented a self-image of exceptionality vis-à-vis other countries in the region. It is upon this master narrative of the nation, as well as upon the doubts and critiques it has generated, that the indigenous demands for the recognition of difference have been forged, and it is upon this narrative that these demands seek to operate.

The Generalization of Mapuche Demands

With the return to democratic rule in 1983, Mapuche political organizations at the supralocal level gained strong momentum. In several provinces and in the Federal Capital, a number of organizations with a variety of strategies and foci emerged. Some, like the Indigenous Advisory Council of Rio Negro (CAI), mobilized demands in the name of the small producers of the province, independent of their Mapuche or *criollo* (nonindigenous) origins. Others, like Nehuen Mapu (NM) in Neuquen, the Bariloche Mapuche Center (CMB) in Rio Negro, and Newentuayiñ (NT) in Buenos Aires, promoted agendas centered on the cultural recuperation of and respect for difference.[9]

By the early 1990s, a number of Mapuche organizations began to coalesce around a series of demands. Progressively, the rejection of the Quincentenary celebrations created growing opportunities to bring together indigenous leaders with differing political trajectories and from various generations. In 1992, *Taiñ KiñeGetuam* (TKG; To become one again) was founded with the purpose of coordinating the organizations that sought to articulate a shared political and ideological project through which to represent the Mapuche People as a whole.

The cultural politics of these efforts have coalesced around three central axes. First, cultural innovation has sought to strengthen the very idea of a Mapuche Originary People-Nation as a site of collective identification that transcends the national boundaries of Chile and Argentina and that cannot be fully explained by concepts such as tribe, ethnicity, or ethnic minority.[10] Second, cultural politics have sought to achieve state recognition of Mapuche rights to a territory instead of the deeds to the lands occupied by the community. Third, they have sought to identify concrete instances in which they can exercise the right to autonomy and self-determination. Supported by a strong demand for the respect of cultural difference intended to delimit the contours of other indigenous and nonindigenous communities, including Argentines, these axes are in continuous development in and through the many practices and initiatives linked to the recuperation of Mapuche culture—its rituals and ancestral knowledge, and particularly *Mapuzungun*, "the word of the earth."[11]

As a coalition of organizations built around a set of shared positions and objectives but at the same time respectful of the diverse strategies and characteristics of its member associations, TKG between 1992 and 1995 was able to integrate diverse groups, particularly from the provinces of Neuquen and Rio Negro, and establish channels of communication and collaboration with communities and organizations in La Pampa, Buenos Aires, and Chubut. In contrast to other organizations that also claim to represent a Mapuche political base, TKG's demands were centralized around a notion of indigenous rights as collective human rights that, in order to be fully recognized, would have required a rethinking not only of existing state geographies of inclusion, but also of the political economy of diversity that these geographies presuppose and create, including a revision of the principles around which states themselves are organized.[12]

A number of factors contributed to TKG's fragmentation. While some member organizations returned to their individual work following several important redefinitions, the Mapuche Confederation of Neuquen (CMN) and NM remained united under the umbrella of the Directorate of Mapuche Organizations (COM), which continues to represent the people, communities, and demands of the province of Neuquen. Over time, the Directorate of Parliament of the Mapuche People of Rio Negro also emerged as an articulation of diverse organizations advancing demands on behalf of people of Mapuche descent.[13]

At the same time this reconstruction of alliances among Mapuche organizations was taking place, there were two important attempts to further articulate both the demands of specific indigenous groups and a common platform that could unite them. In May 1996—as an initiative of indigenous organizations such as the Indigenous Association of the Argentine Republic (AIRA) and with the support of NGOs such as the National Team for Indigenous Ministries (ENDEPA)—the Program for Participation of Indigenous People (PPI) was launched, using resources provided by the national government. The main objective of this project was to generate broader debate among various indigenous constituencies regarding implementation of Article 75–17 of the national constitution (Carrasco 1997). At the same time, and within the context of a World Bank–sponsored training project targeted at indigenous populations, indigenous leaders of the southern region (members of COM) used the opportunity to launch a regional discussion forum with representatives of the Mapuche, Tehuelche, and Selk'nam/Ona peoples. Having the same explicit objectives as the PPI, this forum was able to incorporate a number of leaders who for a variety of reasons had not participated in that initiative (Briones and Carrasco 2000).

Relying on experience acquired in a number of specific political struggles, both the PPI and the Patagonia Forum organized events that pointed to the emergence of First Peoples as collective political subjects seeking to find viable ways of articulating the demands for indigenous autonomy with the growing erratic initiatives coming from the state and looking to have a broader impact on the policies of the federal government in this arena. What one also sees at this juncture is the tendency of indigenous leadership to focus on specific struggles and demands—some new, others long-standing—in their specific localities of origin. In most cases, indigenous organizations adopted strategies that targeted provincial governments as their immediate interlocutors, yet these strategies left room for appeals to the federal government as ultimate guarantor of the existing juridical frameworks.

The Provincialization of Demands

In contrast to the representative projects of Mapuche organizations in the first half of the 1990s, which claimed to speak for the Mapuche People as a whole, starting in 1997 there was a shift in strategy favoring the articulation of specific communities and organizations and the building of coalitions within each province. The uneven success of these efforts appears to be linked to the equally uneven organizational trajectories and experiences that constitute the symbolic capital of indigenous leaders and of activism within each province. An interesting question that emerges from this conjuncture is whether the apparent fragmentation is the result of the failure of previous attempts to unify and consolidate organizations or of a strategic decision taken in order to create more effective relationships between leaders and their political bases at a moment when the federal apparatus for dealing with indigenous people's concerns was being downsized. To elaborate upon this question, I want to examine the form and content of the declarations and actions of Mapuche activists in the provinces of Chubut, Rio Negro, and Neuquen, focusing on press releases, denunciations, and requests for support that circulated electronically within the diverse support networks linked to the indigenous struggles.

Chubut Province

When compared with Rio Negro and Neuquen, the Chubut case has two relevant particularities. On one hand, some of the communities in the province explicitly recognize their mixed Tehuelche/Mapuche makeup. The emergence, on the other hand, of an urban-based association such as the October 11th Organization of Mapuche Tehuelche Communities, which sought to articulate the demands of different communities and groups in the province, takes place relatively late.

The statements of indigenous leaders in Chubut reveal a certain tendency to publicize very specific cases or to elaborate lists of the diverse problems affecting the communities of the province. The first tendency is clearly exemplified by the case of the Pillan Mahuiza community, which was brought to public attention in May 2000. In this case, the recuperation of 250 hectares of land by some families in the Corcovado area of the community is presented as a response to a twofold aggression. The first is "the enclosure using wire fences by the Chubut Provincial Police" that isolates "our cemetery." And the second is a response to "the government's boycott and its stubborn negation of our rights"—a boycott that besides being recently "intensified" is also measured by "its effect on the policies of the Corcovado Electricity Cooperative, which is refusing to provide us with services, using the excuse that we do not have property titles." Yet while at the time of these statements the land recuperation had been under way for five months, it was a specific event that triggered the signatories' plea for the solidarity "of organizations that support indigenous peoples, human rights, and of the men and women of good will who, much like us, dare to dream, to struggle and to build a better future for all of us." Through the "testimonies of some *pu lamguen* [brothers and sisters]," it had been learned that "when people attempted to bring their animals onto the recuperated lands, they had been threatened with repression and arrest by the Police" and told that "it would not take much for these threats to become a sad reality."

In concrete terms, this declaration makes a series of demands on the provincial government and requests that people send "letters or emails expressing their rejection" to the president of the Republic, the governor of Chubut Province, and the general coordinator of the National Institute for Indigenous Affairs. The demands, focused on putting an end to the provocation and on achieving recognition of the legitimacy of the land invasion, are based not only on the recuperation of the cemetery as part of the cultural patrimony of the group, but also on the right to a have a decent place to live.

On the occasion of Indigenous Week, which is celebrated in Argentina every year on April 19, the October 11th Organization coordinated two events, described in the following communiqués. On April 17, 2000, a "Mapuche Gathering took place in the city of Esquel (Chubut)." At this event, participants presented an assessment of the situation and an explanation of the objectives of the event, which were accompanied by a set of "immediate demands on the provincial and national governments."[14] Participants also emphasized the demand for a "speedy solution" to the conflicts over land that "affect our communities today." These conflicts were enumerated one by one and were usually followed by accusations regarding the presence of strangers on the lands and demands for titles and other measures. The statement concludes by affirming that "it is impossible to celebrate a week dedicated to First Peoples in light of such an evaluation" and also remarks that "we continue to stand firm by our demands because we are convinced that we will be able to transform a racist state into one that recognizes the cultural diversity that exists in the country."

On April 20 and 21, a "Mapuche-Tehuelche Gathering" took place in the city of Rawson, Chubut. This event brought together "brothers and sisters from the various communities and representative organizations of the Mapuche people in the Province of Chubut," under the slogan, "United for Our Rights." In addition to stating that they "wanted to reaffirm the conclusions and demands that emerged at the Mapuche-Tehuelche gathering in the city of Esquel . . . with the presence of brothers from the northeast of the province," they incorporated the voice of an urban community from the eastern part of Chubut Province which was demanding the return of a cemetery and of the "remains of our ancestors." This call was made primarily to the provincial government, based on the notion that Argentina is a "racist state" that needs to be transformed so that the nation can recognize "the cultural diversity that exists in the country."

In general terms, it is interesting that these documents from Chubut make little if any explicit references to existing juridical frameworks, either at the national or provincial level. The documents call on the "governors of this province," hoping they will arrive at "conclusions which reflect the feelings of the Mapuche people—the Tehuelche from Chubut Province—in a serious and mature way." Their objective is to inaugurate a "new relationship based on respect and recognition" that can make cultural diversity a source of wealth and interchange, and never again one of negation and repression.

Rio Negro Province

Building on the organizational experience developed in the province starting in 1984, on the creation of the Council for the Development of Indigenous Communities mandated by provincial indigenous law 2287/88,[15] and on the comparatively recent coordination of groups and communities through the indigenous initiative of the Directorate of the Parliament of the Mapuche People in Rio Negro, the shape of indigenous struggles in this case reveals some interesting differences when compared to those in Chubut and Neuquen.

The first of these is the increase in the number of recipients. Although the provincial government remains the main addressee, these documents may also be addressed, depending on the specificities of each case, to both municipal and federal authorities. On a number of occasions, there were polemics that directly involved other sectors of civil society.[16]

There were also specific accusations and requests for assistance centering on specific conflicts in which specific communities were involved, much as in Chubut and Neuquen. Although for different reasons, most of these communities are involved in litigation, either as a way to protest the granting of community lands to private enterprises for commercial exploitation, as in the case for Lof Leufuche de Paso Córdova, or to drive out "intruders" from community lands, as in the case of Lof Casiano from the Ingeniero

Jacobacci Mapuche community and the Kom Kiñe Mu community from Arroyo las Minas.

There are a number of notable aspects to these claims. In each case, local communities generate multiple declarations, communiqués, or transcripts written either by the community itself or its legal advisors, by the Directorate of the Parliament of the Mapuche People of Rio Negro, or sometimes by other Mapuche organizations from the province that are supporting the particular case.[17] At the same time, some of the signatories position themselves in a double role as members of a particular organization or as counselors of the Council for the Development of Indigenous Communities (CODECI).

While some documents abound with judicial details that describe the legal stages of the conflict, most of them contextualize it in the broader juridical frameworks (provincial, national, and international) upon which the indigenous position is based—either by enumerating the indigenous rights that have been violated or the legal provisions that have not been thoroughly applied. It is also common for some documents to denounce forthcoming provincial policies that are perceived to be motivated by the governments' commitments to local economic interests or to international financial agencies like the World Bank. In any case, three points regarding these texts need to be highlighted. First, besides framing the demands for the resolution of specific conflicts in terms of existing legislation, the texts firmly invoke the institutionalized political commitments between the government and the indigenous leaders of the provincial indigenous organizations or between the government and the provincial Mapuche organizations themselves. Second, the texts propose concrete alternatives for the resolution of conflicts in the context of existing legislation. Finally, it is interesting to note how the Directorate of the Parliament of the Mapuche People of Rio Negro alternates between demands that employ the rhetoric of the defense of indigenous rights made possible by the 1994 Constitutional Reform and specific demands for state assistance which operationalize the measures of "assistance and protection" stipulated by the indigenist legislation of the 1980s.

In the opinion of some of its members, these oscillations reflect the varied composition and trajectory of the directorate's member organizations as well as the political weight that accompanies the fact that some members of the directorate also participate as counselors in the Organ of Implementation of the provincial Indigenous Law. These two options are not unrelated to the chain of equivalencies which were historically nurtured at the provincial level by successive hegemonic interpellations—a chain in which "the Mapuche problem" operates as an index signifying and contextualizing that of the most vulnerable and dispossessed sectors of the population (Briones 1999). In this context, it comes as little surprise that Article 53 of the provincial indigenous legislation of 1988 establishes that "the present law will be applicable to rural inhabitants in need whose situation is similar to that of indigenous people."

In any case, amidst multiple accusations and demands, what appears to predominate in this province are the demands for the full implementation of the existing juridical architecture rather than demands that this architecture be modified to make room for more adequate notions of Mapuche "needs and interests." As we will see, it is this latter line of argument that predominates in the statements of the COM of Neuquen.

Neuquen Province

In Neuquen, a number organizations with indigenous philosophy and leadership are currently working to promote the rights and improve the living conditions of the Mapuche People. All of them organize events that, in different ways and to different degrees, question the state's past and present practices and geographies of inclusion. In their strategies, they mobilize both the ideal visions engendered by recent juridical reforms as well as those generated by the everyday practices of political and civil society. In the interest of brevity, I will focus here on the events and campaigns organized by the COM—a coalition which, as we have seen, comprises the CMN and NM— whose projects tend to have the greatest impact and visibility in the public sphere at the provincial, national, and international level.

Supporting the demands of communities and actively participating in numerous battles over specific disputes and rights have been important parts of COM's organizational experience. The involvement of six communities from the Alumine Department in what became known as the Pulmari Case, for example, has led to a highly conflictive process that has been ongoing for over six years. During this time, not only has the notion of indigenous territory been elaborated vis-à-vis the notion of "lands traditionally occupied," but the organization put forth a proposal for a "protected indigenous territory" and cooperation based on "a Mapuche idea in progress." The group has been successful in securing financial support from the World Bank.[18]

At the same time, support for Lof Kallfvkvra in his struggle to obtain juridical personhood through the elaboration of a statute based on "Mapuche institutionality" rather than on the organizational frameworks imposed by existing laws has generated numerous opportunities for thinking about notions of indigenous autonomy and self-rule. The resolution of the *Nor Feleal* (Internal Tribunal) with respect to a crime of grave injury committed in that community led to a "conflict of competency" (Falaschi 2000) between the Mapuche community tribunal and a local court. The episode helped to open a debate about the relationships among autonomy, indigenous law, juridical pluralism, and the administration of justice—a debate which generated elements that were later used by legal experts in their deliberations regarding the reform of the Procedural Penal Code of Neuquen Province.[19]

Another arena of sustained conflict has been the accusations on the part of the communities of Kaxipayiñ and Paynemil about the pollution of communal water with heavy metals and other toxic residues from the extraction of hydrocarbons in their region. As a result of the death of livestock and the intoxication of children and adults, both communities—and more recently the communities of Gelay Ko and Wiñoy Folil—have organized numerous events and campaigns directed at the "three powers" of the federal, provincial, and local governments, at the oil companies, at international financial institutions (the IMF and the World Bank), at the labor unions, at environmental organizations, and at Neuquen society more generally, demanding that each sector assume its respective responsibilities to avoid "harm to the environment, the destruction of culture, the theft of resources and the economic dependency" tied to the expansion of the oil industry. In this context, the COM's support has emphasized a notion of "cultural-ecological debt" linked to the negation of their constitutional rights to be consulted about and to participate in the management of the natural resources in their communities.

Alongside the production of numerous documents, all of these conflicts have involved either dialogue or confrontation with representatives from the three branches of the provincial and national governments as well as with civil society organizations and international solidarity groups. At various times, COM achieved a sustained presence of indigenous issues in local and even national media, and it was not unusual for COM activists or their legal advisors to publish editorials in newspapers with provincial circulation.

Looking at COM's trajectory over time, it would seem that the purpose of their strategy to focus on specific cases and turn them into nationally known struggles has advanced their political standing in three ways. First, they have put the existing juridical framework into action, taking the initiative to implement the rights which authorities evoke more often than they enforce. Second, their activities have been nourished by a reflexive cultural production that has imbued general concepts such as people, autonomy, and territory with local meaning. And finally, having already explored the limits of existing legal frameworks, they have proposed appropriate modification as circumstances have evolved.

What needs to be highlighted here is that in this series of documents, there is a dual tendency that becomes increasingly visible—to present proposals as well as demands, on the one hand, and to frame these proposals within a critical understanding of the functioning of the state and the nation, on the other. The proposals seek to involve nonindigenous civil society without renouncing the strong claims of difference and structures of belonging. The tendencies described are readily apparent in the resolutions of the *xv Gvlamtuwvn*, or Parliament, that took place in December 2000 with the purpose of revitalizing the leadership of the CMN,[20] as well as in a previous manuscript (Coordination of Mapuche Organizations 1999) that was taken up at the event.

Briefly, the *xv Gvlamtuwvn* resolved to demand that, besides incorporating the indigenous rights recognized by the national constitution, there be a reform of the provincial constitution in order to "enable the *further recognition of rights and instititions*, to strengthen those rights in practice in light of the bicultural reality of the province of Neuquen" (emphasis added). The proposal states that "given the qualitative and quantitative importance of the Mapuche People in the province," the reformed constitution should also include the "recognition of the organizations and institutions of the

Mapuche People of Neuquen." References are made to *Meli Wixan Mapu* (MWM), also known as the Parliament of the Mapuche People of Neuquen, the structure and functioning of which are discussed in a document of 1999 that already reveals the tendency toward the provincialization of political organization and indigenous demands I have been describing.[21]

Seen in its entirety, however, the central strategy in the proposal focuses on the status that "exisiting national legislation" affords indigenous Argentine communities in order to establish the grounds for a possible constitutional reform in Neuquen. Interestingly, this struggle for a space within the province has been accompanied by a rethinking of concepts and frameworks that transcend the local level and that are far from consensual among nonindigenous political elites and juridical professionals. Working from what Blommaert (1997) would call an ideology of the "fixed text" of the national constitution—a stable, clear, precise semantic unit with transparent meanings—this proposal is simultaneously attempting to channel the course of discourse (Villalón and Angelieri 1997) regarding the Mapuche question in Neuquen in and through the metadiscursive strategy of limiting the interpretations of the federal juridical framework that may be considered valid.[22]

Yet promoting the idea of the people as a "collective entity with a differentiated culture and spatiality" creates an interesting tension within the tenets of Neuquen-based activism. While on one hand it suggests a strong relationship among group, patrimony, and place, it also condenses and responds to "the flexibility that characterizes living cultures." In this respect, insisting that the majority of indigenous people "live in the capital cities or in the localities closest to their communities" functions as a way to introduce complexity into the debates in order to elaborate forms of representation that are not limited "to the peasant or to the rural" (COM 1999).

Provisional Analyses and Reformulations

In the course of this project, a number of paradoxes have emerged. Following the constitutional reform of 1994, the Argentine state has signaled that it wants to implement new geographies of inclusion. Through its actions, however, it has shown itself to be incapable of generating effective solutions to the socioeconomic and political exclusion of sectors that are exercising an increasingly "low-intensity" form of citizenship (O'Donnell 1993). For their part, the indigenous movement, which at one time was able to establish and represent a unified Mapuche people at a national level, is now experiencing the provincialization of indigenous demands and the fragmentation of coalitions.

The first issue leads one to ask whether the conversion of aboriginality into a legislative issue has produced deep changes in the practices of political and civil society. Without detracting from the visibility acquired by the indigenous question in the past few years, a brief analysis of these practices suggests that both the federal and provincial governments are far from incorporating into their policies and practices a set of coordinated practices through which their constitutional commitments on this issue could be honored. While Hale and Millamán (in this volume) rightly emphasize the paradoxical effects of a "neoliberal multiculturalism" that is at once intensifying the flexibility of capital and at the same time magnifying cultural differences, I would suggest that in the Argentine case these processes are anchored in a cosmetic reformulation of the geographies of exclusion which leaves the existing political economy of diversity intact.

The second issue, however, raises a crucial question. Is the provincialization of demands an effect of an "induced agency"?[23] or has the experience accumulated by indigenous activists over the years shown them the necessity of making such a change? Have they realized perhaps that a "strategic multiplicity" (Hale 1996) may allow them to represent homogeneities and differences simultaneously and at multiple levels more effectively than a global "strategic essentialism"[24] as well as help them to counter the closures imposed by a "strategic authenticity"?[25]

In order to answer these questions, it is necessary to weigh the explicative value of these concepts in terms of both the *Darstellung* (the symbolic representation of the world) and the *Vertretung* (political representation) that they evoke (Spivak 1988). By focusing my closing remarks on these points, I also want to reflect on the risks of anthropological and indigenous politics of representation, taking into account a factor that is rarely considered within the circuits of academic knowledge production, a factor I am calling the aporia of "the glass half empty or half full."

Darstellung, or the Symbolic Re-presentation of the World

When it comes to analyzing the successes and failures of indigenous activism, many observers, including myself, experience a certain discomfort with regard to the ways in which our indigenous interlocutors re-present the social limits that separate them from the nonindigenous population. There is a shared concern about the possible reification or hardening of identities that have stronger links to historical and politically contingent expressions than to essential or primordial attributes, although this does not mean they are arbitrary. On this question, there are two debates I would like to bring to the fore.

First—and at least in my case—my concern with not revealing politically sensitive information has led me to focus my analyses on public documents, most of which are intended for nonindigenous audiences. These kinds of cultural texts are characterized by an articulation of social boundaries that tends to be much more assertive than reflexive with respect to the causalities of their own production and the blurring of these boundaries that emerges in informal conversation with the same individuals. Following the logic employed by Hanna Verber in her examination of the notion of "self-orientalization" (Jackson 1996), I wonder to what degree we engage the task of making explicit that the practices we consider "essentializing" emerge in contexts that favor or enable this kind of reflexivity, or whether we voice generalized opinions about situations that should, above all, appear as "specific instances of the manipulation of images on the part of a few indigenous spokespersons who are operating under pressure within a hostile medium" (Verber 1998:389).

Second—and taking into account the importance of whether the world is being re-presented for oneself or for strangers—I wonder if what we consider to be a remedy for the risks of strategic essentialism should lead us to recognize a multiplicity that involves the simple proliferation of new levels of essentialism, or whether such a task requires making room for unduly emphasized points of tension around each and every one of the different subject positions that are recognized or marked. Let's concentrate, for example, on what in our case appears to be the most all-encompassing form of essentialism. In this case, and although based on a logic of binary oppositions, the very idea of Originary Mapuche People-Nation has not precluded the emergence of particular logics of articulation with groups deemed to fall outside that category: for example, the discourses that link to the problems of small-scale producers in Rio Negro or the efforts in Neuquen to imagine the characteristics and policies of a truly pluriethnic and intercultural state for *all* citizens.

At the same time, Mapuche organizations have been in a process of re-historicizing their notions of belonging in a number of ways. This leads me to believe that their strategic essentialism—including the either overt or covert practices of racialization that have accompanied the transformation of membership into a legislative matter—has less to do with their dehistoricization of interethnic relations, as Handler points out (1985:171), than with the fact that nationalism and ethnicity are social phenomena constituted not simply by cultural differences, but also by a particular theory of cultural difference. In this context, it appears that the foremost challenge facing both Mapuches and ourselves is the deconstruction of the broader social theories that today are animating the hegemonic recognition of diversity within a "new order" that, since the end of the Cold War, has enabled the "free expression of differences," but has also constructed a variety of fundamentalisms as its archenemy.

Finally, rather then naturalizing indigenous experience as such, when indigenous activists call for a commitment to ideological decolonization, they are recognizing that their life experience has been mediated by a *Wigka*, or nonindigenous, re-presentation of the world. In this context, they also understand that the possibility to produce signification from outside the stigmatizing reality which has shaped their experience depends less on their ability to privilege specific experiences as such, and more on their ability to rethink their experience from a Mapuche re-presentation of the world.

Amidst all these questions, the formulation of a notion of a People that is broad enough to incorporate the diversity of circumstances and experiences—rural and urban, peasant and proletarian—constitutes a kind of strategic essentialism that enables a space for the strategic multiplicity which concerns Hale. Yet this strategy does not resolve the question raised by Mallon regarding the ways in which, in the name of a strategic authenticity, specific sectors police the boundaries of permissible identities. As Ranger (1989) and Desai (1993:122) both point out, counterinventions tend to privilege some at the expense of other *others*, making their emancipatory or oppressive character dependent on the work, the relative success, the context, and the objectives of those who are imagining/inventing the specific contours of belonging. Yet this exceeds the arena of the symbolic re-presentation of the world and its subjects and leads us to questions regarding the political representation of the constituents whose needs and interests are at stake.

Vertretung, or Political Representation of Constituents

The formation of a moral and intellectual leadership is a process that requires the formulation of *abstract*, general demands that can encompass *specific* demands. In this process, groups of leaders are constituted as such in a double labor of articulation, which involves the construction of particular sectors as a relatively homogenous political base or constituency despite their inevitable heterogeneity as well as the mobilization of this base behind a notion of the common good.

The critiques of strategic essentialism or the limitations of strategic authencity focus on the identity politics of indigenous organizations and on the construction on consensus and consent within particular groups. Yet these detract attention from two other aspects that, because they play a central role in this internal dynamic of representation, need to be incorporated into this debate. While the first of these acquires importance owing to the fact that the efficacy of movement is related not only to its identity politics but also to its politics of influence, inclusion, and reform,[26] the other is linked to the need for indigenous leaders to acquire legitimacy outside the boundaries of the group, since his or her representativity is permanently questioned by and from multiple state institutions and other organizations, each "according to their own criteria of 'appropriateness.'" In both cases, the disparities within regional formations appear to be—as Hall (1986) suggests—linked to the degree to which these factors determine the tempo and the direction of demands.

Although I am still far from providing a satisfactory explanation of why indigenous demands are being provincialized and of what directions that development is taking, it is significant that the very organizations that at a particular moment saw the fracture of TKG as inevitable—and explain it as a result of the lack of conditions for a comprehensive kind of political representation, the lack of leadership capacity to provide concrete answers to the needs and realities faced by the Mapuche population in the diverse regions in which they live—are now questioning the decentralization program of the National Institute for Indigenous Affairs. Thus, I would like to offer a dual argument that reveals some complex tension, not so much to make this development less ambiguous, but to suggest on the basis of this ambiguity a couple of explanatory clues.

—Despite notable differences in terms of scope, style, and articulation, all Mapuche demands have in some manner exceeded the limits of the hegemonic political arenas within each province. Thus, none of them have been merely "clientelistic requests." Because of the explicit metadiscursive battles that it has unleashed, this process cannot be explained as the result of "induced agency."[27]

—And particularly at a time when federal indigenist policy appears to be retracting and casually suggesting the relevance of administrative decentralization, the debate over whether the provincialization of demands is a response to a growing indigenous consciousness regarding the value of multiplicity or simply a symptom of politically marginal strategies appears to be less relevant than examining the ways in which the diverse lines of critique revealed in contemporary indigenous demands reinscribe historically articulated contradictions at the level of the praxis of the provincial and national government.

While a superficial comparison of the ways in which demands are articulated in each of the three provinces might suggest tremendous differences in the capacities and efficacies of different organizations, one comes to a somewhat different conclusion when one takes into account the political starting points of these organizations and abandons an exclusively instrumentalist notion of the political. In a country that has denied the existence of indigenous people and that even today has difficulties visualizing its internal diversity in positive terms, the very fact that, at a general level, organizations from different provinces have formulated demands on the basis of a politics of identity that takes at its center the idea of a *Mapuche People-Nation* is an accomplishment. This is the result of the success of a politics of influence that has been able to expand the discursive field to a point at which certain ideas that initially provoked fierce opposition—like the very notions of autonomy or People—are now not so far beyond the common sense of both indigenous and nonindigenous people.

With respect to the internal political representativity and the ways in which it has been projected outwards, the efficacy of each organization or of the different coalitions appears to depend less on the inherent contradiction of Mapuche *Darstellung* and *Vertretung*—as Spivak has suggested—and more on a series of other factors. Most immediately, these factors range from the disparity of political assessments and styles of consensus building to the length of time that organizations have been working and the resources they have been capable of mobilizing. In less immediate terms, understanding these factors requires understanding these group trajectories in relation to local styles of interpellation and the construction of hegemony.

Thus, probably not coincidentally, it is in Neuquen that the strongest critiques regarding the limited scope of federal and provincial recognition of diversity have emerged, since it is the only one of the three provinces considered in which, since the late 1950s, there have been forays into what we have defined elsewhere as "tolerant pluralism" (Briones and Díaz 2000). Because it inscribes "Mapuche-ness" as a valued patrimony of provincial identity, COM considers this "official way of doing politics" as a state "legacy and practice" that is as efficient in producing paralyzing agreements with respect to belongings and exclusion as it is counterproductive to the process of indigenous political organization on the basis of their own needs and interests. Thus, it was probably the ability of Neuquen's elite to play with minor concessions as the "benevolent face" of subordination that provided successive provincial governments of the same party with effective and lasting mechanisms to co-opt and even expropriate particular indigenous demands. This "official way of doing politics" paved the way for indigenous activism—a path that now requires explicit confrontation to unmask subtle government strategies that have repeatedly bamboozled their base.

There are, moreover, multiple and obvious differences between the three provinces that I will not address here. Nevertheless, I would like to bring one final point to the discussion, a point which touches upon the ways in which our trajectory as socially inscribed subjects affects our evaluation of that representativity.

On the Anthropological Politics of Representation

When reading academic work on the praxis of indigenous activism, most people, it would seem, oscillate between two perspectives. While some begin by emphasizing its achievements and end by highlighting its limitations or pending challenges, others tend to follow the opposite route. Although pointing to both successes and shortcomings suggests a balanced reading of reality, this order of presentation can lead to different conclusions, depending on whether the same glass appears half empty or half full. What is interesting here is that our premises include the possibility that indigenous praxis—like all subaltern praxis—may be as contradictory as hegemonic practices of subordination, yet we prefer explanations that make these ambiguities less ambiguous. Our political consciousness is apparently having trouble catching up with our discursive consciousness which can now appreciate the capacity of hegemonic processes to proceed without discounting cultural difference.

By sharing this perception, it is not my intention to call for the search for an equidistant point of observation anchored in an impulse to neutralize our trajectories as socially inscribed subjects. For a number of reasons, we empathize with oppositional practices that lead us to highlight their distinctiveness or that are motivated by logics of confluence that can strengthen our appreciation of hybridization processes. Making these trajectories explicit can, however, help us avoid already prescribed paths or reasoning that tend to lead us to one or another conclusion. I would even venture to say that, just as privileging the connections makes us keenly aware of the risks linked to the essentializing of differences, highlighting the particularities leads us to emphasize the dangers of co-optation and to read potential political convergences as accommodation to hegemonic discourse. Subscribing to one or another conclusion, moreover, does not mean we can avoid having the opinion that indigenous people betray "their" cause each time they change course in their political struggle when we as observers believe they *should* maintain it (Ramos 1988).

In this context, denying the preferences that emerge from our political positioning is absurd, yet reproducing that hegemonic double standard that evaluates the "authenticity" of indigenous peoples and their leaders with different criteria (Conklin and Graham 1995) is irresponsible. Here I am referring to the fact that, when it comes time to judge indigenous practices, anthropologists also run the risk of operating from an idealized notion of horizontal, democratic, and face-to-face ties between leaders and their followers. Based on a demand for transparency and immediacy that we generally do not make of other political representatives, this position can even lead us to demand that indigenous people advance particular transformations that no other sector has achieved.

While these are the risks of our explicative propensities, it appears that we still need to generate antidotes so that our anthropological politics of representation of the indigenous politics of representation is consistent with the idea that aboriginality, ethnicity, and race are not essences, but sociohistorical constructions under dispute through multiple kinds of social agency. One possible antibody may be taking particular concepts (induced agency, self-orientalization, type of essentialism, etc.) less as explicative tools than as categories that are descriptive of phases or aspects of the processes we seek to analyze—in other words, as heuristic notions with which to explore movement that may at times be contingent, at times long-lasting, and always grounded in correlations of power.

Moreover, if evaluating the relationships between initial conditions and the directions taken by social action always appears more relevant than assessing the danger of the co-optation of indigenous activism in a vacuum, or highlighting the inherent contradictions in the indigenous *Darstellung* and *Vertretung*, then what happens to the possibility of formulating general explanations?

By proposing to follow these trajectories and taking the diverse conditions of existence and political contexts within which Mapuches attempt to advance their politics of identity, influence, inclusion, and reform as a situated parameter of evaluation, I am not denying that indigenous activism may confront common challenges at the macro level. In fact, it does so to the degree that such activism seeks to recenter transnationalized constructions of aboriginality. What I am suggesting is that, because these are mediated by specific processes of state- and nation-building, and even transnationalized politics and constructions of alterity, they are inscribed within idiosyncratic dilemmas that are often confronted in equally idiosyncratic ways. In this context, the objective of our appeal to the comparative method should be less the isolation of the general characteristics of indigenous activism than the identification of the weight of—and the possible forms of opposition to—its limiting factors.

As I see it, my concern with the possibility of generating historically situated explanations is not a result of my mistrust of anthropological generalization, but a part of an attempt to find axes of comparison that may help establish productive generalizations. In principle, this appears to evoke Geertzian premises, such as the production of thick descriptions instead of codifications of abstract regularities or of generalizations not between but within particular cases (Geertz 1973). Nevertheless, I hope to have established that I am less interested in the thick description of networks of signification than in explaining the emergence, recreation, and transformation of "contact zones" (Pratt 1987) as a field in which the superimposition and the conflict over meanings—as well as the rearticulation of identities, equivalences, and demands—are materializations that are equally possible in the realms of interaction and social control.

Notes

1. It would require, for example, not only a detailed evaluation of the changes in federal indigenous policy that took place within the very process of reform and with the inauguration of a new administration in 1999, but also a linking of these transformations with contradictory initiatives and effects of decentralization policies, which affected an arena much broader than just those linked to "the indigenous question." At the same time, it would require an evaluation of the equivalent changes that have taken place within each provincial government as well as of the trajectories of different indigenous organizations and coalitions, their schisms, and their rearticulations.

2. In January 2001, with funds from the University of Buenos Aires and under my supervision, we launched a research project entitled "Aboriginality, Provinces and Nation: Constructions of Alterity in Provincial Contexts."

3. See Carrasco (2000) and GELIND (2000b) for an analysis of how the constitutional reforms that take place during the same period in several provinces incorporate the amendment of national juridical frameworks. In the specific cases we are concerned with, while some provincial constitutions share the conception and the rhetoric put forth in the national constitution, the reforms in Neuquen (1994), Rio Negro (1988), and Chubut (1994) fall short of the basic guidelines established in the Federal Carta Magna; Neuquen's reform reflects much more reluctance than the reform in

Chubut as far as putting in place the necessary mechanisms to effectively safeguard the recognition that has been granted to all indigenous peoples in the national territory.

4. The concept of the political economy of diversity refers to the complex articulations between the dominant economic system, social structure, juridico-political institutions, and the ideological apparatuses that predominate within a social formation during a particular historical period; more specifically, it points to the ways in which ethnic, racial, regional, national, religious, gender-related, and age differences provide the bases—as Hall (1996) points out—for modes of economic exploitation and for differentiated strategies of political and ideological incorporation of a fractured labor force.

5. In Argentina, moreover, the short-term task of guaranteeing the reelection to the presidency of Dr. Carlos S. Menem.

6. For a history of indigenous activism in Argentina before the transition of 1983, see, for example, Carrasco (1991) and Serbin (1981).

7. For an analysis of the production of national and provincial legislation of the period, see GELIND (2000a).

8. See, for example, Briones (1998a,b,c and in press); Briones and Lenton (1997); Carrasco (1991); Lazzari (2000); Lenton (1992, 1994, 1998); Slavsky (1992); Svampa (1994).

9. Yet the emergence of supralocal Mapuche organization is not only the result of the return to democratic rule. In fact, in 1970, close to thirty Mapuche communities came together to found the Indigenous Federation of Neuquen (known today as the Mapuche Confederation of Neuquen, CMN) with the purpose coordinating and representing "all officially recognized indigenous and tribal federations and groups that are recognized as such by decrees, national or provincial censuses, or any other public document, as well as those that may join in the future on the basis of their traditional forms of organization" (in Falaschi 1994:8).

10. Like so many other indigenous peoples in the Americas, the Mapuche have also ended up in more than one nation-state. The inflexibility with which national borders were imposed progressively diminished cross-border exchanges and eroded a common sense of belonging. This process began to be reversed in the early 1990s, when links were established between Mapuche organizations in the two countries.

11. In contrast to the preoccupations of other indigenous peoples in Argentina, one of the principal concerns of many Mapuche elders and activists is that a significant proportion of their population is monolingual Spanish speakers. Subscribing to a linguistic ideology that establishes intimate links between language, culture, and collectivity, *Taiñ KiñeGetuam* (TKG) and its member organizations have undertaken

numerous activities geared toward the recuperation, teaching and standardization of Mapuzungun. These efforts were accompanied by very substantive discussions regarding the coverage, objectives, and strategies of the "right to bilingual and intercultural education," which is guaranteed by the constitution.

12. My use of the concept of state geographies of inclusion is inspired by Grossberg's proposal (1992) for analyzing the manner in which systems of identification and belonging are produced, structured, and utilized within social formations through the articulations of "machines" that both "differentiate" and "territorialize." According to the author, while "differentiating machines" are linked to the truth regimes responsible for the production of systems of social difference and identity, "territorializing machines" are the result of regimes of power or jurisdiction that locate systems of circulation between "places" or temporary coordinates of belonging that are affectively identified for and by individual and collective subjects. It is around such nodes that subjects articulate their own maps of signification, desire, and pleasure, yet are always shaped by the "structured mobility" produced by existing structures of circulation and of differential access to a determined set of politically articulated historical practices. As they emerge from the strategic interplay between axes of articulation (territorialization) and sites of interruption (deterritorialization) that shape the conditions of possibility for specific kinds of movement (change) and stability (identity), this "structured mobility" enables equally specific modalities of action and agency. According to Grossberg, then, because these axes determine the kinds of places people can occupy, the ways in which they occupy them, the relative spaces that people have to maneuver, and how they are able to maneuver within them, they produce different modalities of action and agency that reflect not only the unequal distribution of cultural and economic capital, but also the differentiated access to the possible life trajectories within which these resources may be acquired.

Starting with this premise, my notion of state geographies of inclusion refers to the historically situated and changing articulations through which state institutions at various levels—including the federal government and each provincial state as pluricentric and multidimensional formations around which different kinds of political discourses and practices condense in the context of the systematic regulation and normalization of the social (Hall 1985)—assess and locate their "internal diversity" within time and space. Within this framework, if the nation-as-state operates as the symbolic territory against which diverse kinds of "internal others" are constituted and circulate, state geographies of inclusion point to that hegemonic cartography that fixes the differential altitudes and latitudes of uniformity and alterity upon which sociocultural hierarchies and systems of circulation of different types of "internal others" are based. By attributing differentiated consistencies and fissures to the (self-)assigned environments of diverse social groups, these geographies of inclusion—which are simultaneously geographies of exclusion—seek to inscribe within the "meaning of belonging" the textures of the demands that will be made (Balibar 1991). Their ability to regulate the political action, conflict, and struggles surrounding subjectivity and agency is the product of a spatiotemporal distribution of uniformities and differences that affects the production, circulation, and consumption of idiosyncratic arguments and practices of belonging of "internal others," "others" that are (self-)constructed as partially segregated around characteristics that are supposedly "theirs" but always defined through a triangulation that distinguishes them and repositions them vis-à-vis the "national subject" (Briones 1998b), as well as vis-à-vis the "provincial subject." With respect to the notion of the political economy of diversity, see note 4.

13. For a description of these processes, the political agendas of TKG, and its member organizations before and after the breakdown of the coalition, see Briones 1999.

14. In this assessment, the participants reaffirmed the necessity of elaborating a "political project for coexistence" based on the institutions and the cultural principles of the Mapuche people. The issues of concerns listed included unemployment, health, education, and land. A good number of the demands revolve around a more general position that the state must implement the rights established by the national and the provincial constitutions, particularly with respect to the "a priori and permanent consultation" with indigenous communities. They also demanded the right to communal property, although not over traditionally occupied lands, but over "ancestral territorial spaces." The assessment also requested logistical and financial support for development policies that would be elaborated and administered by Mapuche-Tehuelche communities themselves and that would bypass the usual intermediaries so that all the resources would reach the communities.

15. This law defines the Council for the Development of Indigenous Communities (CODECI) as its [*autoridad de aplicacion*], attributing to it both a consultative and resolving character (art. 7). The CODECI will be constituted by an executive council comprising three representatives from the Indigenous Advisory Council (CAI) and two from the executive branch of the provincial government, as well as a consultative council comprising seven CAI representatives and seven delegates from the divisions of the executive branch. The designation of the president of the executive council is an attribute of the executive and is to be chosen from the three elected CAI representatives.

16. In April 2000, for example, the Directorate of the Parliament of the Mapuche People of Rio Negro addressed the case of three local clerics who had claimed in a

newspaper interview that "the Araucanos had exterminated the Tehuelches." The directorate's document makes a detailed refutation of their statements, juxtaposing "official history" with the events that "remain present in the memory of our people."

17. In this case, the text often ends with the phrase "*marici weu, marici weu!!*" (Ten times we are alive, . . . ten times we will triumph), a slogan introduced and profusely disseminated by TKG. It appears in current texts of the October 11th Organization of Chubut as well as in those of the COM in Neuquen. For a history of the instrumentalities of this expression, see Briones (1999).

18. For a detailed description of the evolution of this conflict, see Carrasco and Briones (1996) and Briones (1999). With respect to Mapuche conceptions of development and of a "protected indigenous territory," see *Coordinación de Organizaciones Mapuche* (in press).

19. For an analysis of the origins and the negotiations around the Statute of Lof Kallfvkvra, see Briones (1997). For an evaluation of the relationships between Mapuche Law and Penal Justice from COM's perspective, see Nahuel (1999). Some of the repercussions of the conflicts over competency and the reform of the Penal Code can be found in Diez (2000a and 2000b), Falaschi (2000), and Kalinsky (2000).

20. Five resolutions were passed during the event. Because they address complex development issues, these resolutions cannot be thoroughly examined here, but it is relevant to mention that these operate along two central axes. While one involves the proposal of reforms of specific juridical and institutional structures at the level of the national and / or the provincial, the other emphasizes the provincialization of political organization and demands. With respect to the first, four of the resolutions articulate positions with regard to: (1) the imminent reform of Neuquen's Penal Code; (2) the probable reform of the National Civil Code; (3) the contested education reform being implemented in Neuquen; and (4) the long-awaited amendment of Neuquen's constitution. With respect to the second, the fifth and final resolution calls for the elaboration of a "Proposal to reform the Statutes of the Mapuche Federation," given that this was agreed upon "during the years of the military dictatorship [1971]." The purpose of this reform is to bring into agreement "the general principles and the new architecture of our mother organization" at the "moment of the current cultural resurgence," so that the CMN can go "from being an organization that is representative of rural communities to one that is representative of the Originary Mapuche People of the entire province of Neuquen," and an organization in which "the diverse regions of the province would be represented through four zonal organizations that will be known as Territorial Mapuche Entities."

21. According to this document (COM 1999) the MWM is "a space for debate and for the definition of legislative proposals, to be elaborated by a group of Mapuche

representatives elected through a Mapuche Electoral Registry," an "organization that will represent the Mapuche People of Neuquen at the provincial level before the state and the world," with a kind of representation based on the notion of "the People and not limited just to rural inhabitants," since "an indigenous person does not cease to belong to an Indigenous People simply because he lives in the city."

22. In concrete terms, the COM begins with the notion of "ethnic and cultural preexistence" framed in the constitution in order to formalize "Argentine indigenous peoples" as "autonomous entities within the State," with "the right to constitute themselves as Subjects of Public Law . . . political-administrative entities organized around their own traditions and sociocultural identity and, based on this, to fashion themselves [through the law] and make decisions over their affairs without straying from the collective destiny of the nation" (COM 1999).

23. Veber (1998:387) defines "induced agency" as the actions and discourses that are crafted in order to accommodate hegemonic expectations.

24. While "strategic multiplicity" operates on the basis of its ability to create the spaces for the staging of fluid identities and solidarities (Hale 1996), the "strategic essentialism" that Spivak sees as inevitable (1990) is associated by Stuart Hall (1993:110–11) with risks, leaving little space for hybrid forms or a logic of articulation, naturalizing, and dehistoricizing difference, and privileging "experience" itself, as if there was any lived experience outside the horizons of representation.

25. According to Florencia Mallon, while "strategic marginality" consists of giving voice to "other *others*" (1996:178), "strategic authenticity" implies a commitment to a notion of authenticity which relegates those *others* to the margins within the group, denying them their right or ability to occupy a position of exemplarity within it (Mallon 1996:173–74). Along these lines, Mallon also points out that the counter-hegemonic intellectuals within these movements often attempt to open new spaces within limited political arenas, allying themselves with "traditional" ethnic leaders in order to safeguard the limits of a particular ethnic identity based on limited criteria of belonging (Mallon 1996:175).

26. Cohen and Arato (1992:526, 552) maintain that no movement can strategically advance the position of its political bases without engaging in four types of politics. Leaders must first commit themselves to a "politics of identity" that enables the redefinition of cultural norms, individual and collective identities, and appropriate social roles—as well as modes of interpretation and the form and content of local and national discourses. They must also practice a "politics of influence" that, as an attempt to transform the universe of political discourse, must make room for new and necessary interpretations, identities, and norms. These leaders must also participate in "politics of inclusion" that, through its orientation toward political institutions,

seeks the recognition of its constituents as new political actors and at the same time secures benefits for those they claim to represent. Finally, they must promote a "politics of reform" in order to democratize economic and political institutions.

27. Here I am referring not to the demands made as "poor citizens," but rather to those made as a "Mapuche People" in these three provinces.

3 Cautions

Cultural Agency and Political Struggle in the Era of the *Indio Permitido*

CHARLES R. HALE

ROSAMEL MILLAMÁN

Introduction

This essay is the product of a dialogue between the coauthors that has resumed after a lapse of more than a decade. We met and worked together in the early 1980s, a very different era, a time when the issue of the day for both of us was the "struggle within." Charlie, a white North American living in Nicaragua, was immersed in activist research on the relations between the Miskitu Indians and the Sandinista state; Rosamel, a Mapuche intellectual and activist from Chile, was aligned with the Chilean Left and its campaign of opposition against the Pinochet military regime. Rosamel, through his involvement in the Pan-American indigenous rights movement, engaged the complexities of the Miskitu people's struggle for autonomy against—and later within—the Sandinista regime in Nicaragua. We both entered U.S.-based graduate programs in anthropology soon thereafter. Despite our very different backgrounds, we developed an affinity based on strong support for visions of political transformation that leftist forces such as the Sandinistas offered Latin America, on the conviction that indigenous rights could best be advanced by working within these broader movements, and on our growing disillusionment at the enormous difficulties facing this struggle within.

Fifteen years later, in 2002, indigenous movements face a radically different set of political challenges; these are the subject of our comparative analysis in this essay. The Latin American Left confronts profound disarray, both in organizational strength and, more important, in political vision. While all evidence points to widespread and growing popular discontent with the neoliberal political-economic model that has taken the continent by storm, it is much less clear that opposition electoral movements have well-formulated alternatives to offer. Social movements that more consistently defend alternative political visions often do so at the expense of remaining oppositional and therefore relatively marginal and powerless. At the same time, this disarray—or some might say crisis—of the Left brings opportunities; chief among them is the impetus and necessity to rethink the terrain of the political. In some of the most creative and perceptive of such revisionist thinking, the touchstone has been culture. In contrast to the homogenizing and unitary leftist notion of the "national-popular," culture (or cultural politics) signals an attentiveness to difference, particularity, prerogatives to contest internal hierarchies within a given political movement.[1] In the face of the colossus of neoliberal capitalism, expressions of cultural difference and demands for cultural rights often signal fissures, spaces for maneuver that open onto more expansive and transformative forms of political struggle. This last point, as we understand it, informs a central argument of this volume and gives a historically specific meaning to the term *cultural agency*.

We have conceived this essay to engage in critical dialogue with this notion of cultural agency and with the associated argument about the prospects for transformative political struggle. If *culture* has become a political and analytical keyword, then indigenous movements should provide a privileged site from which to assess and understand the full implications of the more generalized proposition. Leaving aside for a moment the great heterogeneity among indigenous movements, we can affirm a basic continuity between the 1970s (if not the 1570s) and 2002: the struggle to defend indigenous culture—a way of seeing the world and, in a more materialist sense, a distinctive organization of daily life. This would suggest, in turn, that a close look at indigenous movements should afford special insight into the possible trajectories of cultural struggle in the present era. We take up this challenge, using our knowledge of indigenous movements in Chile and Guatemala as empirical grounding. While the exercise in part confirms the assertion, it also gives us reason for pause, uneasiness, and qualification of the general argument about cultural agency. Although in previous moments, the notion of struggle for indigenous culture could be more directly associated with an unencumbered space of opposition, this is no longer the case. It now has become an idiom of governance, deployed by the very neoliberal institutions that are also the targets of oppositional struggle. It is no longer as common for these powerful actors and institutions to assert that "indigenous peoples have no culture" or that "they must undergo cultural change to become more like us, or remain forever marginal." On the contrary, the predominant affirmation now is to recognize indigenous culture and identity as integral parts of a multicultural society, to affirm that indigenous peoples have special rights and needs, and to assign the state (or its surrogate) the responsibility for meeting these obligations. Indigenous culture has moved from becoming the object of disdain to the subject of political recognition and desire, from control through marginalization to governance through visibility. This transition is far from complete and, in any case, could never be seamless. Even in its present partial state, however, it raises a central analytical problem very different from the one that consumed our energies in the early 1980s. Then we grappled with the prospects for struggle from within a "culture-blind" Left; now, we must confront the paradox that "cultural rights" is both a battle cry of opposition to neoliberal regimes and a leading idiom through which these same regimes domesticate and govern their opponents.

In this essay we attempt to come to terms with this paradox through a comparative analysis of indigenous politics in two very different settings. The Mapuche now are thought to comprise only about one-tenth of Chile's total population of fifteen million, while the Maya make up 50 to 60 percent of Guatemala's twelve million. In economic terms the two countries occupy opposite poles of the Latin American experience: Chile, with a dynamic productive base and a GDP of roughly $63 billion, has managed to reap some modest benefits from global economic integration; Guatemala, by contrast, with a GDP of about $20 billion, is in the doldrums of economic stagnation and extreme poverty. In the discourse and policies of the state, Guatemala has moved much further toward embracing neoliberal multiculturalism, while in Chile the legacy of a *criollo*-dominant centralist state, inclined to assimilate the Mapuche rather than govern through recognition, remains much stronger. Despite these and many other divergences, the comparison also identified common patterns that sustain a unified line of argument. Both countries experienced, in roughly the same time period, a bloody confrontation between military dictatorship and well-organized forces of the Left; in both cases, great numbers of indigenous peoples joined leftist sociopolitical movements, and in both they faced growing disillusionment, leading many (but not all) to a sharp break and a reorientation toward autonomous cultural-political struggle. In both countries, a return to democracy came with full-fledged endorsement of neoliberal economic policies and an unprecedented recognition (albeit uneven and reluctant) of indigenous peoples as valued members of a multicultural society and as collective subjects of rights grounded in cultural difference. This recognition, in turn, has given rise to a sociopolitical category in both countries that we refer to as the *indio permitido*.

The term *indio permitido*, borrowed from our Bolivian friend and colleague Silvia Rivera Cusicanqui, refers to the identity category that results when neoliberal regimes actively recognize and open space for collective indigenous presence, even agency.[2] The term is a provocative one, true to Cusicanqui's intellectual style, but also highly productive as a stimulus to thinking. The category *indio permitido* does not emerge from thin air in the current moment; it evokes echoes of past formulations, most notably in the Anglo world: the dichotomy good-noble / bad-savage (Berkhofer 1978); the Latin American counterpart might be the docile indigenous laborer in juxtaposition with the treacherous insurrectionary Indian[3] (Stavenhagen 1992). There are, however, three novel features of the current moment that we want the term to call forth. First, the construction of the category *indio permitido* has drawn extensively on cultural-political fragments from indigenous rights movements themselves—demands, discourses, cultural affirmations, political sensibilities—with some degree of active participation (though rarely leadership) of indigenous intellectuals. Second, the *indio permitido* is a rights-bearing collective subject, a negotiated space with prerogatives, but also with clear limits that make effective governance possible. Third, people who occupy the category *indio permitido* command a measure of respect and cultural sensitivity from members of the dominant culture; increasingly, the *indio permitido* has become the subject of active cultural-political desire. All this suggests that people in the dominant culture (*Mestizos*, *ladinos*, *criollos*) who interact with the *indio permitido* would be unsettled by our continued use of the word *indio* in this phrase, having conscientiously replaced it with the more respectful *indígena*, Maya, or Mapuche. We preserve the word to signal that, in a structural sense quite apart from individual intentionality, this newfound respect may be only skin-deep.

The central analytical issue raised by the notion of *indio permitido* concerns the deployment of culture and processes of cultural agency in its construction. Recognition of indigenous people by neoliberal states involves the active and explicit affirmation of indigenous culture and the creation of a category within which indigenous people are encouraged to be themselves, to express their cultural particularities, to pursue their culturally specific rights and interests.[4] This being the case, we may need a new metaphor with which to talk about cultural struggle. The image of a fissure in the system, from which oppositional cultural struggle emerges, may misrepresent the extent to which indigenous culture has become a shared idiom for advancing starkly divergent political projects. Rather than allowing the phrase *cultural struggle* to invoke a more or less direct association with *cultural resistance*, we think about culture as being the terrain on which political struggle unfolds and as providing the language of contention for that struggle. While there are some domains (for example, indigenous spirituality) where indigenous cultural affirmation has remained unambiguously separate and oppositional and some contexts in which the state's claim to recognize and respect indigenous culture is utterly spurious, the strong trend is otherwise. As indigenous culture passes from being the *battle cry* of one side in the struggle to being the *battleground* on which both sides meet and fight it out, activists and intellectuals alike need new analytical resources to make sense of the challenges that lie ahead.

Mapuche Struggles in Dictatorship and Democracy

Viewed comparatively with the other Latin American states, Chile belongs to the group (along with Uruguay and Argentina) in which the tenets of neoliberal multiculturalism are least accepted among political economic elites.[5] Chile has not passed the ILO Convention 169; legal and political reforms affirming Chile's status as a multicultural society with differentiated citizenship rights for indigenous peoples have been relatively anemic and limited; critiques of racism and collective critical introspection on the historical formation of white-mestizo identity have been faint to nonexistent. The relative silence and inaction on issues of race and culture in Chile—especially in contrast to countries such as El Salvador, Nicaragua, and Colombia, where percentages of Black and indigenous peoples in the population are similar or even smaller—correspond to a number of factors we cannot fully explore here. We attempt only to summarize the key features of Mapuche organization since the 1970s, of Mapuche relations with the Chilean state, and of the state's responses to Mapuche demands. In so doing, we only indirectly invoke the principal structural factors that help explain the striking invisibility of Mapuche people and their claims to rights in Chilean national politics—the strong centralist tradition, the power and influence of a democratic Left, the pervasive ideology of the European immigrant—stopping well short of a systematic explanation. At the same time, this narrative will demonstrate the advance, albeit halting and still limited, toward the construction of a Chilean *indio permitido*, with the attendant opportunity and menace for the Mapuche movement.

While the Chilean (and indeed to a large extent the Latin American) Left looks to the government of Salvador Allende of 1970–73 as a golden era during which an alternative political vision grounded in equality and social justice reached to the four corners of the society, from a critical indigenous perspective, this is only partly true. Allende's project of democratic socialism transformed Chilean society, inspired the poor and excluded, and drew many, including many Mapuche, into the fold of political support and participation. Yet control of this project, both in the sense of fixing its contents and guiding its implementation, remained definitively in the hands of Mestizos, generally party loyalists, often from Santiago. While some important changes in the legal-political framework were implemented during these three years—most notably the Indigenous Law 17.729—these did not begin to transform the basic precepts of ethnocentric socialism. Demands for Mapuche autonomy and for rights grounded in cultural difference were relegated to regional political matters, subordinated to the political authority of official Mestizo Left political forces. The politics of culture referred not to indigenous (or any other) cultural particularities, but to the overarching project of the cultural transformation of the Chilean nation and society. The cultural struggle of the Mapuche was regularly conflated with this broader process and rarely valued or even recognized as a goal in its own right.

There was barely time for these criticisms to congeal or be articulated, much less become the basis for struggle from within, before the Allende government came to a brutal end in the military coup of 11 September 1973. In the first years following the coup, the Pinochet regime had no discernable policy toward the Mapuche, no differentiated treatment in relation to Chilean citizens in general. Pinochet divided Chilean society into friends and enemies of the regime, repressing the latter with evenhandedly efficient brutality. The marked centralism of the Chilean political system, newly accentuated under Pinochet, may ironically have worked in the favor of

Mapuche in this first phase of the military dictatorship. Being situated on the extreme periphery (regionally and culturally) brought a measure of relief from the repressive arm of the state.

By the end of the 1970s the Pinochet regime began to articulate a specific policy toward the Mapuche, and its thrust was a return to the punishing assimilationist ideology of times past. The Chilean economy in this period was to become a model of neoliberal reform, designed by the radical monetarist theorists Milton Friedman, Arnold Harburger, and their ilk, implemented by fiat, backed by the full force of a repressive state to assure compliance. In notable contrast to latter-day neoliberal reforms, which have well-developed social and cultural counterparts to economic policy, this was a stripped-down economic neoliberalism, which conceived of the citizen-subject in strictly individual and culture-blind terms and made social policy a direct corollary of the logic of the market. Perhaps the best example of policy toward the Mapuche, consistent with this approach, was Decreto Ley No. 2.568, promulgated in 1979, which redefined Mapuche people's relationship to the land. It undermined the bases for collective property ownership, introduced provisions to return to large landholders property that had been redistributed in Allende's agrarian reform, and, most important, attempted to turn the Mapuche into individual farmers whose property could be bought and sold on the market.[6] In the vision of these early neoliberal reforms, Mapuche cultural difference was simply an impediment to progress and therefore, by force or fate, destined to disappear.

This onslaught of cultural-political aggression, combined with the cumulative effects of political repression, gave rise to a wave of Mapuche cultural resistance. The Mapuche Cultural Centers (CCMs) began modestly as local gathering places where Mapuche people could discuss urgent issues of the day and support one another. Given the threat of repression, the meetings took on a semiclandestine form, often taking place in churches or other safe places; discussion of the most sensitive issues was conducted in Mapundungun, the Mapuche language. Meetings would start with the *Nguillatún*, a ritual ceremony of prayer and gratitude to the spiritual powers. At first there were no leaders, no hierarchy beyond the local level. The emphasis on Mapuche culture developed in part, ironically enough, as a measure of physical security. The Pinochet regime responded ferociously to any sign of political opposition but did not view *cultural* expression as political, and in any case assumed that Mapuche culture was frail and in decline, in no position to pose a political threat. The gatherings caught on and grew like wildfire and soon became a regional movement. By the early 1980s, CCMs existed in some three thousand Mapuche communities, with a loosely coordinated agenda of collective cultural self-affirmation, indigenous self-government, and resistance to the agrarian law and other external threats. An organization outside the country—the Comité Exterior Mapuche, or CEM—led by Mapuche people in exile, lent international support to the CCMs. This was a moment of unprecedented cultural-political unity.

Success attracted attention. Soon the broader forces of opposition to Pinochet discovered the CCMs and came to understand the great potential power of Mapuche cultural politics. Many Mapuche leaders responded positively to the idea of alliance, framed around the goal that everyone shared: bringing an end to the Pinochet regime and a return to democracy. This alliance was consummated in the early 1980s in a general political atmosphere of increasing agitation, mobilization, and frontal resistance against the regime. Mapuche people, organized locally, played a major role in these efforts. As the CCMs became absorbed within the leftist opposition movement, however, tensions grew. Leftist forces, organized in various political parties, wanted to place their *militantes* (party cadres) in key leadership positions. Especially given the ongoing threat of political repression, they often made decisions secretly, involving only a select few, in a leadership style that mimicked, ironically enough, the central state they opposed. Most serious of all, these leaders of the Mestizo Left showed a surface respect for Mapuche culture which turned out to be a façade that barely concealed their deep underlying disdain. They viewed the Mapuche as valuable allies, but not as a "fundamental force" of opposition; they bemoaned the "low cultural level" and "ideological primitivism" of the Mapuche (Necochea 1984); they could not accept (or even understand) the Mapuche inclination to pursue shared political objectives through separate forms of cultural-political struggle. The effort at alliance and common cause, though valuable and productive in many ways, ended in deep, generalized disenchantment.

Here, we can be more candid and precise if we personalize the narrative, with a brief interlude in which Rosamel writes in the first person. *I broke with the Left in 1985. Not all Mapuche intellectuals and leaders made this break, and many of those who did acknowledge valuable aspects of the alliance. We learned an enormous amount, from specific tactics of political mobilization to the importance of framing our analysis with a critical structural understanding of Chilean capitalism and global political economy. But the longer I stayed on within the alliance, the more tired and irritated I became with the sheer ignorance, the lack of respect, and the outright racism—whether intentional or unconscious—that* militantes *of the leftist political parties displayed toward the Mapuche. On the assumption that much of the problem was* desconocimiento *(lack of knowledge), we devoted major energy to education, in programs such as the* Trabajos Voluntarios de Verano *(Summer Voluntary Work), in which hundreds of youth from the cities spent summers working in Mapuche communities. We discussed the issues in innumerable workshops and meetings. These efforts seemed to make a difference. At some point, however, it became clear that much more than* desconocimiento, *the fundamental problem revolved around organizational structure and political culture. They practiced "democratic centralism," with power assigned to an inner circle in which Mapuche leaders would never have a real voice. I experienced this exclusion personally in the early eighties, when I was elected by a great majority of a national congress of the* CCMs *as their leader, only to find the next day that I had been replaced by a* militante. *Eventually, out of sheer exhaustion from responding to problems such as this one, I left the alliance.*

The Mapuche movement for cultural-political rights participated in the final years of struggle for return to democracy (1988–89) much more as an autonomous force, working in coalition with others, but maintaining its own political identity. In any case, by this time confidence in the legitimacy of the organized Left had plummeted, both for internal reasons and in response to the global collapse of actually existing socialism. The broad coalition that successfully engineered the plebiscite and then brought Patricio Aylwin to the presidency was centrist in character and clearly committed to basic continuity with the neoliberal economic ideology that had reigned for the previous decade. Yet Aylwin's *Concertación* government (1990–94) also promised to address the agenda put forth by Mapuche organizations, beginning with the much-publicized meeting during the presidential campaign, which resulted in the Acuerdo el Imperial (1989).[7] True to these campaign commitments, in the first months of his tenure, Aylwin formed a *Comisión Nacional de Pueblos Indígenas* (CONAPI), designed to be a voice for indigenous demands within the government; and he recruited a number of prominent Mapuche leaders to his administration. Later the Aylwin government pushed through a new indigenous law (19.253) which dismantled the worst of the assimilationist thrust of the previous regime, granted basic cultural recognition, established the *Corporación Especial de Pueblos Indígenas* (CEPI) charged with bringing development to Mapuche communities, and opened discussion on collective rights. Quite apart from the effectiveness of these various initiatives—which in most cases was minimal or even counterproductive—they marked the beginning of a new era: governance through recognition.

These patterns continued under the presidency of Eduardo Frei (1994–98), but in time the contradictions deepened. New laws passed during the Frei administration assigned rights to water and subsoil resources exclusively to the state; Frei initiated a series of megadevelopment projects in the southern region, which the Mapuche perceived as direct violations of their aspirations to territorial rights. These economic initiatives came with at least minimal acknowledgment of Mapuche interest and newly opened space for Mapuche participation; this was even more the case for the neoliberal social and political reforms (Aylwin 2001). In each instance, some Mapuche leaders accepted the offer to participate, at times out of sheer opportunism, but often in the hope of achieving broadly distributed benefits. Central government decentralization, a standard component in the neoliberal reform package throughout the hemisphere, is illustrative. According to government rhetoric, decentralization was designed to "contribute to the democratic development of the country, devolving decision-making power and resources from the central government to regional and community representatives, for the economic, social, and cultural development in keeping with existing social values and practices, in order to promote growth with greater equity and autonomy."[8] The apparent convergence of this statement of purpose with the long-term goals of the Mapuche movement was undeniable; but the risks of participation—from increased state control at the local level, to fragmentation of Mapuche organizations, to the further dilution of Mapuche cultural resistance—would soon become all too clear.

Reflection on the past decade of Mapuche organization and struggle under democratic governments reveals a striking paradox: while the Mapuche movement for cultural-political rights has made considerable progress, taking advantage of newly gained political freedoms in many ways, Mapuche organizations were more unified and their methods of struggle more sharply defined under the dictatorship. At the crux of this paradox, we contend, lies the politics of culture. With the first initiatives to include Mapuche people as collective actors in the political process, the democratic governments also took steps to recognize Mapuche culture, to affirm the importance of cultural sensitivity and particularity in a whole range of programs, from health and education to decentralized local government. "Mapuche culture," once a potent encapsulating symbol of autonomy and resistance, has become a terrain of struggle where opposing forces contest meanings and negotiate the distribution of power, positions, and benefits. In response to the risks inherent in this current phase of struggle, the Mapuche movement has developed in two new and important directions. First, Mapuche organizations have placed renewed emphasis on the material bases of indigenous culture, shifting away from individual and communal demands for resources toward demands for territory and toward the consolidation of their historic territorial identities: *Lafkences* (people of the coastlands), *Nagches* (people of the lowlands), and *Wenteches* (people of the highlands). Second, Mapuche organizations have called for a return to the local, a reference both to spatiality—the rural community—and to a political domain guided by autonomous principles of Mapuche culture. These two initiatives share a logic of cultural-political differentiation: keep the Mapuche separate, at least in the first instance, from *lo winka* (the non-Mapuche).[9]

Both initiatives, but especially the renewed emphasis on rights to territory and resources, set the stage for heightened political tensions. Since the mid-1990s groups of Mapuche—at times organized at the community level, at times led by regional organizations—have repeatedly been in conflict with the state and the private sector over questions of territory and natural resources (Aylwin 2001). Whether the particulars involve forestry or mining companies, projects of infrastructure such as dams and roads, or agribusiness, the basic principle is the same: Mapuche have become increasingly vocal in their demands to control the territory they have traditionally occupied and to make the decisions regarding the development of that territory (Millamán 2001). Not only does this set of demands remain unresolved, there is no basis within the existing legal-political framework even to address them, beyond ad hoc negotiations when a particular conflict arises. The *retorno a lo local*, though less overtly conflictive and apparently less threatening, is potentially more radical than the claim to territory. This involves taking full advantage of the space opened through the policies of decentralization but redirecting energies toward a much broader objective: strengthening the grassroots cultural bases of Mapuche identity and thereby building the organizational bases for territorial autonomy from the bottom up. Although these efforts often work through the *winka* political-administrative unit, the *municipio*, they are clear that the *municipio* is only a means to very different ends: to consolidate the Mapuche local administrative unit, the *Lof*, and to recuperate traditional forms of political authority, grounded in the principles of Mapuche culture.

Although the past five years have seen both dramatic victories and gradual progress toward this vision of autonomous cultural-political change, the formidable barriers have also become more apparent. The struggle against the Ralco dam, led by the Quintreman sisters, has become a potent symbol of successful mobilization and resistance against the megadevelopment initiatives characteristic of neoliberal economic policies. In the *municipio* elections of 2000, three Mapuche mayors were elected, and one was reelected. Local electoral efforts were launched in many other *municipios* and laid important groundwork, even though they did not win. Regional Mapuche organizations such as the Consejo de Todas las Tierras and the Coordinadora Arauco-Malleco consistently support the politics of territorial identities, despite the open confrontation that results with the state and *winka*-controlled political parties. At the national level, Mapuche organizations gained an unprecedented opportunity to consolidate a political agenda through the efforts of the Comisión de Trabajo Autónoma Mapuche (COTAM), established by the state to study the demands put forth by the indigenous movement. Yet in each instance of progress—and the ones mentioned here are only a small fraction of the total—there are difficulties, obstacles, potential reversals.

Paradoxically, while the major obstacle to advancing the goal of Mapuche cultural-political autonomy is the state and the *winka* political-economic elites, the most effective expression of this opposition comes increasingly from the *indio permitido*. Despite its ineffective and watered-down character, Indigenous Law 19.253 created a space for indigenous participation in the state, an offer that has never been flatly declined. The state promotes intercultural values in the design of social policy (health, education, social welfare) and recruits competent, committed Mapuche intellectuals to implement these programs. The space of local politics, even in the presence of strong efforts toward Mapuche autonomy, is profoundly ambiguous: to be elected mayor is to be interpellated by the state, imbued with characteristics of the *indio permitido* that only the most resolute and creative manage to subvert.

To make matters more complicated still, these two cultural-political categories—*indio permitido* and *Mapuche autónomo*—are starkly dichotomous only in the abstract; in practice they overlap, blur into one another, shift in relation to one another according to context. One way to think about the politics of Mapuche cultural struggle, especially since the return to democracy, is as a multifaceted effort to make this boundary more distinct and impermeable, to prevent the *indio permitido* from colonizing the space of Mapuche autonomy. Yet here another facet of the complexity comes into focus: while the category of the *indio permitido* directly undermines the integrity of Mapuche autonomy, it also has opened channels of resources, legitimacy, and political will that have helped make the autonomy movement viable in the first place. The blurred line between the two categories, in short, is both a threat and a source of sustenance. The great challenge of Mapuche struggle is to confront this paradox head-on, accepting the fact that these two spaces, though sharply dichotomous in indigenous political discourse, can never be kept so neatly separate in practice.

The Maya Movement in Guatemala: Up from the Ashes

In the same period that Rosamel consummated his break with the Chilean Left, Charlie was studying a closely related set of issues in Nicaragua. Why had the Miskitu Indians risen up, so early on and with such militancy, against the Sandinista revolutionary government? Under what terms might a negotiated solution involving Miskitu autonomy within the revolutionary state be possible? Collective work on these questions, with Rosamel serving as representative of the U.N.-affiliated NGO Indigenous World Association, solidified our affinity. We then lost contact for nearly a decade, as Rosamel finished his graduate studies and returned to teaching, research, and activism in southern Chile, and Charlie shifted his energies from Nicaragua to Guatemala.

In 1994, when Charlie began his research in Guatemala, the Maya cultural rights movement was on a path of rapid expansion and political ascendancy. Although the country formally had returned to democratic government in 1985, in practice, the transition from military rule was much more gradual, uneven, and incomplete. Yet even in the initial years after the 1985 elections, when the armed forces still maintained near-absolute control over the political arena, Maya cultural rights activists, enjoying a semblance of autonomy from the state apparatus, emerged as prominent voices of civil society. The trajectory of the Maya movement since that time and the crossroads it currently faces have striking parallels with the Mapuche. Perhaps even more so than in the Mapuche case, in Guatemala the phrase *indigenous culture* has ceased to be a distinct encapsulating symbol of Maya collective affirmation and resistance, becoming instead an attribute that nearly all political forces in the society (except perhaps the extreme Right) affirm, desire, and seek to define.

During the first decade after the democratic opening of 1985, cultural rights activism played a central role in Maya cultural-political struggle and gave the main points of reference for the character of "the Maya movement."[10] In part, this emphasis emerged from the same conditions that underlay the extraordinary success of the Mapuche CCMs under Pinochet: in an atmosphere of ongoing political repression and state surveillance, activities and demands that were "merely" cultural appeared less threatening, less political, more distanced from the revolutionary forces that persisted at the margins. Language rights, education respectful of Maya identity and history, affirmation of Maya religion and spirituality, and general recognition of Maya culture became the issues of the day, dominating discussion and activism in the political arena; more discreetly, some of these same Maya activist-intellectuals would explain in a Gramscian vein that through cultural struggle they were laying the groundwork for radical political transformation. "Political change," one Maya friend commented in the early 1990s, "advances to the beat of the marimba."

In part, also, the prominence of cultural rights activism corresponded to a conceptual divide, never completely clear and always contested, between two notions of Maya cultural-political struggle. In contrast to pan-Maya cultural rights activism, another arena of indigenous political organization, especially prominent in rural areas, continued to focus on issues that had been central to the discourse and demands of the leftist insurgency: respect for human rights and an end to political repression, critique of neoliberal economic policies, and, especially, rural people's rights to land and resources (Camus and Bastos 1992). In some cases (for example, the historic peasant organization Comité de Unidad Campesina, or CUC), the supposedly Maya organizations that advanced this agenda remained organically linked to the *ladino*-controlled Left, while others (for example, the Coordinadora Nacional Indígena Campesina, or CONIC) had consummated a sharp and public break, for reasons very similar to those that Rosamel describes in the previous section. Regardless, many analysts of Guatemalan identity politics associated this second tendency with the Left, reserving the term *Maya* exclusively for the first. Foreign scholars tended to follow suit, producing by the end of the 1990s at least three major ethnographies of Maya cultural politics—Nelson 1999, Warren 1998, Fischer 2001—none of which devote sustained attention to this second tendency. Throughout the 1990s, Maya activists and intellectuals themselves would acknowledge this divide, at times using harsh words for their counterparts, but in other contexts denying its salience, arguing that Maya culture united them.

Whether aligned or at odds, whether tensions were acknowledged or denied, the relationship between contemporary Maya movement and the Left has exerted profound influence on both; curiously, this relationship has remained largely unanalyzed.[11] We know, for example, the Mayas entered the antigovernment guerrilla movement massively in the early 1980s, and that indigenous civilians suffered horribly from the brutal state repression that followed. Yet scholars are just beginning to explore the complex individual and collective consciousness that guided this participation, a task that requires us first to clear aside the "between two armies" narrative frame, which turns indigenous actors into hapless victims.[12] We know that indigenous participants began to leave the guerrilla movement in waves soon after joining, whether out of ideological disillusionment or a more pragmatic assessment that the army was winning the war. Yet we know very little about the Mayas who stayed, their struggles within the *ladino*-controlled political-military hierarchy. When pan-Maya cultural rights organizations went public in the late 1980s, their sharp disassociation from the Left was often portrayed (and commonly understood) as an expression of an autonomous flow of Maya-centric organizing which began much earlier and was temporarily interrupted by the violence. For some, surely, this held true. But for many others, this account suppressed an intense prior formative experience *within* the Left, downplayed or denied not only for security reasons, but also to accentuate the discourse of autonomous cultural struggle. This sharply differentiated narrative proved extremely hard to sustain into the 1990s, however, because the Left moved so quickly and substantively toward endorsement of the same cultural rights discourse that supposedly marked the division between *lo Maya* and *lo popular*.

Left-aligned social movements had "Mayanized" so effectively by the mid-1990s that they could assume a major leadership role as Maya spokespeople in the peace process. When negotiations between the guerrillas and the government yielded a major indigenous accord in 1995, followed by the definitive peace the next year, international funding for Maya cultural rights and political participation flowed abundantly, channeled largely through the umbrella organization Coordinación de Organizaciones del Pueblo Maya de Guatemala (COPMAGUA). Within two or three years of its inception in 1995, COPMAGUA was controlled by Maya member organizations organically linked to the Left. When COPMAGUA collapsed in the summer of 2000 under the weight of authoritarian abuse and misuse of funds, many *ladino* (and some Maya) observers pointed to a crisis in Maya culture. It is more accurate to view the COPMAGUA debacle as a punctuating episode in the long-term cycle of alliance-estrangement between Mayas and the *ladino*-controlled Left. In any case, one conclusion is beyond dispute: with the Left's return to democratic politics in the 1990s, adding to the wide array of social movements in which indigenous Guatemalans participated, "Maya culture" lost its claim to being a singular, or even predominant, political valence and became the site of constant, profound contestation.

The state's endorsement of multiculturalism, especially with the rise of a well-defined neoliberal ruling coalition in 1994, made the scope of this contestation wider still. This shift may have been less momentous in Guatemala than in other countries of Latin America because—as we have learned from recent revisionist historical work[13]—Guatemalan ruling sectors have always been strikingly ambivalent about the idea of assimilating indigenous people to the dominant culture, preferring arrangements that operated according to an implicit principle of separate and unequal. It may be that, paradoxically, remnants of these sensibilities and practices subtly infused later initiatives to recognize Guatemala as a multicultural society. Regardless, it is now possible to trace a series of state initiatives, beginning with the return to democratic rule in 1986, which laid the groundwork for what would become, by the late 1990s, a full-fledged cultural-political project of neoliberal multiculturalism. In some cases, one can even find faint, perverse echoes of these initiatives in the previous moment of brutal military rule.[14] A short list of the most prominent state initiatives include the far-reaching initiative of decentralization (1986); the approval of the Academia de Lenguas Mayas de Guatemala (1987–90); the founding of the Fondo Indígena de Guatemala (1990); the passage of the ILO Convention 169 (1994); the signing of an indigenous peoples Peace Accord (1995); and the flood of programs, funding, mobilization that followed in the name of the Maya people.

While all these initiatives in part responded, in conception and implementation, to the organized collective voices of Maya people themselves, we would be seriously remiss to accept that analytical resting place. Especially considering their cumulative effects, these initiatives form part of a creative, productive process which in turn gave rise to the social category of the *indio permitido*. This category transmits a straightforward message: one can affirm Maya culture and identity while also reinforcing the legitimacy and authority of the *ladino*-controlled state. Some Mayas who occupy this category actively fight the message, and a few actually manage to subvert it; others submit to the contradiction; no one occupies the category innocently, escaping completely its effects.

The rise of the *indio permitido* within the Guatemalan political arena has not gone uncontested. There are Mayas of various social positions who simply refuse to partake or who have political sensibilities and demands that, from the perspective of governing groups, fall clearly out of bounds. More important and more prominently in political terms, a significant sector of the governing elite dissents, finding even the *indio permitido* too risky or unpalatable. A *ladino* capitalist and financier closely associated with the administration of Alvaro Arzú referred to these holdouts as *los feudales*, in contrast to people like himself, *los modernizantes*.[15] The *feudales* harbor racism toward Indians as in times past and favor frankly assimilationist, *ladino*-centric notions of citizenship rights and nation building. Economically, the *feudales* tend to be more close to traditional agroindustrial activities (for example, coffee) rather than new bases of wealth (for example, finance, commerce).

The odd and deceptive feature of this divide, however, is that the *feudales* rarely meet Maya leaders in public discussion or debate; the racial and class distance in most cases is too great. Their principal adversaries, rather, are the *modernizantes*, with whom they debate in public and with whom they no doubt carry on the discussion in more candid terms in social and family gatherings. Such a debate arose, for example, in response to the referendum of May 1999, intended to introduce a series of constitutional reforms that would incorporate key elements of the 1996 Peace Accords. Vigorous opposition to the reforms by a well-organized group of *feudales* focused almost entirely on the points related to indigenous rights helped to defeat the referendum. This episode, although full of complexities beyond the reach of our analysis here,[16] illustrates the basic point nicely: the category of the *indio permitido* is compelling in part because it is the product of sustained, at times fierce, political struggle *among* competing factions of the elite, each with pretensions to dominance. The leadership role of the *modernizantes* in opening the space is also what makes it risky and menacing for indigenous rights activists to occupy: by defending Maya culture, *modernizantes* also acquire weighty influence in the process of fixing the limits on cultural struggle, of deciding what meanings of "cultural rights" are permissible.

Faced with the rising political investment in the category of the *indio permitido* by *ladino*-controlled forces across the political spectrum, Maya-led efforts to achieve cultural-political rights stand at a crossroads. A number of serious, substantive goals of Maya cultural rights can be advanced by working within the space of the *indio permitido*, under relatively favorable political conditions. Mayas who opt for this path—among them many highly competent, experienced intellectuals—generally argue that they are making good use of the experience, in accordance with deeper and largely autonomous Maya cultural values and interests. In another variant of this same path—less and less frequent among intellectuals, but still prevalent at the grassroots—is for Mayas to occupy the category of *indio permitido* within the Left; far from the urban centers, amid pervasive critical poverty, many Maya peasants show a disconcertingly low level of concern for the cultural rights agenda of the urban-based movement. Yet in this case, also, the consequences are unpredictable, especially given what appears to be a steady "Mayanization" of the social base of the Left. Once the category of the *indio permitido* is occupied by real social actors, the question "who is using whom" must remain open, subject to case-specific empirical analysis.

However this question is resolved in any particular case, there remains a great divide in relation to an alternative path, one which rejects the category of the *indio permitido* altogether and insists on negotiating its own terms of engagement with the state and with other *ladino*-controlled political forces, including the Left. This alternative path, clearly outside the permissible, faces daunting obstacles of political opposition, repression, and delegitimation; it is widely perceived and portrayed as radical and intransigent by political elites who call for moderation. Yet it has the great advantage of being able to formulate a political vision less constrained and influenced by the precepts of neoliberal multiculturalism. The organization that best illustrates this path in Guatemala today is the Coordinadora Nacional Indígena y Campesina (CONIC), a peasant-based and Maya-controlled national organization that broke from the Left in the early 1990s. CONIC is the major force behind the wave of occupations of large landholdings, conceived as a means to respond to the structural crisis in agroindustrial production (especially coffee) and to the corresponding destitution of rural dwellers.[17] It will be important to trace the notions of Maya cultural struggle that emerge from such spaces: are they diluted and displaced by Left-inflected conceptions of class struggle, as many observers aligned with pan-Mayanists contend? Or do they represent a counterhegemonic *retorno a lo local* and reaffirmation of grassroots Maya culture, parallel to the process described earlier in the case of the Mapuche? While there is not yet enough research on this process to address such questions, it is safe to frame these questions with a preliminary assertion: on the forty-odd *fincas* in the Guatemalan *altiplano* presently (the end of 2002) under occupation, the *indio permitido* is nowhere to be found.

Concluding Reflections

The analysis generated by the comparisons of Mapuche and Maya cultural struggles over the past two to three decades fixes on a shift in the way indigenous culture is politicized. It is helpful to think about this shift in terms of two distinct moments, even if in practice the two are overlapping and intertwined. In the first moment, when indigenous people primarily faced policies of exclusion and forced assimilation, the collective affirmation of rights grounded in indigenous cultural difference was, in its own right, a radical and challenging political act. This is the moment of mobilization for, as Eva Dagnino (1998) terms it, the "right to have rights," characterized by an intense and concerted investment in collective representation of cultural difference (Hall 1988). This is the same moment that Lowe and Lloyd (1998) invoke in the *Politics of Culture in the Shadow of Capital*, when they describe how fissures in the dominant political-economic system emerge as cultural incongruities, which in turn provide the entrée for oppositional cultural-political struggle. We certainly do not intend to portray culture in this first moment as a purely oppositional or uncontested space; it is always otherwise. We do want to mark a time when broader conditions imbued the collective self-affirmation of indigenous culture with a potent political valence: an act of protest against the prevailing assumption that modernity and development would bring about the demise of indigenous people; a resolute reminder that Indians, as rights-bearing collective subjects, are here to stay. This moment is nicely illustrated by the early years of proliferation of the CCM in Chile, when the Pinochet regime was so convinced of its own assimilationist ideology that it didn't even perceive Mapuche culture as political. Aided by this misrecognition, the CCM movement generated an unusual sensation of unity, as if the act of cultural self-affirmation encapsulated Mapuche political aspirations and, to some extent, those of non–Mapuche as well.[18]

We draw a sharp contrast with the second moment, when an array of nonindigenous political forces began to make the affirmation of indigenous culture, and the notion of rights grounded in cultural difference, their own. This recognition marks the emergence of a new or substantially reformulated cultural-political category: the *indio permitido*. The organized Left in both countries makes this discovery, a shift we portray in fairly instrumental terms: an attempt to reposition and regain political legitimacy, the most recent in a long history of grappling with the consequences of its own culture- (and color-) blind vision of universal emancipation. Although using the term *indio permitido* to refer to cultural-political categories within both the Left and the neoliberal establishment, we do not conflate the two. The shift is much harder to account for and has more far-reaching political consequences because it has occurred as an integral part of the ascendancy of neoliberal political and economic reform.

The cultural project of neoliberalism, we contend, includes the recognition of indigenous peoples as bearers of special rights to be protected, either to help them compete in the rigors of globalized capitalism or, if this is deemed impossible, to relegate them to the sidelines, allowing the game to proceed unperturbed. Other dimensions of the neoliberal reforms—such as decentralization, the emphasis on civil society associations and on democratic citizen participation—though framed more broadly, also have shaped the category of the *indio permitido*. In some contexts, this has created wide room for maneuver, for accomplishing concrete goals of the indigenous movements, with the state's (and the multilateral funders') blessings. Our point is not to minimize these accomplishments, much less to draw conclusions about individuals who occupy the space of the *indio permitido*, but rather to call for sustained analysis of what this category—appropriately occupied—does. We argue, first, that it lends a new, much-needed legitimacy to the government in question, both internally and, more important, in the estimation of the multilateral funding agencies on which they depend; second, the considerable investment in multiculturalism, in a package of rights for indigenous peoples, comes with an equally weighty investment in the boundary that separates permissible from proscribed rights, acceptably moderate from radically threatening social transformation; third, the emergence of the *indio permitido* has transformed the terrain of cultural struggle, making indigenous culture an asset across the political spectrum with the aim of winning support or at least avoiding the embarrassment of appearing *feudal*—as the Guatemalan businessman put it. Although ongoing processes of racialization, combined with class dynamics, place limits on the reach of this inclusion, it already has gone far enough, in Chile and especially in Guatemala, to destabilize the political valence of indigenous cultural rights; in place of its relatively clear previous meaning, the phrase is now best understood as an open and hotly contested question.

In the face of these transformations, a prominent response in both indigenous movements under study here involves a return to the local. In some cases, this surely could be a formulaic discourse of urban leaders, who regularly invoke an imaginary space of authentic culture to bolster their own legitimacy. In some cases, also, this could signal an earnest but probably illusory attempt to recover the essence of indigenous culture, still untouched and uncontaminated by *lo winka* or (its Guatemalan counterpart) *lo kaxlan*, and to rebuild from there. According to yet another interpretation, more consistent with the argument put forth here, the return to the local is a strategic move to spaces where the terms of struggle over representations of indigenous culture and rights are more advantageous. To conceive of this space as radically outside, completely separate from the category of the *indio permitido*, could inadvertently reinforce the divide between the permissible and the subversive, on which that category depends. Another way to think about the objective of this return to the local is to wreak havoc with the divide itself, to find a strategy of cultural-political struggle that could rearticulate a wide range of indigenous demands and political sensibilities, while doing battle with the neoliberal state's pretensions to shape and control that agenda. Concretely, this is why we both place so much importance on the increasing prominence—among both the Mapuche and the Maya—of demands for land and local autonomy. They give substance to the return to the local, while having the potential to change the subject: away from the question of more or better-defined rights—the trap of the *indio permitido*—toward an alternative logic of cultural-political struggle, grounded in a modest affirmation of collective identity and belonging, a minimally decent standard of material well-being, and a vehement rejection of structural inequality and oppression. Such an alternative logic, were it to prosper, might also offer more promising bases from which to reopen the perennial dialogue on the relationship between indigenous movements and the Left, which planted the seeds of this essay, some twenty years ago.

Notes

1. For two examples of recently published volumes that capture the prominence of cultural politics and struggle, see Jordan and Weedon 1995 and Duncombe 2002.

2. Cusicanqui coined this term during workshop discussions at the University of Texas in the spring of 2001. To our knowledge, the term has not appeared in print.

3. For an overview of dominant culture perceptions of indigenous people in Latin America, see Stavenhagen 1992; for a more specific analysis of the fear of the insurrectionary Indian, see Hale forthcoming.

4. For a cogent analysis of a parallel process outside of Latin America, see Povinelli 2002.

5. For a useful Latin America wide overview of the shift, see Van Cott 2000.

6. Specifically, the law states that the divided (indigenous "reservation") lands will no longer be considered indigenous lands, and the people living on those lands will no longer be considered indigenous (Cap. 1, Art. 1b). Cited in Boccara 2001.

7. Unfortunately, after Aylwin was elected, the Chilean Parliament passed an indigenous law that gutted the most important provisions of this agreement. For an analysis of the law, in the context of state policies toward the Mapuche more generally, see Aylwin 2002.

8. "Bases para una política de decentralización," a seminar presented by a representative of the Chilean government, as recorded in the notes of Rosamel Millamán, 2000, Temuco.

9. "Wi" = new and "inka" refers to the Inka empire that governed the region before the arrival of the Spaniards. *Winka* therefore literally means, "the new Inkas," or the Spaniards. It has evolved to refer more generally to any nonindigenous Chilean.

10. The publication that best captures the political sensibility of these early years is COCADI 1988.

11. The argument put forth here draws heavily on the Guatemala report section of a study of Black and indigenous organizations sponsored by the Ford Foundation. For a summary of that study's findings, see Gordon, Hale, and Anderson 2000. The section on "the national context" of indigenous politics in Guatemala, written by Hale, remains an unpublished manuscript.

12. The best-known representative texts here are Stoll 1993, 1999. For a more sophisticated version of the same argument, see Le Bot 1995.

13. Arturo Taracena Arriola with the collaboration of Gisela Gellert, Enrique Gordillo, Tania Sagastume, and Knut Walter, *Etnicidad, Estado y nación en Guatemala, 1808–1944* (Antigua, Guatemala: CIRMA, 2002).

14. See, for example, during the year of Efraín Ríos Montt's rule (1982–83), the creation of special seats for "representantes étnicas" in the Council of State. Ríos Montt also referred to Guatemalan society as consisting of "20 nacionalides diferentes," although he regularly contradicted this assertion with calls for "un proyecto de nación" in the singular. The point, of course, is not to expect even a minimal level of coherence or accountability in these speech acts, but rather to note that they introduced novel elements into the discourse emanating from the state. For an analysis along these lines, see Cojtí Cuxil 1989, esp. 152–53, notes 2 and 3.

15. For an elaboration of these categories, see Hale 2002.

16. Not all indigenous leaders supported the referendum because of disagreements on the conception of key indigenous rights provisions. According to many observers, the Arzú administration's support for the referendum was lukewarm, whether out of conviction or political calculus. More broadly, the referendum's defeat was a portent of the rise of the Frente Republicano Guatemalteco (FRG), a right-wing populist coalition that capitalized on indigenous and lower class *ladino* animosity toward the *modernizantes*. The relationship of the FRG political bloc, which won the presidency in 2000, to neoliberal multiculturalism in this essay will have to remain an open question. For an analysis of the referendum, see Mendoza 2001.

17. This is a very recent phase of agrarian politics in Guatemala about which very little has yet been written. We draw heavily on personal communication with Irmalicia Velasquez Nimatuj, presently conducting dissertation research on the topic.

18. These remarkable cases in which the political assertion of a minority indigenous population encapsulates and galvanizes the political sensibilities of a broader (nonindigenous) sector of the society have occurred in other contexts as well, notably Colombia and Ecuador.

The Crossroads of Faith: Heroism and Melancholia in the Colombian "Violentologists" (1980–2000)

SANTIAGO VILLAVECES-IZQUIERDO

A quick glance inside any bookstore in Colombia reveals an overwhelming number of titles about war, peace, and violence. Next to the beautiful coffee-table books that pose as proof of a flourishing industry—proudly displayed on center tables and in windows—stand endless shelves marked by a discrete label that reads *Temas Colombianos* (Colombian themes). As one stops and lets the eye wander upward, right, downward, left, and upward again, one is confronted with a printed reflection of contemporary Colombia: besides the usual volumes on local political scandals and economic analysis, the shelves are stacked with innumerable books on violence that stand as uncanny paper artifacts that reflect more than what they mean. A closer look, as the eye stops on a cover, a title, or an author, discloses the intricate web that knits the disruptive itinerary of violence: the fictionalized testimonies that talk about violence in the 1950s or the new violence unleashed around the coca planta-tions (*chagras*) that are spread throughout the uneven geography of the country, the journalistic accounts of the emergence of adolescent assassins, or *sicarios*, in the margins of the big cities, the political and historical analyses that scrutinize former and failed negotiations with guerrilla groups, the sociological analyses that unveil the connections between drug lords and paramilitary activities, and, more recently, the accounts and testimonies re-garding what some have called the newest and most profitable industry in the country, kidnapping.

As varied and multiple as the books on violence are their authors.[1] The spectrum is wide and shows how Colombians have learned to seriously en-gage in what has become not only our heaviest burden but also our major constructor of national identity. In the mid 1980s, a literature boom marked the end of an epoch of conscious neglect, giving way to new times in which coming to terms with a legacy of violence became intricately intertwined with the marketing strategies of the local editorial presses. The careful selec-tion of material strictly endorsed by some publishers became a flaw. Random writers appeared who published books that exalted the characteristics of one of the social agents involved in the conflict; others, less engaged, simply compiled dispersed documents and made a name for themselves. But on the shelves of the bookstore one also finds a systematic production of narrative building around the elusive yet so insistently present manifestations of disseminated violence. Publishing testimonials and fictionalized accounts, Arturo Alape and Alfredo Molano have made their way onto the best-seller lists of the country. Others, like Gonzalo Sánchez, Alejandro Reyes, Alvaro Camacho, and Eduardo Pizarro, have followed the academic path inaugurated in the public university by the sociologist Orlando Fals Borda and by Father Camilo Torres in the sixties, of explaining a sustained and increasing violence as a molding force of the cultural and political history of the country. Although many other academics have built their professional lives around research on Colombian violence, it is this last group of intellectuals that I am concerned with here.[2] In particular I am interested in exploring the complex shifts in intellectual positioning and intellectual production that, induced by ever-changing political and institutional contexts, have made up, and driven to the ground, a failed project of the "violentologists."

The history of Colombia has been deeply marked by violent formations that shape the social, cultural, and political spheres. During the past twenty years Colombia's violence has taken on unforeseen dimensions, bringing about a deeper fragmentation of the country, a more acute confrontation between old and new violent actors, and a felt need for a political solution to the multiple conflicts that have been shaping the country's modernity. Such has been its force that violence in Colombia has become a key constructor of national identity. From the time of Julio Cesar Turbay Ayala's administration (1978–82) to that of Andrés Pastrana (1998–2002), a group of social scientists popularly known as violentologists have moved from radical critiques of the state to state consultancies and bureaucracies and from there to exile. In this essay I explore how these intellectuals, while constructing narratives about violence, shape themselves as agents of change. In so doing I expose the types of identities they adopt as well as the types of utopias they defend. In engaging such questions I aim to understand how the violentologists' own gaze can accommodate certain types of critiques while rendering others invisible. To talk about intellectuals today, as Edward Said (1996) suggested some years ago, is to talk about local histories in global contexts, about processes of state formation and nation building, about dynamic relations between intellectuals and institutions; but it is also to talk about the dynamics in the consolidation of the social sciences, the solidification or fragmentation of European canons and thus the solidification or fragmentation of worldviews, memories, and representations that are mediated by such categories. Throughout this essay I touch on each of these issues. Overall, I suggest the need for interrogating expert knowledge and cultures, particularly in contexts in which democratic consolidation is at bay. What intellectual positions might have a better chance of contributing to the building of democracy?

The violentologists enunciate their own identity while positioning themselves within particular cultural and political spaces. Not a linear movement, this process of identity formation is subject to historical contingencies of paradoxical politics and cultural negotiation. Embedded in battlefields of power and signification as they are, the violentologists are constantly reasserting their own standing as they try to make sense of a reality that shifts rapidly and unexpectedly. Different sites of enunciation are at work in construing a multilayered universe that shapes and determines who the violentologists are, where they speak from, and what they represent. First, violence becomes cultural capital as a historical marker of Colombia; from such a space the word of the academics stands as a systematic effort to bring signification to historical and contemporary formations of violence. Parallel to this process I highlight how the institutionalization of violentology as a field of knowledge and as a niche within the public university opens the doors for some intellectuals to become power and culture brokers reestablishing a long-lost connection between intellectuals and power holders. Finally, I show how the rise of the violentologists enunciates the perversity, persistence, and obliqueness of terror as constructor of modern life in Colombia. In weaving together these sites, I hope to disclose a field in which violence, power, and history come into play in the shaping of an intellectual endeavor.

Three particular moments have shaped contemporary Colombia, each with its own effects over the community of violentologists. A first moment (circa 1965–82), heavily marked by the Doctrine of National Security, saw the social sciences stigmatized as a cradle of insurgency, and the relationship between the armed forces / executive branch and the public university reached its lowest level. A second moment (1982–94), marked by the tragic rupture of peace negotiations with the M-19 guerrillas and the explosion of multiple violence (paramilitary and narcoterrorism joined the existing violence of guerrillas and armed forces), was a period in which the public university and its departments of social sciences were seen by the executive branch as the "natural places" in which to seek informed diagnosis and policy recommendations for the containment of violence: this is the time of the political instrumentalization of research. Finally, a third moment (1995–2000) was marked by a profound polarization of society and the explicit inability of the state to maintain national unity. During these years the paramilitary expanded its activities into the entirety of Colombian territory, and guerrilla warfare degenerated into brutal, indiscriminate killing of civilian populations. The intellectuals who served in the state bureaucracy or as counselors of presidential advisors and ministries were either assassinated or forced into exile.

During the administration of Belisario Betancur (1982–86), the growing need to grant a general amnesty to guerrilla groups opened the way for a massive circulation of literature on violence. As the topic was democratized in the mid eighties, a vast array of possibilities emerged for those who wrote about conflict in Colombia. While serving as minister of interior in the Virgilio Barco administration (1986–90), Fernando Cepeda, a political scientist trained at Harvard, pushed for the need to establish direct links between academia and the decision-making spheres of the government. On that basis, and owing to a reformulation of the peace initiative of the former administration, the first commission for the study of violence, the Comisión de Estudios sobre la Violencia, was formed in 1987. Its members, most of whom had ongoing research projects on violence funded by the Instituto Colombiano de Ciencia y Tecnología (Colciencias)—the Colombian version of the National Science Foundation (NSF)—saw the culmination of their work in a published report presented to the government, *Colombia: Violencia y Democracia* (1987). In an interview with Alvaro Camacho, a member of the commission, a journalist from the periodical *Semana* asked, "What do you all have in common?" Camacho, in a lighthearted tone, responded, "We, the violentologists, are all the most peaceful people in the world." Ten years later, Eduardo Pizarro, a prominent violentologist and former director of the IEPRI, shrewdly remarked, "A bad joke of Camacho's that by chance was published by a journalist from the weekly magazine *Semana*. And so the word finally gained status. Recently, I saw a book published in Germany by a Bolivian author who writes about violence in Colombia and Peru. In the book, Mancilla, the author, already writes about the German violentologists." Over time, the relationship between academia and government as well as the public exposure of the violentologists deepened. In 1986, the Instituto de Estudios Políticos y Relaciones Internacionales (IEPRI), the first systematic academic approach to violence, was established at the Universidad Nacional. The IEPRI became not just a renowned center of intellectual production but also a well-reputed publishing house. The IEPRI publishes two periodicals, *Análisis Político* and *Síntesis*; it has published more than seventy books, most of them a result of its ongoing research. Additionally, the IEPRI has pursued other promotional strategies such as columns in the two major Colombian newspapers (*El Tiempo* and *El Espectador*), weekly radio programs, and, from 1994 to 1995, a half-hour television program. During the nineties, the institute's internal structure was diversified: to its one active area of research in 1986 (Violence and Illegality) were added three more (Educational Policy and Political Culture since 1990; Governance, Democracy, and Human Rights since the early 1990s; and International Relations since 1995). Important formal and informal ties with the presidency, the ministries, and presidential advisors were sought in all these areas.

After years of open confrontation between academia and the establishment, such repositioning was understood, in the words of Gonzalo Sánchez, as a new cultural pact between intellectuals and the state, a pact that paralleled a political willingness within the power elite to initiate peace negotiations with the guerrillas.[3] The significance of such a pact was that it reestablished a long-lost connection between the power of the word and the word of power. During the times of *La Colonia*, and under the best tradition of a Catholic monarchy, all forms of education were in the hands of the Church. Political power and religious doctrine were intertwined in an educational system for those who could prove purity of blood and were therefore entitled to the right of rule: access to higher education was a privilege granted only to descendants of Spaniards and Creoles. During the 1600s, two of the most prestigious universities were founded by the clergy: the Pontificia Universidad Javeriana by the Jesuits in 1623 and the Colegio Mayor de Nuestra Señora del Rosario by the Franciscans in 1654. Soon the first degrees of doctor in theology and jurisprudence were awarded, uniting in the lawyer the secular and the religious ruling principles. In 1826, sixteen years after Independence, the first public universities were created by presidential decree. In an effort to build the newly born Republic, higher education was to include not only theology and jurisprudence, but also medicine, philosophy, and natural sciences. Nevertheless, the privileged status of jurisprudence as the discipline that brought both power and social prestige was not diminished. The lawyer embodied three ruling principles: the ability to construct and manipulate social rules and order (through jurisprudence), the control of the means of economic accumulation and social prestige (through land tenure), and the capacity to access, expand, and naturalize its own cultural capital (through academia). By the end of the nineteenth century that fusion was so well developed that the Argentinian diplomat Miguel Cané characterized Colombia as a republic of ruling scholars: a nineteenth-century Latin American version of Plato's ideal.[4]

The process of modernization solidified the need for an increasing compartmentalization of knowledge and technologies. Reforms to higher education in the mid-1930s democratized access to intellectual debates, and with this the long-standing equation of lawyer and intellectual was broken. This rupture worked against future intellectuals in that it limited access to power, social recognition, and prestige to lawyers, leaving the intellectual with nothing but the hope to forge a future out of his cultural capital. Still today, as they were one hundred years ago, lawyers are considered to be a sort of secular priest in whose hands lie the fate and destiny of the country. With social prestige, recognition, and access to power secured, the lawyer has become naturally self-confident; and the Law, that seemingly eternal symbol of the sacredness of power, has been taken as a form of social mobility for all of those who were not born in the right places.[5] It is not by chance that many of today's older generations of intellectuals had a degree in law. Nonetheless, their decision to engage in social research rather than legal practice undermined their possibilities of achieving a life of comfort and stability. Instead, it triggered a cost that for some has been extremely high. The structural fragility of higher education and its low wages, combined with a lack of social visibility and prestige, have become a heavy burden for the development of stable and solid intellectual communities. Not surprising is the explicit or implicit lingering feeling of social debasement in the Colombian intellectual. The turn of the twentieth century is still thought of nostalgically as the time when power takers and knowledge holders were once united.[6] Today, the only feasible possibility of duplicating such a union is either by entering the state bureaucracy[7] or by making an exponential commitment to well-paid consultancies within state agencies—primarily those of the executive branch, that is, offices of presidential advisors, supraministries, and ministries. Both moves—joining the bureaucracy or investing most of their time in consultancies—apparently allowed intellectuals to efficiently overcome the social and economic burdens born of marginalization and lack of recognition.

The perversity and persistence of Colombia's history of terror and exclusion in conjunction with the cultural and political inability of its elite to integrate a nation have laid the groundwork for the invention of a field of knowledge that tragically reflects the transforming forces of disseminated violence. In the mid-eighties the coining of the term *violentologist* highlighted not only the traversing velocity of violence as it molds cultural and institutional worlds, but also a taxonomy that identifies and differentiates a peculiar type of intellectual. Such a classification floats along two basic axes, one thematic, the other institutional, that address how such intellectuals talk about violence as well as where they talk from and for whom. These two axes not only define the violentologist as a power and culture broker who interprets a social drama to key sectors of the Colombian high bureaucracy, but also are pillars in the construction of the violentologist's self-representation. The production of particular symbolic goods, the colonization of spaces once demonized (government and state institutions), and the garnering of public visibility have laid the foundation for the violentologists' active intervention in processes of state formation.

Intellectuals and State Formation

In 1978, when Turbay was inaugurated as president, the presidential abuse of state of emergency legislation rapidly climaxed. A month after taking office, Turbay issued the infamous Estatuto de Seguridad, expanding the judicial powers of the military while censoring radio and television. During this period many intellectuals were tortured and forced into exile as the military continually identified the Universidad Nacional as a seedbed of subversion. The public university reacted radically to an increased militarization of its campuses during the seventies, and many intellectuals censored themselves. The public proscription and mystification of any topic connected to violence as well as the death threats that came if the taboo was broken led many intellectuals to have visceral reactions against the state apparatus.[8] Nevertheless, amidst such restrictions, an important pool of research around the period of *La Violencia* (1944–65) flourished in the department of history at La Nacional.[9] The works produced during the seventies followed two paths. The first was interested in exploring *La Violencia* as the result of a power struggle among elites that, combined with a weak and fragile state formation, led to a dissociation between the political spheres and the changing circumstances in the social and rural contexts, a dissociation that could only be addressed through the exercise of violence.[10] A second path was committed to exploring the socioeconomic factors that associated violence with capitalist development and modernization of agriculture; or with a strategy of the dominant classes to frustrate democratic processes of access to land, especially in the coffee-growing regions of the country.[11]

With the end of Turbay's presidency a radical shift occurred in both the way in which the government related to the guerrillas and the way in which it reestablished a connection with the intellectuals of La Nacional. The inauguration of Betancur's administration in 1982 held the promise of opening a national dialogue in search of peace with all the guerrillas,[12] a promise that has since become a major issue in all presidential debates and policy-making decisions. This political shift opened spaces for a needed public debate on violence, amnesty, peace, and conflict negotiation. In 1985, Marco Palacios, then-rector of the Universidad Nacional, took up this opportunity by appointing a commission to explore the possibility of creating a master of arts program in political studies and international relations. Sánchez, by then professor in the department of history, a prolific researcher on the period of *La Violencia*, and one of the most prominent violentologists, chaired the commission. In March 1986, the commission's final report recommended the creation of a research institute that would "contribute to the formation of a political culture committed to the building of consciousness on issues of peace, the development of democracy, and the strengthening of international ties."[13] The IEPRI, as noted earlier, was born in July 1986, and since then it has become a highly visible space in the public arena as well as the most important point of reference on topics that range from short-term political analysis to drug trafficking, guerrillas, and conflict management. Such visibility has been paralleled by the state's commissioning of policy-oriented reports and consultancies to the institute.

In a recent paper, Sánchez explained the shift in the intellectuals' positioning toward state and guerrillas as a movement from what he calls a "critical intellectual" toward an "intellectual for democracy."[14] This local typology has been accepted by the violentologists and thus serves as an axis for a cohesive process of narration that not only imprints an identity on an otherwise heterogeneous group, but also reflects their own understanding of political activism in a highly contested reality. Sánchez's "critical intellectual" is characterized by an independence from the state and political parties and a silent, implicit empathy with the revolutionary ideals of the guerrillas. This type of intellectual, highly critical of the state apparatus and ideologically connected to the multiplying struggles of social movements and margins, emerged during the sixties within the newly created sociology department of the Universidad Nacional. Two issues were paramount in the shaping of such intellectuals. On one hand was the strong self-critique within the discipline triggered by Fals Borda, founder of the department of sociology, who questioned the detached and objectifying forms of sociological research through his *investigación acción-participativa*, an epistemological and methodological move that allowed researcher and informant to share common political standings. On the other hand, the research and consultancies the department had undertaken under the auspices of state agencies and international donors (for example, the Ford Foundation, Fulbright, UNESCO, and the universities of Wisconsin and Münster) were disclosing a further, more complex reality that called upon the need for radical changes in land tenure, power distribution, and social welfare. The failure of the "critical intellectuals" stemmed both from their way of engaging violence as a congealed process that had to be dissected and classified in order to be comprehensible, and even more so from the state's repressive apparatus.

In sharp contrast with the "critical intellectual," Sánchez's "intellectual for democracy" emerges as a by-product of the policy shifts that since the mid-eighties have reassessed the state's responses to political violence. This is the intellectual that circulates within high bureaucracy, the intellectual that is hired by ministries and special advisors to the president, the organic intellectual of power. In the words of Alejandro Reyes, a violentologist himself,

If one doesn't believe in the guerrilla's project, then the only alternative is to frame our work on violence under an effort to construct the state. In other words, the Colombian context has pushed us to be the state's organic intellectuals. It really doesn't matter if we are based in a public or private university, in any case the intellectual is perceiving himself as an intellectual of the state, and that is because the state is simultaneously the cause as well as the alternative to violence. We know in theory that conflict resolution ends with broad agreements of state consolidation that give room to the actors in conflict—guerrillas, paramilitaries, and so on; that is why I keep a close eye on the dynamics that are unfolding throughout the country, and although I've been one of the few from the IEPRI that hasn't accepted positions within the state, a good part of my work is contributing to generate debates that, without doubt, are helping strengthen the state. And I am not fooling myself in saying this. I think that the historic mission of Latin American intellectuals, living under such precarious states and societies, is that of contributing to the construction and strengthening of the state. That is why I am not scandalized when I see people that do research on violence make a transit to the state for a few years and later return to academia. Even if they don't return one can see this as an input of academia to the qualification of state bureaucrats.[15]

For Sánchez this new type of intellectual allows for the engagement with state functions without necessarily renouncing the intellectual's intrinsic critical nature. This would be a perspective in which it is the intellectual's own function, not the site of action (academia, state, society), that matters.[16] Unfortunately, the recent history of Colombia shows otherwise: the sites of enunciation do matter, and it is precisely because they do that intellectuals at times have been forced to go into exile, silenced, killed, or caught in the allures of power. What I want to highlight here is the paramount importance of building an awareness of the situational and tactical positioning of the intellectual, even more so in highly volatile and contested realities.

Heroes and Antiheroes, or the Tensions Between the Sublime and the Contingent

The contemporary history of the violentologists in Colombia has been marked by a tragic pendular movement between a self-perceived heroism and a deeply felt failure. The structural fragility of higher education, its low wages and economic vulnerability combined with a lack of social visibility and prestige, have become heavy impediments to the development of stable and solid intellectual communities. The Colombian intellectual has learned to negotiate a paradoxical existence in constant tension between the ideals of reason and social transformation and the exclusions and stigmas imposed by a parochial and self-centered elite. The cocoon that intellectuals have spun to cope with such in-betweenness has been that of assuming a heroic agency as mechanism that allows for the mobilization of their own burdens toward a sublime (serving the people, society, democracy). The major drama of such a move has been the impossibility for creating communal selves: the violentologist usually remains an absolutely private individual whose claims to represent the whole are best fulfilled when he acts as an isolated, self-interested individual (an ethos aligned with that of expansive capitalism).[17]

The movement from "critical intellectual" to "intellectual for democracy" is a movement from the heroism of an enlightened voice for the oppressed to an enlightened voice for the state.[18] In both cases the intellectual is engaged in a self-referential process of redemptive sacrifice, disarticulated from social movements, from alternative political and cultural formations, from emerging forms of social and cultural critique. These two types of heroism revolve around the same axis: the relationship between intellectuals and state; and it is precisely this fixation that has led to the repeated failures of these intellectuals. Once censored and persecuted by state terrorism, then blinded by the shining corridors of the palace, then persecuted and killed by disseminated violence, the violentologists tragically seem to be caught in the spiral of the eternal return: always pushed back to their original condition as antiheroes, as displaced. And the tragedy deepens when these intellectuals, experts in violence, fail to recognize the full extent of the social drama that brings them together with the internally displaced populations of the country. Can they recognize the sameness of the natures of these two displacements? If so, can they identify and recognize the authoritarian, exclusive nature of a state that, echoing the self-centeredness of its elite, has always perpetuated its cultural inability to build a nation, to embrace difference? The state is a god that always deceives, wrote Said (1996), but it seems that for the violentologists it is still a god that might redeem.

The violentologists' heroism is founded on their ascription to alien models of social transformation, nation building, and state formation rooted in European historical and sociological contexts; these are far distant from the colonial legacies that have actually informed not only what is imagined to be state but also the role within such visions that the intellectual has endorsed (for example, their function in the consolidation of state institutions in postdictatorial situations). On the other side, despite their fine-tuning with European epistemologies and state models, the violentologists have become extremely parochial in their belief in the uniqueness of Colombian state formation. They have failed to identify the traces of colonial legacies present in all third world countries which form hybrid states, half in Europe and half in the former colony, that even today reproduce the same authoritarian and exclusionary practices, the same cultural inability to construct community while embracing difference.[19] The late Gonzalo Guillén, a Colombian social scientist, wrote in the early seventies a local history of state formation that builds precisely on these issues.[20] In his book Guillén discloses the colonial legacies that construct the Colombian modern state as well as their performative enunciation through state institutions and practices. Unfortunately, the violentologists, caught in what Walter Mignolo calls the "coloniality of power," have put aside such insights.[21] What is at stake here is more than the construction of an academic/intellectual authority; what is at stake is the production and circulation of contesting visions about the nature, capacities, and inadequacies of the Colombian state in its responses to violence and in its challenges for building or allowing for the emergence of a viable nation.

All these misrecognitions are at the crux of the tension between the sublime heroism and the historically shaped social burdens and stigmas that Colombian intellectuals have to bear. The violentologists' fantasy drive seems to be shaped upon a deep desire to become elite: a mimesis with power that would allow them access not only to the shaping of state institutions and policy-making spheres, but also to the inner circles of that same elite that censors, marginalizes, and persecutes everything that it sees as different, including the community of violentologists! The tragedy unfolds as the charismatic nature of the violentologists (their felt sense of revelation and heroism), sustained and nurtured by their own belief in the substantial quality of an abstract idea (the state), is precisely frustrated by such conviction. While betting the farm on the state as ultimate reference point and unifying force of political practice, the violentologists misrecognize what really underlies such mystification: the disunity of power as well as the history and relations of subjection that such mystification endorses. In a personal interview in 1995, when the insertion of the "intellectual for democracy" into high state spheres was at its height, Eduardo Pizarro made reference to these paradoxes and ambiguities:

Building the team for the first commissioned report was very complex. Most of us were academics with a strong critical standing against the state. Our first discussions were obviously on the legitimacy of our role as members of a governmental commission that was asking from us instrumental formulas for the contention of violence. The book that resulted from the 1987 commission (*Colombia: Violencia y Democracia*) was quite unique since it served the purpose of highlighting the diverse causes of violence, with very little diagnosis but with many recommendations. In doing so we consciously accepted a solely instrumental approach. The book had a very profound impact not so much on the ways violence was understood, but rather on the relationship that was built between intellectuals and state. Since then, a massive transit of intellectuals to the state begins, and with it new debates around intellectual co-optation. We've been struggling to build an intellectual community for the past twenty years, and now the state has the potential of absorbing it, and that has a very deep cultural impact over the future of Colombia. Our felt need to contribute to democratic building led us to pragmatic positions engaged with policy making rather than with a deeper comprehension and critique of our own realities. And this shift is not as heroic as many would like to think. Today we are more interested in influencing short-term political processes rather than cultural constructions, if one can make that distinction. Our pragmatism has led us to seek influence in the decision-making spheres, and our lack of critical positioning has diverted us from culture. We've become imprisoned in our own impoverishment.

Since then our most intense debates here at the Institute have been centered on the legitimacy of us being counselors of the prince rather than maintaining a constructive but critical standing towards the establishment. The crux of such debates lies in the way the state can instrumentalize knowledge in order to construct its own imaginary. How can we perform without being instrumentalized by a power elite? I think that we have been colonized and used by that elite. In the end, one thinks one is contributing to the construction of democracy, but maybe one is contributing to construct a different thing altogether. We want to make the transit to the state because we want a decent salary, we want power, social prestige, because we are fed up by the elite's contempt toward the Colombian intellectual, who, like the artist, becomes in their imagination simply a loser. One can build heroic justifications that validate the need of moving toward the state, but this only shows a deep desperation of the Colombian intellectual, who in desiring to influence political processes finds himself blocked by deeply rooted obstacles.[22]

Modernity's Disenchantments: Melancholia, Marginalia, and Truncated Agencies

From the mid-eighties until the mid-nineties the expectations the violentologists held of the state seemed to be just right. They were active mediators between high government and guerrilla and extreme right paramilitary organizations. Many of them were making their passage to state positions, as special advisors for peace negotiations or as high-ranking bureaucrats in the attorney general's office. Following such transits, the violentologists began to play a key role in the efforts that the Barco and Cesar Augusto Gaviria (1990–94) administrations invested in bringing about a modernization of the state. At a time when political violence was thought to be overdiagnosed, the executive branch was asking for the input of the violentologists in building strategies for conflict management. The violentologists' main function became that of technocrat in the negotiations and peace treaties, which were thought of as the by-product of a practical comprehension of what some had called "the architecture of negotiation."[23] In-depth research was left aside, and funds and intellectual efforts were channeled to satisfy the increasing demands of the executive. The state then became the violentologists' main funder and main client, and thus an audience that always clamored for satisfaction.[24]

The golden years came abruptly to a halt with the administrations of Ernesto Samper (1994–98) and Pastrana. The increasing intensification of the conflict in conjunctiion with what Sánchez has called the "gangsterization of the guerrillas" has triggered new formations of violence—more disseminated, fragmented, and decentered—that have surpassed any former analysis or expectation. As Sánchez mentioned in one of our conversations,

"All of us have fallen into an incapacity for recognizing the fact that violence has indeed changed, and because of this lack of recognition we have compromised ourselves with the wrong debates." The cost of that mistake has been extremely high. Isolated from any alternative social movement, the violentologists were trapped in their own illusion: caught between "palace wars" that endorsed either a negotiated peace with the guerrillas or more militaristic responses to conflict, the violentologists soon became "legitimate" war targets for all those interested in promoting further radicalization of the conflict.[25] Having no protection from the state, they were left on their own:

> There are moments in which the intellectual world feels deeply threatened, more so when threats from various places converge. One sees people threatened by the guerrillas because they defend positions that are different from the guerrilla's own positions, because they defend positions that although politically questionable are, foremost, academic. There are also threats from the paramilitary that have consequences over segments of intellectuals. One knows that in this country not only famous people have had to leave, but many have left silently, especially those committed to the defense of human rights. . . .
>
> The last months have been that. A moment of convergence of all these things, with people one knows. Obviously this produces a great impact on the community of intellectuals, a sense of paralysis. The academic community feels more intimidated. Albeit the spaces we've tried to create, spaces of autonomy, debate, the intellectual community feels more pressure, feels pushed to have a standing. This is the drama of intellectuals today. I believe that the intellectual must have a clear position on the major issues of the country, but another thing is feeling that one is pushed, because of threats, to say certain things and to keep others silenced.[26]

Today, the tragedy of the violentologists couldn't be more acute: their utopias lost, their lives and agencies truncated, the social foreclosures deepened. Within such a context, self-censure, uncertainty, economic recession, and violence have triggered not only forced exiles but also a deep fragmentation within the already fragile world of the Colombian social sciences. The pendular movement between heroism and failure once again resolved in favor of the latter. Embodying the consciousness of the defeated, the violentologists have become melancholy subjects, isolated, grieving for a lost ideal, still attached to the illusion of the redemptive capacities of the state, and carrying the heavy burden of living in a context with no clear cultural alternatives.[27] The Colombian state is dead, and from that fact the deepest tragedy unfolds: the violentologists invested in defending a ghost, a mask that was to dissolve with the first bullet, with the first death threat. The crossroads of Faith! In Sánchez's words, "You feel the threats not in an abstract manner but with your whole body. And I feel that the rest of the intellectual community has this same perception. Then the phrases of precaution begin: You have to be careful . . . we can't talk about this. . . . This can happen to us . . . this is going to happen to us . . . this is happening to us."[28]

The silencing of the violentologists has paved the way for a more forceful insertion of an already ascending transnational trend: that of explaining violence from "hard-edged" disciplines with "nonideological" bias and more "technical" approaches to reality. A new heroism was on the rise, heavily marked by an oversimplification of violence and an instrumentalization of culture. Funded and endorsed by the World Bank, the Inter-American Development Bank, and the Organization of American States, among others, epidemiology and economics have become the key disciplines for legitimating policies for the containment of disseminated violence. Understanding violence as a state problem of public health or as a process of individual decision based on a cost-benefit analysis encourages less compromising views on the part of the establishment at the same time that it allows the circulation of narratives more functional for political manipulation.[29] The deepening of the conflict in Colombia and the increasing polarization of society call for an urgent bridging between state institutions and policy-making spheres with social movements, ex-centric political and cultural initiatives, and emerging forms of social and cultural critique. Unfortunately, the failure and pursuant silencing of the violentologists and the consolidation of the new technical rhetoric on violence work perversely in tandem to further frustrate the possibilities for a more profound and polyphonic understanding of a problem that concerns all.

Reassessing Commonalities, Breaking Parochialisms

Latin American democracies today operate on the basis of two opposing but complementary realities. The first, rooted in the terrain of the imagined, focuses on the rhetorics of postauthoritarian regimes, democratic participation, and the need for institutional consolidation. The second, founded on political practice, focuses on the need to sustain, through the use of extensive and unaccountable force, cohesion in an increasingly fragmented, ruptured, and exclusive society. As globalization imprints itself on Latin America and neoliberal "adjustments" keep deepening social and economic inequalities, the possibility of viable democracies in Latin America seems to be slipping away. The failure of the nation-state to incorporate and enforce its primary functions as provider of justice and security has led the way for the consolidation of parallel systems of order, security, and justice which, while often illegitimate, operate as real alternatives in the interstices of the nation-state. Colombia is an extreme manifestation of a broader Latin American pattern. The expansion of narcotraffic, the deepening of state corruption, and the increasingly evident collapse of the justice system raise serious questions regarding the viability of state institutions across Latin America. The challenge that the region as a whole faces today demands a creative reinvention of the state's architecture: one that can democratically foster the recomposition of the nation as well as provide alternative mechanisms for coping with multiple fin-de-siècle terrors; one that can genuinely fight against radical individualism and its accompanying rhetoric of heroism. Such reinvention can only come through the displacement of the state as center of enunciation and consequently by allowing the emergence of new loci of enunciation. As Mignolo points out, "One thing is to criticize the complicity between knowledge and state while inhabiting a particular nation-state, and another to criticize the complicity between knowledge and state from the historical exteriority of a universal idea of the state forged on the experience of a local history: the modern, European experience of the state."[30] The latter path opens up possibilities for destabilizing the status quo and its unchallenged traditions, symbols, solidified memories, and practices, its monumentalism, its sacred texts, subjects, and explanations.

The misrecognitions of the violentologists and their incapacity to recede from teleological and heroic agencies blocked their capacity to generate counterhistories denouncing not only the exclusionary nature of state formations and practices, but also the state's own cultural inability to engage with difference. In their quest for democratic ideals they forgot to interrogate the history of the Colombian state, the hegemonic ideologies that crosscut state practices and institutions. Today in Colombia, as perhaps in other countries in the hemisphere, what is at stake is the possibility for reimagining the nation's topography while challenging, as the Guatemalan intellectual Enrique Sam suggests, "nationalistic histories that focus on the development of the modern state (like Sánchez's intellectuals for democracy) and materialistic histories that see foreign imperialism and class conflict as the only driving forces (like Sánchez's critical intellectuals)."[31] What I am arguing is the need to relocate expert languages, knowledge, and cultures in order to expose their own particular locus of enunciation as a double bind between objectivity and "global designs,"[32] on one hand, and local histories and social, cultural, and historical experiences of alterity, on the other. Furthermore, there is an urgency to destabilize expert knowledge and cultures as builders of a modernity and a nation-state that, while mirroring European ideals, deeply undermine the role of local histories in constructing alternative visions of state and nation, alternative visions of more plausible futures.

Notes

1. Roughly one can group these authors into three distinct categories. The first one, based on testimonial accounts, began with Arturo Alape and continued throughout the eighties and nineties with the prolific writings of Alfredo Molano, German Castro Caycedo, Olga Behar, and Alonso Salazar. The second category, maybe more persistent and varied, is based on fictional accounts that explore the depths and nuances of an increasing pervasive violence; such authors as Manuel Mejía Vallejo, García Márquez, and, more recently, Fernando Vallejo are among its practitioners. Finally, the third group, the locus of analysis in this paper, is characterized by historical, political, and sociological analysis started in the sixties by Fals Borda, Álvaro Guzman, and Javier Torres, and continued in the eighties and nineties by Daniel Pecaut, Gonzalo Sánchez, Álvaro Camacho, Eduardo Pizarro, Alejandro Reyes, and others associated with the Instituto de Estudios Políticos y Relaciones Internacionales (IEPRI) at the Universidad Nacional de Colombia. These last authors are referred to in this paper as violentologists.

2. This group of political scientists, sociologists, and lawyers not only was the first generation of middle-class intellectuals trained abroad (in the United States, France, England, and Germany), but also formed an academic community that began to structure its project around the relationship between history, state, politics, and violence.

3. See Sánchez, 1998:134.

4. The schools of law not only trained the state's nobility but also became the natural spaces in which contemporary intellectual debates flourished. Throughout the nineteenth century a sustained discussion was held on whether or not it was legitimate to teach Jeremy Bentham's texts in the schools of law. For some, Bentham's texts were basic for laying the foundations of liberal ideology and for undermining the union between power and religion; for others, the utilitarian model was a clear opposition to the constitutional mandate that accepted Catholic faith as the moral base of the nation (see Jaramillo 1982). Cultural capital, combined with social and economic capital, held the lawyer as architect of state, builder of social order, and regent of national (or an imagined national) unity.

5. Today, the other competing and extensive form of social mobility is the one that comes through rapid wealth accumulation from corruption and / or drug-related activities (traffic, money laundering).

6. For example, in the cases of Salvador Camacho Roldán, José María Samper, and Miguel Samper (the last two ancestors of Colombia's president and lawyer Ernesto Samper).

7. Former and current members of the IEPRI have been on leave while taking state positions: for example, Jorge Orlando Melo, former presidential advisor for human rights and later director of the Biblioteca Luis Angel Arango (Colombia's central bank library); Alvaro Tirado, ambassador to Switzerland; Hernando Valencia Villa, former deputy attorney general for human rights; Iván Orozco, former auxiliary attorney general of the nation; Pilar Gaitán, former private secretariat for human rights at the Ministry of Defense; and Martha Ardila, former director of a program in the Ministry of External Affairs.

8. At the time, the perpetrators of terror were easily identifiable: the outbreaks of political violence, social control, and repression were sponsored only by the security forces of the state following the widely spread doctrine of National Security. In the following decades such clarity was reversed, as indiscriminate and decentered violence was unleashed *not only* by the state but by other social actors (guerrillas, paramilitary organizations, narcotraffic).

9. This period was characterized by extreme political violence in rural Colombia that unleashed an uncontained terror and bloodshed that killed more than eight hundred thousand peasants.

10. See, for example, Arrubla 1978, Fals 1968, Gilhodés 1976a, Palacio 1980, and Pecault 1976.

11. See, for example, Fajardo 1977, 1981; Gilhodés 1976b; and Kalmanovitz 1978.

12. At the time, six guerrilla groups were in arms (Fuerzas Armadas Revolucio-

narias de Colombia [FARC], Ejército de Liberación Nacional [ELN], Ejército Popular de Liberación [EPL], Movimiento 19 de Abril [M-19], Movimiento Quintin Lame, and the Partido Revolucionario de los Trabajadores [PRT]).

13. See IEPRI 1996

14. See Sánchez 1998.

15. Personal interview, 1995.

16. See Sánchez 1998:136.

17. This comes in sharp contrast with the conscious moves that other intellectuals, speaking from either the academia or from NGOs have chosen to follow: by aligning themselves or by promoting strategic partnerships with subaltern agents these *other* intellectuals have become circumstantial activists (see Marcus 1998), invested in the promotion of new tools for the political leverage of marginalized subjects or / and experiences (displaced populations, women, violence, memory, and trauma, to name a few). See, for example, Riaño 2000, Meertens 1998, Rodriguez 2000, Sánchez-Blake 2000, Vásquez 1998.

18. An exception to such a characterization would be Fals Borda's suggestion for an *investigación acción–participativa*.

19. See, for example, Chaterjee 1993.

20. See Guillén 1996 (1978).

21. Coloniality of power is the "correlation between epistemology and colonization in the constitution of Europe as a geopolitical and economic entity from which the rest of the world is measured, studied, and classified." Mignolo 2000:213.

22. Personal interview, 1995.

23. See Bejarano 1995.

24. Compare this with cases in which the audiences of the intellectual are not power holders but disempowered agents that seek new partnerships for expanding their own political leverage while gaining other visibilities through the transit of their own counter / hegemonic discourses into more centered / public spheres.

25. In 1999, Jesús Antonio Bejarano, the key theorist of the "architecture of negotiation," was assassinated, presumably by the FARC. The same year Eduardo Pizarro, former director of the IEPRI, was seriously wounded in an assassination attempt presumably ordered by paramilitary groups.

26. Gonzalo Sánchez. See Galindo and Valencia 2000:249–50 (my translation).

27. This same situation was lived by the intellectuals in the former German Democratic Republic during the period of reunification. See Lepenies 1992.

28. Gonzalo Sánchez. See Galindo and Valencia 2000:255 (my translation).

29. See, for example, the extremely impoverished use of sociological concepts appropriated by economic rhetoric in Lederman, Loayza, Menéndez 1999. In par-

ticular, their understanding of social capital as a compound variable composed of "regional dummy variables indicating groups of countries according to geographic location or stage of development (with the idea that countries in a region share certain cultural traits that in turn affect their social capital), and, second, the numbers of telephones per capita and radios per capita in the country (which diminish the costs of social interactions)" (5).

30. See Mignolo 2000.
31. Cited by Warren 1998:145.
32. See Mignolo 2000.

Afterword: A Fax, Two *Moles*, a Consul, and a Judge

MARY LOUISE PRATT

The phone rings early one morning at the home of the Mexican consul in a California city. His assistant needs him urgently in court. She has been called in in the case of a fourteen-year-old Mexican girl who is pregnant. The father is a twenty-six-year-old man, also from Mexico. Both are undocumented. The judge has ruled as she normally does in such cases—the pregnant girl should become a ward of the state for her own protection; the baby would almost certainly be put up for adoption; the man should be charged with statutory rape, imprisoned for fifteen to twenty years, then deported. The young girl speaks no English. She does not speak Spanish either. She is indigenous, a Mixteca from the state of Oaxaca. So is he. Through interpreters the story unfolds. The two are from the same village; among the Mixteco it is common for girls to marry at fourteen, often to older men, in unions arranged between families.[1] In the village, the man said, the matrimonial rituals and necessary exchanges had taken place in good order; he had come north to find work and sent for her to join him. Now they were starting a family.

Lives were on the line. For the judge, a crime had taken place, a girl was pregnant at a far too young age, and her life chances were unfairly limited. She was not old enough to make such decisions for herself. She needed to be protected and given a chance at a life of her own. The perpetrator should be punished. The consul saw a human tragedy in the making. Swallowed up by the social service system, knowing neither Spanish nor English, the girl would be isolated and torn forever from everything that was hers, including her child. Her prospects would be grim, and she would be unlikely ever to reconnect with her family. For the young man, were he to survive a U.S. prison sentence at all, losing his wife and child in this way would destroy his status in the village and devastate relations among their families. The judge and the consul were both right; both were following the rules.

The girl's parents, it turned out, were also working in the United States. The consul telephoned the mother in the state of Washington and the father in New York. Yes, they confirmed, they had arranged the union. Back in the village, the agreed-upon animals had been delivered from one family to the other. The girl's grandmother had prepared the ritual *mole* (a special dish of chicken in a complex sauce made with chocolate and chile) and delivered it to the groom's family. The groom's family had likewise prepared their *mole* and sent it via a courier to the bride's parents in the United States. The consul called the state-sponsored center for the study of indigenous cultures in Oaxaca. A researcher faxed a letter confirming that the union indeed constituted a marriage in the community and that the forms described, particularly the exchange of *moles*, were the authorized ones. The judge listened, read, understood, wondered what to do. The consul offered a solution: Let me marry them here, he said, as their consul. Case closed—but what happened? A Mixteco marriage was authorized by Mexican law in the United States, though it violated U.S. law and social norms; a fourteen-year-old girl was embarked on a life that she had probably not chosen for herself and which would offer her few choices along the way; three lives and a family were saved from human disaster; a community's longstanding social forms were respected. Which gets it right? All of the above, but mainly, in this case, the last two.

This book, *Cultural Agency*, would have us attend to the role of scholars, social movements, and states in this story. A scholar faxed the letter affirming and legitimating (in an act of cultural agency) the account given by the witnesses. That scholar was salaried as a state-sponsored researcher, but his work continually placed him in the position of advocacy for indigenous communities against racism and indifference from the state. Indigenous movements had educated him in this role. The consul, a state employee informed by indigenous social movements and shaped by the Mexican democratic uprising of the 1960s, told the story over dinner to a pair of U.S.-based scholars who he knew would be fascinated by it. These scholars, from different disciplines, had their roots in the intellectual formations connected to movements for racial justice, decolonization, and gender equality. Both had binational identities.

One of them happened to be writing an afterword for a book on cultural agency. She retold the story in her afterword to demonstrate the entanglements, discontinuities, and ambivalences that tend to characterize the fields in which acts of cultural agency occur. The story thus entered a circuit of scholarly communication, one of the tracings on an artful, risk-ridden, intensely human circuit board that includes a court exchange with Mixteco-Spanish-English interpreters, phone calls to rural Washington and New York City, a fax from a scholar to a consul, an explanation by a consul to a judge, two illegal border crossings, one *mole* commissioned in the United States and delivered in Oaxaca, another made in Oaxaca and delivered in the United States, a wedding required in one place but not the other, and a trinational dinner party. One of the strengths of the approach offered in this book is to bring the circuit board into view.

It is irresistible to read *Cultural Agency* as an instance of its own subject matter; to read it in the book's own terms, as a cultural intervention that seeks to promote, legitimate, and energize certain practices in the interest of reinforcing democratic life; as an act not derived from a fixed program but created from within the situation in which it intervenes. In titling itself as it does, *Cultural Agency* makes a foundational gesture. The thing to be founded is a scholarly praxis, a blueprint for academic work committed to advancing energetic, creative, nonharmonious but nonviolent democratic relations. In thus defining a project, cultural agency tries to break out of the uneasy stasis into which cultural studies seems to have gravitated. Beginning as a radical upstart that defied hierarchies of high and low, art and everyday, first world and third world, cultural studies developed into an eclectic, tolerant, elastic space open to methodological experimentation and engaged scholarship but also available to less energetic work that sidesteps seriously challenging questions.[2] The terms *cultural citizenship* and now *cultural agency* have come into play to define projects that seek to be more specific about their direction, objectives, and politics while retaining flexibility about objects of study.[3] In both cases the commitment is to the promotion of democratic social relations and to the flourishing of culture and creativity as a means of sustaining them.

Why culture? Sylvia Wynter, in a manifesto for a new humanism, offers an explanation going back to the nineteenth century.[4] Then, she says, "Culture took the place that Reason had played in the Classical episteme," as the criterion for defining and valuing the human. It was, she sustains, a radically democratizing move. Initially the shift produced a hierarchization of cultures, just as Reason had been used to distinguish between groups who had it and groups who did not. Yet the study of languages and cultures outside the West challenged the hierarchies. From the 1960s on, decolonization and democratization movements did their work on the idea of culture, making it into a vehicle for articulating what Wynter describes as "a humanitas now conceived as isomorphic with the global human rather than with merely its Indo-European expression"(50). From this standpoint cultural studies is the emergence of this global human in knowledge. The genealogy of cultural studies lies in the engaged intellectual endeavors of feminism, ethnic studies, anti-imperialism, and class analysis.

Cultural agency names both an object of study—"moments and manners of acting up," to cite Sommer's lively phrase—and a particular positioning of scholars in relation to the cultural agents and agencies they study. The scholar in this model is neither a producer of knowledge whose job is to assemble truthful, disinterested assertions about the world, nor is she the interpreter of texts who elucidates and explains symbolic expressions, though both of these are often part of the enterprise. Cultural agency's image of scholars is as self-conscious interveners whose work is described by a set of transitive verbs: anticipate, promote, energize, reinforce. The approach rejects the view of academic study as parasitic on other people's world-changing activity. While such parasitism (*vampirism* is the word the authors use) may exist, it is not inevitable. The cultural agency approach insists on academic study and cultural activism as reciprocal and mutually beneficial enterprises. Each illuminates the other and gives it legitimacy, recognition, vitality; each makes use of the other and consents to be made use of in these ways. These mutual relationships and the circulations of meaning, insight, and value they create justify the scholarly enterprise and give it life. Often they place the scholar in the role of translator and mediator crisscrossing the fertile divide between activists and scholars, interpreting to one community what another has said.

The scholar of cultural agency is thus being a cultural agent. The contributors to this book exemplify several variants. Barbero and Sommer work at formulating manifestos for the enterprise. García Canclini and Godenzzi are directly engaged in government policymaking and the discussions that surround it. They work with the power of cultural and educational policies in the pursuit of social justice and strong democratic public life. Their task of translation is threefold: bringing scholarly arguments, policy discussions, grassroots knowledge, and experience into play with each other. Hernández-Reguant and Ramos analyze and critique government cultural policies with a view to influencing what comes next and showing the need for alternatives. Taylor and Arias write out of research and fieldwork on particular projects of political-cultural intervention which they regard as successful. Making these known outside their local and national contexts, and known to each other, counteracts the entirely plausible tendency to see neoliberalism as an over-whelming homogeneous force bulldozing everything in its path. They re-mind us that life must be made meaningful locally, that place and memory have force. Matory and Villaveces study instances of scholarly interventions gone awry due to failures to reflect on the webs of relationships in which the scholars were enmeshed. As a result, work overcenters the researcher and loses political potency. Hale and Millamán take up one of the vectors that inheres in the approach—its commitment to the struggles of nondominant and subaltern groups. (Half the contributions in this book are about indige-nous and African-based social groups.) These struggles, they point out, are often not homogeneous but are themselves terrains of struggle, where con-flicting aspirations and relationships interact. This is particularly true, they point out, in the neoliberal state, which uses the language of democracy, difference, rights, identity, and multiculturalism to achieve, in Hale's apt phrase, "governance by recognition." The implications for scholars are sev-eral: to be competent, they must learn to navigate these terrains and avoid oversimplifying; their scholarly interventions are interventions in these in-ternal struggles; scholars are as enmeshed as anyone else in the dynamics of co-optation and compromise; and the interests of scholars may be incompat-ible at points with those of particular movements, especially if they seek autonomy. Overall, the question is whether and how a cultural agency ap-proach can distinguish its interventions and objectives from those of the neoliberal state, especially at the points where the two use the same language. One answer may be Sommer's insistence on nonviolent conflict as the thing democracy thrives on. The neoliberal state by contrast opts for a mask of consensus overlaying great social violence wrapped in silence.

In calling forth the scholar as a cultural agent, this volume seeks a path out of the long-acknowledged sense of despair and paralysis that has gripped engaged intellectuals since the late 1980s. In this respect it echoes another foundational study, J. J. Gibson-Graham's *The End of Capitalism (as we knew it): A Feminist Critique of Political Economy.*[5] Gibson-Graham argues that scholars must refuse to reproduce totalizing narratives "rendered in a language and an image of noncontradiction," such as accounts in which capitalism explains everything and "everything comes to mean the same thing." Such accounts are likely to seem coherent and plausible but lead only to an ethically grounded despair and paralysis. Capitalist societies, they argue, are riddled with noncapitalist modes of production and with relations and activities that are not functional for capitalism. These may appear trivial to the analyst, but the analyst should think twice about them, for the apparent triviality may be an effect of the workings of the totalizing narrative in the analyst. The task of critical scholars is to seek to tell the story otherwise, including to override their own intuitions at times. They should identify in the existing world elements of the worlds they would like to see come into being. This requires attending to disharmonies, unintended consequences, alternative formations, however trivial they may initially appear. In Gibson-Graham's formulation, in their acts of describing the world scholars are also making it; in their descriptions of the world they are accountable for the worlds those descriptions imply. Sommer reaches a similar conclusion by a different route: "It is easier, after all, to be right about a bad situation than to make a difference in it." The rejection of despair is one reason these projects focus away from the negative capabilities of scholarship, from the damage it can do.

With debts to feminism and ethnic studies, projects like Gibson-Graham's and Sommer's also rise from the ashes of what scholars themselves see as the crushing defeat of Left revolutionary aspirations since 1989, the year in which the Berlin Wall and the Sandinista government in Nicaragua fell and Chile's highly compromised return to democracy took place. The apparent defeat of heroic, utopian, sacrificial revolutionism along with new triumphs from the Right produced profound despair and disorientation among socially committed scholars and intellectuals. Cultural studies became for many the terrain on which to regroup. The regrouping is taking place around projects which, like cultural agency, are implicitly anti-utopian, antiheroic, antitragic, and anti-universalist. Parameters and objects of study are defined from within the situations under study; the distinction between reform and revolution is simply set aside; no image of a peaceful, harmonious society occupies the offing. Like *cultural agency*, the term *cultural citizenship*, for example, has no generalizable referent. It refers to whatever are the constitutive elements of belonging and unbelonging for the inhabitants of a given social context. Like cultural agency, cultural citizenship faces the difficulty of distinguishing valid social change from co-opted management of difference, knowing that the distinction can be analytical but not always empirical.

Absences are inevitable, especially in an initial volume. Two conspicuous ones are women's movements and religiosities, two of the most dynamic and varied cultural arenas in Latin America and the world today. Across the great range of women's organizations and emergent religiosities, what relations are to be found to the goals of a thriving democratic life? Where are the potentials for significant change? Where is change actually occurring? The answers, this book predicts, will be multiple, varied, and local. The variants and locales can enter into relationships with each other, however, and these relations can be strengthening, affirming, illuminating, clarifying. To say they can be only that, however, would, as Gibson-Graham warns, reduce everything to the same thing. To have accountability, they would say, scholars-cum-cultural-agents must also exercise judgment and seek out instabilities, disharmonies, unintended consequences in their corpuses and in their own work. Irritants of the state, they will need to be irritants of each other as well.

Notes

1. The Mexican-American musician and singer Leila Downs tells the story of her Mixteca mother, who fled just such an arrangement as a girl of fifteen. Having developed a talent for singing, she was able to leave her village and make a life for herself in Mexico City, where she eventually married a North American biologist. After the marriage broke up, she returned to the village, where she owns a business. Her daughter sings in Spanish, English, and Mixteco.

2. Despite its amorphous and decentered character, cultural studies seems to pose enough of a threat to traditional disciplines that it has not been encouraged to institutionalize itself in the United States, either within existing entities or in new ones.

3. For an initial engagement with cultural citizenship, see Renato Rosaldo, *Culture and Truth* (Boston: Beacon Press, 1989); elaboration of the concept can be sampled in

two recent collections, W. Flores and R. Benmayor, eds., *Latino Cultural Citizenship* (Boston: Beacon Press, 2001) and R. Rosaldo, ed., *Cultural Citizenship in Island Southeast Asia* (Berkeley: University of California Press, 2003).

4. Sylvia Wynter, "The Ceremony Must be Found: After Humanism," *boundary 2* 12 (1984):19–70, see esp. 46.

5. J. J. Gibson-Graham, *The End of Capitalism (as we knew it): A Feminist Critique of Political Economy* (New Brunswick: Rutgers University Press, 1995). J. J. Gibson-Graham is the combined name of a joint author.

Afterword: Spread It Around!

CLAUDIO LOMNITZ

In Jewish tradition, what the authors of this book call cultural agency is a godly attribute: "Blessed is He whose words are acts." This description of God implies, by default at least, that most people do not do as they say, that their acts fall short of their stated intentions, or, at the very least, that people talk a lot before acting. These very human attributes are acknowledged in another well-known saying: "Man thinks, God laughs" (or, to put it in a more contemporary way, "People think, God laughs"). Puzzled, baffled, stumped, scheming, wily, interpretive, reflexive: these are human states. Perhaps some of the authors of this book would echo Nietzsche and call them "all too human," but let us refrain from doing so at this time and simply note that the Judeo-Christian tradition elevates "cultural agency" above these human qualities.

And yet we know with some precision, from reading J. L. Austin and others since, that *performative* statements, statements that "do things with words," are a kind of enunciation next to various other sorts of propositions and tropes: Say "I do" at the right time and place and, by golly, you're married! Respond, instead, to the question "What do you think about marriage?" and no amount of moaning will grant you a divorce.[1] In other words, there are contexts for cultural agency, and contexts for reflection, rumination, cultivation, and inconsequential expression. This book reflects on cultural agency in the Americas, so I will focus these brief remarks on a few general aspects of that context.

In Latin America there is a longstanding tendency to sublimate cultural agency as the only true and acceptable form of intellectual production. Missionary practice runs deep there, and so does revolution. As a consequence, Latin American intellectuals generally seem to agree that the object of cultural production is not to understand the world, but to change it. The intellectual is thus a kind of visionary or healer. A most impressive and perfected example of the magic of Latin American cultural agency is Paulo

Freire's pedagogical method, in which "the oppressed" learn to read and transform their consciousness in a single sweep.[2] I call this method magical because it is, literally, an example of sympathetic magic: the manipulation of the word *is* the transformation of the world.

And we might argue that Latin American intellectuals have put too much stock in it. Liberals of the nineteenth century magically did away with the effects of three hundred years of colonial degradation by writing ever-more-awesome constitutions. Even today, for example, Mexicans have the constitutional right to work, but whom do they sue if they are unemployed? To which government office can they take their case and get it resolved? More famously for sure, the so-called Indian problem was solved at the stroke of a pen—about as often and as successfully as alchemists transubstantiated lead into gold. In their turn, Marxist zealots generated democracy, abundance, and gender and racial equality in propaganda campaigns ("ready . . . aim . . . SING!," as Tom Lehrer once put it). But let's get off of this Magical Mystery Tour for a moment and inspect the conditions of this penchant for enchantment.

On the question of the conditions for cultural agency, it is useful to distinguish between an ideological propensity to favor cultural agency and a set of material conditions for intellectual production that might have a similar effect. For example, the scriptwriter in Mario Vargas Llosa's *Tía Julia y el escribidor* had to belt out at least one chapter of his radio soap per day. This mode of production, arguably an example of (mass-mediated) cultural agency—insofar as a successful *novela* provides narratives that are discussed and then redeployed by radio listeners in their own social practice—is different from literary writing, which is sheltered from the daily appetites of the market. Both sorts of production may end up circulating in an ample public, true, but the former needs constantly to monitor and respond to the public's desires, while the latter has greater freedom to propose ideas and terms that may not have immediate acceptance.

The first form of production has a relatively unmediated connection to its patrons, whether these are the broad public of a soap opera or a bureaucracy of planners at the Ministry of Health, while the latter has more buffers in between—call these academic institutions, endowed trust funds for cultural production, or independent resources.

I think readers can guess where I am going. In most Latin American countries, cultural production has quite a direct connection to the market: university salaries are in most cases insufficient to sustain full-time employment; independent sources of private funding tend to be linked to narrow objectives; and cultural institutions are often at the mercy of a governor, a minister, or a single wealthy patron.

As a result, Latin American intellectuals tend to be "public intellectuals"—they tend to write in the press, appear on television, work for NGOs, or serve as government consultants. To give a blanket endorsement to cultural agency in this context could be to make a virtue out of necessity.

Intellectuals in the United States, on the other hand, often complain of the opposite problems: universities, foundations, academic presses, professional associations are all such well-greased machines that the ivory tower has become a player in a closed-network system of ivory towers. The traveler to that country will at times remark on a kind of melancholic disposition among American academics: an excessive degree of professionalization closes cultural innovators off from a tumultuous world of cultural vernaculars, while the university campus itself appears at times as the very epitome of the place that will never change.

This febrile system of academic production has also led to the (mis?)representation of American society as being profoundly anti-intellectual: whereas in Europe—or in Latin America, for that matter—the death of a great psychologist, historian, or mathematician makes national front-page news, in the United States she will be lucky to make the obituary section of her local paper. Whereas Latin American politicians often wish to appear to be cultured (Mexico's Vicente Fox suffered public humiliation with his botched highbrow celebration of the works of the great Argentine writer "Jose Luis Borgues"), in the United States cultivation, or the appearance of it, seems a surefire formula for loosing an election.

Moreover, attempts to break out of this enclosure sometimes appear to be misguided, timid gestures rather than firm strides. It is difficult, for example, to feel very sanguine about the prospects of Florida Atlantic University's new doctoral program in public intellectual-hood in setting this reality to rights.[3] And yet, one must recognize that, despite the depressing effects that the industrial mode of production has on U.S. academics, and its obvious contrast with the panache of Latin America's bohemians, the American university has had an enormous effect on social change. Claude Lévi-Strauss was not wrong when he compared the American system favorably to the anachronisms of the French intellectual model that are still prestigious in Latin America today:

> We French appear to remain prisoners of an attitude towards science and learning inherited from the nineteenth century, when each area of the intellectual field was sufficiently circumscribed to allow a man endowed with those traditionally French qualities—a broad, general culture, quickness and clarity of thought, a logical mind and literary ability—to achieve a complete grasp of it and, working in isolation, to rethink it in his own way and offer his own synthesis. Whether one applauds the fact or deplores it, modern science and learning no longer admit of this artisan-like approach.[4]

Despite its demotion of the intellectual to a variety of nine-to-five technician, a demotion I believe must be resisted (today's academic is too often treated more like a pack-mule than a racehorse), when it is charged with being irrelevant, the American university can at least point to scientific and technological innovations, to the influence of its humanists and social scientists, and to the recognized value of the educational curriculum. Thus, if Latin American intellectuals may be tempted to glorify cultural agency because it is the natural result of the conditions of production in which most of them operate, U.S. academics may be tempted to forgo the idea entirely and bask instead in the ample credit that its ivory towers have justly earned as agents of change.

This book points to a very different path, a different role for cultural agency in the Americas. It does not seek to glorify Latin American intellectual conditions or stroke the already bloated vanity of its successful intellectuals. Neither does it stoke the fire of nostalgia that the overworked U.S. academic might feel for an artisanal mode of production that is gone.

The conspirator and animator of this volume, Doris Sommer, seeks to use cultural agency as a way of bridging the void between these realities, a proposition that should have obvious attraction both to U.S. and Latin American intellectuals. The stimulating results of this move are visible already in the consolidation of a community of dialogue between humanists, social scientists, and activists, a community that is in evidence in this very volume. The benefits of such a community speak for themselves, and I will dwell on them no further.

There is, however, another aspect of cultural agency as it is being promoted here that deserves some emphasis. This is the commendable *modesty* of the project. Unlike the grand examples of cultural agency that served as blueprints for the reinvention of society, unlike radical "solutions" to society (is society a problem that needs to be solved?), this book accepts that we do, shall, and—at least in the foreseeable future—*should* live in a world of contradiction and multiplicity. The work of cultural agency in this context is not to create a common utopian horizon, but rather to help instantiate, to help press, express, and at times redress contradiction. In other words, in this book cultural agency is not so much conceived as a messianic ideal of godliness or as the defining characteristic of an attainable human utopia, as a necessary effort to give teeth and claws to democratic process.

There is, in all of this, an ethics of cultural production that is a bit reminiscent of Roland Barthes' criticisms of bourgeois aesthetics, with their penchant for appropriation, for packaging, and for mythification. However, the authors of this book are concerned not so much with cultural form and aesthetics as they are with a sociology of unevenly spread resources: a critique of cultural appropriation and of the monopolization of the power to represent. Moreover, and this is the modest and very attractive point—these criticisms must be addressed *in practice*, through humanistic intervention.

It is harder to ignore (or to annihilate!) others when venues of communication are effective and in good repair. And yet the traditional venues of democratic communication have never been sufficient. Think, for instance, of the informal mechanisms of exclusion that operated in the salons and cafes that were the original site of modern democratic expression. Think of the uneven access to representation in radio and television today, and of the limited readership of the press. These inequalities are tied up with uneven levels of education and uneven access to resources and with cultural and linguistic heterogeneity. Given this variety of barriers to collective expression, a broad, humanistic approach to cultural agency makes a great deal of sense, since it can draw on a wide range of expressive techniques and traditions to help give intelligible form to local desires, demands, complaints, and expression.

Finally, the authors of this book recognize, express, and instantiate the energetic potential that emerges from an *American* perspective. Our continental inequalities are complementary, being, as they are, born of the same general economy: the exuberance of the one is the scarcity of the other. If the field is played imaginatively, we have enough wiggle room to keep ourselves busy, at least until the coming of the next Messiah.

Notes

1. *How to Do Things with Words*, 2d ed. (1955; reprint Cambridge: Harvard University Press, 1997).

2. *Pedagogy of the Oppressed*, trans. Myra Bergman Ramos (1970; reprint New York: Continuum, 2000).

3. See http://www.publicintellectuals.fau.edu/.

4. *Tristes Tropiques* (1955; reprint New York, 1977), 100.

References

Abarca Cariman, Geraldine. 2000. "Expectativas educativas de los mapuches de Santiago." M.A. Thesis, Cochabamba, Bolivia, PROEIB Andes, Universidad de San Simón.

Abimbola, Wande. 1997. "Ifa Will Mend Our Broken World: Thoughts on Yoruba Religion and Culture in Africa and the Diaspora." Interviews with an introduction by Ivor Miller. Roxbury, Mass.: Aim Books.

Abiodun, Rowland. 1989. "Women in Yoruba Religious Images." *African Languages and Cultures* 2, no. 1: 1–18.

Abu-Lughod, Lila. 1991. "Writing against Culture." In *Recapturing Anthropology: Working in the Present*, ed. Richard Fox. Santa Fe: School of American Research Press.

Academia de Lenguas Mayas de Guatemala. 1990. *Documentos del Seminario: Situación Actual y Futuro de la ALMG*. Guatemala: Patrocinio del Ministerio de Cultura y Deportes.

Acosta, Leonardo. 1986. "La Información de la Televisión y la Televisión como Información." In *Selección de Lecturas sobre la Propaganda*, ed. Nancy Yion. Havana: Facultad de Psicología.

Adams, Abigail E. 1998. "Gringas, Ghouls and Guatemala: Hypogamy and Transnational Kinship in the Post-NAFTA World." *Journal of Latin American Anthropology* 4, no. 1.

Adelaar, Willem. 1991. "The Endangered Languages Problem: South America." In *Endangered Languages*, eds. E. R. Robins and E. Uhlenbeck. Oxford and New York: Berg.

Adorno, T. W. 1966. *Negative Dialektic*. Frankfurt: Surkamp.

——. 1980. *Teoria estética*. Madrid: Taurus.

Agency for International Development (USAID). 1982. *Land and Labor in Guatemala: An Assessment*. Guatemala: Ediciones Papiro.

Agentes de Pastoral Negros. 1990. *Mulher Negra: Resistência e Soberania de uma Raça*. Petrópolis: Vozes and Quilombo Central—Agentes de Pastoral Negros.

Aguirrechu, Iraida, and Nora Madan, eds. 1994. *Diálogo del Gobierno Cubano y Personas Representativas de la Comunidad Cubana en el Exterior*. Havana: Política.

Albert, Bruce. 2000. "Associações indígenas e desenvolvimento sustentável na Amazônia brasileira." *Povos Indígenas no Brasil 1996/2000*, 197–207. São Paulo: Instituto Socioambiental.

Alfonso, A. 1990. *Televisión de servicio público, televisión lucrativa en América Latina.* Caracas: Ministerio de Cultura.

Alonso, Maria Margarita. 1988. "Actualidad y Perspectivas de la Investigación Social de los Medios de Difusión Masiva y la Juventud en Cuba." *Revista Cubana de Ciencias Sociales* 6, no. 18: 91–104.

Alvarado, Arturo. 2000. "El derecho de aprender." In *¿Quién es el otro? Conversaciones para la convivencia*, ed. Marta Bulnes. Lima: Programa FORTE-PE Unión Europea, Ministerio de Educación.

Alvarez, Francisca. 1996. "Las Mujeres Mayas Etnocidas." *El Periodico Domingo.* Nov. 24.

Alvarez, Sonia E., Evelina Dagnino, and Arturo Escobar, eds. 1997. *Cultures of Politics, Politics of Cultures: Re-visioning Latin American Social Movements.* Boulder: Westview Press.

Anderson, Benedict. 1991 [1983]. *Imagined Communities*, rev. ed. London and New York: Verso.

Andrews, George Reid. 1992. "Racial Inequality in Brazil and the United States: A Statistical Comparison." *Journal of Social History* 26: 229–63.

Appadurai, Arjun. 1996. *Modernity at Large: Cultural Dimensions of Globalization.* Minneapolis: University of Minnesota Press.

Arguedas, José María. 1975. *Formación de una cultura nacional indoamericana.* Mexico City: Siglo Veintiuno Editores.

Arias, Arturo. 1990. "Changing Indian Identity: Guatemala's Violent Transition to Modernity." In *Guatemalan Indians and the State, 1521–1988*, ed. Carol Smith. Austin: University of Texas Press.

Arnold, Denise, and Juan de Dios Yapita, eds. 1994. *Jichha nä parlt'a / Ahora les voy a narrar: Elvira Espejo Ayka.* La Paz: UNICEF / Casa de las Américas.

Arriola, Arturo Taracena, with the collaboration of Gisela Gellert, Enrique Gordillo, Tania Sagastume, and Knut Walter. 2003. *Etnicidad, Estado y nación en Guatemala, 1808–1944.* Antigua, Guatemala: CIRMA.

Arrubla, Mario, ed. *Colombia Hoy.* 1978. Bogotá: Siglo Veintiuno Editores de Colombia.

Asturias, Miguel Angel. 1983. *Hombres de Maíz.* San Jose, Costa Rica: Editorial Universitaria Centroamericana.

Austin, J. L. 1997 [1955]. *How to Do Things with Words*, 2d ed. Cambridge: Harvard University Press.

AVANCSO (Association for the Advancement of the Social Sciences in Guatemala). 1995. *Trabajo y Organización de Mujeres: Su influencia en la Construcción de los Significados de la Identidad de Género Femenino.* Texto para Debate No.10. Guatemala City: AVANCSO.

——. 1998. *La Economía de Guatemala Ante el Ajuste Estructural a Comienzo de los '90,* Textos para Debate No.13. Guatemala City: AVANCSO.

Awe, Bolanle. 1997. "The Iyalode in the Traditional Yoruba Political System." In *Sexual Stratification,* ed. Alice Schlegel. New York: Columbia University Press.

Aylwin, Jose. 2001. "Los conflictos en el territorio mapuche: Antecedentes y perspectivas." In *Politicas Publicas y el Pueblo Mapuche,* ed. J. Aylwin, 25–56. Temuco: Instituto de Estudios Indigenas.

——. 2002. *Política Pública y Pueblos Indígenas: El Caso de las Políticas del Estado Chileno y el Pueblo Mapuche.* Temuco, Chile: Instituto de Estudios Indigenas, Universidad de la Frontera.

Azevedo Santos, Maria Stella de. 1993. *Meu Tempo É Agora.* São Paulo: Editora Oduduwa.

Bach, Robert L. 1985. "Socialist Construction and Cuban Emigration: Explorations into Mariel." *Cuban Studies* 15, no. 2: 19–35.

Bakhtin, Mikail. 1981. "Discourse in the Novel." In *The Dialogic Imagination,* ed. M. Holquist. Austin: University of Texas Press.

Balibar, E. 1991. "The Nation Form: History and Ideology." In *Race, Nation, Class. Ambiguous Identities,* eds. E. Balibar and I. Wallerstein. New York: Verso.

Barry, Tom. 1987. *Roots of Rebellion: Land and Hunger in Central America.* Boston: Southend Press.

Barthes, Roland. 1981. *Camera Lucida: Reflections on Photography,* trans. Richard Howard. New York: Hill and Wang.

Bastide, Roger. 1961. *O Candomblé da Bahia.* São Paulo: Editora Nacional.

Bastos, Santiago, and Manuela Camus. 2003. *Entre el mecapal y el cielo: Desarrollo del movimiento Maya en Guatemala.* Guatemala City: FLACSO and Cholsamaj.

Baudrillard, J. 1985. "El éxtasis de la comunicación." In H. Foster and J. Baudrillard, *La postmodernidad.* Barcelona: Kairós.

Bauer, Brian. 1996. *El desarrollo del estado inca.* Lima: CBC.

Bejarano, Jesús Antonio. 1997. "Democracia, conflico, y eficiencia económica." In J. A. Bejarano, Camilo Echandía Castilla, Rodolfo Escobedo, and Enrique León Queruz. *Colombia: Inseguridad, violencia y desempeño económica en las áreas rurales.* Bogotá: Fonade, Universidad esternado de Colombia.

Benhabib, Seyla. 2002. *Claims of Culture: Equality and Diversity in the Global Era.* Princeton: Princeton University Press.

Benhabib, Seyla, ed. 1996. *Democracy and Difference: Contesting the Boundaries of the Political*. Princeton: Princeton University Press.

Bennett, J. "The Aesthetics of Sense-Memory: Theorising Trauma through the Visual Arts." Work in progress.

Berkhofer, Robert F. 1978. *The White Man's Indian: Images of the American Indian from Columbus to the Present*. New York: Knopf.

Berríos, Rodrigo, and Felipe Abarca. 2001. "Ranking de ciudades: De Puerto Madero a Puerto Digital." In *America Economia Publishing*, supplement ilhn 2297, 15 May.

Betancourt, Luis A. 1989. "Radio Swan: La Voz de Cochinos." *Moncada* 24, no. 4: 62–66.

Bhabha, Homi K., ed. 1977. *Nation and Narration*. London: Routledge.

———. 1994."The Other Question: Stereotype, Discrimination, and the Discourse of Colonialism." In Bhabha, *The Location of Culture*. London: Routledge.

Birman, Patricia. 1985. "Identidade social e homossexualismo no Candomblé." *Religião e Sociedade* 12, no. 1: 2–21.

Birringer, Johannes. *Performance on the Edge: Transformations of Culture*. London: Athlone Press, 2000.

Blommaert, J. 1997. "The Slow Shifts in Orthodoxy: (Re)formulations of 'Integration' in Belgium." *Pragmatics* 7, no. 4: 499–518.

Bobbio, Norberto. 1979. "Gramsci and the Conception of Civil Society." In *Gramsci and Marxist Theory*, ed. Chantal Mouffe. London: Routledge and Kegan Paul.

Boccara, Guillaume. 2001. "The Mapuche People: Mobilization and the Reworking of Politics and Territoriality in Post-Dictatorship Chile." In *Etudes rurales*, 163–64: *Terre, territoire, appartenances*, under the direction of Édouard Conte, Christian Giordano, Ellen Hertz. http://etudesrurales.revues.org/document124.html.

Bonfil Batalla, Guillermo. 1990. *México Profundo: Una civilización negada*. Mexico City: Grijalbo.

Borda, Orlando Fals. 1969. *Subversion and Social Change in Colombia*. New York: Columbia University Press.

Borja, Jordi, and Manuel Castells. 1997. *Local y global: La gestión de las ciudades en la era de la información*. Madrid: United Nations for Human Settlements (Habitat), Taurus.

Boswell, Thomas D., and James R. Curtis. 1983. *The Cuban-American Experience. Culture, Images and Perspectives*. Totowa, N.J.: Rowman and Allanheld.

Brait, Beth. 1996. *Ironia em Perspectiva Polifônica*. Campinas, São Paulo: Editora da Unicamp.

Breton, Ph. 1992. *L'utopie de la communication*. Paris: La Découverte.

Briones, C. 1998a. *La alteridad del "Cuarto Mundo": Una deconstrucción antropológica de la diferencia.* Buenos Aires: Ediciones del Sol.

——. 1998b. "Construcciones de aboriginalidad en Argentina." Presented at *Indigenismo na América Latina, o estado da arte* Conference. Universidad de Brasilia. November 23, 24.

——. 1998c. "Construcciones de aboriginalidad en Argentina." Paper presented at the Seminar "Indigenismo na América Latina: O estado da arte," organized by Alcida Rita Ramos, Departamento de Antropologia, Universidade de Brasília, November 23–24.

——. 1999. "Weaving 'the Mapuche People': The Cultural Politics of Organizations with Indigenous Philosophy and Leadership." Ph. D. diss., University of Texas at Austin. Ann Arbor, Michigan: University Microfilms International.

——. In press. "Mestizaje y Blanqueamiento como Coordenadas de Aboriginalidad y Nación en Argentina." *RUNA*, Universidad de Buenos Aires, vol. 23.

Briones, C., and M. Carrasco. 2000. "(Neo)indigenismo estatal y producciones indigenas en Argentina (1985–1999)." XII Reunião da Associação Brasileira de Antropologia. Forum no. 6 "Organizações Indígenas, Práticas e Legislações Indigenistas." Coordinators: Priscila Faulhaber, Stephen Baines, Antônio Carlos de Souza Lima. Brasilia, July 15–19.

Briones, C., and R. Díaz. 2000. "La nacionalización / provincialización del 'desierto.' Procesos de fijación de fronteras y de constitución de 'otros internos' en el Neuquén." *Actas del V Congreso Argentino de Antropología Social.* "Lo local y lo global: La antropología ante un mundo en transición," part 3, pp. 44–57. La Plata: Entrecomillas.

Briones, C., and D. Lenton. 1997. "Debates parlamentarios y nación: La construcción discursiva de la inclusión / exclusión del indígena." *Actas de las Terceras Jornadas de Lingüística Aborigen*, Instituto de Lingüística, FFyL-UBA, pp.: 303–18.

Brunner, J. J. 1994. *Bienvenidos a la modernidad.* Santiago: Planeta.

Brunner, J. J., C. Catalán, and A. Barrios. 1989. *Chile: Transformaciones culturales y conflictos de la modernidad.* Santiago: FLACSO.

Buarque de Holanda, Sérgio. 1989 [1936]. *Raízes do Brasil.* Rio de Janeiro: José Olympio.

Bueno, Salvador. 1995. "Significance of Cuban Culture Day." *Granma Internacional* 30, no. 41: 13–10 / 18.

Bunster-Burotto, Ximena. 1986. "Surviving Beyond Fear: Women and Torture in Latin America." In *Women and Change in Latin America*, eds. June Nash and Helen Safa. South Hadley, Mass.: Bergin and Garvey.

Butler, Judith. 1995. "Collected and Fractured: Response to *Identities*." In *Identities*, eds. Kwame Anthony Appiah and Henry Louis Gates, Jr. Chicago: University of Chicago Press.

Butler, Kim D. 1998. *Freedoms Given, Freedoms Won: Afro-Brazilians in Post-Abolition São Paulo and Salvador*. New Brunswick: Rutgers University Press, 1998.

Cabrera, Lydia. 1983 [1954]. *El Monte*, 5th ed. Miami: Collección del Chicherekú.

Cadena, Marisol de la. 1998. "Silent Racism and Intellectual Superiority in Peru." *Bulletin of Latin American Research* 17, no. 2: 143–64.

——. 2000. *Indigenous Mestizos: The Politics of Race and Culture in Cuzco, Peru, 1919–1991*. Durham: Duke University Press.

Calderon, F., et al. 1996. *Esa esquiva modernidad:Desarrollo, ciudadanía y cultura en América Latina y el Caribe*. Caracas: Nueva Sociedad.

Camus, Manuela, and Santiago Bastos. 1992. *Quebrando el Silencio*. Guatemala: FLACSO.

Cantor, Judy. 1999. "A Portrait of the Artist as a Communist Bureaucrat: An Interview with Abel Prieto, Cuba's Minister of Culture." *Miami New Times* 14, no. 11, June 24.

Carneiro, Édison. 1986 [1948]. *Candomblés da Bahia*, 7th ed. Rio de Janeiro: Civilização Brasileira.

——. 1967. *Antologia do Negro Brasileiro*. Rio de Janeiro: Editora Technoprint S.A./ Ediouro Grupo Coquetel.

Carrasco, M. 1991. "Hegemonía y Políticas Indigenistas Argentinas en el Chaco Centro-Occidental." *América Indígena* 51, no. 1: 63–122.

——. 1997. "Procesos organizativos, producciones culturales y aboriginalidad en Argentina." II Reunión de Antropología del Mercosur Fronteras Culturales y Ciudadanía. "Territorialidad y Políticas Indigenistas en los Países del Mercosur." Piriápolis, Uruguay.

——. 2000. *Los derechos de los pueblos indígenas en Argentina*. Asociación de Comunidades Indígenas Lhaka Honhat y Grupo Internacional de Trabajo sobre Asuntos Indígenas. Serie Documentos en Español # 30. Buenos Aires: VinciGuerra Testimonios.

Carruthers, Mary. 1990. *The Book of Memory*. Cambridge: Cambridge University Press.

Caruth, Cathy, ed. 1995. *Trauma: Explorations in Memory*. Baltimore: Johns Hopkins University Press.

Caruth, Cathy.1996. *Unclaimed Experience: Trauma, Narrative, and History*. Baltimore: Johns Hopkins University Press.

Carvalho, José Murilo de. 1990. *A Formaçpo da Almas: O imaginário da República no Brasil*. São Paulo: Companhia das Letras.

———. 2000. "Dreams Come Untrue." *Daedalus*. Special issue on *Brazil: Burden of the Past. Promise of the Future*, 129, no. 2: 57–82.

Castellanos de Ponciano, Carlos González, and René Poitevin. 1992. *Mujeres, Niños, y Ajuste Estructural*. Debate #18. Guatemala City: FLACSO.

Castro, Fidel. 1961a. *Words to Intellectuals*. Havana: Consejo Nacional de Cultura.

———. 1961b [1984]. "Homenaje al Periódico *Revolución*." In *Pensamiento Revolucionario y Medios de Comunicación Masiva*, ed. Ana Nuñez Machín. Havana: Editora Política.

———. 1961c. [1984]. "Discurso en la Primera Reunión Nacional de Orientadores Revolucionarios." In *Pensamiento Revolucionario y Medios de Comunicación Masiva*, ed. Ana Nuñez Machín. Havana: Editora Política.

———. 1980. *Speech at the Plaza de la Revolución*. 1 May.

———. 1999. *Capitalismo Actual*. Havana: Editora Política.

CECMA (Centro de Estudios de la Cultural Maya) 1996. "Mujeres Mayas." *Iximulew* in *Siglo Veintiuno*. Aug. 9.

CEH (United Nations Commission for Historical Clarification). 1999. *Guatemala: Memory of Silence*. http://hrdata.aaas.org/ceh/report.

Certeau, Michel de. 1986. *Heterologies: Discourse on the Other*, trans. Brian Massumi. Minneapolis: University of Minnesota Press.

———. 1988. *The Practice of Everyday Life*, trans. Steven F. Rendall. Berkeley: University of California Press.

Chatterjee, Partha. 1990. "The Nationalist Resolution of the Women's Question." In *Recasting Women: Essays in Colonial History*, eds. Kumkum Sangari and Sudesh Vaid. New Brunswick: Rutgers University Press.

———. 1993. *Nation and Its Fragments: Colonial and Postcolonial Histories*. Princeton: Princeton University Press.

Chihuailaf, Elicura. 1999. *Recado confidencial a los chilenos*. Santiago, Chile: LOM Ediciones.

Chuquimamani, Rufino. 1988. "¿Quién soy?" In *Quiénes somos? El tema de la identidad en el Altiplano*, eds. R. Montoya and L. E. López. Lima: Mosca Azul Editores, and Puno: Universidad Nacional del Altiplano.

Claparede, Edouard. 1911. "La question de la 'mémoire' affective," *Archives de psychologie* 10: 361–77.

COCADI. 1988. *Cultura Maya y Politicas de Desarrollo*. Chimaltenango: Ediciones COCADI.

Cohen, J., and A. Arato. 1992. *Civil Society and Political Theory*. Cambridge: MIT Press.

Cojtí Cuxil, Demetrio. 1989. "Problemas de la 'Identidad Nacional' Guatemalteca." In *Cultura Maya y Politicas de Desarrollo*, ed. COCADI. Chimaltenango: Ediciones COCADI.

Collahua Juárez, Irene. 2000. "Un idioma propio que no podemos negar." In *¿Quién es el otro? Conversaciones para la convivencia*, ed. Marta Bulnes. Lima: Programa FORTE-PE Unión Europea, Ministerio de Educación.

Collier, Jane. 1997. *From Duty to Desire*. Princeton: Princeton University Press.

Conklin, B., and L. Graham. 1995. "The Shifting Middle Ground: Amazonian Indians and Eco-Politics." *American Anthropologist* 97, no. 4: 695–710.

Coordinación de Organizaciones Mapuche. 1999. "Reconocimiento Institucional del Pueblo Mapuche de Neuquén. NUEVO MILENIO, NUEVA CONSTITUCION, NUEVA RELACION." MS.

——. In press. "Pulmarí: Protected Indigenous Territory." In *Contemporary Perspectives of the Native Peoples of Pampa, Patagonia and Tierra del Fuego: Living on the Edge*, eds. C. Briones and J. L. Lanata. Bergin and Garvey Series in Anthropology. Westport, Conn.: Greenwood.

Corrêa, Mariza. 2000. "O Mistério dos Orixás e das Bonecas: Raça e Gênero na Antropologia Brasileira." *Etnográfica* 4, no. 2 : 233–65.

da Cunha, Gomes, and Gail D. Triner. 1999. "Race, With or Without Color? Reconciling Brazilian Historiography." *Educación y Política en América Latina* 10, no. 1: 1–23.

Dagnino, Evelina. 1998. "The Cultural Politics of Citizenship, Democracy, and the State." In *Cultures of Politics, Politics of Cultures: Re-visioning Latin American Social Movements*, eds. S. E. Alvarez, E. Dagnino, and A. Escobar, 33–63. Boulder: Westview Press.

Da Matta, R. 1979. *Carnavais, Malandros e Heróis: Para uma sociologia do dilema brasileiro*. Rio de Janeiro: Zahar Editores.

Daniel, Yvonne. 1995. *Rumba, Dance and Social Change in Contemporary Cuba*. Bloomington: Indiana University Press.

Dantas, Marcelo. 1994. *Olodum: De bloco afro a holding cultural*. Salvador, Bahia: Grupo Cultural Olodum, Fundação Casa de Jorge Amado.

——. 1995. "Baiano teatro da vida." In *Trilogia do Pelô*. Salvador, Bahia: Edições Olodum.

Dary Fuentes, Claudia. 1991. *Mujeres Tradicionales y Nuevos Cultivos*. Guatemala City: FLACSO.

Davis, Lennard J., ed. 1997. *The Disability Studies Reader*. New York: Routledge.

Degler, Carl N. 1971. *Neither Black nor White: Slavery and Race Relations in Brazil and the United States*. Madison: University of Wisconsin Press.

Degregori, Carlos Iván, ed. 2000. *No hay país más diverso. Compendio de anthropogia peruana*. Lima: PUCP, IE.

De la Hoz, Pedro. 2001. "Lo cortés no quita lo valiente." *Granma*, 8 April.

Delgado, Guillermo. 1996. "Entre lo popular y lo étnico: Notas de un debate para un debate." In *Pueblos Indios, Soberania y Globalismo*, ed. Stefano Varese. Quito: Ediciones Abya-Yala.

Desai, G. 1993. "The Invention of Invention." *Cultural Critique* 24: 119–42.

Diaz-Polanco, Hector. 1987. *Etnia, Nación y Política*. Mexico: Juan Pablo Editorial.

Diez, F. 2000a. "Costumbre Jurídica Indígena y Diversidad Cultural en el Anteproyecto de Código Procesal Penal del Neuquén." MS.

——. 2000b "Reparación, Costumbre Indígena y Diversidad Cultural." MS.

Douglas, Mary. 1966. *Purity and Danger*. London: Routledge and Kegan Paul.

Drago, T., ed. 1989. *Integración y comunicación*. Madrid: Turner.

Duany, Jorge. 1988. "After the Revolution: The Search for Roots in Afro-Cuban Culture." *Latin American Research Review* 23, no. 1: 244–55.

——. 2000. "Reconstructing Cubanness." In *Cuba, the Elusive Nation*, eds. Damian J. Fernandez and Madeline Camera Betancourt. Gainesville: University Press of Florida.

Duncombe, Stephen. 2002. *Cultural Resistance Reader*. London: Verso.

Dussel, Enrique. 1995. "Eurocentrism and Modernity: Introduction to the Frankfurt Lectures." In *The Postmodernism Debate in Latin America*, ed. J. Beverley. Durham: Duke University Press.

Enloe, Cynthia. 1990. *Bananas, Beaches, and Bases: Making Feminist Sense of International Politics*. Berkeley: University of California Press.

Erlanger, Steven. 2001. "Italy's Premier Calls Western Civilization Superior to Islamic World." *New York Times*, September 27.

Fadipe, N. A. 1970 [1939]. *The Sociology of the Yorùbá*. Ibàdàn, Nigeria: Ibàdàn University Press.

Falaschi, C. 1994. *La Confederación Indígena Neuquina: Reseña histórica, parlamentos, estatuto*. Serie La Tierra Indígena Americana no. 4. Prólogo: Raúl Díaz. Neuquén: IREPS-APDH.

——. 2000 "La *IURIS-DICTIO* de los Pueblos Originarios a partir del 'caso Calfucurá,' Neuquén." MS.

Falla, Ricardo. 1992. *Masacres de la Selva: Ixcan, Guatemala (1975–1982)*. Guatemala: Editorial Universitaria, Universidad de San Carlos de Guatemala.

Felman, Shoshana, and Dori Laub. 1992. *Testimony: Crisis of Witnessing in Literature, Psychoanalysis, and History*. New York: Routledge.

Fischer, Edward F. 2001. *Cultural Logics and Global Economics: Maya Identity in Thought and Practice*. Austin: University of Texas Press.

Fischer, Edward F., and R. McKenna Brown, eds. 1996. *Maya Cultural Activism in Guatemala*. Austin: University of Texas Press.

Fitzpatrick, Peter. 1995. "Comment on 'Talking Culture: New Boundaries, New Rhetoric of Exclusion in Europe' by Verena Stolcke." *Current Anthropology* 36, no. 1: 14–15.

Flores, W., and R. Benmayor, eds. 2001. *Latino Cultural Citizenship*. Boston: Beacon Press.

Fontaine, Pierre-Michel. 1981. "Transnational Relations and Racial Mobilization: Emerging Black Movements in Brazil." In *Ethnic Identities in a Transnational World*, ed. John. F. Stack Jr. Westport, Conn.: Greenwood Press.

Fontanille, Jacques. 1998. *Sémiotique du discours*. Limoges: Presses Universitaires de Limoges.

Fornet, Ambrosio. 1997. "Soñar en Cubano, Escribir en Ingles." *Temas* 10: 4–12.

Forster, Cindy. 1996. "The Neoliberal Assault Begins: Guatemalan Labor Confronts Free Trade." *Report on Guatemala*. Fall

Frank, Luisa, and Philip Wheaton. 1984. *Indian Guatemala, Path to Liberation: The Role of Christians in the Indian Process*. Washington: EPICA Task Force.

Frederick, Howard H. 1986. *Cuban American Radio Wars: Ideology in International Telecommunications*. Norwood, N.J.: Ablex.

Freeman, Derek. 1983. *Margaret Mead and Samoa: The Making and Unmaking of an Anthropological Myth*. Cambridge: Harvard University Press.

Freire, Paulo. 2000 [1970]. *Pedagogy of the Oppressed*, trans. Myra Bergman Ramos. New York: Continuum.

Freyre, Gilberto. 1986 [1933]. *The Masters and the Slaves*, trans. Samuel Putnam. Berkeley: University of California Press.

Fry, Peter. 1986. "Male Homosexuality and Spirit Possession in Brazil." *Journal of Homosexuality* 11, nos. 3–4: 137–53.

Fuentes, Carlos. 1990. *Valiente Mundo Nuevo: Épica, utopía y mito en la novela hispanoamericana*. Mexico City: Fondo de Cultura Económica.

Fuentes, R. 1994. "La investigación de la comunicación: Hacia la post-disciplinariedad en las ciencias sociales." In *Medios y mediaciones*. Mexico City: Iteso.

Fuss, Diana. 1996. *Identity Papers*. New York: Routledge.

Gaceta Oficial. 1980. "Decreto 74 del 22 de Agosto de 1980." *Gaceta Oficial de la República de Cuba* 67, September 8.

Gadamer, Hans-Georg. 1991. *Verdad y método*. Salamanca: Ediciones Sígueme.

Galindo, Mauricio, and Jorge Valencia. 2000. *En Carne Propia*. Bogotá: Intermedio Editores.

Galvani, Walter. 2000. *Nau Capitânia: Pedro Álvares Cabral, como e com quem começamos*. Rio de Janeiro: Record.

Garces, Abelardo, Leo Bueno, et al. 1998. *Encuesta Para Auto–Evaluar su Cubanidad*. www.accespro.net / leobueno / cubanidad.html.

Garcia, Daniel, ed. 1995. *Cuba: Cultura e Identidad Nacional*. Havana: Unión.

Garcia, Maria Cristina. 1996. *Havana, USA: Cuban Exiles and Cuban Americans in South Florida, 1959–1994*. Berkeley: University of California Press.

García Canclini, N. 1982. *Las culturas populares en el capitalismo*. Mexico City: Nueva Imagen.

——, ed., 1987. *Políticas culturales en América Latina*. Mexico City: Grijalbo.

——. 1990. *Culturas híbridas*. Mexico City: Grijalbo.

——, ed. 1994. *El consumo cultural en México*. Mexico City: Conaculta.

——. 1999. *La Globalización Imaginada*. Buenos Aires: Paidos.

Garcia Canclini, N., and C. Moneta, eds. 1999. *Las industrias culturales en la integración latinoamericana*. Mexico City: Grijalbo / SELA / UNESCO.

Geertz, C. 1973. *The Interpretation of Culture: Selected Essays*. New York: Basic Books.

GELIND (Grupo de Estudios en Legislación Indígena: C. Briones, M. Carrasco, D. Lenton, and A. Siffredi). 2000a. "La producción legislativa entre 1984 y 1993." In *Los derechos de los pueblos indígenas en Argentina*, ed. M. Carrasco. Asociación de Comunidades Indígenas Lhaka Honhat and International Working Group on Indigenous Affairs. Serie Documentos en Español no. 30. Buenos Aires: Vinci-Guerra Testimonios.

——. 2000b. "El espíritu de la ley y la construcción jurídica del sujeto 'pueblos indígenas.'" VI Congreso Argentino de Antropología Social, "Identidad Disciplinaria y Campos de Aplicación." Facultad de Humanidades, Universidad Nacional de Mar del Plata, and Colegio de Graduados en Antropología. September 14–16.

Gereffi, Gary, ed. Forthcoming. *Who Gets Ahead in the Global Economy: Industrial Upgrading in Theory and Practice*.

Gibson-Graham, J. J. 1995. *The End of Capitalism (as we knew it): A Feminist Critique of Political Economy*. New Brunswick: Rutgers University Press.

Gilhodes, Pierre. 1970. "Agrarian Struggles in Colombia." In *Agrarian Problems and Peasant Movements in Latin America*, ed. Rodolfo Stavenhagen. Garden City, N.Y.: Doubleday.

Gilliam, Angela. 1998. "The Brazilian *Mulata*: Images in the Global Economy." *Race and Class* 40, no. 1: 66.

Gilroy, Paul. 1993. "The End of Antiracism." In *Race, Culture, and Difference*, eds. A. Rattansi and J. Donald. London: Sage.

——. 2000. *Against Race: Imagining Political Culture beyond the Color Line*. Cambridge: Harvard University Press.

Gimenez, G., and R. Pozas, eds. 1994. *Modernización e identidades sociales*. Mexico City: UNAM.

Gleich, Utta von. 1989. *Educación Primaria Bilingüe Intercultural en América Latina*. Eschborn, RFA: GTZ.

Gomes da Cunha, Olivia Maria. 1998. "Black Movements and the 'Politics of Identity' in Brazil." In *Cultures of Politics, Politics of Cultures: Revisioning Latin American Social Movements*, eds. Sonia E. Alvarez, Evelina Dagnino, and Arturo Escobar. Boulder: Westview Press.

González, Jennifer. 1995. "Autotopographies." In *Prosthetic Territories*, eds. Gabriel Brahm and Mark Driscoll. Boulder: Westview Press.

González, Leila. 1985. "The Unified Black Movement: A New Stage in Black Political Mobilization." In *Race, Class and Power in Brazil*, ed. Pierre-Michel Fontaine. Los Angeles: UCLA, Afro-American Studies Center.

Gordon, Edmund T., Charles R. Hale, and Mark Anderson. 2000. *Indigenous and Black Organization in Central America: An Analytical Framework*. Austin: Central America and Caribbean Research Council (CACRC).

Gramsci, Antonio. 1958. *Studi Gramsciani*. Rome: Editori Riuniti.

——. 1973. *Prison Notebooks*, trans. Quintin Hoare and Geoffrey Nowell-Smith. London: Lawrence and Wishart.

Gray, Chris Hables, and Steven Mentor. 1995. "The Cyborg Body Politic: Version 1.2." In *The Cyborg Handbook*, ed. Chris Hables Gray, with Heidi J. Figueroa-Sarriera and Steven Mentor. New York: Routledge.

Green, James N. 1999. *Beyond Carnival: Male Homosexuality in Twentieth-Century Brazil*. Chicago: University of Chicago Press, 1999.

Green, Linda. 1999. *Fear as a Way of Life: Mayan Widows in Rural Guatemala*. New York: Columbia University Press.

Greenhouse, Linda. 2003. "In a Momentous Term, Justices Remake the Law, and the Court." *New York Times*, July 1.

Grossberg, L. 1992. *We Gotta Get Out of this Place: Popular Conservatism and Postmodern Culture*. New York: Routledge.

Grossberg, L., C. Nelson, and P. Treichler, eds. 1992. *Cultural Studies*. New York: Routledge.

Grossman, David. 2001. "Terror's Long Shadow." *The Guardian*, September 20.

Grosso, José Luis. 1999. "Indios Muertos, Negros Invisibles: La identidad 'Santiagueña' en Argentina." Ph.D. diss., Universidade de Brasília, Brazil.

Grosz, Elizabeth. 1994. *Volatile Bodies: Toward a Corporeal Feminism*. Bloomington and Indianapolis: Indiana University Press.

Guanche, Jesús. 1996a. *Componentes Etnicos de la Nación Cubana*. Havana: Unión.

———. 1996b. "Etnicidad y Racialidad en la Cuba Actual." *Temas* 7: 51–59.

Guillén, Fernando. 1996 [1979]. *El Poder Político en Colombia*. Bogotá: Planeta.

Guimaraes Vásquez, Lerner. 2000. "Conocer cómo funciona el mundo." In *¿Quién es el otro? Conversaciones para la convivencia*, ed. Marta Bulnes. Lima: Programa FORTE-PE Unión Europea, Ministerio de Educación.

Gunder Frank, Andre. 1970. "The Development of Underdevelopment." In *Imperialism and Underdevelopment*, ed. Robert Rhodes. New York: Monthly Review Press.

Gutierez, L., and L.A. Romero. 1985. *Sectores populares y cultura política*. Buenos Aires: Sudamericana.

Habermas, J. 1986. *Teoria de la acción comunicativa*. Madrid: Taurus.

———. 1989a. *El discurso filosófico de la modernidad*. Madrid: Taurus.

———. 1989b. *The New Conservatism*. Cambridge: MIT Press.

Halbwachs, Maurice. 1992. *On Collective Memory*, ed. and trans., Lewis A. Coser. Chicago: University of Chicago Press.

Hale, Charles. 1996. "*Mestizaje*, Hybridity and the Cultural Politics of Difference in Post-Revolutionary Central America." *Journal of Latin American Anthropology* 2, no. 1: 34–61. Special Issue: "Mestizaje," ed. C. Hale.

———. 2002. "Does Multiculturalism Menace?: Governance, Cultural Rights, and the Politics of Identity in Guatemala." *Journal of Latin American Studies* 34: 485–524.

———. 2003. "La Efervescencia Maya y el Imaginario Político Ladino en Guatemala." In *Guatemala: Futuros Alternativos*, ed. C. Arenas. Guatemala: AVANCSO.

Hall, Stuart. 1977. "Culture, the Media, and the Ideological Effect." In *Mass Communications and Society*, eds. James Curran et al. London: Arnold.

———. 1985. "Signification, Representation, Ideology: Althusser and the Post-Structuralist Debates." *Critical Studies in Mass Communication* 2, no. 2: 91–114.

———. 1986. "Gramsci's Relevance for the Study of Race and Ethnicity." *Journal of Communication Inquiry* 10, no. 2: 5–27.

———. 1987. "Cultural Studies: Two Paradigms." In *Culture, Ideology and Social Process*, eds. T. Bennett, G. Martin, C. Mercer, and J. Woollacott, 19–37. London: B. T. Batsford and Open University Press.

———. 1988. "New Ethnicities." In *Black Film, British Cinema*, ed. K. Mercer. ICA Documents #7.

Hall, Stuart. 1993. "What Is This 'Black' in Black Popular Culture?" *Social Justice* 20, nos. 1–2: 104–14.

Hannerz, Ulf. 1999. "Comment on 'Writing for Culture: Why a Successful Concept Should Not Be Discarded' by Christoph Brumann." *Current Anthropology* 40: 18–19.

Handler, R. 1985. "On Dialogue and Destructive Analysis: Problems in Narrating Nationalism and Ethnicity." *Journal of Anthropological Research* 41, no. 2: 171–82.

Harbury, Jenifer. 1994. *Bridge of Courage: Life Stories of the Guatemalan Compañeros and Compañeras*. Monroe, Maine: Common Courage Press.

Harding, Rachel E. 2000. *A Refuge in Thunder: Candomblé and Alternative Spaces of Blackness*. Bloomington and Indianapolis: University of Indiana Press.

Hart Dávalos, Armando. 1983. *Cambiar las Reglas del Juego*. Havana: Letras Cubanas.

———. 1988. "La Cultura Se Expresa en la Defensa de la Identidad." *Cuba Socialista* 32, no. 2: 23–31.

———. 1998. "40 Años de Revolución." Talk delivered at the University of Havana, November 18.

Harvey, David. 1990. *The Condition of Postmodernity: An Enquiry into the Origins of Cultural Change*. Cambridge, Mass., and Oxford: Blackwell.

Healey, Mark Alan. 1998. " 'The Sweet Matriarchy of Bahia': Ruth Landes' Ethnography of Race and Gender." *Dispositio / n* 23, no. 50: 87–116.

Heliodora, Barbara. 1992. "Monotonia em montagem oca e um show de percussão: *Brida* e *Ó Paí, Ó.*" *O Globo*, March 13.

Hendricks, Janet. 1991. "Symbolic Counterhegemony among the Ecuadorian Shuar." In *Nation-States and Indians in Latin America*, eds. G. Urban and J. Sherzer, 53–71. Austin: University of Texas Press.

Hendrickson, Carol. 1995. *Weaving Identities: Construction of Dress and Self in a Highland Guatemala Town*. Austin: University of Texas Press.

Hernández, Isabel. 1992. "Le calme règne sur le Cône Sud: Le génocide des Indiens." In *Notre Amérique métisse: Cinq cents ans après les Latino-Américains parlent aux Européens*, eds. Anne Remiche-Martynow and Graciela Schneier-Madanes. Paris: Éditions La Découverte.

———. 1995. *Los Indios de Argentina*. Quito, Ecuador: Abya-Yala.

Hernandez Valdes, Emilio. 1997. "Pase de Revistas." *Temas* 10: 117–26.

Herschmann, Micael, and Carlos Alberto Messeder Pereira. 2000. "E la nave va . . . As celebrações dos 500 anos no Brasil: afirmações e disputas no espaço simbólico." *Estudos Históricos* 26: 203–15.

Hershberg, Eric. 2002. "Latin American Studies Sans Political Science?" Paper presented at the conference "The New Latin Americanism: Cultural Studies Beyond Borders." University of Manchester, U.K.

Herzfeld, Michael. 1997. *Cultural Intimacy: The Social Poetics of the Nation-State.* London: Routledge.

Huyssen, A. 1987. "Guía del postmodernismo." *Punto de vista*, no. 29. Buenos Aires.

IEPRI. 1996. IEPRI: 10 Años. Memorias. Bogotá: Universidad Nacional de Colombia.

ISA, Instituto Socioambiental. 2000. "O que os brasileiros pensam dos índios?" *Povos Indígenas no Brasil 1996/2000*, 57–62. São Paulo: Instituto Socioambiental.

Iturralde, D. 1997. "Demandas indígenas y reforma legal: Retos y paradojas." *Alteridades*, Volume "Estado Nacional, Autodeterminación y Autonomía" 7, no. 14: 81–98. Mexico City: UAM.

Jackson, J. 1996. "The Impact of Recent National Legislation in the Vaupés Region of Colombia." *Journal of Latin American Anthropology* 1, no. 2: 120–51.

Jackson, Peter A. 2000. "Reading Rio from Bangkok: An Asianist Perspective on Brazil's Male Homosexual Cultures." Review article. *American Ethnologist* 27, no. 4: 950–60.

Jain, Sarah S. 1999. "The Prosthetic Imagination: Enabling and Disabling the Prosthesis Trope." *Science, Technology and Human Values* 24, no. 1: 31–54.

Jameson, J. 1985. "Postmodernismo y sociedad de consumo." In H. Foster and J. Baudrillard, *La postmodernidad*. Barcelona: Kairós.

Jara, Rebeca, and Elisabel Diaz. 1997. *Commercialización versus Identidad: Una Experiencia Afirmadora*. Radio Taino report.

Jaramillo, Jaime. 1982. "El Proceso de Educación del Virreinato a la Epoca Contemporánea." In *Manual de Historia de Colombia*, volume 3. Bogotá: Procultura.

Johnson, Barbara. 2000. "Using People: Kant with Winnicott." In *The Turn to Ethics*, eds. Marjorie Garber, Beatrice Hanssen, and Rebecca Walkowitz. New York: Routledge.

Jonas, Susanne, Ed McCaughan, and Elizabeth Sutherland Martinez, eds. 1984. *Guatemala: Tyranny on Trial*. San Francisco: Synthesis Publications.

———. 1991. *The Battle for Guatemala: Rebels, Death Squads, and U.S. Power*. Boulder: Westview Press.

Jordan, Glenn, and Chris Weedon. 1995. *Cultural Politics: Class, Gender, Race and the Postmodern World*. Oxford: Blackwell.

Kalinsky, B. 2000. "El Derecho Penal en ámbitos interculturales: Comentario a un caso de conflicto entre el derecho indígena y el derecho oficial." MS.

Kearney, Michael. 1996. *Reconceptualizing the Peasantry: Anthropology in Global Perspective*. Boulder: Westview Press.

Knight, Alden. 2000. "Tackling Racism in Performing Arts and the Media." In *Afro-*

Cuban Voices, eds. Pedro Perez Sarduy and Jean Stubbs. Gainesville: University Press of Florida.

Kulick, Don. 1998. *Travestí: Sex, Gender and Culture among Brazilian Transgendered Prostitutes*. Chicago: University of Chicago Press.

Kurzman, Steven. 2001. "Presence and Prosthesis: A Response to Nelson and Wright." *Cultural Anthropology* 16, no. 3: 374–87.

Kutzinski, Vera M. 1993. *Sugar's Secrets: Race and the Erotics of Cuban Nationalism*. Charlottesville: University Press of Virginia.

Labriola, Antonio. 1907. "Gramsci's Teacher." In *Socialism and Philosophy*, trans. Ernest Untermann. Chicago: Charles Kerr.

Lachatañeré, Rómulo. 1992 [1939]. *El Sistema Religioso de los Afrocubanos*. Havana: Editorial de Ciencias Sociales.

Laclau, Ernesto. 1996. *Emancipation(s)*. London: Verso.

Laclau, Ernesto, and Chantal Mouffe. 1985. *Hegemony and Socialist Strategy: Toward a Radical Democratic Politics*. London: Verso.

Landes, Ruth. 1994 [1947]. *The City of Women*. Albuquerque: University of New Mexico Press.

———. 1940. "A Cult Matriarchate and Male Homosexuality." *Journal of Abnormal and Social Psychology* 35, no. 3: 386–97.

———. 1953. "Negro Slavery and Female Status." *Mémoires de 1'Institut Français d'Afrique Noire* 27: 265–68.

Landi, O. 1982. *Crisis y lenguajes políticos*. Buenos Aires: Cedes.

———. 1988. *Reconstrucciones: Las nuevas formas de la cultura política*. Buenos Aires: Puntosur.

———.1992. *Devórame otra vez:¿Qué hizo la televisión con la gente, qué hace la gente con la televisión?* Buenos Aires: Planeta.

Larsen, Neil. 1996. "Brazilian Critical Theory and the Question of 'Cultural Studies.'" In *Reading the Shape of the World: Toward an International Cultural Studies*, eds. Henry Schwarz and Richard Dienst. Boulder: Westview Press.

Lazzari, A. 2000. "El 'indio argentino' y la 'reparación histórica': Ensayo preliminar para una genealogía del indigenismo argentino." VI Congreso Argentino de Antropología Social, "Identidad Disciplinaria y Campos de Aplicación." Facultad de Humanidades, Universidad Nacional de Mar del Plata, and Colegio de Graduados en Antropología. September 14–16.

Leão Teixeira, Maria Lina. 1987. "Lorogun—Identidades sexuais e poder no candomblé." In *Candomblé: Desvendando Identidades*, ed. Carlos Eugênio Marcondes de Moura. São Paulo: EMW Editores.

Le Bot, Yvon. 1995. *La guerra en las tierras Mayas: Comundiad, violencia y modernidad en Guatemala, 1970–1992.* Mexico: Fondo de Cultura Económica.

Lederman, Daniel, Norman Loayza, and Ana María Menéndez. 1999. "Violent Crime: Does Social Capital Matter?" MS.

Lent, John A. 1990. *Mass Communications in the Caribbean.* Ames: Iowa University Press.

Lenton, D. 1992. "Relaciones Interétnicas: Derechos Humanos y Autocrítica en la Generación del '80." In *La problemática Indígena: Estudios antropológicos sobre pueblos indígenas de la Argentina,* eds. J. Radovich and A. Balazote, 27–65. Buenos Aires: CEDAL.

———. 1998. *Transformaciones en el discurso gubernamental sobre el indígena: Argentina, 1930–1955.* Informe Final de Beca de Iniciación. FFyL(UBA).

Lepenies, Wolf. 1995. *Ascensão e Declínio dos Intelectuais na Europa.* Lisboa: Edições 70.

Levenson-Estrada, Deborah. 1994. *Trade Unionists Against Terror: Guatemala City 1954–1985.* Chapel Hill: University of North Carolina Press.

Lévi-Strauss, Claude. 1969. *Elementary Structures of Kinship.* Boston: Beacon Press.

———. 1977 [1955]. *Tristes Tropiques.* New York: Atheneum.

Lewis, Bernard. 2001. "Jihad vs. Crusade." *Wall Street Journal,* September 27.

Lima, Délcio Monteiro de. 1983. *Os Homoeróticos.* Rio de Janeiro: F. Alves.

Lipietz, Alain. 1987. *Mirages and Miracles: The Crises of Global Fordism,* trans. David Macey. London: Verso.

Liss, Sheldon. 1987. *Roots of Revolution.* Lincoln: University of Nebraska Press.

Lowe, Lisa, and David Lloyd. 1998. *Politics of Culture in the Shadow of Capital.* Durham: Duke University Press.

Luiz, Macksen. 1992. "No compasso contagiante do Olodum." *Jornal do Brasil,* March 13.

Lyotard, J. F. 1984. *La condición postmoderna: Informe sobre el saber.* Madrid: Cátedra.

———. 1988. *La diferencia.* Barcelona: Gedisa.

Machado, Dario. 1986. "Medios de difusión masiva y trabajo ideológico." *Cuba Socialista* 20: 87–114.

Magioli, Ailton. 1992. "O Teatro da Cidadania pelo Olodum." *Diário da Tarde,* July 15.

Mallon, F. 1996. "Constructing *Mestizaje* in Latin America: Authenticity, Marginality, and Gender in the Claiming of Ethnic Identities." *Journal of Latin American Anthropology* 2, no. 1: 170–81.

Manach, Jorge. 1978 [1928]. *Indagación al Choteo.* Miami: Universal.

Mani, Lata. 1990. "Contentious Traditions: The Debate on Sati in Colonial India." In *Recasting Women: Essays in Colonial History*, eds. Kumkum Sangari and Sudesh Vaid. New Brunswick: Rutgers University Press.

——. 1992. "Cultural Theory, Colonial Texts: Reading Eyewitness Accounts of Widow Burning." In *Cultural Studies*, eds. Lawrence Grossberg, Cary Nelson, and Paula Treichler. New York: Routledge.

Mannheim, Bruce. 1999. "El arado del tiempo: Poética quechua y formación nacional." *Revista Andina* 33, no. 1: 15–64.

Mannheim, Bruce, and Denis Tedlock. 1996. "Introduction." In *The Dialogic Emergence of Culture*, eds. D. Tedlock and B. Mannheim. Urbana: University of Illinois Press.

Marcus, George. 1998. *Ethnography through Thick and Thin*. Princeton: Princeton University Press.

Marcus, G., and M. Fhischer. 1986. *Anthropology as Cultural Critique*. Chicago: University of Chicago Press, 1986.

Marinas, José M. 1995. "La identidad contada." In *Destinos del relato al fin del milenio*. Valencia: Archivos de la Filmoteca, Monográfico.

Marmelo, Jorge. 2000. " 'Brasil: outros 500' vai dar origem a documento reivindicativo: Núbia, a Tupinambá que resiste." *Público* (Portugal), February 29 (via Internet).

Marramao, G. 1988. "Metapolítica: Más allá de los esquemas binarios." In *Razón, ética y política*. Barcelona: Anthropos.

Martín Barbero, J. 1980. "Retos a la investigación de comunicación en América Latina." *Comunicación y cultura*, no. 10. Mexico City.

——. 1987. *De los medios a las mediaciones: Comunicación, cultura y hegemonía*. Mexico City. Gustavo Gili.

——. 1988. "Euforia tecnológica y malestar en la teoría." In *Dia-logos de la Comunicación*, no. 20. Lima.

——. 1989. "Innovación tecnológica y transformación cultural." *TELOS*, no.10. Madrid.

——. 1992. "Panorama bibliográfico de la investigación latinoamericana en Comunicación." *Telos*, no. 19. Madrid.

——. 1994. "Identidad, comunicación y modernidad." In *Posmodernidad en la periferia. Enfoques latinoamericanos de la nueva teoría cultural*, eds. H. Herlinghaus and M. Walter. Berlin: Langer Verlag.

Martín, José Luis. 1995. "Tendencias Temáticas de las Ciencias Sociales en Cuba." In *Cuba: Cultura e Identidad Nacional*, ed. Daniel Garcia. Havana: Unión.

Martinez Heredia, Fernando. 1995. "Izquierda y Marxismo en Cuba." *Temas* 3: 23.

Materiales sobre la Propaganda. 1980. "Camaguey: Análisis del Contenido de la Programación Radial." *Materiales sobre la Propaganda* 8 (26): 9–18.

Matory, J. Lorand. 1988. "Homens montados: Homossexualidade e simbolismo da possessão nas religioes afro-brasileiras." In *Escravidão e Invenção da Liberdade*, ed. by João José Reis. São Paulo: Brasiliense.

——. 1991. "Sex and the Empire That Is No More: A Ritual History of Women's Power among the Oyo-Yoruba." Ph.D. diss., University of Chicago.

——. 1994. *Sex and the Empire That Is No More: Gender and the Politics of Metaphor in Oyó Yorùbá Religion.* Minneapolis: University of Minnesota Press.

——. 1999. "The English Professors of Brazil: On the Diasporic Roots of the Yoruba Nation." *Comparative Studies in Society and History* 41, no. 1: 72–103.

——. Forthcoming. *Man in the "City of Women": Tradition, Transnationalism, and Matriarchy in the Afro-Brazilian Candomblé.* Princeton: Princeton University Press.

McAllister, Carlota. 2002. "Good People: Revolution, Community, and Conciencia in a Maya-K'iche' Village in Guatemala." Ph.D. diss., Johns Hopkins University.

Medin, Tzvi. 1990. *Cuba: The Shaping of Revolutionary Consciousness.* Boulder: Lynne Rienner.

Meertens, Donny. 1998. "Víctimas y sobrevivientes de la guerra: Tres miradas de género." In *Las Violencias: Inclusión creciente*, eds. Jaime Arocha, Fernando Cubides, and Miriam Jimeno. Bogotá: Centro de Estudios Sociales, CES.

Menchú Tum, Rigoberta. 1984. *I, Rigoberta Menchú: An Indian Woman in Guatemala*, ed. Elisabeth Burgos-Debray, trans. Ann Wright. London: Verso.

Mendoza, Carlos. 2001. "Guatemala, más allá de los Acuerdos de Paz: La democracia en un país multicultural." Washington, D.C.: Woodrow Wilson International Center for Scholars.

Mies, Maria. 1991. *Patriarchy and Accumulation on a World Scale: Women in the International Division of Labor.* London: Zed Books.

Mignolo, Walter. 2000a. "Diferencia colonial y razón postoccidental." In *La reestructuración de las ciencias sociales en América Latina*, ed. Santiago Castro-Gómez. Bogotá: Pensar, Instituto de Estudios Sociales y Culturales, Pontificia Universidad Javeriana.

——. 2000b. "Colonialidad del poder y subalternidad." *Hueso Húmero*, no. 36: 91–118.

——. 2000c. *Local Histories / Global Designs: Coloniality, Subaltern Knowledges and Border Thinking.* Princeton: Princeton University Press.

Millamán, Rosamel. 2001. "Mapuches Press for Autonomy." NACLA 35, no. 2: 10–12.

MINUGUA (Missión de Verificación de las Naciones Unidas en Guatemala). 2000. "Informe de Verificación, Situación sobre los compromisos laborales de los Acuerdos de Paz." Guatemala City: UN Publishing. June.

Mohanty, Chandra Talpade, Ann Russo, and Lourdes Torres, eds. 1991. *Third World Women and the Politics of Feminism*. Bloomington: Indiana University Press.

Moingt, Joseph. 1992. *L'homme qui venait de Dieu*. París: Les Èditions du Cerf.

Moore, Robin. 1997. *Nationalizing Blackness: Afrocubanismo and Artistic Revolution in Havana, 1920–1940*. Pittsburgh: University of Pittsburgh Press.

Moraga, Cherrie. 1983. *Loving in the War Years: Lo que Nunca Pasó por sus Labios*. Boston: South End Press.

Morley, D. 1986. *Family Television, Cultural Power, and Domestic Leisure*. London: Comedia.

Mosse, George. 1985. *Nationalism and Sexuality*. Madison: University of Wisconsin Press.

Mouffe, Chantal. 1979. "Hegemony and Ideology in Gramsci." In *Gramsci and Marxist Theory*, ed. Chantal Mouffe. London: Routledge and Kegan Paul.

Nahuel, J. 1999. "Derecho mapuche y justicia penal." Editorial, Río Negro daily. September 25.

Necochea, Ramirez. 1984. *Origen y Formación del partido comunista de Chile*. Moscu: Editorial Progreso.

Nelson, Diane. 1994. "Gendering the Ethnic-National Question; Rigoberta Menchú Jokes and the Out-skirts of Fashioning Identity." *Anthropology Today* 10, no. 6: 3–7.

———. 1996. "Maya Hackers and the Cyberspatialized Nation State: Modernity, Ethnostalgia, and a Lizard Queen in Guatemala." *Cultural Anthropology* 11, no. 3: 287–308.

———. 1999. *A Finger in the Wound: Body Politics in Quincentennial Guatemala*. Berkeley: University of California Press.

———. 2003. " 'The More You Kill the More You Will Live': The Maya, 'Race,' and the Biopolitical Economy of Peace in Guatemala." In *Race, Nature, and the Politics of Difference*, ed. Donald Moore. Durham: Duke University Press.

Nichols, John Spicer. 1996. "Effects of International Propaganda in U.S.–Cuban Relations." In *Communications in Latin America: Journalism, Mass Media and Society*, ed. Richard R. Cole. Wilmington, Del.: Scholarly Resources.

Niño-Murcia, Mercedes. 1995. "Política del purismo lingüístico en el Cuzco." *Lexis* 19, no. 2: 251–88. Lima: Pontificia Universidad Católica del Perú.

Nora, Pierre. 1994. "Between Memory and History: Les Lieux de Mémoire." In

History and Memory in African-American Culture, eds. Genevieve Fabre and Robert O'Meally. New York: Oxford University Press.

Nun, J. 1982. "El otro reduccionismo." In *América Latina: Ideología y cultura*. San José, Costa Rica: FLACSO.

Nuñez Machín, Ana, ed. 1984. *Pensamiento Revolucionario y Medios de Difusión Masiva*. Havana: Editora Política.

O'Donnell, M. 1993. "Estado, Democratización y Ciudadanía." *Revista Nueva Sociedad* 128: 62–87.

Oglesby, Elizabeth. 2002. "Politics at Work: Elites, Labor, and Agrarian Modernization in Guatemala, 1980–2000." Ph.D. diss., University of California, Berkeley.

Ogundipe-Leslie, 'Molara. 1985. "Women in Nigeria." In *Women in Nigeria Today*, eds. S. Bappa, J. Ibrahim, A. M. Imam, F. J. A. Kamara, H. Mahdi, M. A. Modibbo, A. S. Mohammed, H. Mohammed, A. R.Mustapha, N. Perchonock, and R. I. Pittin. London: Zed Books.

Okediji, O. O., and F. O. Okediji. 1966. "Marital Stability and Social Structure in an African City." *Nigerian Journal of Economic and Social Studies* 8, no. 1: 151–63.

Oliveira, Lucia Lippi. 2000. "Imaginário histórico e poder cultural: As comemorações do Descobrimento." *Estudos Históricos* 26: 183–202.

Ong, Aihwa. 1997. "'A Momentary Glow of Fraternity': Narratives of Chinese Nationalism and Capitalism." *Identities* 3, no. 3: 331–66.

———. 1987. *Spirits of Resistance and Capitalist Discipline: Factory Women in Malaysia*. Albany: SUNY Press.

Ortiz, Fernando. 1975. *Un catauro de cubanismos*. Havana: Editorial de Ciencias Sociales.

———. 1991 [1940]. *Contrapunteo cubano del tobacco y el azúcar*. Havana: Editorial Ciencias Sociales.

———. 1991. *Estudios etnosociológicos*. Havana: Editorial Ciencias Sociales.

———. 1996 [1939]. "Los Factores Humanos de la Cubanidad." In *Fernando Ortiz y la Cubanidad*, ed. Norma Suarez. Havana: Unión.

———. 1996 [1940]. "Del Fenómeno Social de la Transculturación." In *Fernando Ortiz y la Cubanidad*, ed. Norma Suarez. Havana: Unión.

Otzoy, Irma. 1996. "Maya Clothing and Identity." In *Maya Cultural Activism in Guatemala*, eds. Edward F. Fischer and R. McKenna Brown. Austin: University of Texas Press.

Oyewumi, Oyeronke. 1997. *The Invention of Women: Making an African Sense of Western Gender Discourses*. Minneapolis: University of Minnesota Press.

Pacini Hernandez, Deborah, and Reebee Garofalo. 1999. "Hip-Hop in Havana: Rap,

Race, and National Identity in Contemporary Cuba." *Journal of Popular Music Studies* 11 / 12: 18–47.

Paggi, Leonardo. 1974. "Gramsci's General Theory of Marxism." In *Gramsci and Marxist Theory*, ed. Chantal Mouffe. London: Routledge and Kegan Paul.

Palacio, Marco. 1979. *El café en Colombia, 1850–1970: Una historia económica, social y política*. Bogotá: Editorial Presencia.

Pantoja, Julio. "Los Hijos, Tucumán veinte años después." Web site at http://julio-pantoja.com.ar/Reportajes/HijosTodos.htm.

Parker, Richard D. 1998. *Beneath the Equator: Cultures of Desire, Male Homosexuality, and Emerging Gay Communities in Brazil*. New York: Routledge.

Partido Comunista de Cuba. 1976. *Sobre los Medios de Difusión Masiva: Tesis y Resoluciones*. Havana: PCC.

Paul, Lois. 1974. "The Mastery of Work and the Mystery of Sex in a Guatemalan Village." In *Women, Culture, and Society*, eds. Michelle Zimbalist Rosaldo and Louise Lamphere. Stanford: Stanford University Press.

Payeras, Mario. 1983. *Days of the Jungle: The Testimony of a Guatemalan Guerrillero, 1972–1976*. New York: Monthly Review Press.

———. 1997. *Los Pueblos Indígenas y la Revolución Guatemalteca: Ensayos Etnicos*. Guatemala City: Luna y Sol.

Paz, Octavio. 1979. *Corriente alterna*. Mexico City: Siglo XXI.

Pécaut, Daniel. 1978. *Orden y Violencia en Colombia 1930–1954*. Bogotá: Siglo XXI.

Peres, Phyllis. 1997. *Transculturation and Resistance in Lusophone African Literatures*. Gainesville: University Press of Florida.

Pérez Firmat, Gustavo. 1989. *The Cuban Condition: Translation and Identity in Modern Cuban Literature*. Cambridge: Cambridge University Press.

Pérez Sáinz, Juan Pablo, ed. 2002. *Encadenamientos globales y pequeña empresa en Centroamerica*. San José: FLACSO—Costa Rica.

Pérez Sáinz, Juan Pablo, Manuela Camus, and Santiago Bastos. 1992. *Todito, Todito es Trabajo: Indigenas y Empleo en la Ciudad de Guatemala*. Guatemala City: FLACSO.

Peters, Julie Stone. 1995. "Intercultural Performance, Theatre Anthropology, and the Imperialist Critique: Identities, Inheritances, and Neo-Orthodoxies." In *Imperialism and Theatre: Essays on World Theatre, Drama and Performance 1795–1995*, ed. J. Ellen Gainor. London: Routledge.

Peterson, Kurt. 1992. *The Maquiladora Revolution in Guatemala*. New Haven: Orville H. Schell, Jr., Center for International Human Rights at Yale Law School, Occasional Paper Series, 2.

Phelan, Peggy. 1993. *Unmarked: The Politics of Performance*. New York: Routledge.

Piccini, M. 1987a. *La imagen del tejedor: Lenguajes y políticas de comunicación*. Mexico City: G. Gili.

———. 1987b. "Industrias culturales, transversalidades y regímenes discursivos." In *Dia-logos de la Comunicación*, no. 17. Lima.

Poitevin, René. 1993. *Guatemala: La Crisis de la Democracia—dudas y esperanzas en los golpes de estado de 1993*. Facultad Latinoamericano de Ciencias Sociales-Guatemala Debate No. 21. Guatemala City: FLACSO.

Polar, Antonio Cornejo. 1980. *Literatura y sociedad en Perú: La novela indigenista*. Lima: Lasontay.

Povinelli, Elizabeth A. 2002. *The Cunning of Recognition: Indigenous Alterities and the Making of Australian Multiculturalism*. Durham: Duke University Press.

Pratt, M. L. 1987. "Linguistic Utopias." In *Linguistics of Writing*, eds. N. Fabb and A. Duranti. Manchester: Manchester University Press.

———. 1991. "Arts of the Contact Zone." *Profession* 91: 37.

———. 1992. *Imperial Eyes: Travel, Writing and Transculturation*. London and New York: Routledge.

Prieto, Abel. 1994. "Culture, Cubanidad, Cubania." In *Conferencia: "La Nacion y la Emigracion." Ponencias*.

Quijano, Aníbal. 1999. "Colonialidad del poder, cultura y conocimiento en América Latina." In *Pensar (en) los intersticios: Teoría y práctica de la crítica postcolonial*, eds. Santiago Castro-Gómez, Óscar Guardiola-Rivera, and Carmen Millán de Benavides. Bogotá: Pensar, Instituto de Estudios Sociales y Culturales, Pontificia Universidad Javeriana.

Rama, Angel. 1982. *Transculturación narrativa en América Latina*. Mexico City: Siglo Veintiuno Editores.

Ramírez, S. 1987. *Culturas, profesiones y sensibilidades contemporáneas en Colombia*. Cali: Univalle.

Ramos, Alcida Rita. 1994. "The Hyperreal Indian." *Critique of Anthropology* 14, no. 2: 153–71.

———. 1998. *Indigenism: Ethnic Politics in Brazil*. Madison: University of Wisconsin Press.

———. 2002. "Cutting through Class and State: Sources and Strategies of Self-representation in Latin America." In *Indigenous Movements, Self-Representation, and the State in Latin America*, eds. Kay Warren and Jean Jackson, 251–79. Austin: University of Texas Press.

———. 2003. "Pulp Fictions of Indigenism." In *Race, Nature, and the Politics of Difference*, eds. Donald S. Moore, Jake Kosek, and Anand Pandian, 356–79. Durham: Duke University Press.

Ranger, T. 1989. "The Invention of Tradition in Colonial Africa." In *The Invention of Tradition*, eds. E. Hobsbawm and T. Ranger, 211–62. Cambridge: Cambridge University Press.

Rawls, John. 1993. *Political Liberalism*. New York: Columbia University Press.

Ray, Sangueeta. 1996. "Rethinking Migrancy: Nationalism, Ethnicity, and Identity in *Jasmine* and *The Buddha of Suburbia*." In *Reading the Shape of the World: Toward an International Cultural Studies*, eds. Henry Schwarz and Richard Dienst. Boulder: Westview Press.

Riaño, Pilar. 2000. "Remembering Place: Memory and Violence in Medellín, Colombia." MS.

Ribeiro, René. 1969. "Personality and the Psychosexual Adjustment of Afro-Brazilian Cult Members." *Journal de la Société des Américanistes* 58:109–20.

Ridley, Matt. 1999. *Genome*. New York: Harper Colllins.

Risério, Antônio. 1981. *Carnaval Ijexá*. Salvador, Brazil: Corrupio.

Roach, Joseph. 1996. *Cities of the Dead: Circum-Atlantic Performance*. New York: Columbia University Press.

Rodrigues, Edson. 1994. "Márcio Meirelles explica proposta do Novo Vila." *A Tarde*, November 6, 13–14.

Rodríguez, Clemencia. 2000. "In the World of the Father: Women Gambling with Death. Life Stories of Colombian Women in Violent Contexts." MS.

Rodriguez, José Luis. 1990. "Aspectos Económicos del Proceso de Rectificación." *Cuba Socialista* 44, no. 2: 86–101.

Roncagliolo, R. 1996. "La integración audiovisual en América Latina: Estados, empresas y productores independientes." In *Culturas en globalización*, ed. N. García Canclini. Caracas: Nueva Sociedad.

Rosaldo, Renato. 1989. *Culture and Truth*. Boston: Beacon Press.

——, ed. 2003. *Cultural Citizenship in Island Southeast Asia*. Berkeley: University of California Press.

Rowe, William. 1996. *Hacia una poética radical: Ensayos de hermenéutica cultural*. Rosario, Argentina: Beatriz Viterbo Editora.

Rowe, W., and V. Scheling. 1991. *Memory and Modernity: Popular Culture in Latin America*. London: Verso.

Rozada, Hamile. 1987. "Entre Nota y Nota: El Universo Musical de Radio Taino." *Clave* 7: 20, 21.

Rueda, A. 1998. "Representaciones de lo latinoamericano: Memoria, territorio y transnacionalidad en el videoclip del rock latino." Thesis, Univalle, Cali.

Said, Edward. 1996. *Representaciones del Intelectual*. Barcelona: Paidos.

Salazar, Ernesto. 1977. "An Indian Federation in Lowland Ecuador." Copenhagen: International Work Group for Indigenous Affairs, Document 28.

Sánchez, Gonzalo. 1998. "Intelectuales . . . poder . . . y cultura nacional." In *Análisis Político*, no. 34, May / August. Bogotá.

Sánchez-Blake, Elvira. 2000. *Patria se Escribe con Sangre*. Bogotá: Antropos.

Sanchez Ruiz, E. 1986. "La crisis del modelo comunicativo de la modernización." In *Réquiem por la modernización*. Guadalajara: University of Guadalajara.

Sangari, Kumkum, and Sudesh Vaid, eds. 1990. *Recasting Women: Essays in Colonial History*. New Brunswick: Rutgers University Press.

Santilli, Márcio. 2000. *Os Brasileiros e os Índios*. São Paulo: Editora Senac.

Sassen, Saskia. 2001. "La ciudad global: Una introducción al concepto y su historia." In *Mutaciones*. Contributors Rem Koolhaas, Harvard Project on the City, Stefano Boeri, Multiplicity, Sanford Kwinter, Nadia Tazi, and Hans Ulrich Obrist. Barcelona: Actar. English trans., New York: Actar, 2001.

Schechner, Richard. 1985. *Between Theatre and Anthropology*. Philadelphia: University of Pennsylvania Press.

Schlesinger, Ph., et al. 1987. *Los intelectuales en la sociedad de la información*. Barcelona: Anthropos.

——. 1990. "Identidad europea y cambios en la comunicación: De la política a la cultura y los medios." *Telos*, no. 23. Madrid.

Schmucler, H., and M. C. Mata, eds. 1992. *Política y comunicación: Hay un lugar para la política en la cultura mediática?* Córdoba: Catálogos.

Schüler, Donaldo. 2001. *Na Conquista do Brasil*. Cotia (São Paulo): Ateliê Editorial.

Schwarz, R. 1987. "Nacional por sustracción." *Punto de vista*, no. 28. Buenos Aires.

Scott, James. 1985. *Weapons of the Weak*. New Haven: Yale University Press.

——. 1990. *Domination and the Arts of Resistance: Hidden Transcripts*. New Haven: Yale University Press.

Segato, Rita Laura. 1991. "Uma vocação de minoria: A expansão dos cultos afro-brasileiros na Argentina como processo de reetnicização." *Dados, Revista de Ciências Sociais* (Rio de Janeiro) 34, no. 2: 249–78.

Serbin, A. 1981. "Las organizaciones indígenas en la Argentina." *América Indígena* 41, no. 3: 407–33.

Serres, Michel. 2001. *Hominescence*. Paris: Le Pommier.

Sieder, Rachel, Megan Thomas, George Vickers, and Jack Spence, eds. 2001. *Who Governs? Guatemala Five Years After the Peace Accords*. Cambridge: Hemisphere Initiatives.

Silverstein, Leni M. 1979. "Mãe de Todo Mundo: Modos de Sobrevivência nas Comunidades de Candomblé da Bahia." *Religião e Sociedade* 4: 143–69.

Simon, Jean Marie. 1988. *Eternal Spring, Eternal Tyranny*. New York: W. W. Norton.

Singer, Paul. 1995. "Radiografia da 'Democracia Racial' Brasileira." In *Racismo Cordial, A mais completa análise sobre o preconceito de cor no Brasil*, eds. Cleusa Turra and Gustavo Venturi, Racismo. São Paulo: Editora Ática S. A.

Slavsky, L. 1992. "Los Indígenas y la Sociedad Nacional: Apuntes sobre política indigenista en la Argentina." In *La problemática Indígena: Estudios antropológicos sobre pueblos indígenas de la Argentina*, eds. J. Radovich and A. Balazote. Buenos Aires: CEDAL.

Smith, Carol, ed., with Marilyn Moors. 1990. *Guatemalan Indians and the State 1540–1988*. Austin: University of Texas Press.

Sobchack, Vivian. 1995. "Beating the Meat / Surviving the Text, or How to Get Out of this Century Alive." *Body and Society* 1: 205–14.

Sodré, Muñiz. 1983. *A verdade seducida: Por un conceito de cultura no Brasil*. Rio de Janeiro: Codecrí.

Sommer, Doris. 1991. *National Romance, Foundational Fiction*. Berkeley: University of California Press.

——. 1999. "No Secrets for Rigoberta." In *Proceed with Caution, When Engaged by Minority Writing in the Americas*. Cambridge: Harvard University Press.

Sontag, Deborah. 1997. "Albita Takes Her Country Music to the Top." *New York Times*. March 11.

Spitta, Silvia. 1995. *Between Two Waters: Narratives of Transculturation in Latin America*. Houston: Rice University Press.

Spivak, Gayatri. 1988. "Can the Subaltern Speak?" In *Marxism and the Interpretation of Culture*, eds. Cary Nelson and Lawrence Grossberg. Urbana: University of Illinois Press.

——. 1990. *The Post-Colonial Critic: Interviews, Strategies, Dialogues*. London: Routledge.

Squef, E., and J. M. Wisnik. 1983. *O nacional e o popular na cultura brasileira: Música*. São Paulo: Brasiliense.

Stavenhagen, Rodolfo. 1992. "Challenging the Nation-State in Latin America." *Journal of International Affairs* 45, no. 2: 423–40.

Stephen, Lynn. 1991. *Zapotec Women*. Austin: University of Texas Press.

Stolcke, Verena. 1995. "Talking Culture: New Boundaries, New Rhetorics of Exclusion in Europe." *Current Anthropology* 36, no. 1: 1–24.

Stoll, David. 1993. *Between Two Armies in the Ixil Towns of Guatemala*. New York: Columbia University Press.

——. 1999. *Rigoberta Menchu and the Story of All Poor Guatemalans*. Boulder: Westview Press.

Stone, Allucquere Rosanne. 1995. *The War of Desire and Technology at the Close of the Mechanical Age*. Cambridge: MIT Press.

Suarez, Norma, ed. 1996. *Fernando Ortiz y la Cubanidad*. Havana: Unión.

Svampa, M. 1994. *El Dilema Argentino: Civilización o Barbarie, De Sarmiento al revisionismo peronista*. Buenos Aires: Ediciones El Cielo por Asalto.

Sweet, James H. 1996. "Male Homosexuality and Spiritism in the African Diaspora: The Legacies of a Link." *Journal of the History of Sexuality* 7, no. 21: 184–202.

Tabares, Sahily. 1987. "Radio Taino: Rescate de la Esencial Cubania." *Verde Olivo* 28, no. 20: 60–61. 21/5.

Taussig, Michael. 1987. *Shamanism, Colonialism, and the Wild Man: A Study in Terror and Healing*. Chicago: University of Chicago Press.

———. 1993. *Mimesis and Alterity: A Particular History of the Senses*. London: Routledge.

Taylor, Diana. 1991. "Transculturating Transculturation." In *Interculturalism and Performance*, eds. Bonnie Marranca and Gautam Dasgupta. New York: PAJ Publications.

———. 1997. *Disappearing Acts: Spectacles of Gender and Nationality in Argentina's "Dirty War."* Durham: Duke University Press.

Teillagorry, Jacqueline, and José León. 1990. "Nadie Puede Quitarnos la Esperanza." *Alma Mater* 322, no. 9: 9.

Terena, Marcos. 2000. Interview in *Caros Amigos*, April: 36–41.

Texier, Jacques. 1979. "Gramsci, Theoretician of the Superstructures: On the Concept of Civil Society." In *Gramsci and Marxist Theory*, ed. Chantal Mouffe. London: Routledge and Kegan Paul.

Theweleit, Klaus. 1989. *Male Fantasies*. Minneapolis: University of Minnesota Press.

Torre, Carolina de la. 1995. "Conciencia de Mismidad: Identidad y Cultura Cubana." *Temas* 2: 111–15.

Touraine, A. 1992. *Critique de la modernité*. Paris: Fayard.

Trexler, Richard C. 1995. *Sex and Conquest: Gendered Violence, Political Order, and the European Conquest of the Americas*. Ithaca: Cornell University Press.

Trinh T., Minh-ha. 1986. "She, the Inappropriated Other." *Discourse* 8.

Trouillot, Michel-Rolph. 1995. *Silencing the Past: Power and the Production of History*. Boston: Beacon Press.

Turner, Victor. 1957. *Schism and Continuity in an African Society: A Study of Ndembu Village Life*. Manchester: Manchester University Press.

———. 1969. *The Ritual Process*. Chicago: Aldine.

———. 1983. "Carnaval in Rio: Dionysian Drama in an Industrializing Society." In *The*

Celebration of Society: Perspectives on Contemporary Cultural Performance, ed. Frank Manning. Bowling Green, Ohio: Bowling Green University; London, Ontario: Congress of Social and Humanistic Studies, University of Western Ontario.

———. 1986. *El fin de la modernidad*. Barcelona: Gedisa.

———. 1992. *From Ritual to Theater: The Human Seriousness of Play*. New York: PAJ Publications.

Valderrama, R., and C. Escalante, eds. 1981. *Gregorio Condori Mamani: Autobiografía*. Cuzco: Centro Bartolomé de Las Casas.

Van Cott, Donna Lee. 2000. *The Friendly Liquidation of the Past: The Politics of Diversity in Latin America*. Pittsburgh: University of Pittsburgh Press.

Veber, H. 1998. "The Salt of the Montaña: Interpreting Indigenous Activism in the Rain Forest." *Cultural Anthropology* 13, no. 3: 383–413.

Various authors. 1987. *Colombia: Violencia y Democracia*. Bogotá: Instituto de Estudios Políticos y Relaciones Internacionales, Universidad Nacional de Colombia.

Vásquez, María Eugenia. 1998. "Bitácora de una militancia." B.A. thesis, Universidad Nacional de Colombia, Bogotá.

Vattimo, G. 1989. *La sociedad transparente*. Barcelona: Paidos.

Veja Magazine. 2000a. "De nau a pior." May 3: 44–50.

———. 2000b. "Fiasco maravilhoso: As comemorações dos 500 anos naufragam em ritmo de samba-enredo." Cover story.

Viegas, Susana de Matos. 2000. "Tupinambá em carne o osso." *Público* (Portugal), March 27 (via Internet).

Villalón, M. E., and S. Angeleri. 1997. "The Practice of Retort: Exchanges Leading to the Caracas Peace Dialogues." *Pragmatics* 7, no. 4: 601–23.

Villaveces, Santiago. 1998a. "Entre pliegues de ruinas y esperanzas: Viñetas sobre el IEPRI." In *Análisis Político*, no. 34, May / August. Bogotá.

———. 1998b. "Violentologists and Magistrates: Questions of Justice and Responses to Violence in Contemporary Colombia." Ph.D. diss., Rice University.

Viotti da Costa, Emilia. 1989. *Da Senzala à Colonia*, 3d ed. São Paulo: Editora Brasiliense.

Wagley, Charles. 1963 [1952]. "Introduction." In *Race and Class in Rural Brazil*, ed. Charles Wagley. New York: UNESCO / International Documents Service, Columbia University Press.

Wallerstein, Immanuel. 1999. "La cultura como campo de batalla ideológico del sistema-mundo moderno." In *Pensar (en) los intersticios: Teoría y práctica de la crítica postcolonial*, eds. Santiago Castro-Gómez, Óscar Guardiola-Rivera, and Carmen Millán de Benavides. Bogotá: Pensar, Instituto de Estudios Sociales y Culturales, Pontificia Universidad Javeriana.

Warren, Kay. 1992. "Transforming Memories and Histories: The Meaning of Ethnic Resurgence for Mayan Indians." In *Americas: New Interpretive Essays*, ed. Alfred Stepan. New York: Oxford University Press.

———. 1998. *Indigenous Movements and Their Critics: Pan-Mayan Activism in Guatemala*. Princeton: Princeton University Press.

Weiss, Judith, et al., 1993. *Latin American Popular Theater: The First Five Centuries*. Albuquerque: University of New Mexico Press.

Williams, Raymond. 1977. *Marxism and Literature*. New York: Oxford University Press.

Willis, David. 1995. *Prosthesis*. Stanford: Stanford University Press.

Wilson, Richard. 1995. *Maya Resurgence in Guatemala: Q'eqchi Experiences*. Norman: University of Oklahoma Press.

Wimberly, Fayette. 1998. "The Expansion of Afro-Bahian Religious Practices in Nineteenth-Century Cachoeira." In *Afro-Brazilian Culture and Politics: Bahia, 1790s to 1990s*, ed. Hendrik Kraay. Armonk, N.Y.: M. E. Sharpe.

Winant, Howard. 1992. "The Other Side of the Process." In *On Edge: The Crisis of Contemporary Latin American Culture*, ed. George Yúdice with Jean Franco and Juan Flores. Minneapolis: University of Minnesota Press.

Wolf, M. 1990. "Tendencias actuales del estudio de medios." In *Comunicación social 1990, Tendencias*. Madrid: Informe Fundesco.

Wolin, Sheldon. 1996. "Fugitive Democracy." In *Democracy and Difference: Contesting the Boundaries of the Political*, ed. Seyla Benhabib. Princeton: Princeton University Press.

Wynter, Sylvia. 1984. "The Ceremony Must Be Found: After Humanism." *boundary 2*, no. 12: 19–70.

Yúdice, George. "Postmodernity and Transnational Capitalism in Latin America." In *On Edge: The Crisis of Contemporary Latin American Culture*, ed. George Yúdice with Jean Franco and Juan Flores. Minneapolis: University of Minnesota Press.

Yurchak, Alexei. 1997. "The Cynical Reason of Late Socialism: Power, Pretense, and the *Anekdot*." *Public Culture* 9: 161–88.

Zhang, Xudong. 1998. "Nationalism, Mass Culture and Intellectual Strategies in Post-Tiananmen China." *Social Text* 55, no. 16: 2.

Zimmerman, Klaus. 1995. "Formas de agresión y defensa en el conflicto de las lenguas española y portuguesa con las lenguas amerindias." In *Pueblos y medios ambientes amenazados en las Américas*, eds. M. Mörner and M. Rosendhal. Actas I del 48o Congreso Internacional de Americanistas. Stockholm: Instituto de Estudios Latinoamericanos.

Contributors

Arturo Arias is a distinguished novelist, scholar, and professor of Latin American literature and past president of the Latin American Studies Association.

Claudia Briones, Argentine anthropologist and professor at the University of Buenos Aires, is a beacon for other cultural agents through her engagements with a range of theories and peoples.

Néstor García Canclini is Professor of Anthropology at the Iztapalapa campus of the Autonomous Metropolitan University (UAM) in Mexico. He is author of numerous books, including *Latinoamericanos buscando un lugar en este siglo*, *La globalización imaginada* and *Culturas híbridas: Estrategias para entrar y salir de la modernidad*.

Denise Corte has recently completed her doctoral studies in the Department of Theater and Performance Studies at the University of Maryland. She is currently working on a federally funded project that examines the rekindling of Brazil's cultural politics, formulated by the newly appointed Minister of Culture, "tropicalist" pop star Gilberto Gil, concerning the promotion of diversity and the demarginalization of hip-hop music and performance.

Juan Carlos Godenzzi is an anthropologist and the Director of Bilingual Education for Peru's Ministry of Education.

Charles R. Hale is Associate Professor of Anthropology and Latin American Studies at the University of Texas, Austin. He is the author of *Resistance and Contradiction: Miskitu Indians and the Nicaraguan State, 1894–1987*.

Ariana Hernández-Reguant is Assistant Professor of Media Studies at the University of California, San Diego.

Claudio Lomnitz is Professor of History and Anthropology at the University of Chicago. He is the author of *Exits from the Labyrinth: Culture and Ideology in Mexi-*

can National Space. His research and teaching focus on the historical sociology of politics and culture in modern Mexico, with special emphasis on the ways in which national states mediate economic modernization and capitalist development.

Jesús Martín Barbero is Professor and founder of the School of Communication, Universidad del Valle (Colombia), and one of Latin America's leading communication theorists. His book publications include *De los medios a la mediación* and *Procesos de comunicación y Matrices de la Cultura*.

J. Lorand Matory is Hugh K. Foster Associate Professor of Anthropology and of Afro-American Studies at Harvard University. He is the author of *Sex and the Empire That Is No More: Gender and the Politics of Metaphor in Oyo Yoruba Religion* and his forthcoming book, *The Trans-Atlantic Nation Tradition, Transnationalism & Matriarchy in the Afro-Brazilian Candomblé*, concerns gender and nationalism in and around an Afro-Brazilian religion known as Candomblé.

Rosamel Millamán is Professor of Anthropology at the Catholic University of Temuco in Chile.

Diane M. Nelson is Associate Professor of Anthropology at Duke University and author of *A Finger in the Wound: Body Politics in Quincentennial Guatemala*.

Mary Louise Pratt is Silver Professor of Spanish and Portuguese at New York University. She is the author of *Imperial Eyes: Travel Writing and Transculturation* as well as numerous essays and reviews on topics that range from verb forms in the African Kikuyu language, through ideology and speech-act theory, to new visions in culture and citizenship and the "traffic in meaning."

Alcida Rita Ramos is Professor of Anthropology at the University of Brasilia. She has defended indigenous peoples, particularly Yanomami, acting as expert witness to the Brazilian Attorney General's Office and as mediator between the Sanumá and emergency medical teams working to combat epidemic malaria. She is the author of *Sanumá Memories: Yanomami Ethnography in Times of Crisis*.

Doris Sommer is Ira Jewell Williams, Jr. Professor of Romance Languages and Literatures at Harvard University. Her previous books include *Bilingual Aesthetics: A New Sentimental Education* (Duke, 2004); *Proceed with Caution, When Engaged by*

Minority Writing in the Americas; and the edited collection *Bilingual Games: Some Literary Investigations.*

Diana Taylor is Professor of Performance Studies and Spanish at New York University. She is the author of *Theatre of Crisis: Drama and Politics in Latin America, Disappearing Acts: Spectacles of Gender and Nationalism in Argentina's "Dirty War,"* and *The Archive and the Repertoire.* She is the Founding Director of the Hemispheric Institute of Performance and Politics, funded by the Ford Foundation and the Rockefeller Foundation.

Santiago Villaveces-Izquierdo is an anthropologist who received his Ph.D. from Rice University in Houston, Texas. He has conducted extensive research on conflict and democracy in Colombia as well as at the Universidade Federal do Rio de Janeiro. Most recently, he served as the Law and Human Rights Advisor for the Asia Foundation, an NGO based in Jakarta, Indonesia, that works on law reform and civil society.

Index

Brazil: Bahia region of, 127, 133–35, 203, 204, 214–15, 220n.4, 230, 234, 242, 246n.1; borrowing and aesthetic imitation in, 215, 227n.42; Pedro Álvares Cabral and, 230, 246n.1; campaign for direct elections in, 229–30; creation myth of, 232; democracy in, 203; European migration to, 126; gender definitions in, 130–33; informal economies of, 208, 224n.26; national holidays of, 240; nationality ritual enactment, 244; Northeastern Regionalism in, 126, 127–28; northeastern region of, 126; Porto Seguro protests in, 234, 236, 237, 239, 241–42, 244–45; Portuguese language in, 230; quincentennial of, 230, 234–37, 244–45; race in, 122, 127, 128, 203, 210–11, 214, 219n.1, 220n.2, 241; responses to Indian protests in, 236–37; state indifference in, 229–30, 245. *See also* Bahia, Brazil; Bando de Teatro Olodum (BTO, Olodum theater group); Candomblé

Briones, Claudia, 7–8, 18

Burgos-Debray, Elizabeth, 109

Bussi, Antonio Domingo, 73–74, 76

Cabral, Pedro Álvares, 230, 237, 246n.1

Camacho, Álvaro, 306, 308, 322n.1

Candomblé: the *adé* (passive homosexuals) and, 122, 124, 130–33, 142n.39; Black Mother and, 127, 128, 129, 132; *caboclo* worship and, 123, 125, 133; Casa Branca and, 123, 126, 133; cult matriarchate in, 122–23, 125, 130, 141n.18; in *Essa é a nossa praia*, 226n.35; female-headed temples and, 126–27, 128, 129; homosexuality and, 122, 130–31, 142n.39, 143n.42; indigenous personality theory and, 131; Jeje nation and, 123–26, 129, 133; marriage metaphors in, 134; masculinity as divine authority in, 130; Nagô nation and, 123–24, 125, 126–27, 133; Oyo-Yoruba people and, 133–35, 136; Quêto/Nagô denomination of, 122, 123. *See also* Priesthood

Capitalism, 87, 102–6, 119n.5, 282, 312, 331

Cardoso, Fernando Henrique, 234, 236, 237, 238–39

Carneiro, Édison, 124, 125, 126–27, 133, 138

Caruth, Cathy, 53, 78

Castellanos, Orlando, 184

Castro, Fidel, 181, 182, 192

Castro Caycedo, Germán, 322n.1

Catholic Church, 27n.48, 60, 80n.8, 168, 235–36, 242–43, 250, 309

Censorship, 42, 188–90, 312

Center for the Study of Mayan Culture (CECMA), 111–12, 113

Centro de Investigaciones Regionales Mesoamericans (CIRMA), 170

Certeau, Michel de, 5, 222n.12

Chatterjee, Partha, 101, 110

Children: cultural transmission to, 112, 153; of the disappeared, 56–57, 59 (fig. 4), 73–78, 74 (figs. 15, 16, 17); education of, 155–56; murder of, in Pelourinho, 207, 208, 212, 223n.19

Chile: *criollos* and, 283; democracy in, 283, 286, 289, 331; 11 September 1973 military coup, 12–13, 286; GDP of, 283; indigenous people recognized in, 283–84; multiculturalism in, 296–97; neoliberalism in, 285, 287; presidential regimes in, 1, 286–88, 287, 294, 300. *See also* Mapuche people

Cholsamaj, 111–12

Chubut province, 249, 256–58, 272n.3, 275n.14

Citizenship, 31–32, 43, 222n.12, 245, 252, 328, 332n.3

Cojtí Cuxil, Demetrio, 170, 171–72, 173

Collier, Jane, 104, 105, 110–11

Collor de Mello, Fernando, 230

Colombia: book trade in, 305–6, 322n.1; Catholic Church in, 309; colonial legacies in, 316; corruption in, 321; cultural agency in, 1–2; elites in, 309–10, 312–13, 323n.12; guerilla warfare in, 307; intellectuals as consultants to government of, 308, 311, 313–15, 317–18, 323n.7; law schools in, 310, 323n.4; local histories of, 321–22; peace negotiations in, 309, 312–13, 323n.12; university education in, 309–10, 312, 313, 322n.1. *See also* Violentologists

Language (*continued*)
malan Mayan Language Academy (ALMG),
110, 112; Mapundungún, 254, 273n.11; of
Maya, 170–71, 294; monolingualism,
27n.48, n.50, 112; multilingualism in
Peru, 16, 153–55, 159; Portuguese, 230;
Quechua, 11, 12, 16, 150–51, 153–55,
160; queer uses of, 27n.48; of radio broad-
casts, 183, 184, 195; semiotics, 44, 45,
157–58, 165–66; Spanish, 160, 168, 171,
195, 273n11; young generation's knowl-
edge of, 35
Laub, Dori, 53
Lefebvre, Henri, 225n.27
Levinas, Emmanuel, 7
Lévi-Strauss, Claude, 100–101, 337
Lewis, Bernard, 24n.32
Local culture, 13–14, 34, 39, 43, 291, 301–2,
330
Lux de Coti, Otilia, 171, 173–74
Lyotard, J. F., 40–41

Madres de la Plaza de Mayo: Aparición con
vida, 66; performance protest of, 54–55;
photography and, 62–64, 72, 75; spectacle
of, 56, 62–64; wearing faces on the body,
78. *See also* Memory; Photography
Magalhães, Antonio Carlos (ACM), 234, 235,
246n.3
Mallon, Florencia, 266, 277n.25
Mañach, Jorge, 186, 200n.6
Mani, Lata, 96, 97
Mannheim, Bruce, 149, 157
Manolín, El Médico de la Salsa, 201n.17
Mapuche Cultura Centers (CCMS), 287–88,
289, 294, 300
Mapuche people: Patricio Alwyn and, 289–
90, 303n.7; autonomy for, 286, 292–93;
borders of, 253, 273n.10; in Chubut province, 256; coalition building of, 18, 254,
255–56; COM (Directorate of Mapuche
Organizations) and, 254, 255, 260, 261,
262, 269, 277n.22; constitutional reform
and, 250–52, 255, 272n.3; cultural activism of, 249, 287–89, 290, 292–94, 300; as
indio permitido, 284–86, 292–93, 297–99,
300–302, 304n.16; Mapundungún and,

254, 273n.11; Rosamel Millamán on, 11,
18, 19, 264, 288–89, 293, 330; organizations of, 253–54, 258–59, 263, 275n.15,
n.16, 276n.21, 287–89, 294, 300; Pinochet
regime and, 286–87; politics of influence
and, 268–69, 271, 277n.26; representation
of the world (*Wigka*), 266–67; Rio Negro
province and, 249, 253, 254, 258, 259,
272n3, 275 nn.15, 16; Spanish language
and, 273n.11; state government and, 287–
88, 292–93; Taiñ KiñeGetuam (TKG) and,
253, 254, 267, 273n.11, 276n.17; Tehuelche people and, 255, 256–58,
275n.14, 276n.17; territorial rights of, 186,
187, 291–93; urban migration of, 156–57;
voluntary work programs (Trabajos Voluntarios de Verano) and, 289; World Bank
funding of, 261. *See also* Land rights;
Neuquen province
Martí, José, 183, 185–86
Martín Barbero, Jesús, 5, 9, 12, 14–15, 94
Maya: in Chile, 296–98; conspiracy and, 16–
17, 168–69; Coordinadora Nacional Indi-
gena Campesina (CONIC), 120n.11, 295,
299; cultural rights activism of, 95, 111–
13, 294–95; education of, 168; ethnic
groups of, 168, 173; feminization of men,
104–5; national identity and, 102, 109–
11, 176; political activism of, 171–72;
population of, in Guatemala, 283; Secretariat for the Maya Woman and, 171;
Spanish language and, 168, 173
Media, the: Afro-Brazilians in, 210–11; Brazilian Indians' protests and, 236; COM
activism and, 262; cultural capital commu-
nicated through, 88; intellectuals in, 308–
9, 336; national identity and, 46–47; Portuguese relations with Brazil in, 239;
transnational cooperation and, 34–35. *See
also* Music; Radio broadcasts; Television;
Young people
Memoria gráfica de Abuelas de Plaza de
Mayo, 64, 65 (fig. 6), 66
Memory: archival, 55–56, 57, 59 (fig. 4), 63,
64, 73–76, 74 (figs. 15, 16, 17), 75, 80n.6;
culture and, 149; erasure and, 75, 158;
force of, 330; historical, of indigenous

peoples, 275n.16; invented history and, 242; Memoria gráfica de Abuelas de Plaza de Mayo and, 64, 65 (fig. 6), 66; museums and, 83, 84, 88; nationhood and, 43; nostalgia and, 126, 128, 139, 183–84; spectators to, 64, 65 (fig. 6), 66; surrogation and, 57, 59, 60; transmission of, 53, 54, 55–56, 80n.6; trauma and, 15, 52–56, 57, 59 (fig. 4), 61–66, 65 (fig. 6), 73, 76–77, 80n.6. *See also* Performance; Photography

Menchú Tum, Rigoberta, 4, 9, 108–10, 115, 120n.10, 171–72, 174

Mestizos, 39, 127, 128, 167–68, 176, 240–41, 286, 288

Mexico: arranged marriages in, 326–28, 332n.1; audiovisual industries in, 84; cultural agency in, 335; cultural history of, 83–84; Día de la Raza and, 240–41; music in, 17, 84, 87–88

Mexico City: business environment in, 84–85, 87; cultural capital of, 83, 84–87; educational level in, 84–85; multicultural population of, 85

M-19 guerillas, 308, 323n.12

Miami, Florida, 181, 183–84, 189–90

Mignolo, Walter, 148–49, 150, 316, 321

Millamán, Rosamel, 11, 18, 19, 264, 288–89, 293, 330

Miskitu Indians, 293

Mixteco, Mexico, 326–28, 332n.1

Mockus, Antanas, 1–2

Modernity: communication and, 40–41; economic component of, 42; feminism and, 32, 98, 113, 114–15, 122, 129; individualism and, 110; language and, 154; in Latin America, 37–38; mass culture and, 41; Mayan identity and, 105; *La Mujer Maya* and, 101; nontraditional exports and, 103, 106; technology and, 38, 39–40; women and, 95–97, 113

Modernizantes, los, 297, 298, 304n.16

Modernization: education reform and, 310; *los feudales* and, 297–98; Ladino state and, 168; socioeconomic factors of violence and, 312

Moingt, Joseph, 165

Molano, Alfredo, 306, 322n.1

Monteiro de Lima, Délcio, 131

Moreno Vega, Marta, 139

Morrison, Toni, 6

Movimento dos Sem Terra (MST), 234, 235, 237, 239, 244

Movimiento 19 de April (M-19), 308, 323n.12

Movimiento Quintin Lame, 323n.12

Mujer Maya, La, 93; activism of, 110–17, 120n.11; feminism and, 113, 114–15; labor of, 103–5, 112, 119n.5; Rigoberta Menchú Tum and, 4, 9, 108, 109, 120n.10; pronatalism of, 111, 112–13, 115; as prosthetic, 95–96, 98, 100, 102, 104–5, 109, 111, 119n.5; as symbol of resistance, 109; tradition embodied in, 95–96, 100–102, 111, 112

Multiculturalism, 39, 47, 85, 87–88, 285, 297, 299

Music: Afrobahian, 215; in Cuba, 183–84, 188–90, 189, 195, 197–99, 201n.17; from Mexico, 87–88; racial identity and, 195, 197–98, 201n.17; Radio Taino and, 183; reterritorialization of, 221n.5; rock bands and, 17, 47–48; transnational influences on, 195, 197–99, 201n.17

Nagô nation, 123–24, 125, 126–27, 133

National Consultation Committee for BIE, 159–64

National identity: audiovisual industries' impact on, 34–35; common culture and, 186; of Cuban exiles, 181–82, 187–88; indigenous peoples as anachronism and, 252; literature and, 186; melting pot imagery and, 252–53; music and, 188–90, 195, 197–99, 201n.17; nationalist discourse and, 201n8; territory and, 186, 187, 291–93; transnationalism and, 187, 193–94; whiteness and, 126, 210, 219n.1, 252. *See also* Tourism

National Institute for Indigenous Affairs, 257, 268

Neoliberalism: capitalism and, 87, 102–6, 119n.5, 282, 312, 331; consensus and, 330; cultural project of, 301; economic policies of, 287, 292, 295; multiculturalism and, 39, 47, 85, 87–88, 285, 297, 299; telecommunications and, 42, 46

Tehuelche People, 255, 256–58, 275n.14, 276n.17

Teiexeira, Leão, 130, 132

Television: Brazilian Indians' protests on, 236, 244; community operation of, 39; investment in, 41–42; local culture and, 43; in Mexico, 84; satellites and, 41–42; transnational market strategies and, 43; violentologists on, 309

Terena, Gildo, 235

Theater: Turner's drama analysis and, 244–45; popular theater in Salvador, Bahia, 221n.7; *Santiago* (play), 11, 16, 23n.31; Teatro campesino, 3; Yuyachkani (theater collective), 11, 12. See also *Trilogia do Peló*

Tourism: in Cuba, 184, 196; *La Mujer Maya* and, 101, 119n.5; in Pelourinho, 208, 213, 217, 224n.24; racism and, 224n.24; Radio Taíno and, 182–83

Tradition: cosmopolitanism and, 116–17, 184, 185; Cuban culture and, 184; of dress, 101, 102; feminism and, 113, 114–15; folklore and, 37, 214, 236; gender equality and, 114; innovation and, 41; modernity and, 115–16, 184; *La Mujer Maya* and, 95–96, 100–102, 111, 112

Transnationalism: Afro-Brazilian religion and, 122; capitalism and, 87, 102–6, 119n.5, 282, 312, 331; imperialism and, 45; market strategies for, 43; music and, 195, 197–98, 197–99, 201n.17; national identity and, 187, 193–94

Trauma, 15, 52–56, 57, 59 (fig. 4), 61–66, 65 (fig. 6), 73, 76–77, 80n.6

Trilogia do Peló: Bai, bai Peló, 208, 209, 213, 224n.24; black culture in, 209, 225n.30; *Essa é a nossa praia*, 206–7, 209–10, 211, 226n.35; *Ó pai, ó*, 207–8, 212, 223nn.18, 20; racial identity in, 209, 210–12; redressive action in, 208, 224n.21; spaces examined in, 212, 217–19, 226n.36, 228n.50; stereotypical representations in, 211, 213, 226n.35; transculturation in, 218; women in, 211, 212, 226n.36

Tucumán's children of the disappeared, 57, 59 (fig. 4), 73–76, 73–76, 74 (figs. 15, 16, 17)

Tupinambá, 242

Turbay Ayala, Julio César, 306, 311, 312

Turner, Victor, 131, 206, 223nn.14, 16, 224n.21, 244–45

Union of Afro-Brazilian Sects, 138

United Nations, 109, 172, 219n.1, 250, 293

United States: border crossings of, 191–92, 193; intellectuals in, 336–37; involvement of, in Latin America, 67, 78, 106, 119n.7, 181, 182; Peace Corps of, 119n.9; radio broadcasts from, 182–83. *See also* Cuban exile community

University of Saskatchewan, 174

Vampirism, 9, 94, 106, 329

Vargas Llosa, Mario, 335

Vasconcelos, José, 216

Vásquez, Lerner Guimaraes, 155

Vattimo, G., 41

Vega, Pastor, 188

Verber, Hanna, 265

Vertretung, 249, 264, 267–70, 271

Vicente Menchú Tum Foundation, 172

Villaveces-Izquierdo, Santiago, 18, 19, 330

Violencia, La (1944–65), 312, 323n.9

Violentologists: assassination attempts on, 324n.25; guerillas and, 313–14; heroisms of, 315–17, 319–20, 320, 321, 324n.17; ideological position of, 313; as intellectual community, 306–7, 322nn.1, 2; local histories and, 321–22; in the media, 308–9; as state consultants, 311, 317–18, 323n.7, 324n.24; use of the term of, 311. *See also* names of individuals (e.g., Alape, Arturo)

Warren, Kay, 17, 28n.51

Wigley, Mark, 98

Williams, Raymond, 9–10, 13, 25n.37

Wilson, Richard, 112

Winant, Howard, 219n.1, 222n.10

Women: agency of, 97–98; clothing as identifiers of, 171; cult matriarchate and, 122–23, 125, 126, 141n.18; disappearances of, during the Dirty War, 57; education of, 112, 151–53; feminism and, 32, 98, 114–15, 122, 129, 132, 331; and the feminization of men, 104–5, 130–33; gender stereotypes of, 104, 105, 111, 112, 119n.5, 242; labor of, 103–5, 112, 119n.5; modernity on, 95–97; in national narratives, 226n.36; as priests, 123, 125, 126–30, 132, 134, 135; *Trilogia do Peló* portrayals of, 211, 212. *See also* Madres de la Plaza de Mayo; *Mujer Maya, La*

World Bank, 255, 259, 261, 320

Wynter, Sylvia, 328–29

XEL-HUH Coalition in Quetzaltenango, 172

Xicox, Olga, 114, 115

Xiquín, Calixta Gabriel, 171

xv Gvlamtuwvn (Parliament), 262, 276n.20

Yoruba, 121, 133–36, 137–39, 203, 204

Young people: armed insurgency and, 107; cultural identity and, 12, 193–94; cultural nationalism and, 190; frustrations of, 35; language knowledge of, 12, 35; music of, 195, 197–98, 199, 201n.17; national identity and, 190–91, 192, 193–94, 197–98; popular culture and, 190–91, 192; radio broadcasts for, 185, 195, 196; rock and roll industry and, 47–48; social movements and, 107; Test of Cubanidad and, 190–91, 192, 193; voluntary work programs (Trabajos Voluntarios de Verano) and, 289; on Yuyachkani (theater collective), 12

Doris Sommer is Ira Jewell Williams Jr. Professor of Romance Languages and Literatures at Harvard University. Her previous books include *Bilingual Aesthetics: A New Sentimental Education* (Duke, 2004); *Proceed with Caution, When Engaged by Minority Writing in the Americas*; and the edited collection *Bilingual Games: Some Literary Investigations.*

Library of Congress Cataloging-in-Publication Data

Cultural agency in the Americas / Doris Sommer, editor.

p. cm.

Includes bibliographical references and index.

ISBN 0-8223-3487-9 (cloth : alk. paper)

ISBN 0-8223-3499-2 (pbk. : alk. paper)

1. Latin America—Cultural policy. 2. Arts and society—Latin America. 3. Art and state—Latin America. 4. Social change—Latin America. 5. Globalization—Social aspects—Latin America. I. Sommer, Doris, 1947–

F1408.3.C83575 2005

306'.098—dc22   2005021628